1963

University of St. Francis
GEN 977.3 S671w
Snyder
John Francis Snyder

977.3
S671w

33916

LIBRARY
College of St. Francis
JOLIET, ILL.

John Francis Snyder:
Selected Writings

Dr. John Francis Snyder

John Francis Snyder:
Selected Writings

Edited by CLYDE C. WALTON

with a Biographical Essay
by PHYLLIS E. CONNOLLY

and an Appraisal of Snyder's Archaeological Work
by MELVIN L. FOWLER

THE ILLINOIS STATE HISTORICAL SOCIETY · SPRINGFIELD · 1962

LIBRARY
College of St. Francis
JOLIET, ILL.

THE ILLINOIS STATE HISTORICAL SOCIETY

OFFICERS · 1961–1962

Mrs. Doris P. Leonard, Princeton, *President*
Robert G. Bone, Normal, *Senior Vice-President*
Clyde C. Walton, Springfield, *Executive Director*

VICE-PRESIDENTS

Gunnar Benson, Sterling
Dr. A. V. Bergquist, Park Ridge
David Davis, Bloomington
Gordon B. Dodds, Galesburg
Mrs. John S. Gilster, Chester
Mrs. William Henry, Jr., Cambridge
King V. Hostick, Springfield
George M. Irwin, Quincy

Donald F. Lewis, Bethalto
Karl B. Lohmann, Champaign
Herman G. Nelson, Rockford
Mrs. Theodore C. Pease, Urbana
Philip L. Shutt, Paris
J. Robert Smith, Carmi
Robert M. Sutton, Urbana
Gilbert G. Twiss, Chicago

DIRECTORS

[TERM EXPIRES IN 1962]

Virginia R. Carroll, Galena
Mrs. Ralph Gibson, Cairo
William A. Pitkin, Carbondale
Philip D. Sang, River Forest
Donald F. Tingley, Charleston

[TERM EXPIRES IN 1963]

O. Fritiof Ander, Rock Island
Eleanor Bussell, Lacon
Sibley B. Gaddis, Mt. Sterling
Mrs. Paul Hatfield, Harrisburg
Ebers Schweizer, Chester

[TERM EXPIRES IN 1964]

Burton C. Bernard, Granite City
Newton C. Farr, Chicago
Richard S. Hagen, Galena
Victor Hicken, Macomb
Frank J. Kinst, Elmhurst

LIVING PAST PRESIDENTS

Jewell F. Stevens, Chicago
Wayne C. Townley, Bloomington
Irving Dilliard, Collinsville
Elmer E. Abrahamson, Chicago
C. P. McClelland, Jacksonville
Philip L. Keister, Freeport
J. Ward Barnes, Eldorado

Arthur Bestor, Champaign
John W. Allen, Carbondale
Ralph E. Francis, Kankakee
Alexander Summers, Mattoon
Marvin H. Lyon, Jr., Moline
Ralph G. Newman, Chicago
Glenn H. Seymour, Charleston

Copyright © 1962 · *Illinois State Historical Society* · Springfield, Illinois · *Printed in the U. S. A.*

977.3
S671w

PREFACE

Dr. John Francis Snyder (1830–1921) was a notable historian and archaeologist and one of the founders of the Illinois State Historical Society. Plans for publishing this tribute to him have been underway for several years. Funds for the project were bequeathed to the Illinois State Historical Society by Dr. Snyder's daughter, the late Miss Isabel Snyder of Virginia, Illinois.

Though many of Dr. Snyder's early works have long been out of print, they are still in demand by historical and archaeological students. Not only was Dr. Snyder a good research man, but he wrote with flair, and his personality flavors all his work. He was at once flamboyant and withdrawn, irascible and patient, logical and prejudiced; but he was, withal, one of Illinois' first historical and archaeological scholars. Without the research materials of the mid-twentieth century, he spent endless hours at the correspondence that was required for ferreting out the information that makes his work so valuable. Unfortunately, not all of his correspondents were as conscientious as Dr. Snyder, and they, not he, were generally responsible for the errors of fact that do occur in his writings. Though the doctor was meticulously careful in assembling facts, his procedure in interpreting those facts might shock his modern counterparts, for his history is full of purpose and passion. A violent partisan on every issue–political, social, scientific– he expressed his prejudices freely. As a result of this approach, his writing is never colorless, noncommittal prose. He is always committed–sometimes unwisely but always vividly, dramatically, elegantly. Herein lies the charm of his work.

In general, the historical writings chosen for this book represent substantial original contributions to Illinois historiography and are virtually free of factual error. His "Forgotten Statesmen of Illinois" series, which appeared in the *Transactions of the Illinois State Historical Society*, is still used as source material by biographers of famous early Illinoisans, and, even today, it is in some instances the only source material available. (One or two otherwise remarkable sketches from that series were passed over for this collection because of such minor errors as incorrect page citations or legislative vote tallies.) This volume also includes several articles of lesser importance, selected because they illuminate Snyder's own personality or because they are the kind of historical trivia that fascinated him (the Robinson story, for example).

The archaeological selections were made and arranged by Melvin L. Fowler, curator of North American prehistory at Southern Illinois University, who also wrote the appraisal of Snyder's archaeological work and compiled the archaeological section of the bibliography.

v

339/6

Mrs. Phyllis E. Connolly, author of the biographical essay, was formerly a historical research editor on the staff of the Illinois State Historical Library and editor of *Illinois History* magazine.

Unless otherwise stated, footnotes appearing in the original articles are numbered in these reprints; the current editor's notes are indicated by symbols. The text and style of the original notes have been left unchanged. Dr. Snyder frequently used abbreviated book titles, and these too have been left unchanged if the books are easily identifiable. Although he always sought perfection (once he wrote a friend that he abhorred typographical errors), his transcriptions of quotations from other authors are often inexact. He seldom distorted meaning, but his transcriptions frequently vary from the original in matters of capitalization, punctuation, and abbreviation. When possible, quotations have been checked against the original source, and faulty transcriptions corrected. All such changes have been noted. The drawings illustrating Dr. Snyder's original articles have been copied and renumbered to facilitate reproduction, and captions have been added. All illustrations are in one section following page 274. With these minor exceptions (and the correction of such unmistakable typographical errors as transposed letters), the articles in this volume are verbatim reprints. Consequently, archaic and incorrect spellings are common.

The editor wishes to express his thanks to Mrs. Janice Metros Johnston, a former Library staff member, for her invaluable assistance in helping to make the selections for this volume; to Mrs. Norma Darovec, who prepared the line drawings, after Dr. Snyder's originals; and to Mrs. Ellen Whitney, James N. Adams, and Howard F. Rissler, of the Library's editorial staff, who helped see the book through the press. Mr. Hubert H. Hawkins, secretary of the Indiana Historical Society, has graciously permitted us to reprint a section of James B. Griffin's study, *Additional Hopewell Material from Illinois*, which appeared in Volume 2 of the Indiana *Prehistory Research Series*. He also furnished the illustrations for that section.

CLYDE C. WALTON

CONTENTS

Part III

PIONEER ILLINOIS ARCHAEOLOGIST: JOHN FRANCIS SNYDER

Part IV

SELECTED ARCHAEOLOGICAL WRITINGS

ILLUSTRATIONS

ILLUSTRATIONS

PART I

Physician Extraordinary
John Francis Snyder

A BIOGRAPHICAL ESSAY

By Phyllis E. Connolly

FEW MEN practice with any degree of success more than one profession in their lifetimes. But before he died, on April 30, 1921, at the age of ninety-one, John Francis Snyder, a resident of Virginia, Illinois, had achieved financial success as both a physician and lawyer and had won national recognition as an archaeologist and historian. He possessed "an intellect that was both broad and deep (in fact the very Mississippi of minds) capable of grasping great things . . . [and] of retaining them, and then of imparting knowledge to others in a most fascinating way."[1]

Dr. Snyder was the famous son of a renowned father—Adam Wilson Snyder, a leading Illinois politician in the 1830's and early 1840's. The father of Adam W. Snyder (for whom the latter was named) was an Alsatian immigrant who eventually, after fighting in the Revolutionary War, settled in Connellsville, Fayette County, Pennsylvania. There, on October 6, 1799, Adam Wilson Snyder was born, the oldest child of Adam Snyder and his second wife, Margaret Hartzell Schaeffer.[2]

In the hope of finding greater opportunity, Adam W. Snyder set out for Ohio at the age of seventeen to join his half-brother who had a farm in Preble County. On the way Adam stopped to inquire about lodgings at a small general store near Mount Vernon, Knox County, Ohio. The proprietor, David McFarland, took such a liking to the dusty, footsore traveler that he offered him a job clerking. Young Snyder promptly accepted. The following spring he became acquainted with Jesse B. Thomas, a federal judge in Illinois Territory, who was visiting relatives in Mount Vernon. Judge Thomas

1. A. R. Lyles, "Dr. John Francis Snyder, 1830–1921," *Journal of the Illinois State Historical Society*, XIV (April–July, 1921): 239.

This essay is based largely upon the Snyder Collection in the Illinois State Historical Library, Springfield. The collection consists of six legal-size file drawers of correspondence received by Dr. Snyder and occasional letters written by him, plus the many scrapbooks he kept on various subjects, his medical account books, the family Bible, the diary of his trip to California, 1850–1852, and miscellaneous books from his library. Unless otherwise stated, all references are to items in the Snyder Collection. I should also like to thank Miss Margaret A. Flint, assistant state historian, and Mr. S. Ambrose Wetherbee, reference librarian, both of the Illinois State Historical Library, for their assistance in locating needed information.

2. John Francis Snyder, *Adam W. Snyder, and His Period in Illinois History, 1817–1842* (2d and rev. ed., Virginia, Ill., 1906), 419–20.

had decided to set up a wool-carding business in Cahokia, Illinois, and asked Snyder (who, it is thought, had learned the trade) to take charge of it. Adam agreed, and in June, 1817, he arrived in Cahokia.[3]

The carding mill operated only in the summer, and during the winters of 1817 and 1818 Adam W. Snyder read law in Thomas' office. In 1818 he acted as the Judge's agent while Thomas was in Washington, D.C., serving as one of Illinois' first two United States senators. In February, 1820, Adam Wilson Snyder—not yet old enough to vote—was admitted to the Illinois bar.[4] Two years later he was appointed prosecuting attorney of the First Judicial District, a post he resigned after one year "for the reason that in criminal practice he much preferred the defense of offenders . . . than their prosecution—because the former paid best." [5]

In October, 1820, Snyder married Adelaide Perry. The bride was the daughter of his first law client, Adelaide Saucier Perry, whose husband, Jean François Perry (or Perrey), had emigrated from France in 1792, and whose grandfather, Captain Jean Baptiste Saucier, had designed Fort de Chartres. Adelaide Perry was born January 24, 1803. Her formal education, conducted by her father, was abruptly terminated by his untimely death in 1812 at the age of forty-six. When she was married, Adelaide Perry could speak, read, and write only French, but she later learned English.[6]

Adam W. and Adelaide Snyder had seven children, of whom only three lived to maturity. They were William Henry, Frederick Adam, and John Francis. William was born July 12, 1825. He was graduated from McKendree College in Lebanon, Illinois, in March, 1843, and subsequently studied law in Belleville in the office of Gustavus Koerner (later lieutenant governor of Illinois). He was appointed postmaster of Belleville in 1845 and admitted to the bar in December, 1846. A few months later he enlisted in the army to fight in the Mexican War. Upon his return to Belleville he became active in Democratic politics. In 1850 and again in 1852 he was elected to the lower house of the Illinois General Assembly, and in 1854 he was elected prosecuting attorney for St. Clair County. Two years later he was an unsuccessful candidate for the office of secretary of state. In 1857 he was elected judge of the circuit court for the area including St. Clair County. He was

3. *Ibid.*, 21–22, 14–15, 23.
4. *Ibid.*, 34–35, 46.
5. *Ibid.*, 50.
6. *Ibid.*, 426–33.

defeated for Congress in 1868. In 1869 he was elected to the Illinois Constitutional Convention. He was again elected circuit judge in 1873 and 1879, declining to run for re-election in 1885. He died December 24, 1892.[7]

Frederick Snyder was born December 28, 1827. He, like his elder brother, was a graduate of McKendree College and a student of the law, being admitted to the bar in the spring of 1847. He also served in the army during the Mexican War. In 1849 he contracted gold rush fever and went to California. He had little success as a miner, however, and after some time joined the editorial staff of the *Alta California*, a San Francisco newspaper. In 1852 he was elected on the Democratic ticket to the California legislature. When his term expired, he moved to El Dorado County, and together with an old Belleville friend, Daniel W. Gelwicks, founded a newspaper, *The Mountain Democrat*, at Placerville. On July 23, 1854, he died of sunstroke at Lake Tahoe.[8]

John Francis Snyder was born March 22, 1830, at his mother's home in Prairie du Pont, St. Clair County, Illinois.[9] The Snyder family was then residing on a farm five miles south of Cahokia and one mile west of Sugar Loaf, a high point on the bluffs near the boundary separating St. Clair and Monroe counties. When John was three years old, his parents moved to Belleville, for Adam W. Snyder thought the climate of the American Bottom unhealthful and the location of the farm too "remote from his professional interests."[10] In 1830 he had been elected to the state senate, and in the late summer of 1832, after serving in the Black Hawk War, he was re-elected to that body. In Belleville, Snyder opened a law office, and his knowledge of German (his father's native language) quickly brought him many clients from Belleville's large German population. But politics was his absorbing interest. In 1836 he was elected to Congress (he had been defeated in the congressional election two years previously by Governor John Reynolds). In 1840 Snyder was once again elected to the state senate and was also chosen a presidential elector. Two years later he became the Democratic candidate for governor of Illinois, but he died on May 14, 1842, before the election took place.[11]

7. *Ibid.*, 424.
8. *Ibid.*, 424–25.
9. Snyder Family Bible.
10. Snyder, *Adam W. Snyder*, 150.
11. *Ibid.*, 99, 49, 211, 332, 385, 394.

5

The loss of his father was a severe blow to twelve-year-old John. Years later he wrote, "I spent a great deal of my time, in those closing, gloomy, days in my father's room; for my devotion to him amounted well-nigh to worship, and I—'Bully,' as he called me—occupied a large part of his affections and pride." [12] John's feelings toward his mother, however, were more ambivalent. On the positive side he commented that "she had a sterling sense of honor and honesty, and the keenest appreciation of right and justice. She abhorred debt—and drunkeness. . . . Extravagance was as distasteful to her as debt; and she always gauged her expenses by her income. Always truthful herself, she detested a liar. . . . She was very sympathetic, kind and charitable." [13] On the other hand, he complained, she was "an inveterate scold" and had a "violent temper" that "filled us boys with shame." [14] Her moods were extreme: "At times she was a jubilant optimist; but most generally a gloomy pessimist. When I came to know her well it appeared to me her normal condition was that of abject mental misery." [15]

In many respects Dr. Snyder's temperament resembled that of his mother. William H. Snyder wrote his brother on more than one occasion not to let the blues get the best of him.[16] A friend, George D. Elgin, wrote John on December 4, 1854, mentioning the latter's "habitual gloom" and exclaimed, now that Snyder was married, "Heavens—what a change! Last year ready to die for misery—& this—to die for happiness!" Snyder evidently suffered periods of depression the rest of his life. On September 27, 1890, he noted the occasion of his thirty-sixth wedding anniversary with the remark, "How much better it would have been all around if I had been laid in the grave on, or before . . . [our wedding] day. What an awful struggle life has been." [17]

Snyder had an irascible temper, was quick to anger and slow to forgive. He was extraordinarily opinionated and did not hesitate to express himself on any and all subjects. For years he feuded with some of the leading historians of the state.[18] He was also an assiduous writer of "letters to the

---

12. John F. Snyder, "Some Account of My Family and Self: Notes Jotted Down at Odd Times" (unpublished MS), 108.
13. *Ibid.*, 139–40. The misspellings are Dr. Snyder's.
14. *Ibid.*, 141.
15. *Ibid.*, 139.
16. William H. Snyder to John F. Snyder, Aug. 29, Sept. 17, 28, 1853.
17. Account Book C.
18. *Freeport Daily Journal*, Aug. 28, 1909, in Personal Scrapbook D, 32–33.

editor" of a number of newspapers, and he carefully preserved all of his published materials (along with other items that interested him) in a series of scrapbooks which he began in 1841 and continued until his death eighty years later. In "Personal Scrapbook A—1841–93" one finds articles which Dr. Snyder contributed to the *Missouri Republican* between 1881 and 1889 on such varied topics as the explorations of Hernando de Soto, the mound builders, Black Hawk, snakes, crows, and "Hannibal" (an elephant belonging to P. T. Barnum).[19] He also wrote many letters to the *Republican* concerning the correct pronunciation of "Arkansas," which he claimed should be accented on the second syllable—"Ar-kan'sas." The editor of the newspaper decided against Snyder, but the determined doctor would not concede defeat. In the margin beside the Arkansas clippings he wrote, "Still, none but an ass will pronounce it Arkan*saw*."[20]

Snyder's formative years were spent in Belleville. His father's home, according to John, was "the finest in town,"[21] and the family had several slaves.[22] When Adam W. Snyder was at home, he entertained many of the state's political leaders; among them, Judge Walter B. Scates, Orlando B. Ficklin, Colonel John D. Whiteside, Usher F. Linder, Stephen A. Douglas, David Blackwell, Zadoc Casey, Thomas Carlin, Thompson Campbell, and William H. Bissell.[23] The Snyders were also acquainted with John Reynolds, governor of Illinois from 1830 to 1834, a resident of Belleville, and, though both were Democrats, a political rival of Adam Snyder's.

In 1836 John F. Snyder, then six years of age, began his formal educa-

19. Personal Scrapbook A, 214–16, 216–22, 226–28, 261–63, 263–65, 267–70.
20. *Ibid.*, 230.
21. Snyder, "Notes," 97.
22. *Ibid.*, 60.
23. *Ibid.*, 66–67. Scates was Illinois attorney general, 1836; judge of the Third Judicial Circuit, 1836–1841; justice of the Illinois Supreme Court, 1841–1847, 1854–1857. Ficklin was elected to the Illinois General Assembly, 1834, 1838, 1842, 1878; he was a member of Congress, 1843–1849, 1851–1853. Whiteside was elected to the state house of representatives, 1830, 1832, 1834, 1844; to the state senate, 1836; and was state treasurer, 1837–1841. Linder, Illinois attorney general, 1837–1838, was elected to the legislature, 1836, 1846, 1848, 1850. Blackwell was a Belleville lawyer; he was elected to the General Assembly in 1820, 1824, and 1826 and served as Illinois secretary of state, 1823–1824. Douglas, Illinois' famed "Little Giant," served in the United States Senate, 1847–1861. Casey was in the General Assembly from 1820 to 1830; he was lieutenant governor, 1830–1833, and a member of Congress, 1833–1843. Carlin was governor of Illinois, 1838–1842. Campbell was secretary of state, 1843–1846, and a member of Congress, 1851–1853. Bissell, also a Belleville lawyer, served in Congress, 1849–1855, and was the first Republican governor of Illinois, 1857–1860. (Biographical information from *Historical Encyclopedia of Illinois*, edited by Newton Bateman and Paul Selby, Chicago and New York, 1900.)

tion,[24] attending a series of subscription schools in Belleville.[25] Letters to and from John indicate that he was a student at McKendree College at least from January, 1844, through March, 1845.[26] The next year he was appointed deputy postmaster of Belleville.[27] His brother William was the postmaster, and evidently his brother Fred was also employed at the post office. When the two older boys left for the Mexican War in 1847, John took charge,[28] but he soon tired of the work. On November 17, 1847, he wrote Fred that he had to do both of their jobs and was chopping wood, making fires, and even sleeping in the post office. Moreover, he complained, the job didn't pay well; if he could find another, he would take it. Evidently he was unsuccessful, for he wrote letters dated from the Belleville post office as late as June, 1848. In the meantime, however, he had continued to look for another position, inquiring of several St. Louis firms whether they needed salesmen.[29] He also wrote Congressman Robert Smith and Senator Sidney Breese about the possibility of an appointment as a hospital steward on a ship of the United States Navy, having, he stated later, "a great desire to see the world, and at the same time get a knowledge of the practice of medicine free of expense."[30] But neither Breese nor Smith could help him.[31] He was nevertheless determined to be a doctor, and during the school year 1849–1850 he studied at McDowell's Medical College, St. Louis.[32]

Still, his "desire to see the world" persisted. In the summer of 1849 Frederick Snyder had gone to California along with a party of other Belleville men, and John "was crazy" to go there, too. On April 1, 1850, he left Belleville and started the long trek across plains and desert to what he hoped would be his El Dorado. His traveling companions were fellow-townsmen: a tailor named Henry Johnson and three brothers, Jake, Sam, and Tim Hinckley.[33]

John kept a diary in which he noted events and sights of the trip west

24. Personal Scrapbook D, 101.
25. Personal Scrapbook B, 216.
26. John W. Parker to Snyder, Jan. 18, 1844; John F. Snyder to Frederick A. Snyder, Feb. 22, 1845.
27. A. G. R. to Snyder, Dec. 21, 1846.
28. John F. Snyder to Frederick A. Snyder, May 6, 1847.
29. A. S. Bragg to Snyder, April 11, 1849; Stratton and Barnes to Snyder, May 9, 1849.
30. Note in Snyder's handwriting on the back of Breese to Snyder, March ?, 1849.
31. Breese to Snyder, March ?, 1849; Smith to Snyder, Jan. 5, 1849.
32. Personal Scrapbook B, 3–4.
33. Handwritten copy of Snyder to Chicago Herald, Jan. 19, 1890, in ibid., 17–30.

and of his subsequent two-year stay in California. The journey lasted almost four months and was anything but dull. Four days away from home John was thrown by his mule; the next day he narrowly escaped death when a companion's gun was accidentally discharged. That night, to make a fire, the little party took some fence rails that were stacked conveniently by the trail. The next day the irate owner of the rails signed a warrant for their arrest, but the "Belleville boys" escaped retribution when the plaintiff was unable to find a constable to serve them with the warrant. At Fort Kearny, which they reached May 17, John left the Hinckley boys, who owned the rapidly tiring team, and joined another party with which he remained until July 14. He then struck out on his own again, though he joined a third group for the trek across forty-five miles of desert. After the first five miles the water supply gave out. Under the blazing sun, parched with thirst, John found himself dreaming of ice cream, beer, mint juleps, and the well back home. Once that grueling experience was behind him, he proceeded across the mountains on foot, driving the mule which carried his provisions. On July 26 he arrived in Sacramento without a penny and with feet so sore he could scarcely walk. Two days later he set off for the mines. On the thirty-first he found Sam Hinckley near Georgetown, California, and on August 3 he began mining with a group from Belleville.[34]

For almost two years he remained in California, working with his friends in the mines when the weather was good, sitting around his cabin "reading, writing, and playing cards"[35] in the rainy season. During these periods of enforced leisure the transplanted Illinoisan ate so much that he complained of getting fat[36] and drank to such an extent that eventually he "took the pledge" of temperance, commenting, "I am fond of good liquor . . . [but] the passion [for it] gradually but firmly gains on me."[37] (He disliked temperance societies, however, describing them as "all humbug."[38]) He also detested the hard work required of miners, though he conceded that the relative freedom of his employment was attractive: "The work in the mines is very hard and the life we lead most villainous, though very independent. We have no bosses to grumble at us or discharge us, no taxes to pay or no govern-

34. Typescript of Snyder's California diary, entries of April 4, 5, 6, May 17, 18, July 14–15, 26, 28, 1850.
35. *Ibid.,* Nov. 24, 1850.
36. *Ibid.,* Jan. 2, 1851.
37. *Ibid.,* Jan. 30, 1851.
38. *Ibid.,* June 20, 1851.

ment agents to support. We go to work when and where we please and quit when we please. But the only attraction this country has for me is its climate—none other. The gold I would like to have but the 'getting of it' is attended with rather too much hard labor to detain me in the mines very long." [39]

Yet Snyder remained in California mining gold for another seventeen months. The reason was elementary—he needed money. He was determined to finish his medical education. And he was equally determined to prove to the folks back home that his California venture was a success. To his diary he confided, "I have lived . . . [in Belleville] in prosperity; I cannot bear the idea of returning there in adversity." [40] The young man was, in fact, haunted by a fear of failure. He had a recurring dream: he arrived home penniless only to find that no one liked him or was glad to see him, and, in consequence, he decided to return to the mines. [41] His sensitivity to public opinion in Belleville also led him to write home elaborate accounts of his activities, knowing that his letters would in all likelihood be published in the local newspaper. When his cabin was robbed by Indians, he wrote home about the incident, commenting in his diary, "I made a great tale of it." [42] Shortly before sailing for home he noted, "I wrote a letter to William [his brother] giving him a rather highly colored (but untrue) account of my operations." [43]

The amount of cash that Snyder deemed necessary to have on hand before returning to Illinois gradually but steadily diminished as the length of his stay in California increased. In February, 1851, the figure was $1,000; a month later it was down to $700. By June $500 was his goal. [44] But the summer's profits were meager. Not until February, 1852, did Snyder and his partners find gold in abundance. Then suddenly they cleared over $900 in one week. John was jubilant: "I am now worth a *thousand* dollars for the first time in my life. With this and no bad luck I can certainly complete my medical education." [45] His luck held good; within six months he was on his way home. Sailing from San Francisco on May 16, 1852, he reached New York (by way of Panama) just twenty-seven days later. After a visit

39. *Ibid.*, Jan. 22, 1851.
40. *Ibid.*, Jan. 28, 1851.
41. *Ibid.*, April 30, 1851; May 20, 1852.
42. *Ibid.*, May 20, 1851.
43. *Ibid.*, April 23, 1852.
44. *Ibid.*, Feb. 5, March 7, June 2, 1851.
45. *Ibid.*, Feb. 21, 1852.

with relatives in Pennsylvania, he finally reached Belleville on July 2.[46]

In the fall of 1852 he resumed his studies at McDowell's Medical College, St. Louis, and in February, 1853, he passed his examination qualifying him as a doctor of medicine.[47] During the winter he was also laying plans for the future. In January he applied for—and received—a post with the army as physician to the Delaware Indians, but he was assailed by doubt. Should he, he asked his brother, accept the post? He was "very anxious to get back to California, and scarcely . . . [knew] what to do." School would be over on March 1, and he had to decide before then.[48] What brother William's advice was is not known; but whatever adventures, if any, the young doctor had with the Delaware were brought speedily to a close, for by March 31, 1853, only a few weeks after his graduation, John Francis Snyder was established as a practicing physician in Orleans, Missouri.[49] In April his friend George Elgin wrote him, "I had not expected so speedy & tragic a *denoument* [*sic*] to your military career."

Snyder's residence in Orleans was also short-lived. By October of the same year he was settled in Bolivar, Polk County, Missouri,[50] a town that was to remain his home for eleven years. At the time of his arrival in Bolivar the twenty-three-year-old physician was, according to an acquaintance, "tolerably large in stature, [had a] strong intellect, [was] of prepossessing manners, and not what the ladies would call handsome, though he had the good fortune to win the affections as well as the hand of one of Bolivar's fairest and most beautiful daughters."[51] She was Annie Eliza Sanders, and she married the doctor on September 27, 1854.[52]

Miss Annie was evidently quite a catch. Some six months before the wedding one of Snyder's friends urged him, "Woo—love, and win her—and wear her through life. She will make you a choice wife—will be the means of settling you down in a regular . . . way."[53] Another friend commented, "Miss Annie is a lady who [*sic*] I have ever considered an exception to her sex in this part of the civilization. I esteem her verry [*sic*] highly as much so

46. *Ibid.*, June 12, July 2, 1852.
47. John F. Snyder to William H. Snyder, Oct. 23, 1852; Feb. ?, 1853.
48. John F. Snyder to William H. Snyder, Jan. 29, 1853.
49. Dr. J. A. Lindsey to Snyder, March 31, 1853.
50. William B. Cowan to Snyder, Oct. 24, 1853.
51. W. A. Ruyle to *Bolivar Herald*, Feb. 19, 1885, in Personal Scrapbook A, 233–34.
52. Snyder Family Bible.
53. A. G. Blake to Snyder, March 18, 1854.

as any one."[54] The marriage also met with William Snyder's approval. Six days before the wedding he wrote his brother, "I have every reason to believe that you are about to be happily married. I am assured of the worth, morally, intellectually and socially of your intended." (Unfortunately, John did not have reciprocal feelings toward William's wife, Jane Champion of Belleville, whom he described as a paranoiac.[55])

Annie Eliza bore her husband four children. The oldest, Frederick (named for his deceased uncle), was born September 13, 1855, and died April 24, 1937.

The Snyders also had three daughters: Adel, born October 7, 1857, died November 20, 1943; Nelle, born September 10, 1859, died January 5, 1920; and Isabel, born May 17, 1864, died March 21, 1952.[56]

Marriage did not, however, have the settling effect upon Dr. Snyder so earnestly hoped for by his friends. He seems not to have cared for Bolivar, and he was constantly investigating the feasibility of establishing a practice in another community. Early in 1855 he decided to move to Buffalo, Missouri, but a fellow-physician's warning that the townsfolk there would provide him with a heavy practice and "doubtful pay"[57] seems to have deterred him. Two years later he took an extended trip through the Southwest. He dallied with the thought of locating in Camden, Arkansas,[58] then decided to move to Springfield, Missouri,[59] but for unknown reasons he remained in Bolivar.

Certainly his life there was active, indeed strenuous. In addition to keeping up his medical practice, Dr. Snyder was, like his father and brothers before him, active in Democratic politics. By 1856 he seems to have been chairman of the Polk County Democratic Party.[60] He was also one of a group of volunteers who fought against John Brown at Osawatomie, Kansas, on August 30, 1856, an activity about which he later wrote: "I glory in the title of Border Ruffian, and I thank God that the opportunity has offered

54. J. Atkisson to Snyder, May 25, 1854.
55. Personal Scrapbook B, 61.
56. Snyder Family Bible. Birth dates of the two youngest daughters were obtained from their death records in the Illinois Department of Public Health, Division of Vital Statistics, Springfield.
57. Dr. B. Barrett to Snyder, March 20, 1855.
58. John A. Pile to Snyder, June 15, 1857.
59. J. B. Chandler to Snyder, July 7, 1857.
60. Questionnaire from the chairman, National Democratic Resident Committee, to county chairmen of the Democratic Party, July 2, 1856.

itself for me to raise my arm in defense of Law and Order." [61] Within a few months he had applied for, received, and turned down an appointment with an Indian agency,[62] but in December, 1857, he accepted a commission as colonel in the Missouri militia.[63] In his spare time he wrote for the local newspaper, the *Bolivar Courier,* and even, for a time, served as its editor.[64] He was also engaged in the study of law and in April, 1859, was admitted to the bar.[65] Thereupon he stopped practicing medicine—which he did not care for and which evidently did not provide him with an income he deemed adequate—and devoted his time to working as a lawyer and land agent.[66]

In 1858 Dr. Snyder engaged in an extremely bitter election campaign when he was a candidate for the state legislature on the Democratic ticket. His platform advocated preservation of the Union and elimination of the slavery question from politics. In a circular to the voters of Polk County, dated July 20, 1858, he stated: "I am totally opposed to the agitation of the slavery question in any shape, believing that that question should rest entirely with the slaveholders who will ultimately find a solution for it in the laws of political economy, climate, of production and expediency. I regard the institution of slavery as a matter of individual interest exclusively, and consequently I think it ought never to be made an element in politics." [67]

His opponents thought otherwise. They also attacked his lack of religious beliefs (the doctor was an agnostic and had no love for established churches, being particularly bitter against Methodists and Catholics) and his disdain for Polk County, claiming he had once stated that "a majority of the citizens

61. Undated letter in Snyder's handwriting in the 1856 correspondence file. William H. Snyder, in a letter to his brother dated Oct. 27, 1856, referred to a picture of John in Border Ruffian costume. In 1910 the doctor wrote his recollections (highly colored) of the Battle of Osawatomie for the *Missouri Historical Review;* the account was published in the Jan., 1912, issue.

62. William H. Snyder to John F. Snyder, April 10, 1857.

63. Commission signed by Gov. R. M. Stewart, dated Dec. 28, 1857.

64. Clippings in Personal Scrapbook A, 67–71. The editor of the *Jefferson City Examiner,* Sept. 1, 1859, took note of Snyder's retirement as editor of the *Courier* and stated that under his leadership the paper had been "an able and vigorous exponent of Democratic principles" (clipping in *ibid.,* 76).

65. Judge Foster P. Wright to Snyder, April 19, 1859.

66. In Personal Scrapbook A, 107, is a notice that John F. Snyder was acting as "Attorney at Law, Land Agent and Collector." In a letter from W. Pitt to Snyder, dated May, 1859, the writer speaks of Snyder's having changed his profession "from necessity" and because he "disliked" medicine. The Snyder correspondence files from 1859 through 1864 are filled with letters to Snyder from clients.

67. Personal Scrapbook A, 74–76.

of Polk were not worthy of being associated with by genteel people."[68] The attacks were effective, and Snyder was defeated.[69]

Nonetheless, he continued to be active in the Democratic Party and was a delegate from Polk County to the Missouri Democratic convention in 1860. He served as a member of the committee on resolutions, where he was, he said later, a "'Fire-eater,' against . . . Douglas Democrat[s]."[70] When the national Democratic Party split, Snyder followed the southern wing, publicly stating that "the vote of Missouri should be . . . cast for [John C.] Breckinridge and [Joseph] Lane."[71]

Dr. Snyder never pretended to be anything but sympathetic to the institution of slavery. Not only had he fought against John Brown in Kansas in 1856, but the following year he traveled through Arkansas and Texas, where he was favorably impressed by the treatment and condition of the slaves he saw toiling on large plantations. Characteristically, he sent voluminous letters to newspapers back in Missouri describing his impressions. From Camden, Arkansas, he wrote: "I passed a few days . . . on a plantation that employed a hundred and eighty active field hands, and . . . [they were] jolly [and] contented. . . . They went to the fields cheerfully and enlivened their labors with their peculiar original songs all day."[72] He was willing to concede that "the life of a plantation slave at best is a wretched one, at least so it appears to a person reared in the North." But, he continued, "cotton and sugar *must* be produced, and . . . none but slaves can produce them." Therefore, he stated, "we must at least admit slavery to be a *necessary* evil, and one that must be tolerated in the cotton and sugar growing countries for many days yet. I have now traveled many hundred miles in slave territory, and with a few exceptions have invariably found the slaves contented, cheerful, and happy—well fed, well worked, and well clothed."[73]

68. "To the Voters of Polk County" (circular), in *ibid.*, 72–73.
69. W. A. Ruyle in *Bolivar Herald*, Feb. 19, 1885 (clipping in *ibid.*, 233–34). Dr. Snyder's mother was a Catholic and attempted, unsuccessfully, to rear her sons in that faith. In his "Notes" (144) Snyder expressed his "contempt and detestation" for her belief in what he termed "absurd and senseless superstitions." Years earlier he wrote, "By observing the great & universal hypocracy [sic] of Churchmen generally (and Methodists in particular) I have come to the conclusion to look on religion itself as a complete humbug" (California Diary, Feb. 16, 1851).
70. "Proceedings of the Democratic Convention of Missouri," an account copied by Snyder from the *Missouri Democrat* (St. Louis), in Personal Scrapbook A, 106.
71. Unidentified newspaper clipping, Oct. 4, 1860, in *ibid.*, 107.
72. April 24, 1857, in *ibid.*, 53.
73. May 20, 1857, in *ibid.*, 55.

In the hectic months between Lincoln's election and the firing on Fort Sumter, Snyder spent some time on patrol along the Missouri border,[74] serving as commander of the Polk County Rangers.[75] Missouri was torn asunder by unionists and secessionists, and in the struggle Snyder unhesitatingly joined forces with the Southern cause. Writing to an Illinois friend, Jo Sargent, on April 18, 1861, he flatly stated: "If Missouri is to take any active part in this horrid civil war . . . I shall of course take the field, and stake everything I have, life included, upon the issue. Still, however, I hope the matter may yet be compromised and the horror of a general war avoided." But such, of course, was not to be. Joining the Fourth Cavalry of the First Division of Missouri Confederate forces, Snyder was elected major of that body's First Battalion.[76] Within a short time he was appointed ordnance officer of the Second Missouri Division.[77] In the following two years he fought in the battles of Wilson's Creek, Pea Ridge, Helena, and Corinth.[78] By early 1863, however, he decided that "the Confederacy had collapsed,"[79] and he left the Southern army. Returning to Bolivar, he resumed his law practice.

But conditions there were "squally."[80] When, on July 24, 1864, a client, James Beck, asked if Snyder would go to New Mexico to settle an estate, the lawyer willingly agreed. After a few months in Santa Fe, however, he was ready to return to the Middle West. Already several of his friends had moved to Illinois, and he, too, decided to leave Missouri for his native state. He visited Ripley, Rushville, Pleasant View, Chandlerville, and Beardstown before choosing Virginia, later the seat of Cass County, for his home. The town, he was informed, had two doctors—one an elderly Democrat, the other an energetic Republican—and the Democrats wanted a younger physician.[81]

Virginia was Dr. Snyder's home for the rest of his life. To support himself and his family he resumed the practice of medicine. In 1866 he was elected to the Morgan County Medical Society,[82] and in 1890 the Cass

---

74. A. C. Orrick to Snyder, Dec. 2, 1860.
75. Miss Wear to Captain Snyder, undated letter in 1860 correspondence.
76. Affidavit signed by Perry Little, Assistant Adjutant General, July 4, 1861.
77. General Order No. 56, signed by Gen. J. S. Rains, July 15, 1861.
78. John F. Snyder, "The Capture of Lexington," *Missouri Historical Review*, VII (Oct., 1912): 1, 8.
79. Note in Snyder's handwriting in Personal Scrapbook A, 234.
80. P. J. Bond to Snyder, May 11, 1863.
81. *Virginia* (Ill.) *Enquirer*, Oct. 9, 1913, in Personal Scrapbook D, 92.
82. Unidentified clipping, July 16, 1866, in Personal Scrapbook A, 118.

County commissioners appointed him county physician.[83] But he still had no love for medicine, at one time confiding to a friend that he found his profession "obnoxious." [84] Certainly working conditions were not ideal. He made his rounds, mostly in the country, on horseback and in all kinds of weather over roads that were little better than tracks of mud. Often he had to treat patients by mail, as in the case of a Champaign man who wrote, "I believe that I have heart disease of some form or other and would like to know if you can perscribe [sic] for me without an examination." [85] And while today his fees seem modest,[86] many patients paid only when the doctor threatened to sue, while some completely defaulted.

Still, Dr. Snyder's income was sufficient to support his family and to permit him to pursue his various avocations—natural history, geology, archaeology, and history—in each of which he achieved a degree of fame. In 1869 he was offered the post of assistant Illinois state geologist but was forced to decline because the "salary was insufficient." [87] Three years later he was elected to the American Association for the Advancement of Science.[88] (He was already a member of the Academy of Science of St. Louis.[89]) In later years he was elected to membership in the National Geographic Society,[90] the Wisconsin Natural History Society,[91] the Northern Indiana Historical Society,[92] and the Missouri Historical Society.[93]

Dr. Snyder also continued to be active in the Democratic Party and in 1878 was elected to the state legislature from the Thirty-sixth District—Cass, Menard, Brown, and Mason counties.[94] In the General Assembly he served on the finance, penitentiary, education, geological survey, and libraries com-

83. Account Book C.

84. Lyles, "Snyder," 241.

85. Gridley to Snyder, Jan. 8, 1899. A few days earlier the doctor received a letter from a Mrs. Millner describing her symptoms in graphic detail and requesting him to send her medicine.

86. Snyder's schedule of fees in Account Book A lists the following charges: prescription and medicine, $1; visit in town, $1.50; visit in the country, $2 plus 50¢ per mile after the first mile; consultation, $5; obstetrics, $10 up to ten hours, then $1 each additional hour; pulling teeth, $1; reducing fractures, $5–$25; amputations, $5–$100.

87. Virginia Courier, Nov. 12, 1869, in Personal Scrapbook A, 147.

88. Boston Daily Advertiser, Aug. 20, 1872, in ibid., 178.

89. B. F. Shumard(?) to Snyder, Sept. 23, 1856.

90. Certificate of election, July 6, 1899.

91. Charles E. Monroe to Snyder, Jan. 30, 1903.

92. George A. Baker to Snyder, Oct. 14, 1899.

93. Charles P. Pettus to Snyder, July 12, 1905.

94. Macomb Eagle, Sept. 14, 1878, in Personal Scrapbook A, 203.

mittees.[95] The measures he introduced in the legislature reflected his chief interests—amendment of the board of health law (he described the boards of health and agriculture as "superlative frauds and humbugs"[96]), improved enforcement of the laws providing for the prevention of cruelty to animals and the preservation of game and fish, and a resolution "inquiring into the propriety of purchasing the library of the late Hon. Sidney Breese" (United States senator and justice of the Illinois Supreme Court).[97] Practical politics, however, evidently lost its appeal for the doctor, and he declined to run for re-election.[98] Perhaps in 1879 he was too absorbed in a project involving former Governor John Reynolds' *Pioneer History of Illinois*. Snyder hoped to publish a new edition of the venerable work, but eventually he turned the project over to the Fergus Publishing Company in Chicago with the comment, "No money in it."[99]

And all this time he was collecting—anything and everything that appealed to him. In 1893 some of his "antediluvian relics" were placed on exhibit at the World's Columbian Exposition in Chicago,[100] and his "country museum"—a small building by his home in which he exhibited his collection—came to attract statewide notice:

The first room is a library, three sides being lined with books . . . of history and scientific observation; one compartment being filled with volumes pertaining to our own state. . . . Here also are to be seen some historical relics; some bonds and treasury notes of the defunct Confederacy; specimens of the old State bank notes; old continental notes printed by Benjamin Franklin, all neatly framed and under glass.

From this library room, you step into the long annex, known as the museum proper. Here . . . [are] regular rows of stones, corals, shells, starfish and insects . . . specimens of marine life, crabs, lobsters, sea urchins, etc. . . . skulls of many of our small animals and birds. . . . On the floor repose the vertebrae[,] ribs and other bones, of a seventy foot Greenland whale, whose lower jaw bones, measure nintean [*sic*] feet. . . . The ponderous pelvic bones of a Mastodon, that were washed out of a ravine in the eastern part of the county also occupy space on the floor. . . . [T]he walls of the room all around are adorned with heads and horns of buffalo, elk, deer, sheep and goats, and cases of stuffed birds are artistically

95. Unidentified newspaper clipping in *ibid.,* 207–8.
96. Note in Snyder's handwriting in *ibid.,* 214.
97. *Petersburg Observer,* Feb. 15, 1879, in *ibid.,* 208.
98. Unidentified newspaper clipping in *ibid.,* 212.
99. Note in Snyder's handwriting to accompany clipping from *Illinois State Register* (Springfield), Aug. 15, 1879, in *ibid.,* 209.
100. Unidentified newspaper clipping in *ibid.,* 287.

placed around. . . . Near the ceiling in the back part of the room, hangs a birch-bark canoe from the head waters of the Mississippi. Also cases filled with neatly labeled specimens of fossils, minerals, ores, crystals, and other geological specimens.[101]

But the largest number of items in the doctor's collection were Indian relics:

In this interesting department we find a large case of the utensils and tools of stone, bone and shell, with specimens of pottery and woven fabrics and skulls of the cliff-dwellers from the cliffs of the Mesas [sic] Verde. . . . Beyond this is an upright case of ghastly, grinning skulls of old native Americans, dug up from the ancient graves and mounds in this vicinity and . . . Tennessee. In different cases are displayed perhaps five thousand flint implements of all and every kind. . . . Other cases contain many curious vessels and vases of pottery ware taken from the mounds; stone pipes of varied designs, some very rude and some very brightly polished; armlets, beads and other ornaments . . . and implements of native copper hammered into shape with stones.[102]

Many, if not most, of his Indian objects Dr. Snyder obtained while excavating mounds built by prehistoric Illinois Indians. He was particularly intrigued by the Cahokia mounds and helped to map and survey them.[103] In 1894 he opened a large mound near the Illinois River in Brown County. He continued to excavate in the area, and in 1897 he reported his findings in a paper at the meeting of the American Association for the Advancement of Science.[104] He corresponded at length (characteristically) with scientists on the staff of the Smithsonian Institution in Washington, D.C., which published some of his archaeological findings. The curator of ethnology, O. T. Mason, wrote the doctor on April 5, 1902, that he was "well thought of in the Institution." This opinion was shared by the chief of the Bureau of Ethnology, W. H. Holmes, although the latter told Snyder on one occasion that he should "have pulled in . . . [his] horns."[105] In January, 1897, Dr. Snyder assumed the editorship of a monthly archaeological magazine entitled *The Antiquarian*. The low price of the publication was designed to attract the "working, thinking, investigating" portion of the middle-income

101. Woman's Edition, *Virginia Gazette*, Jan. 31, 1896, in Personal Scrapbook B, 99–100.
102. *Chicago News-Record*, July 8, 1892, in Personal Scrapbook A, 274.
103. Warren King Moorehead, "John Francis Snyder," *Dictionary of American Biography*, XVII: 389. On any but archaeological matters this sketch is highly inaccurate.
104. *Beardstown Enterprise*, Nov. 25, 1897, in Personal Scrapbook B, 190.
105. Quoted in Robert E. Elkin, "John Francis Snyder and Illinois Archaeology" (Master's thesis, University of Illinois, 1949), 8.

group, although, the editor stated, he intended to place the magazine "on the level of the leading science publications of our country." [106] Two years later, unfortunately (and through no fault of the doctor's), the magazine was bankrupt.[107]

But Snyder, now approaching seventy, continued to write on archaeology. The noted archaeologist Warren King Moorehead asked the doctor on at least two occasions to contribute to archaeological volumes.[108] Moorehead, in fact, had such a high opinion of Dr. Snyder that he described him as "the ranking pioneer in archaeology of the state of Illinois." [109]

As the years passed, Snyder's fears concerning the future of archaeology in his native state increased. Foreseeing that valuable prehistoric Indian mounds, as yet hardly explored, would be plowed under as ribbons of steel and concrete spread across the state, the "weekend archaeologist"—as he was called—delivered an impassioned plea at the first meeting of the Illinois State Historical Society, January 6, 1900, for the preservation of Illinois antiquities and the granting of state aid to insure their adequate investigation. (A sore point with him was the subsidy of archaeological expeditions by Illinois universities in foreign lands while prehistoric Indian sites in the state lay virtually ignored.[110]) He also continued to add to his collections and would have liked to present his "museum" to the state of Illinois. But he demanded that a fireproof building be constructed to house his specimens, and this was never done. Illinois College in Jacksonville also refused to meet his condition,[111] and eventually he sold the entire collection to J. W. Seever and Jesse J. Allard of St. Louis, who planned to integrate the items into two museums in that city.[112]

As he grew older, Dr. Snyder increasingly devoted his time to reading and writing Illinois history. In 1899 he prepared a paper for the Morgan County Medical Society on early Cass County doctors which was afterward serialized in the *Virginia Gazette*. Later he re-did the biographical sketches, correcting errors and adding new material.[113] He then wrote a similar series

106. *Virginia Gazette*, Jan. 15, 1897, in Personal Scrapbook B, 172–73.
107. Elkin, "Snyder," 80.
108. Moorehead to Snyder, Oct. 21, 1899; Oct. 19, 1903.
109. Moorehead, "Snyder," 389.
110. *Chicago Record-Herald*, Oct. 18, 1903, in Personal Scrapbook C, 99–101.
111. Lyles, "Snyder," 240.
112. *Virginia Gazette*, Jan. 27, 1911, in Personal Scrapbook D, 49–50.
113. Personal Scrapbook B, 233–45 and *passim*.

for the *Gazette* on Cass County poets.[114] He also collected material on early Illinois newspapers,[115] a source of historical information Dr. Snyder deemed of greatest importance. He once told the Illinois Press Association that "the newspaper, day by day, week by week, mirrors all phases of human life and prints with fidelity all transpiring events of interest within its sphere of activity. . . . Its pages are the best possible source from which students of history and of social and political problems can obtain their material."[116]

At the time he was working on these varied projects, Dr. Snyder was also engaged in writing two biographies. The first was *John Baptiste Saucier*, a study of the doctor's great-great-grandfather, which appeared in 1901. Two years later he published the story of his father, *Adam W. Snyder, and His Period in Illinois History, 1817–1842*. While this work cannot be called objective, it is vastly entertaining, for the doctor wrote in a crisp and colorful style. Moreover, he was acquainted with many of the people about whom he wrote, and he did not hesitate to express his very definite opinions about them. Describing his Belleville neighbor John Reynolds, he wrote:

In some respects he was a living paradox, a strange mixture of sense and nonsense, possessing many sterling traits, with some reprehensible faults. He was neither a great or specially gifted man, but nevertheless, an extraordinary character whose successful career must be accepted as evidence that he possessed genius of a certain order. There was about him none of that force, commonly styled "personal magnetism," so essential for a leader of men; nor were his powers of mind of that lofty or transcendent kind that command the admiration and following of the multitude. But, an adept in the knowledge of human nature and human motives, he gained and held the confidence and support of the people, more by the exercise of consummate tact and craftiness than of talents of higher order. . . . He was always gentlemanly in appearance and apparel, with modest but ungraceful manners. With neither high culture nor refinement, claiming to be one of the humblest of the people, and constantly practicing the arts of electioneering—of which he was a perfect master—he never descended to masquerading in linsey hunting shirt and coonskin cap to gain the rabble's favor.[117]

For those historians who seek to divorce personal opinion from the writ-

---

114. Personal Scrapbook C, 20–46.
115. J. K. Van Demark to Snyder, Dec. 2, 1903; John S. Harper to Snyder, Dec. 3, 1903; J. N. Gridley to Snyder, Dec. 8, 1903; Eb Spink to Snyder, Dec. 14, 1903; and others.
116. "The Relation of the Public Press to the Illinois State Historical Society," a speech delivered to the Illinois Press Association on May 14, 1903, by Dr. John F. Snyder, reprinted in the *Virginia Enquirer*, Personal Scrapbook C, 90.
117. Snyder, *Adam W. Snyder*, 298–99.

ing of history Dr. Snyder would undoubtedly have felt profound contempt.

In 1889 the Illinois General Assembly created the Illinois State Historical Library as a repository for "all books, pamphlets, manuscripts, monographs, writings, and other material of historic interest and useful to the historian, bearing upon the political, physical, religious or social history of the State of Illinois." [118] Dr. Snyder's appointment as one of the three trustees to govern the Library was urged upon Governor Joseph W. Fifer by several newspapers and by John M. Scott, a justice of the Illinois Supreme Court. Despite the doctor's affiliation with the Democratic Party, a group of Republicans from Virginia also interceded with the Republican governor on the doctor's behalf. [119] But to no avail. The governor, according to one of Snyder's friends, "endorsed your qualifications for the place, but said it would get up a row among his political friends to appoint you." [120]

Nevertheless, ten years later Dr. Snyder joined with the Library's trustees—Judge Hiram W. Beckwith of Danville; Dr. Edmund J. James, president of Northwestern University, Evanston; and George N. Black of the Springfield Public Library—and others to issue a call to establish an Illinois State Historical Society. [121] At the organizational meeting Judge Beckwith was elected president of the Society; Dr. Snyder, vice-president; and Evarts B. Greene, professor of history at the University of Illinois, secretary. [122] Dr. Snyder continued in his post until 1903, when he was elected the Society's president. [123] The following year he was re-elected. [124]

At that time membership dues in the Society were one dollar a year, and officers and directors of the organization (as well as the trustees of the Historical Library) soon realized that they could not carry on much of a program so long as their activities were restricted by the limited revenue received from membership dues. Another perplexing problem was the relationship between the Historical Library, a state agency, and the Historical Society, a private organization usually, though not necessarily, having among its directors the

118. "The Illinois State Historical Library," *Journal of the Illinois State Historical Society,* LI (Winter, 1958): 428.

119. *Virginia Gazette,* June 14, 1889; *Quincy Whig,* June 19, 1889; Scott to Snyder, June 23, 1889, reprinted in the *Gazette;* all in Personal Scrapbook A, 265–67.

120. William Epler to Snyder, Feb. 10, 1903.

121. "Call for an Illinois Historical Society," clipping in Personal Scrapbook B, 246.

122. Unidentified newspaper clipping in *ibid.,* 248.

123. *Illinois State Journal* (Springfield), Jan. 28, 1903, in Personal Scrapbook C, 71.

124. *Virginia Gazette,* Feb. 5, 1904, in *ibid.,* 109.

three trustees of the Historical Library. The officers were, however, divided as to the means of overcoming their difficulties.

Dr. Snyder believed that the only solution lay in a radical reorganization of the Society and the Library. He wanted the legislature to create a State Department of History, of which the Society and the Library would be separate and equal divisions, headed by an executive officer who would serve as both librarian of the Historical Library and secretary of the Historical Society. The proper functions of the Library, Snyder contended, were the acquisition and preservation of historical material,[125] while those of the Society were the stimulation of historical research and the publication of subsequent findings and of documents relating to the history of the state.[126] At one time he also felt that the State Department of History should operate a historical museum.[127]

The trustees of the Historical Library, however, did not agree with Dr. Snyder's plans. Instead, led by Judge Beckwith, they secured the passage of an act (May 16, 1903) by which the Historical Society was made a department of the Historical Library and the Library trustees were empowered to use Library funds to meet the incidental expenses of the Society. This included publication of the Society's annual volume of *Transactions* and, after its founding in April, 1908, the quarterly *Journal of the Illinois State Historical Society*. This act, Beckwith assured Dr. Snyder, was not what the judge wanted, "but believe me . . . it was the best the Legislature could do at the time." [128]

But Dr. Snyder chafed under what seemed to him the increasing direction of the Society by the Library trustees. In January, 1904, he submitted his resignation as president of the Society but was prevailed upon to withdraw it.[129] In succeeding months, however, the doctor's disenchantment only increased. The legislature was to meet in 1905, and on December 19, 1904, the doctor resubmitted his proposed bill for the creation of a State Depart-

125. Proposed "Bill for an Act to define and establish union of the State Historical Society and State Historical Library and promote their public usefulness," enclosed in letters from Snyder to directors of the Illinois State Historical Society, Dec. 19, 1904.

126. Snyder to John H. Burnham, Jan. 3, 1905.

127. Unidentified newspaper clipping, reprinting "The Illinois State Department of History," an address given by Snyder at the annual business meeting of the Illinois State Historical Society, Jan. 23, 1902.

128. Beckwith to Snyder, Aug. 20, 1903. The act of May 16, 1903, still governs relations between the Library and the Society.

129. Jessie Palmer Weber to Snyder, Jan. 9, 13, 1904.

ment of History to the Society's thirteen other directors, requesting their comments. (Dr. Snyder as president of the Society was the fourteenth director.) Eight of the thirteen, including Mrs. Jessie Palmer Weber—then librarian of the Historical Library and secretary of the Society—approved of Dr. Snyder's bill in whole or in part.[130] One director, George N. Black, who was also a trustee of the Library, evidently did not reply. Three of the remaining four directors—Professor George W. Smith of Southern Illinois Normal College, Carbondale; Professor Evarts B. Greene of the University of Illinois; and Dr. Edmund J. James, recently chosen president of the University of Illinois and a trustee of the Library—were strongly opposed to the doctor's plans. M. H. Chamberlin, the other director and third trustee of the Library, seems to have tried to reconcile Snyder and James, but without success.[131] On January 3, 1905, President James wrote the doctor that he could not support the bill. That month Snyder again submitted his resignation as president of the Historical Society, stating that the trustees of the Historical Library "were at variance with every effort he had put forth."[132] Privately he blamed Dr. James (as he had Judge Beckwith before him) for having reduced the Society to an appendage of the Library.[133] When in 1910 James resigned his post as trustee, Dr. Snyder clipped the newspaper announcement and sent it to his friends with the comment, "Thank God, I can now attend a meeting of the society."[134]

Despite his eighty years Dr. Snyder continued his many activities, contributing articles to the Society's *Journal,* writing voluminous articles for, and letters to, newspapers, and pasting clippings in his many scrapbooks. The years were taking their toll, however. The scrapbook pages that once were covered with sentimental poems and reminiscences of pioneer life in Illinois, of prospecting in California, and of digging in prehistoric Indian mounds, now contained little but obituaries—first of friends, then of family.

---

130. Those directors besides Mrs. Weber who supported Snyder's proposed bill were John H. Burnham, Bloomington; Judge Joseph O. Cunningham, Urbana; David McCulloch, Peoria; William H. Collins, Quincy; Edwin E. Sparks, professor of history, University of Chicago; Alfred Orendorff, Springfield; and Rev. C. J. Eschmann, Prairie du Rocher.

131. James to Snyder, Dec. 19, 1904; Smith to Snyder, Dec. 23, 1904; Greene to Snyder, Dec. 24, 1904; Chamberlin to Snyder, Jan. 2, 1905. Judge Beckwith died Dec. 23, 1903, and Chamberlin, president of McKendree College, Lebanon, was appointed to replace him.

132. *Daily Journal* (no town indicated), Jan. 26, 1905, clipping in Personal Scrapbook C, 119.

133. Snyder to Burnham, Jan. 3, 1905.

134. *Springfield Evening News*, April 19, 1910, in Personal Scrapbook D, 40.

On January 17, 1918, Annie Eliza Snyder died, followed two years later by her daughter Nelle.[135] And on April 30, 1921, the doctor himself passed away.

Dr. Snyder was stubborn, opinionated, and irascible. But he was more than that. He was also "a wonderful character, robust, able, courageous, original, versatile, brilliant. He was one of the really big men of Illinois, big physically, big emotionally and big intellectually. He was a pioneer and a frontiersman, a digger and a delver, a scout and an explorer in history and in science and in literature. When a man like that dies, the state and society suffer a loss that can never be replaced."[136]

135. Snyder Family Bible.
136. *Belleville News-Democrat,* May 2, 1921, reprinted in *Journal of the Illinois State Historical Society,* XIV (April–July, 1921): 245.

PART II

Selected Historical Writings

LIBRARY
College of St. Francis
JOLIET, ILL.

33916

CAPTAIN JOHN BAPTISTE SAUCIER
AT FORT CHARTRES IN THE ILLINOIS
1751–1763

Reprinted from *Transactions of the Illinois State Historical Society*, XXVI (1919): 215–63; originally printed by Smith and Schaefer of Peoria, Illinois, 1901. The 1919 version was reprinted "with Some Additions, and Correction of Certain Errors in the First Edition."

Preceding the text in the *Transactions* is the following preface by Dr. Snyder:

Every intelligent man should learn all he can of his ancestry, and transmit that knowledge to his descendents, in order that the traits and tendencies of the stock, if elevating, may be emulated; if degrading, may be corrected and improved.

This view prompted the writing of the biographical sketch, here presented, of Captain John Baptiste Saucier of the French Army, who assisted in designing the plans of the second Fort Chartres, in the Illinois, and superintended its construction.

Since the first edition of this little work was published, in 1901, diligent investigation of the Saucier family history has resulted in the discovery of new facts, and elimination of several errors in the original text. This revised edition is therefore believed to be substantially correct, and an inconsiderable, but reliable, contribution to the early history of Illinois.

Documentary evidences verifying many of the statements herein related, were lost nearly a century ago in the destruction by fire of his son's residence.

The known facts, and family legends, concerning Captain Saucier, have been collected, in this narrative form, by one of his descendents, to perpetuate the name and history of a brave soldier and honorable, upright citizen.

VIRGINIA, ILL.   J.F.S.

CHAPTER I. *The Sauciers in France*

At the beginning of the Eighteenth Century Monsieur Jean Beaumont Saucier—or Saussier, as the family name was then spelled[1]—was a prominent and prosperous merchant in the quaint old city of Orleans, in France. He was descended from a line of merchant ancestors, who had transacted business at the same place, the eldest son succeeding his father, from time immemorial. He had been carefully trained in the mercantile art by his father, Beaumont

---

1. See Note A [p. 80 below] in the Appendix. The French descendents of this family retain the original spelling of the name—Saussier—pronounced So-se-a. [Although "John" appears in this title, Snyder usually used the French "Jean."]

Saucier, who had, on retiring from business, a few years before, transferred to him the real estate, goods, credits and good will of the old establishment.

Jean Beaumont Saucier was then, in 1700 about twenty-five years of age; was happily married, and in the enjoyment of life's chief blessings, in the venerable family home situated midway between the house of Joan D'Arc and the ancient city wall. His only brother, Felix Xavier Saucier, a few years his senior, had chosen the military profession, and was then an officer in the Royal Guards at Versailles.

In the passing of time, with its swiftly shifting scenes and ceaseless changes, two sons were born to Monsieur and Madame Jean Beaumont Saucier; the first receiving the name of Louis Beaumont Saucier, and the other that of Paul. The thrifty young merchant was then blessed with possession of all the choicest gifts of life—health, success in business, friends in abundance, and angelic wife and two promising children. The world seemed to him radiant with joy, and the future full of buoyant hope. But suddenly a deep shadow fell upon his bright and happy home; caused by one of those subtle strokes of Fate, or inexorable Law, so difficult to reconcile with generally accepted doctrines of Omniscient mercy and goodness. By an accidental fall, down a tortuous stairway in the rambling old mansion, the young wife and mother received injuries that caused her death in a few hours.

M. Saucier was almost distracted by the shock, and for a long time was broken down by the intensity of his grief. But time compassionately assuages the pangs of suffering it inflicts, and mitigates the acutest sorrow. The terrible blow fully tested the young merchant's power of mental endurance; but he survived it, finding solace in the care and education of his children, and preparing them for the great battle of life before them.

The elder of the two, Louis Beaumont, destined to succeed his father, and perpetuate the Saucier mercantile house, received, at Paris, as thorough business training as was at that time practicable to obtain. Paul, who was gifted with his mother's gentle disposition, in course of time, was educated for the Church; and, after taking holy orders, was installed as coadjutor, or assistant priest, in the old Cathedral of his native city.

The time at length approached when M. Saucier, according to ancient family custom, would retire from the active management of his business, and relinquish it to his son, Louis. The thought of leaving the old homestead where he was born, hallowed by so many tender and endearing memories, cast a shadow of melancholy upon his mind, and induced a feeling of indescribable lonesomeness. He had purchased a little estate a few miles from Orleans, and fitted it up to suit his tastes, contemplating passing there the remainder of his days. This change of residence removed him but a few miles from the city; yet, it separated him for the greater part of time from his sons, and isolated him in the silence and solitude of the country, with servants as his only associates. This condition, contrasted with his former active life on the busy, noisy street, with genial, pleasant surroundings, seemed to him intolerable, and suggested—as is often the case with old widowers—the desirability of securing a sympathetic companion to share his elegant retirement.

While revolving the propriety of this momentous step in his mind an amusing incident occurred that dispelled any doubts or misgivings he may have entertained on the subject; and, like a stroke of magic, relieved him of all ennui and despondency. For years horseback riding had been his favorite exercise for the promotion of health, and relaxation from long hours of mental and physical business drudgery.

Mounted on his trusty horse, one fine evening in early summer, he cantered out beyond the limits of the old town, as was his custom, and turned his course into the great forest, preserved there for ages in its primitive wildness, to enjoy a view of nature in one of its grand and majestic forms. As he rode on he became so absorbed in the freshness and fragrance of the budding and blooming shrubs, and the wide-spreading leafy branches of the stately old trees, the chattering of squirrels and songs of birds, and, perhaps, in deep reveries of more tender kind, that he lost all note of time, direction and distance, and wandered on, along by-ways and obscure paths, until the light of day was fast disappearing. Great banks of black clouds now floated up from the south and overspread the sky; and, soon, intense darkness ushered in the approaching night.

He had often before ridden through the forest, and was familiar with the windings of its roads; but now, unable to see any object to guide his course, he realized the fact that he was lost. It was not, however, his first experience of that sort. He had before lost his way in the forest at night, when, trusting to the sagacity of his old horse, the faithful animal had safely and speedily carried him out of the dungeon-like gloom back to his home. He now dropped the reins, and, holding fast to the pommel of his saddle, bowed his head and urged his horse forward. Cautiously and steadily his four-footed servant pursued his course, across ravines, up one hill and down to another, turning now to the right, then to the left, and again straight on through the dense blackness that surrounded them. In his dreamy meandering before sunset, M. Saucier must have penetrated far into the depths of the old woods; for an hour or more had passed since his horse had commenced its unguided effort to retrace his course. So long indeed, that his confidence in the animal's instinct began to waver, and the horrid thought occurred to him that all this groping in the dark had been aimless, and that every step, perhaps, carried them farther into the interior of the vast wilderness. He began mentally to debate the advisability of stopping there, where he was, to await the return of day, when the rumbling of distant thunder, and flashes of blinding lightning, portending an advancing storm, strengthened his resolution to proceed yet a little farther. Just then the clatter of the horses' hoofs, and his accelerated gait, proved that he had reached a broad, well-beaten road. In a few minutes a glimmering light in the distance revived the despairing traveler's drooping spirits.

The light, when approached, was found to emanate from the window of a farm house. M. Saucier, though his horse manifested no disposition to slacken his brisk pace, concluded to stop and dispel his utter bewilderment by inquiring of the inmates of the house his exact whereabouts. Dismounting, he made out a gate that obstructed his course to the light. Securing his horse to the fence, he entered the premises and walked up a graveled way to the veranda, which now the interior light, and fitful lightning, disclosed from the impenetrable darkness. He had advanced to within a few steps of the house, when, to his utter amazement, a female figure came bounding from the door to meet him. She threw her arms around his neck, and kissing him fervently, exclaimed: "Oh, Papa! I am so glad you have come. You were so late getting home, I was fearful you had met with some accident."

Recovering from his surprise, and comprehending the young lady's mistake, he replied, "You are mistaken, Madame; I am not your father; but be not alarmed. I am Monsieur Saucier, a merchant on Rue Dupont, in Orleans; and having lost my way I stopped here on seeing the light in your window, to inquire where I am, and by what road I may the most speedily get back to my home." The young lady was obviously much confused; but regaining her composure, invited her accidental guest into the house, where he at once discovered her identity, and recovered his lost bearings.

30

Much to his relief he saw before him Mam'selle Adelaide Trotier, daughter of his old friend and patron, Jaques Trotier; and was in a house he had frequently before visited, situated on Trotier's farm, not quite a league from the old city wall. The girl explained that her father had gone to town early in the afternoon, and that she was anxiously expecting his return when she heard M. Saucier open the gate and come up the walk; and that she was feeling quite uneasy about his protracted absence; as he was very seldom detained in town to so late an hour. She had scarcely finished her last sentence when a step was heard on the veranda, and the door was opened by M. Trotier, who was no little astonished upon the unexpected meeting with his friend there. Explanations followed, and though the belated merchant was hospitably pressed to remain until morning, he declined, and, mounting his impatient horse, arrived at his own home as the threatened rain began to fall.

The adventures of that evening—most probably that impetuous kiss he received in the dark—wrought a notable change in M. Saucier's train of thought; and, also, in his plans for the future. His depression of spirits vanished and was replaced by marked cheerfulness. His equestrian excursions became more frequent and less extended, usually terminating at the Trotier farm. In short, it was soon noticed by his intimate associates that he had once more capitulated to Cupid, and, when, a few months later, his nuptials with the motherless Mam'selle Adelaide Trotier were announced in the Church, it elicited a variety of gossiping comments, but no surprise. The young lady was twenty-four years of age, handsome, tall and muscular; with some education and much amiability and sweetness of disposition. M. Saucier was then fifty-two years old—a little passed the middle period of life,—but in the prime of vigorous manhood.

The union of a man, some years passed the meridian of his probable existence, to a lady several years less than half his age, is usually—and justly—regarded as a violation of the natural order of things, and a consummate act of folly on the part of both. Yet, marriage under any auspices—the most flattering, or least promising—is always, in its happiness-producing results, a mere matter of lottery—an untried experiment.

CHAPTER II. *The Boyhood and Education of Jean Baptiste Saucier*

Four leagues below Orleans, on the right, or northern bank of the river, is situated the pretty little village Lachapelle; and half a league beyond it, nestled in the vine-clad hills overlooking the picturesque valley of the Loir for miles, was the tasty, yellow-roofed cottage of M. Saucier, where himself and bride were domiciled a few weeks after their marriage. Their ticket in the matrimonial lottery, fortunately, drew the highest prize; for, notwithstanding the disparity of their ages, their natures were compatible, and their days were redolent with unmarred happiness.

The doctrine of special Providence perhaps cannot be sustained; but surely none will deny the special mercy vouchsafed poor humanity by its total impotency to penetrate the future. With this knowledge given to mortals, suicide would depopulate the earth; without hope life would be a dreary blank. Among the many useful articles M. Saucier had taken with him to the country from his town residence, was his factotum, Pierre Lepage, a young man of unexceptionable habits, industrious, honorable, and strictly reliable. Moreover, he was a broad-gauged optimist, with splendid flow of spirits and humor. Pierre was installed as general manager of the little estate, and saw to trimming the vines, pruning the trees, cultivating the garden and miniature fields, and took care of the pigs, the poultry, the cows, and horses. All the day he was busy from dawn till bed-time; and was usually singing or whistling when not talking or laughing; and if not working or eating, was often fiddling or dancing.

The sentiment of love is not contagious as measles or whooping cough, but may be communicated by example or association. Pierre was exposed to this infection, and was a very susceptible subject to its influence. The connubial bliss he daily witnessed in the cottage profoundly impressed him, and strengthened his conviction that it is not best for man to dwell alone. He pondered the matter over for some time, and the more he thought about it the more assiduous he became in his devotions, or rather, in his attendance at church. Heretofore the priest had, on several occasions, reprimanded him for his neglect of this duty, and Pierre always excused himself on the plea of want of time. Now, however, he was, every Sabbath, the first one at the church door, and was a frequent caller at the priest's residence during week days, especially in the evenings. His neighbors, and the villagers, were for a time considerably surprised at this sudden manifestation of zealous piety, and began to surmise that Pierre's sins must be weighing heavily upon his conscience. This view seemed confirmed when he was seen to enter the confessional, supposedly to invoke the holy man's aid in lifting the burden from his sin-stricken soul. But they were mistaken. About all that Pierre had to confess to Father Jarvais was the fact that he was in love with his sister, Mam'selle Marie Jarvais; and that what he needed to ensure his happiness, and incidentally that of the young lady also, was not absolution so much as the good Father's consent to their union. This he obtained, and in due time they were married.

A year and a half had passed since M. Saucier had inducted his blooming young bride in their new home; and the fleeting days and months had brought to her increasing joy and happiness, and rose-tinted anticipations of a future blessing that would add new charms to that home, and gladden the hearts of its inmates. But, oh, how merciful it was for their sanguine hopes that no power could reveal to them the hidden calamity the future had in store for them.

On July 25th, 1726, the event occurred to which they had looked forward with glowing expectations, not unmixed, very naturally, with feelings of grave anxiety. On that day a son was born to them; and, for a short time it seemed that heaven had smiled upon them in the realization of their fondest wishes. The young mother had received the congratulations of her delighted husband and sympathetic friends and relatives around her; and had impressed on her infant's lips an impassioned kiss, when she was suddenly seized with horrible, agonizing convulsions, that continued at short intervals, baffling the skill of able physicians, and unceasing efforts of heroic nurses, until death mercifully relieved her of her suffering.

Marie Lepage, whose honeymoon had scarcely passed, remained resolutely by the stricken young woman's bedside, rendering every service in her power, until the awful scene was closed; and then took charge of the motherless child, constituting herself its foster mother and most affectionate and devoted nurse.

It is needless here to dwell upon the effect of this great bereavement upon Monsieur Saucier. Its crushing shock can much more readily be imagined than described. This pitiless stroke wellnigh bereft his life of every charm and hope. But from the almost intolerable misfortune there yet remained to him one incentive to live, and to continued exertion. The young life consigned to his love and care by the holy affection and confidence of the one who gave her life for it, demanded, and must receive, his unsparing attention for the balance of his declining years.

One bright Sunday morning the babe was taken down to the village church and baptized by Father Jarvais, receiving the name of Jean Baptiste Saucier, after a favored relative of his father, one Jean Baptiste Saucier, who had recently gone to America in the King's service.[2]

Pierre and Marie Lepage enjoyed the special privilege and honor of appointment as his god-father and god-mother. No more willing or faithful sponsors for the motherless child could have been selected. Under the angel-like watchfulness of Madame Lepage he thrived and grew apace, developing robust proportions, and rather more than average activity and intelligence.

Three years then passed over the house of mourning, when the gloom of its great sorrow was measurably dispelled and enlivened by a gleam of joy, this time unattended, or followed, by casualty or disaster. To Pierre and Marie was born a daughter, which event the proud father lost no time in heralding throughout the neighborhood and village. All went well, and the sunlight of love and joy again illuminated the cottage. The time for another baptism was soon at hand. By this time Pierre's exuberance of happiness had settled down sufficiently to permit him to think coherently, and he asked Marie if she had yet thought of a name for their girl.

"Yes, Pierre, I have," she said, "as a testimonial of our respect and affection for the sainted dead, and a token of gratitude to M. Saucier for the kindness and benefits we have received at his hands, I think we should name our child Adelaide; don't you?"

"Indeed I do, Marie," said Pierre, "and for the additional reason that Adelaide was my good old grandmother's name also."

And, so, the child received that name; but for convenience it was abridged to Adel. The two children infused new life and light in the cottage; and it regained much of its former cheerful home-like appearance. They were reared together as brother and sister, sharing alike the love and tender care of the young mother, and of Pierre and the old gentleman. In time they grew strong enough to follow Pierre about when at work in the garden, or among the vines, and to ride with him in the cart to and from the fields. And when

2. See Appendix, Note B. [Pp. 80–85 below.]

34

Marie dressed them out in gay attire, M. Saucier experienced great pleasure and pride in taking them with him in his gig on his frequent visits to the village, where they were petted and admired by friends and relatives. In course of time they daily walked to the village together, when the weather was fair, the boy carrying their dinner basket, and attended the village school, and learned the catechism. It was a long walk, but as other children joined them along the road, they enjoyed the exercise and were benefitted by it. In bad weather, or muddy roads, Pierre bundled them in his cart and took them to the school house, and returned for them when school was dismissed in the evening.

Jean Baptiste rapidly grew to be a manly lad; stout, athletic, and courageous. He learned quickly, was fond of active sports, and, though neither ill-tempered or quarrelsome, was not slow to resent an insult, or redress a wrong. In consequence, he often had occasion to test his muscular power, and was not long in being accorded the pugilistic championship of the school.

Adel was of quiet and retiring disposition, but brave and spirited enough to admire her foster-brother's knightly traits. They were brought up, as their parents and ancestors had been, in the Catholic faith, and together received elementary religious instruction at Father Jarvais' parochial school; and together they knelt at the altar in their first Communion.

But the happy childhood days were fleeting, and the inevitable time at length arrived decreeing their separation, and diverging their young lives into different channels. The boy would ere long have to assume his part in the serious drama of life, and needed to be well prepared for it. He had exhausted the old village teacher's resources and learning, and must seek higher instruction at the Academy in Orleans. He left his home for the first time, and though his destination was but a few miles away, the leave taking left no dry eyes in the cottage. He visited his home at the close of each week; yet, his absence left a dreary void that dampened the hilarity of the family circle.

He was graduated at the Academy at the head of his class, and then accompanied his father to Paris, to visit his uncle, Col. Felix Xavier Saucier, and to see the many attractive sights visible in the splendid metropolis. It is a family tradition that Colonel Saucier bound the boy's hands together behind his back with a handkerchief, when he took him through the great palace at Versailles, in order to restrain his intense desire to touch or handle the swords and other glittering arms he saw there at every turn.

Jean Baptiste was so captivated by the fine martial bearing of Colonel Saucier, and the perfect discipline and gorgeous appearance of his regiment of Royal Guards, that he determined then and there to emulate his uncle's course in the profession of arms; and to consecrate his life to the cause of his king and his country. His natural aptitude for that calling, and erect, soldierly, figure, won the Colonel's admiration and encouragement. After much persuasion he gained his father's consent; then through the influence and efforts of his uncle, was admitted into the Royal Military School as a cadet.

This disruption of home ties—destined to be prolonged indefinitely—cast upon the inmates of the cottage overlooking the Loir a deeper cloud of sadness. M. Saucier wandered about the fields and vineyards aimlessly as though lost, and Adel wept in secret. Pierre was not so jolly as of old, and had frequent moments of serious reflection. And poor Marie, diligent as ever with her routine domestic affairs, often blamed the onions, or mustard, or the dust or smoke, for bringing tears to her eyes that she wiped away with her apron.

Jean Baptiste was too thoroughly engrossed in his studies and duties to be homesick. His excellent scholarship, assiduous application and intellectual alertness enabled him to readily master the curriculum and training of L'Ecole Militaire; from which he emerged at the early age of twenty-two with a commission of Lieutenant of Engineers in the Royal Army.

He returned to his cottage home on a brief leave of absence, arrayed in the tinseled trappings of his newly attained rank, a superb type of physical manhood and gallant soldier. All gazed on him with pride, and feelings akin to adoration. Pierre no longer called him pet names, but doffed his hat in respectful obeisance; and Marie, in happy amazement, addressed him as *Monsieur* Jean Baptiste. Adel could scarcely realize that the handsome young military officer, in showy uniform, now before her, was the impetuous boy companion of her childhood; and she awoke to the consciousness that her sisterly affection for him had somehow changed to a different and loftier sentiment. This discovery caused her to be strangely demure and reserved in his presence. Too soon the limit of his furlough expired; and he received orders from the War Department at Paris, to report for duty at once to Major Makarty at Brienne. Then came the trying ordeal of taking final leave of his dear old home where he had passed all the early and happiest years of his life, and of the loved ones he was destined never to see again.

Feeling his fortitude about to desert him, he tore himself away, after receiving the tremulous blessing of his gray-haired father, the tearful fare-well of big-hearted Pierre, and fervent embrace of his beloved foster-mother, Marie, and lastly, the parting kiss of Adel, now a charming maiden with lustrous black eyes, rosy cheeks and queenly figure, who, with mighty effort, repressed her tears until the young soldier had disappeared down the wind-ing road leading to the village.

It is altogether probable that the order of the Ministre de Marine to the young officer, to join Major Makarty's command for service in America, was in compliance to his own request. The romance and glamour of the new world, centering in highly colored representations of wild, free life on the great Mississippi, were still attracting there many from the better classes of the French people. Moved by the spirit of adventure usually exuberant at his age, and by aspirations for attaining distinction in the service of his coun-try, Lieutenant Saucier did not hesitate to sever the sacred bonds of kindred, home, and friendships, in responding to that call to duty. Two considerations, however, tended to ameliorate the pangs of that sacrifice and his prospective exile; one was the vague hope that his absence would not be of long con-tinuance, and the other that he would meet relatives of his father there who had preceded him to the new empire, one of whom, in particular, a civil engineer, who had long been employed in the construction and preservation of old Fort Chartres.[3]

CHAPTER III. *Fort Chartres in the Illinois*

In the autumn of 1718, Pierre Duque Boisbriant, recently appointed Commandant of the Illinois, by the Company of the Indies, arrived at Kas-kaskia with a detachment of troops for the purpose of constructing a fort in that region to protect the Company's interests there, and the French colonists in that portion of New France. Boisbriant, a Canadian by birth, and cousin of Bienville, then Governor of Louisiana, arrived at Mobile on the 9th of February, 1718. Proceeding to Biloxi he there made his preparations, and then commenced his long voyage up the great river, which he accomplished by fall without incident of note. Gov. Bienville and a colony of French ac-companied him from Mobile to a point on the east bank of the Mississippi,

3. See Appendix, Note B. [Pp. 80–85 below.]

thirty leagues above its mouth, where they founded a post they named Iberville, subsequently re-named New Orleans.

The site selected by Boisbriant for his fort in the Illinois, was near the east bank of the Mississippi, on the flat alluvial bottom land, sixteen miles above Kaskaskia; having a long slough, or lake, the remains of an ancient channel of the river, on the east midway between it and the bluffs four miles away. This slough, he supposed, would add materially to the strategic strength of the position. The fort he erected there was a wooden stockade reinforced on the interior with earth taken from the excavations of the exterior moats. It was completed in 1720, and named Fort de Chartres, as a compliment to the Regent, whose son was Le Duc de Chartres.

This fort was for many years the *chef-lieu,* or seat of civil as well as military government of the Illinois district embracing the territory from the mouth of the Ohio to Canada between the Mississippi and Wabash rivers. In 1731, the Company of the West failed and surrendered their charter to the king. The Illinois was by this act receded to the crown of France.

For the protection of Kaskaskia from threatened incursions of the fierce Chickasaws, below the mouth of the Ohio, a stockade fort, was in the year 1733, erected on the bluff just east of the town, and a portion of the troops at Fort Chartres were sent there to garrison it. This Kaskaskia fort has been known, erroneously, since the conquest of the Illinois by George Rogers Clark, as "Fort Gage." Its name, and the name of its builder, are lost. It was a French fort, and when the disheartening news of the cession of the country by the craven King of France to the English, in 1763, reached the town of Kaskaskia, the indignant citizens set fire to the fort and destroyed it, determined that the hated ensign of England should not float over it. The "Fort Gage" entered by Col. George Rogers Clark, on the night of the 4th of July, 1778, was the stockaded Jesuit buildings in the town, occupied by the British under the command of M. Rocheblave.[4]

It is much to be regretted that so few of the records and official documents

4. Fort Chartres passed into possession of the English in 1765. Seven years later, in 1772, occurred an extraordinary rise of the Mississippi that inundated all the low lands along its borders. The water rose in Fort Chartres to the depth of seven feet. The northwest bastion, and greater part of the western wall fell into the river. The Fort was abandoned by the English, who took possession of the large buildings of the Jesuits in Kaskaskia, surrounding them with a stockade, which they named Fort Gage, and there established their seat of government, military and civil, for the Illinois. At the period of Capt. Bossu's second visit to Fort Chartres, in 1755, the fort on the hill, east of Kaskaskia, was garrisoned by French troops commanded by Captain Montcharvaux. It was destroyed in 1766.

of old Fort Chartres have been preserved to reveal to us the story of its occupants in their daily life; of the stirring events, and strange, thrilling scenes transpiring there; of the busy throngs that came and went; of the military expeditions marching from its gates to repel invasions, or attack distant enemies; of the Indians lounging about its gates, or camped near by; of the joys and sorrows, deaths and griefs, hopes and disappointments of its inmates in their remote exile from civilization.

About the close of the first half of the Eighteenth century France and England were again at war because of a disagreement between Frederick the Great and Marie Theresa [Maria Theresa, Empress of Austria]; and this produced serious disturbances in the settlements in the Illinois. Some Englishmen lurking on the Mississippi were arrested as spies and confined in the dungeon at Fort Chartres. Then rumors came of a contemplated English and Indian attack on the Fort in retaliation. Chevalier de Bartel, the Commandant of the Post was sorely perplexed. The Fort was sadly out of repair, and supplies of all sorts very nearly exhausted. Many of the soldiers of the garrison, tiring of idle confinement had deserted to try free life in the woods and prairies. Many of "the old-time Indian allies were won over by the British, and agreed to destroy the French post during the moon of the fall of the leaf, but they were thwarted by the skill and address of De Bertel." [5]

The peace of Aix-la-Chapelle, in 1748, gave the dissolute King of France, Louis XV, brief respite from contention with England and profitless continental wars, only to sink deeper in vice and debauchery, and to become more completely under control of the beautiful, soulless Madame de Pompadour. He had impoverished France by his profligacy, and support, with his armies and treasury, of his father-in-law's claims to the throne of Poland, and in the wars of the Austrian succession. Meanwhile his American colonies were utterly neglected, and some of his western military posts, including Fort Chartres, on the verge of abandonment. This latter calamity, however, was averted "when," again quoting from Mr. Mason's paper, "the Marquis de Galissonière, Gov.-General of Canada, presented a memorial on the subject to the home government. He [therein] says, 'The little colony of Illinois ought not to be left to perish. The King must sacrifice for its support. The

---

See "The Armament of Fort Chartres," a paper in the 1906 *Transactions* of the Illinois State Historical Society, page 225.

5. Old Fort Chartres. A paper read by Hon. E. G. Mason before the Chicago Historical Society, June 16th, 1880. Fergus Co., Chicago. [This paper and two others are No. 12 of the Fergus Historical Series; the quotations, corrected here, are from pp. 32–33.]

principal advantage of the country is its extreme productiveness, and its connection with Canada and Louisiana must be maintained.'" Again in January, 1750, he "urged upon the King the importance of preserving and strengthening the post at the Illinois, describing the country as open and ready for the plough, and traversed by an innumerable multitude of buffaloes. 'And these animals,' he says, 'are covered with a species of wool, sufficiently fine to be employed in various manufactories!' And he further suggests, and, doubtless, correctly, that 'the buffalo, if caught, and attached to the plow, would move it at a speed superior to that of the domestic ox!'"

The King was at last aroused to a proper understanding of the deplorable condition of affairs in his far western possessions, and decided upon a vigorous policy to defend and retain them. He ordered Fort Chartres to be rebuilt with stone, and garrisoned with a body of regular troops. For the reconstruction of the Fort he appropriated a million of crowns; and ordered large quantities of munitions, and other supplies, to be sent up the Mississippi at once.

In the summer of 1751, Chevalier Makarty,[6] a Major of the Engineer Corps, a rugged soldier of remote Irish descent, arrived at the Fort, from France, with a considerable military force and a large number of artisans and laborers, and boats ladened with tools, ammunition, arms, provisions and clothing. The Major assumed command of the post, and lost no time in beginning the great work he had been sent there to do. In this era of scientific military engineering it is difficult to imagine any reason for locating a defensive work upon such a wretched site as that selected for Fort Chartres. It was situated on sandy, alluvial soil but little elevated above the river's level, and continually subject to the river's encroachments; with a slough between it and the river bank, and a large slough between it and the bluffs; and in the midst of pestilential malarious, mosquito-infested, swamps. And why an

---

6. This is the correct spelling of his name, as written by himself on the parish records of the Church of St. Anne of New Chartres. Of Major Makarty, who was Commandant at Fort Chartres during the very interesting period of its construction, unfortunately but little is known. Of his personal history and characteristics we know absolutely nothing. But meagre mention is made of him in any of our local histories; and the records of his official acts are lost, or stored in the state archives at Paris. In 1753, M. DuQuesne, Governor General, wrote to the Minister of Marine, at Paris, charging Commandant Makarty with illicit sales of liquor to the Indians and French settlers, and advising that he be relieved therefor of his command. But no attention was paid to this charge, and he was not relieved until 1761, and then by his own request; as, at this time, he was incapacitated for active service by reason of disability from rheumatic gout.

Engineer of Chevalier Makarty's presumed attainments erected a splendid fortress, at immense expense on the same ground is beyond comprehension, excepting on the supposition that he acted in obedience to positive instructions. His arrival at the post, with well equipped and well disciplined soldiers and their sprightly officers, accompanied by a small army of skilled mechanics and laborers, and a fleet of keel-boats of stores, produced a great sensation not only at the decayed and nearly deserted post, but all through the settlements in the Illinois. Fort Chartres awoke from its lethargy and was transformed to a scene of busy animation. The hum of a new activity resounded in the forest and distant hills. The *habitants* of the bottom were elated; and the Indians gazed upon the new arrivals in mute surprise.

Captain M. Bossu, who came up the Mississippi with a company of marines, the following spring, 1752, writing from Fort Chartres, says, "LeSieur Saussier, an engineer, has made a plan for constructing a new Fort here according to the instruction of the Court. It will bear the name of the old one, which is called Fort de Chartres." The stockades of the old fort were decayed beyond repair, though the buildings they enclosed were yet tenable and in fair condition. The site chosen for the new structure was not half a league above the old Fort, and but a short distance from the river.[7]

At that point a mission for the Kaskaskia Indians had many years before been established—which was perhaps one reason for locating the new Fort there—and it served as the nucleus of quite a town at the gate of the Fort, subsequently known as Nouveau (New) Chartres.

Chevalier Makarty began operations by sending a large force of workmen to the bluffs at the nearest escarpment of limestone, about four miles east, where they built temporary quarters of logs covered with clapboards, there to blast the rock and cut the detached masses to required dimensions. "The place in the bluff may be seen to this day where the stone was quarried to erect the fort."[8] Another force of laborers, with carts drawn by oxen, con-

7. I acknowledge with pleasure my indebtedness to Hon. H. W. Beckwith, President of the Illinois State Historical Society, for important references corroborating this fact, and correcting the common impression that the new fort, built of stone, was a reconstruction of the old stockade. Captain Bossu, who again visited the fort in 1755, says—in his *Travels en Louisiane*—"I came once more to the old Fort Chartres, where I lay in a hut, till I could get lodging in the new fort, which is almost finished." [See p. 158, Vol. I of the 1771 edition in English. This quotation and that in the text (p. 127, *ibid.*) may have been translated by Snyder from the French edition, since they differ slightly in wording.]

8. Reynolds' *Pioneer History of Illinois*. [Quotation from p. 47.] "The finer stone, with which the gateways and buildings were faced, were brought from beyond the Mississippi." E. G. Mason. ["Old Fort Chartres," 34; quotation corrected.]

veyed the dressed stone, around the end of the slough, in the dry season, to
the builders by the river; and in the wet season to the slough, or lagoon, across
which they were ferried in flat boats, and then taken on to the required place.
Besides these were lime burners, mortar mixers, wood choppers and whip-saw-
yers, carpenters, blacksmiths, boatmen, teamsters, hunters, cooks and servants, comprising, with the soldiers, a population of several hundreds. The
new fort was projected on a more modern plan than the old one, and was
much larger; a quadrangle, comprising an area of four acres. The exterior
walls of massive masonry, thirty inches in thickness at the base, and loop-
holed for musket and artillery firing, rose sixteen feet in height, with square
bastions at each corner, and midway in the west wall was a small gate for
convenience of access to the river landing. The northeastern bastion having
the flagstaff was higher than the others. In the southeastern bastion was
situated the magazine of stone, laid in cement now as hard as flint. It is yet in
sound preservation; its vertical end walls twenty-five feet in height, closing
the arch between. Its floor, seven feet below the surface, and its interior, well
plastered with cement, measuring twenty-five feet by eighteen; and twenty-
two feet from floor to apex of the arch. There were also long lines of barracks, officers' quarters, and store rooms.

The period occupied in building the new fort was one of unprecedented
prosperity for that portion of New France. Kaskaskia, the metropolis of the
Illinois, the center of its widespread commerce, and of its wealth and industries, profited largely by its proximity to the military post. Its citizens of
French lineage, were not distinguished for energy or enterprise, but were
thrifty and self-reliant. With this continuous round of mirth and festivities
they were not unmindful of their own interests. Cahokia, twenty-eight miles
above the fort, on the Mississippi, rivaled Kaskaskia as a trading point, was
almost its equal in population, and its people were as noted for their social
gaieties and generous hospitality. Prairie du Rocher, settled in 1722, and
nestled at the foot of a high perpendicular cliff of the bluffs, four miles southeast of the fort, gained much importance during the construction of the new
fortification. St. Philip, founded by Renault, five miles above the old fort, on
his extensive land grant, had passed the zenith of its growth, and was already
known among the settlers as "Le Petite Village." New Chartres in the parish
of St. Ann, near the main gate of the new fort, gained the proportions of a
considerable town having absorbed the greater part of the population of the

town below, near the old fort,[9] with a large part of that of St. Philip, and comprised the temporary homes of the mechanics and laborers employed on the new structure; also of some of the officers and soldiers having families.

These settlements constituted an isolated community surrounded by Indians, having only periodical communication with the outside world by way of New Orleans, or the northern lakes and Quebec. They were all situated on the alluvial "bottom" of the Mississippi, a region of unsurpassed fertility, teeming with wild fruits and nuts, and overrun by herds of buffalo, deer, turkeys, prairie chickens, and other varieties of game; its numerous lakes and sloughs visited by myriads of water fowls, and alive with the finest of fish. Nature lavishly supplied, in a great measure, the simple wants of the people, and left both old and young to regard the pursuit of pleasure the chief object of existence.

CHAPTER IV. *Social Life at the Fort*

The household of the Commandant, Chevalier de Makarty, consisted, with himself, of his son and daughter, his wife having died some years before of that entailed curse upon humanity, pulmonary consumption. The son, Maurice, acted in the capacity of his father's secretary and personal assistant. The daughter, Eulalie, a tall, slender, handsome girl of twenty summers, with very fair complexion, blue eyes and auburn hair, though French by parentage and education, possessed some marked traits of her father's Celtic ancestry, with the physical constitutional frailties of her deceased mother. As some of the officers in the Chevalier's command were accompanied by their wives and families, she had come with her father and brother, by advice of her physician, in quest of health and vigor that a change of climate might offer.

She was by no means an invalid; and the rough, wild life at the post, for a time, greatly improved her strength and animation. In the quarters she enlivened the garrison with her music and laughter, when not engaged in alleviating the sufferings of the sick by her kind and patient attentions. A great deal of her time was passed in the open air when the weather permitted, as she was much interested in the progress of the work, and in everything she

9. "The site of this village was swept off by the Mississippi; so that not much or any vestage of it remains at this day. This village had its common field, commons for wood and pasture, its church and grave-yard, like the other settlements of Illinois." Reynolds' *Pioneer History of Illinois.* [Corrected quotation from p. 50.]

saw in the strange new country. She had for a companion—who followed her everywhere like her shadow—a mulatto servant, named Lisette, a native of Martinique, a few years her senior in age; strong, agile as a cat, and absolutely fearless. This maid was devoted to her young mistress almost to infatuation. In pleasant weather with bright skies, the two could be daily seen together, mounted on their ponies, galloping over the prairie; or on the high bluff viewing the grand panorama before them; or in a canoe, paddled by the intrepid Lisette, on the broad Mississippi; or fishing on the marais; or gathering wild flowers, nuts, or grapes near the Fort. Occasionally some of the ladies from the officers' quarters joined them, and quite often a gallant officer, then off duty, offered his services as an escort to guard them from harm, and to enjoy the young lady's smiles. Eulalie and her dusky maid needed no countersign to pass the camp sentinels; but were prudently restrained from going beyond the cordon of outriding pickets without an escort of armed horsemen.

The multitude of people at the Fort engaged in the gigantic work, and the number of officers and soldiers quartered there, rendered it an attractive place for all surrounding settlements; not only for sale of produce, and other traffic, but also for social enjoyment and pastimes. The Fort was frequently visited by parties of ladies and gentlemen from Kaskaskia, or Cahokia, or both, to spend the day in rowing, fishing, or picnicing, followed, after candle lighting by dancing.

Strict discipline was at all times enforced by the Commandant of the garrison. The troops were regularly drilled; sentinels and picket guards, or videttes, were constantly on duty, and the distant stone and wood workers and teamsters were guarded by squads of well armed soldiers. These precautions, apart from maintaining discipline and order, were necessary because of the defenseless condition of both forts, the old and the new, during the erection of the latter, in view of the many rumors of Indian hostilities, and possible attacks at any time by the despised English.[10]

10. In 1752 six Indians of the Outagami, or Fox tribe, then residing west of Lake Michigan, came down the country on a hunting expedition, and were captured by the Cahokia Indians, who burned five of them at the stake. The sixth one escaped to return to his people and report the fate of his companions. A council was called, and revenge determined upon. One hundred and eighty bark canoes filled with Foxes and their allies, the Kickapoos and Sioux, descended the river, passing the fort at Cahokia, then commanded by Chevalier de Volsci, at night without being seen. The Cahokias and Michigamis were encamped, as Bossu says, but a league from Fort Chartres. The day on which the avengers arrived happened to be one of the numerous fast days of the Catholic church, when several of the Indians from the village had gone to Fort Chartres to witness the ceremonies of the Church there. They were all who

Lieutenant Jean Baptiste Saucier reported for duty to Major Makarty at Brienne; and there, before sailing with his command from France, received from the Minister of Marine specific instructions regarding the character of fort the king desired to be erected. During the long, tedious voyage across the Atlantic, and the laborious ascent of the Mississippi, the young lieutenant was much in the company of the Major's daughter, Mam'selle Eulalie. And after their arrival at the old Fort, his relations with the Commandant continued confidential and intimate, his assignment as Chief Designer requiring his presence at headquarters much of his time. While there at work the young lady was frequently at his side, assisting in his drawings and calculations; and, when off duty, he was often her companion in morning excursions, and in the evening cotillions and waltzes. This continued association of the handsome young officer and the brilliant girl, in their distant exile, naturally engendered in both sentiments of mutual regard higher and more fervent than mere respect. And indeed, with her, this sentiment gradually deepened to an absorbing passion. He would probably have fully reciprocated this feeling, but for the everpresent image before him of his childhood's playmate, schoolmate, and more than sister, the stately Adel, far away on the sun-kissed hills of the Loire. He admired Eulalie, but loved Adel.

CHAPTER V. *Rescue of Commandant's Daughter*

All through the winter and succeeding summer the adjacent forest resounded with strokes of the woodman's axe and mason's hammer; and heavy blasting of rocky cliffs above Prairie du Rocher was reechoed like distant peals of artillery. The Indians watched the progress of the work in silent amazement, and the Creole settlers were loud in praises of their good and munificent King. The second winter passed pleasantly at the Fort with no cessation of labor in preparing building materials; or interruption of the usual exchange of polite courtesies between the officers and the elite of Kaskaskia and Cahokia. Unrelaxed military vigilance was maintained; and the peace

survived the vengeance of the Foxes, who slew every man, woman and child remaining in the village, excepting a fifteen year old girl who ran to Capt. Bossu for protection and was not molested. Capt. Bossu says he witnessed this massacre "from an eminence near by"; but it is difficult to understand what "eminence" he found there, without it was one of the ancient prehistoric Indian mounds. The Foxes reascended the Mississippi river, firing their guns in triumph as they passed the Cahokia stockade.

and quietude of the post was undisturbed, save by frequent false alarms of Indian uprisings, or English invasions.

The second Easter came and passed, and the snow and ice disappeared. The hickory buds were bursting in the woods tinged with green; and the prairie lark, just up from the south, enlivened the scene with his cheery notes. One beautiful morning in the early spring, Lieutenant Saucier had passed out of the river gate, on a tour of inspection of that portion of the structure, when he was suddenly startled by the discharge of a musket and loud shrieks of the sentinel stationed on the river bank scarcely a rifle shot distant from where he stood. Rushing to the spot he saw the soldier wildly gesticulating and loudly calling for help. Glancing over the river bank, the Lieutenant saw the cause of his agitation—a sight that almost paralyzed him; but only for a moment. Eulalie and her maid, lured by the brilliance of the perfect day to resume their canoe excursions suspended during the long winter, had rowed some distance up the great stream, and returning, when but a short distance from the landing, a puff of wind blew the young lady's hat off into the water. In her effort to recover it she capsized the canoe, and the two girls were struggling for life in the turbid current of the river. Lisette was clinging to the upturned dugout with one hand, and with the other had grasped her young mistress and was endeavoring to support her head above the treacherous waves. The sentinel on duty there, a few yards away, witnessed the accident, but as he had never learned to swim, was powerless to afford help; yet, had the presence of mind to fire his gun to attract assistance.

As the Lieutenant reached the water's edge Lisette lost her hold of Eulalie who sank beneath the surface. Quick as thought, he threw aside his coat and hat and plunged into the stream. He was an expert swimmer, and though encumbered with his clothing, and the water was very cold, he caught the girl as she was disappearing, and, by exertion that only such an emergency could inspire, succeeded in bringing her to the shore.

When Lisette saw her mistress sink she quit the canoe to attempt her rescue; but the Lieutenant, who had by this time grasped the drowning girl, called to the servant to save herself, which she readily did by swimming to the bank. The report of the sentinel's gun and his frantic cries were immediately answered at the Fort by the long roll of the drum, and the company then on duty, led by its officers, came dashing to the place of supposed attack. A hand litter was quickly improvised upon which Eulalie, exhausted, pale

46

and unconscious, but still breathing, was placed, warmly enveloped in several of the coats that nearly every member of the company divested himself of and offered for the purpose. She was hurriedly taken to her apartments, where the post surgeons, aided by all the ladies of the garrison, in time, resuscitated her. From the river bank Lisette, fatigued and, of course, dripping wet, walked briskly behind the litter borne by the soldiers, and could not be induced to lose sight of her mistress until assured that all immediate danger was passed.

Eulalie was saved from death by drowning; but the shock she received, together with the cold immersion, resulted in a severe attack of pneumonia that brought her to the verge of collapse. She was confined to her room for some weeks, for several days in the balance between life and death, the beam finally turning in her favor. The wild roses and sunflowers were in bloom when she had gained sufficient strength to sit in the dearborn, or caleche, cushioned around, for exercise in the prairie in the early mornings and evenings. A cough she had contracted during the Christmas festivities became aggravated and persistent. The melancholy fact that she was now an invalid, with serious pulmonary trouble, was apparent, with but little doubt of its ultimate result.

CHAPTER VI. *Early Navigation of the Mississippi*

Communication with France, by the residents of the Illinois, was at that era slow and uncertain. The best sailing vessels required from two to four months to cross the Atlantic; and often that length of time was consumed in propelling keel boats, or lighter craft, from New Orleans to Kaskaskia, or the Fort. About half the same period of time was necessary for the transmission of despatches and letters from Quebec, by friendly Indians, or hardy Canadian couriers, to the Illinois settlements. Traveling by either route was irksome and laborious, and attended by many dangers, particularly when passing through hostile tribes of Indians.

Lieutenant Saucier called frequently on Eulalie, and by affecting much cheerfulness himself, sought to stimulate her hopes, and inspire her with courage. And her spirits always revived when in his presence, or within sound of his voice.

Several weeks had passed since Eulalie's thrilling experience in the river when, one day, a courier, accompanied by several Indians, arrived at the Fort

47

from Quebec, bringing official despatches from the Governor General, and also from the home government, and European mail for the Fort and surrounding settlements. When the Lieutenant called that evening, as usual, at the Commandant's quarters to enquire how the young lady had passed the day, and to assure her that she looked better, he received, among other letters from France, one with familiar superscription closed with a black seal, which he pretended not to notice as he hurriedly put it, with the others, in his pocket. He soon excused himself on the plea of duty, and, reaching the privacy of his room, tore the black-sealed missive open with trembling hands, and quivering lips. It was from Adel, and its contents caused a conflict of emotions; of profound grief and joy, of sadness and pleasure, that plunged him in deep thought, oblivious to his surroundings for a long time. She informed him of the death of his father; how he calmly passed away with his two sons and military brother by his side; how his priest son had administered to him extreme unction; and how in his last conscious moments he had spoken of, and invoked the blessings of heaven upon his youngest and beloved son, now in the King's service far away in New France. She described the funeral ceremonies, and told of the great concourse of friends of the deceased that followed his body to the grave. She then said that by this sad event her father, Pierre, would be thrown out of employment, as the estate would pass into other hands, and that he had concluded to emigrate to America and try his fortunes there. She added that they had engaged passage in a vessel named L'Etoile du Nord, for New Orleans, and would sail from the port of Brest about the tenth of February. In a postscript she told him he need not answer her letter, as their preparations for leaving the dear old cottage were then nearly completed.

Young Saucier was deeply affected by the death of his father, though he had passed the three score and ten allotted to humanity and succumbed to the inexorable law of nature. His grief was mitigated by the reflection that he would again meet Adel and her dear, dear parents, much sooner than his most sanguine hopes had permitted him to expect.

After entering the military service the Lieutenant was always reticent about his family history and relatives, and confided to no one the profound and sincere love he entertained for Adel. For reasons of his own he mentioned to no one the information Adel's letter had conveyed, excepting to tell of his father's death to Chevalier Makarty.

48

He was now moody, silent and reflective, in such marked contrast with his usual social, jovial disposition, as to attract the notice of his associates, who charitably attributed the change to his tender solicitude for the invalid girl in the Fort, now slowly fading away. How to dispose of Pierre and Marie when they arrived gave him no uneasiness, as he was well able financially to situate them comfortably in any of the neighboring settlements. But there was another matter he could not so easily dispose of, that he now had to consider. He was fully aware of Eulalie's fervent regard for him; now intensified by gratitude for having saved her life at the risk of his own; and his sense of honor upbraided him for permitting her to be longer deceived respecting the true sentiments he entertained for her. He concluded he would frankly tell her that another had a prior claim to his affections. But then, Adel had never spoken or written to him of love, save that of a sister; and, for aught he knew, she might then be the plighted fiancée of another. Having nerved himself to the point of making a full disclosure of his perplexing thoughts and sentiments to Eulalie, he called upon her for that purpose. His resolution, however, failed him when, seated by her bedside, he took her feverish hand in his and looked into her shrunken, haggard face. He saw that her frail condition could not bear such a revelation; and he esteemed her too highly to subject her to the anguish of mind it would cause, and thereby endanger her slender hold upon life, and, so, postponed his intended confession to a more propitious time.

The days sped by and he continued dreamily to discharge his routine duties in silence.

The time had arrived for the annual descent of the fleet of keel boats to New Orleans for supplies for the post. The voyage that year was one of unusual importance, as engineers' reports and other weighty despatches were awaiting transmission to France, and a considerable amount of specie, large supplies, and a company of recruits for the Fort, must be brought up from New Orleans. The annual voyages to and from New Orleans were generally in charge of a subaltern of the Commissary, or Quartermaster's department; and they were by no means mere pleasure jaunts. The loading and unloading of the boats, their navigation, controlling the crews of boatsmen, and guarding against the many dangers by the way, involved grave responsibilities, and entailed many hardships, with much exposure and hard labor; requiring vigilance, prudence and great firmness. The boats commonly employed in this service, called *pirogues* by the French river men, were large, unwieldy, clumsy affairs, constructed of hewed timbers and whip-sawed plank fastened together with wooden pegs. Floating with the current and the use of oars, rendered descent of the stream comparatively easy; but stemming the river's current in its ascent for over a thousand miles was accomplished only by persistent hard work. To surmount the force of the swift current for long stretches of the way, or to pass strong eddies, the boats were "cordeled"; that is, a long line was taken ashore and carried far above, where it was made fast to a tree on the river's bank. The boat was then drawn, by hand, or capstan, to that point; and this was repeated again and again until calmer water was reached, when the oars were once more plied. When practicable, the boats were drawn by the united strength of the crew walking along the shore, as horses draw canal boats. At night, when going up stream, the boats laid by in willow thickets bordering sand bars, or islands, for safety from surprises or night attacks by hostile Indians.

CHAPTER VII. *A Second Visit to New Orleans*

The Commandant was about to detail a non-commissioned officer for that summer's voyage, when he was much surprised by receiving an application from Lieut. Saucier for this duty. While Major Makarty would not have ordered a commissioned officer for this onerous service, he was pleased when Lieut. Saucier volunteered for it; for he knew that it could not be entrusted to anyone more reliable, or more capable to conduct it successfully, and gladly assented to his request.

Having perfected his preparations, the Lieutenant took leave of Eulalie, promising to return as soon as possible, and expressing the hope that he would find her much better when he came. His boats were furnished by the merchants of Kaskaskia and Cahokia, free of charge excepting the transportation down the river of their export produce. Some of them were loaded with lead in bars from Renault's mines at New Potosi, in the Spanish territory across the river; others carried cargoes of furs obtained in trade from the Indians; others with beeswax, dried venison, buffalo meat, and other products of the country. Even at that early day much wheat was raised by the *habitants,* and flour, ground by the water mills, was one of the principal exports of the country.

The Lieutenant's progress, with his fleet, down the river was rapid and without extraordinary incident. The tedium of the voyage was lightened by his anticipations of joy in meeting, at his destination, the loved ones who had left France some months before, and were probably then at New Orleans awaiting his arrival. In imagination he pictured the surprise of Pierre and Marie upon meeting him, and wondered how Adel looked, and what she would say.

Arriving at New Orleans, after securing his boats, he eagerly enquired along the river front for the expected vessel, L'Etoile du Nord, and was grievously disappointed when told that nothing had yet been heard of it. After paying his respects to Colonel Kerlerec, the then Governor of Louisiana, he secured pleasant lodgings, and proceeded industriously to discharge the duties of his mission. The Governor courteously took charge of his despatches, to transmit them, with his own, to the Minister of Marine by special messenger. Overhauling and refitting his boats; keeping his crews of boatsmen under control; receiving, receipting for, assorting and stowing away his cargoes of munitions, and supplies of various kinds, occupied his time for many days. Though he was the recipient of many invitations from the Governor, officers, and citizens, to dinners, balls, and other social entertainments, he declined all that he well could on different pretexts, feeling that in his state of mental anxiety they would afford him no pleasure, and he could not acquit himself as a guest with credit.

He arose every morning with the sun, and took long walks along the river levee, or about the straggling town; and often during the day he scanned the great river southward hoping to catch sight of an incoming ship. Occasionally he was elated by seeing in the distance a sail slowly moving toward the landing. With feverish impatience he awaited its arrival, to be again overcome with disappointment when it proved to not be the vessel he was expecting, nor bringing any news of it. One evening, after an unusually busy day, he again, as was now his custom, sought the river side, with a lingering hope of perhaps gaining some tidings of those he longed to see. As he approached the river he was astonished on seeing a large ship moored near the wharf, from which its passengers and their luggage were being put ashore. The setting sun had touched the line of verdure that fringed the western river bank, and its departing rays converted the broad surface of the stream into a sheet of burnished gold. The resplendent beauty of the scene, however, was lost to the Lieutenant as he hurried to the water's edge to see the name of the vessel. He saw it painted in large letters above the rudder, and almost sank from revulsion of overwrought hope again blasted. The name he read was not "L'Etoile du Nord," but "La Cygne," and, as he soon learned, from Bordeaux, France, having touched on the way in at Fort Royale, in Martinique. Rallying his drooping spirits he clambered aboard to make inquiries for the object of his weary watching. Accosting the Skipper of the vessel, he asked if he could give him any information of "L'Etoile du Nord" that sailed from Brest four months ago. The burly old seaman, apprised by the questioner's uniform, that he was a military officer in the King's service, touched his cap, and answered courteously, regretting that he knew nothing of the ship; but said his Commis (Purser) over there perhaps did; and added, so far as he knew, that craft had not been heard from since it left the French port. The Purser, a brisk young man, busy with pencil and entry book, overheard the question and the Skipper's answer, and without looking up from his book and papers, said, "Is it of the French ship, L'Etoile du Nord, Monsieur is enquiring?"

"Oui, oui," gasped the Lieutenant, "can you tell me where she now is?"

"Yes"; answered the young man, between rapid strokes of his pencil, "she is in the bay of St. Pierre, in Martinique, undergoing repairs, having had a disastrous transit of the ocean. One of her passengers who came aboard this ship at Fort Royale, and has not yet gone ashore, can probably give you any additional information you may desire."

With great effort to appear calm the Lieutenant asked the busy Commis if he would be so kind as to point out to him the person mentioned.

"Certainly, Monsieur; there is the man, in white clothing and broad brimmed hat, sitting on the chest by the main mast."

The individual in white clothing, a middle aged man of gaunt frame, with grizzled hair and thin sallow face, evidently emaciated by prolonged sickness, was instantly confronted by the agitated young officer, who asked:

"Were you a passenger from France on L'Etoile du Nord?"

"Yes, Monsieur, I was," the man dryly answered.

"Tell me, please, were Pierre Lepage and his family on that vessel?" was the next anxious inquiry.

"They were," said the man with ominous emphasis on the "were."

"Can you inform me where they now are?" faintly asked the questioner.

52

"Yes, Monsieur, I can," replied the weary looking individual, "they are all three dead and at the bottom of the sea."

"Mon Dieu—" gasped young Saucier, "that surely cannot be possible."

"Yes; it is indeed possible, and too true. Did you know them, Monsieur?"

To this question the Lieutenant responded that he did.

"Pardon me, Monsieur," added the stranger, eyeing him closely, "may I ask who you are?"

"I am Jean Baptiste Saucier, from Lachapelle, near Orleans, in France, now in the King's military service."

"Ah, yes, yes," remarked the man musingly, "and so you was not slain by the Indians as was reported? I see how you knew Pierre Lepage and wife. They kept house for your father, whom I knew well; and I remember you when a school boy at the village near by your father's place. My name is Isadore Brusier. I lived in Tours, and my business occasionally called me to Orleans, and there I became acquainted with your father and his son Louis"—

"Pardon me, Monsieur Brusier," interrupted Jean Baptiste, "but please tell me of the fate of the Lepages."

"Ah—Mon cher enfant," feelingly replied M. Brusier, becoming quite communicative, now that he knew to whom he was talking, "I have a very sad story to tell you. You have, I presume, heard of the death of your father? Yes; well, after his burial, his estate was sold for partition and passed into possession of strangers; so Lepage concluded to leave France and seek a new home in America. About that time—fortunately after your father['s] death—the report came that you had been killed in battle with the savages. This report, believed by all to be true, very nearly caused Lepage to give up the voyage and remain in France,—and would to God that he had done so! But his preparations were completed, and he went to Brest with his wife and daughter, and took passage on the ill-fated ship on which my brother and myself embarked.

"The voyage, though tedious, was not unpleasant until we had traversed about two-thirds of the way, when we were struck by a terrific storm, coming from the northeast, that continued with unabated fury, for six days. Two of the seamen were washed, or blown away, as was also the main mast; and the ship sprung a leak that threatened to sink us to the bottom. We could do nothing but keep the vessel in line with the course of the gale, and that carried us far out of our way in the direction of Brazil. It is well that L'Etoile du Nord was staunch and well built, else none of us would have ever reached dry land—and not many of us did, as it turned out.

"But we all worked the pumps, night and day, and kept afloat. When the storm at length abated, and the raging sea subsided, the leak in the hull was securely closed, and by crowding on all the sails the two remaining masts could carry, we regained our course and made fair headway, being driven by the African tradewinds. All this was bad enough; but as nothing compared to what fate yet had in store for us.

"What with calms, and storm and very slow sailing we had been on the sea for three months or more. Our supplies of water and provisions were running low; but we were all well, and buoyed up by the expectation of soon sighting some one of the West India Islands. The weather was intensely hot and the little water remaining in our casks was scarcely fit to drink. Suddenly, one day, one of the passengers was taken violently sick, and soon died. Then another was prostrated with the same symptoms and lived but a short time. Then we realized the appalling fact that the plague [11] had broken out among us and we were doomed to destruction by this horrid pestilence. Lepage was among the first victims, and lived but twenty-four hours. He was always jovial and good humored, and by his fine flow of spirits, had materially mitigated the dreariness of the voyage, and greatly aided in sustaining the flagging hopes and courage of all on board throughout all our troubles. We gently lowered his body into the sea; but had no time to indulge our grief, as he was quickly followed by others.

"The terrible disease attacked the strong as well as the weak, the old and the young alike, with pitiless severity. The only mercy it extended was to render its victims speedily unconscious. The ship's captain, surgeon, half the crew, and more than half of the passengers fell before the awful scourge and were consigned to the deep. Madame Lepage, who had been untiring in ministering to the sick and dying, was spared for some time; but, at length she was stricken down and soon breathed her last, following Pierre to an unmarked grave. We were now approaching the West India Islands, and very eager to reach land—any land—so that those of us who survived might abandon the infected vessel and flee to the shore for our lives. Only a day and a night after we had given to the waves the body of Marie Lepage, her daugh-

11. Probably a virulent form of Asiatic cholera.

54

ter, Adel, already exhausted by grief and attention to the sick, was seized by the dreadful epidemic, and quickly succumbed to its deadly virulence. I was bathing her head with sea water, in her death struggles, when all at once I felt very sick. The ship seemed to be rapidly whirling around; everything became dark, and I fell to the deck unconscious.

"When I awoke, as though from a long, troubled sleep, I was in a large shed-like house thatched with palm leaves, on the highlands in the northern part of the island of Martinique, where my brother, who was of the number not attacked by the plague, had me immediately brought from the ship—we having entered the Bay of St. Pierre, in that island a few hours after I had fallen. There he and others took care of me until I recovered. My brother having secured employment at Fort Royale will remain there until winter and then join me here where we will engage in business. As soon as the anchor was dropped in the Bay of St. Pierre my brother had me carried to the highest part of the island—as far as he could go from the death smitten ship—without stopping, and I have seen none of our surviving fellow-passengers since. I learned, however, before leaving Fort Royale, that L'Etoile du Nord was at once deserted by all the survivors aboard, and is still in the Bay of St. Pierre being thoroughly repaired."

CHAPTER VIII. *A Brush with Southern Indians*

Lieutenant Saucier sat as though stupefied while listening to Monsieur Brusier's startling narrative, and only by a mighty effort could he control his emotions when the narrator depicted the closing scene of Adel's young life. How he left the La Cygne and got back to his quarters in the town he never could remember. In the solitude of his room he contended with his great grief through the sleepless, restless, night. He was literally prostrated with the weight of sorrow that taxed all his fortitude to bear. His glowing day dreams were cruelly dissipated, and even hope had vanished and left him dismally alone in the world with nothing further to live for. The next morning was ushered in with rain; and dense black clouds covered the sky like a pall, as though the very elements were testifying their sympathy with the young soldier's woeful wretchedness. Pleading indisposition, he remained in his room and excused himself to all who called on him. In the evening a messenger from the Governor informed him that the company of recruits for the force at Fort Chartres, he was expecting, had arrived, and begged him to call at the executive office next morning to arrange for their transportation up the river. This had some effect to divert his mind from, and somewhat relieve it of, the dark gloom that had fallen upon him.

The next morning, he arose early, as usual, resolved, if possible, not to be overcome by his misfortunes; but to assert his manhood, and continue the conflicts of life with all the firmness he possessed. At the appointed hour he called at the Governor's office with little, if any, external indication of the soul-racking torture he was enduring. Arrangements for additional boats and provisions were perfected in a few days; and then, having neither incentive or desire to longer remain in the melancholy place, he hurried the preparations for his departure as rapidly as possible. In less than a week after his interview with the Governor he was ready to start, courting, rather than dreading, the perils and hardships that he knew awaited him.

As the prevailing winds at that time of the year are from the south, Lieutenant Saucier concluded to try the experiment, when they blew with sufficient force from that direction, of utilizing them in propelling his boats. Accordingly he caused a light, strong and movable mast to be stepped in each of his pirogues, rigged with spars and sails. Several of his recruits, enlisted about the seaport towns of France, were familiar with the management of sailboats, and these he installed as his navigators.

At length all was in readiness, his bills were all settled, his cargoes snugly stowed in the boats, and his round of farewell calls ended. His men were in superb condition for service, and at the dawn of one of the closing days of July, he left New Orleans with his fleet having every sail set and filled by a stiff breeze from the Gulf. Not a sail was furled during the entire day, and they proved valuable adjuncts to the oars. The sun in setting must have passed the new moon, as it appeared in the early twilight a little way above the western horizon, and was pronounced by the sages among the crews, a "dry" moon, augering a propitious voyage and pleasant weather. The river was at that season at its lowest stage, and its current, in consequence, at its slowest rate; so, the progress of the flotilla, if not rapid, was quite satisfactory. In propelling the boats the men had regular relays at the oars, and when off duty, some slept, others fished, and a few, with musical talent, enlivened the toil of their comrades with exhilirating strains of the violin.

Everything went well until the mouth of the Arkansas was passed. Indians at several places along the river, had come to the boats in their canoes in friendship, to beg, or to barter game they had killed for calico and brass ornaments; but though manifesting no unfriendly disposition then they were known to be treacherous and utterly unreliable. To guard against night attacks of hostile savages ashore—for there was no danger whatever from them in midstream, or in day time—keelboatmen cautiously landed on one side of the river in the evening, or on an island, and there made fires and spread their meals. Then extinguishing the fires, resumed their course for a short distance, and tied up on the opposite shore until morning.

On the evening of the fourth day after having passed the mouth of the Arkansas river, the sky became heavily overcast with dark clouds, and the rumbling thunder and vivid lightning were sure harbingers of an approaching storm. The boats that had been lined up on the Arkansas side of the river for the evening repast, were hastily cast loose, and, as customary, rowed to the opposite side, in the rain and darkness, and made fast to the overhanging trees there for the night. Not an Indian had been seen during the day on either side of the river; or any indication of their presence observed anywhere. By the time the boats were secured to the river bank, and the tarpaulins drawn over each, the rain descended in torrents, and continued for the greater part of the night.

At early dawn next morning, the rain had ceased, but the sky was still obscured by clouds, and the air was hot and sultry. The men, glad to escape from the sweltering confinement of the boats, leaped ashore with the first rays of light in the east, and began to kindle fires to prepare their breakfast. A few of them had the precaution to take their arms with them as they left the boats, probably from force of habit. Of this number was Lieutenant Saucier, who never went ashore without his trusty carbine. While all were busily engaged in search of fuel dry enough to feed the flickering fires, they were suddenly assailed by a shower of bullets from the surrounding trees and undergrowth, followed by a chorus of unearthly yells and whoops, as a large band of hideously painted savages rushed wildly upon them. The few Frenchmen armed stood their ground, and with steady aim returned the fire of their assailants as they advanced, then clubbing their guns went fearlessly into the fight. Those without their arms fled to the boats to secure them, and very soon returned with the balance of their comrades who had not before landed, all well armed, and lost no time in coming to the support of those holding the

Indians at bay. They charged upon the horde of red demons, who had not had time to reload their guns, with such fury, that they fell back, and scattered in full retreat. In this brief but spirited engagement the Frenchmen fought with the courage and precision of well-trained veterans. They followed up the advantage their first charge gave them, and advanced in quick time, firing at the retreating foe as long as one of them could be seen. At the first appearance of the Indians, Lieutenant Saucier fired and killed the one nearest him; then seizing his carbine by its muzzle he brained the next one, and struck right and left, at the same time cheering his men on, until his reinforcements came up, when he led them on until the enemy was dispersed. He was twice wounded, but not seriously, and was not aware of having received any injury until the fight was all over. The Frenchmen lost but one man, one of the new recruits was killed, but several of the others were more or less severely wounded. Seven of the Indians were left dead on the ground, and several more so badly wounded they could not escape, and they, the infuriated boatmen despatched without mercy. They breakfasted without further molestation, then pushed off, continuing their voyage, taking with them the body of the dead soldier which they buried at evening on the western side of the river. The wounded were made as comfortable as possible, and they proceeded, with more caution, and without further incident or accident, to their destination.

CHAPTER IX. *Death of the Commandant's Daughter*

The first frosts of early autumn had tinged the dark green maples with scarlet and gold, and the ripening hickory nuts and pecans were beginning to fall, when the long line of boats were drawn up to the Fort landing. The commander of the successful expedition, who had not yet recovered entirely from his wounds, looked haggard and careworn. Leaving the boats, he marched the recruits, not disabled from wounds or sickness, to the barracks, and then repaired to the Commandant's quarters. His knock at the door was answered by Lisette who to his hurried inquiries, told him her young mistress was very low, and daily failing in vitality; also, that as long as she could speak she had asked about him every day, and prayed that she might see him again before she was called away to her mother. Following the devoted servant into the sick chamber he was shocked upon seeing the ravages wrought by the unrelenting disease during his absence. The sunken cheeks flushed with hectic fever, the glistening eyes, the cruel, persistent cough and hot, dry hands, plainly told that the fair young girl was doomed and her life nearing its close. She spoke his name in a husky whisper as she extended her thin bloodless hand, and a gleam of radiant joy lighted her wan features when he pressed it, and implanted a kiss upon her forhead. She was too far exhausted to speak to him; but the mute eloquence of her expression assured him that his presence afforded her real comfort and happiness. Almost heartbroken already by M. Brusier's narrative, the pathetic sadness of Eulalie's condition very nearly overpowered him. All the strength he could command was required to control his feelings while by her side, and not add to her distress by an exhibition of emotional weakness. With great effort he appeared cheerful, and tried to speak to her in the pleasant, airy strain of other days—and partially succeeded. But he could not long sustain this unnatural simulation, and, with a promise to call again in a short time, he took leave of her and hurried to his own quarters, and there found relief in unmanly tears that could no longer be repressed.

The arrival of the boats with stores, mails and recruits, was an exciting event at the Fort. From the Commandant down to the servants, all were elated and eager to hear an account of the voyage, and learn what was going on in the outer world. The pirogues were unloaded and sent back to Kaskaskia; the sick and wounded were carried to their separate wards in the hospital; the munitions were safely placed in the magazine, and other supplies in the store rooms; and the voluminous mail matter promptly distributed. Lieutenant Saucier was weak and still suffering from his wounds, and sorely depressed in mind; but refused to be billeted by the post surgeon to the hospital, and applied himself as diligently as his condition permitted to writing the report of his transactions in New Orleans, and of his fight with the Indians, and all other important incidents of his memorable descent and ascent of the great river. He visited Eulalie every day as often as his duties permitted, and experienced some assuagement of the oppressive affliction he was bearing in silence, by his efforts to soothe and mollify the fleeting hours of her waning life. He recounted his adventures on the river, and told her of amusing incidents and strange sights he had witnessed at New Orleans; and by interesting her in that way sought to detract her attention from the gloom and misery of her mournful fate.

A week, or more, had passed since the arrival of the boats at the Fort, and the commotion that event caused had gradually subsided to the ordinary routine life of the post. One beautiful morning in the mellow haze of lovely Indian summer, the bright sunshine streaming through the invalid's open window, and the soft, invigorating breeze fanned her wasted form, the Lieutenant sat by her side with her small hand clasped in his; her brilliant blue eyes were fixed upon his sad face, a sweet smile played upon her pallid lips, and then, without sigh or tremor, her spirit took its flight, so gently and quietly that, for several moments, those around her could scarcely realize that the struggle was ended.

"Eulalie is dead," was whispered throughout the garrison, and all was hushed; all labor suspended; the flag floating from the highest bastion was lowered to half mast and the great fortress became at once a house of mourning. They draped her cold body in robes of spotless white, and laid it in state in the large hall, where she had, in health, reigned as queen of the dance and joyous festivities, and received the homage of all in her social realm. Then placed in a coffin covered with white velvet, they conveyed her to the church in Kaskaskia, preceded by a guard of honor with arms reversed, the flag craped and drums muffled, followed by all the officers and ladies of the Fort, and a large concourse of civilians from the adjacent settlements. After the sacred offices of the priests she was tenderly consigned to the grave in the village cemetery near the church and buried with military honors.

CHAPTER X. *Defeat of Washington at Fort Necessity*

The grand object to be attained in rebuilding Fort Chartres was the permanent security of French possessions on the Mississippi, and, incidentally, the maintenance of peace. But the great work was not completed when hostilities between England and France again commenced. Their respective military forces in America, ever at variance, were not long in engaging in earnest conflict. In the month of May, 1754, one George Washington, a Virginian, in the service of the English King, commanding a body of militia from his native state, then stationed in Pennsylvania, surprised Coulon de Jumonville with a small detachment of French soldiers, near the Youghiogeny, (not far from the present city of Connellsville, in Fayette county), and defeated him, Jumonville falling at the first fire, shot through the head.[12]

The report of this affair, and its resultant disaster to the French arms, when received at Fort Chartres produced the wildest consternation, and fired the military ardor of the inactive garrison. Neyon de Villiers, the senior Captain of Chevalier Makarty's command, a brother-in-law of Jumonville, asked leave of the Commandant to march to the scene of conflict and assist in avenging the death of his relative and regaining the lost prestige of France in that quarter. This leave he readily obtained; and, with alacrity, began his preparations for the expedition.

To the depressed mind of Lieutenant Saucier the excitement and hazard of this undertaking offered alluring promise of relief. He felt willing to undergo any hardships; or risk any danger that would tend to revive his broken spirits and divert his thoughts from the sad occurrences of the past few months. He volunteered his services, and was granted permission by the Commandant to accompany Capt. de Villiers as one of his Lieutenants. A hundred picked men were selected and fully equipped with everything necessary for the long journey. The boats were overhauled and put in order. Embarking, they proceeded down the Mississippi, then up the Ohio to Fort du Quesne, where they joined the force of Coulon de Villiers, an elder brother of the Captain. They there organized their men in four companies under trusted officers, and sallied forth in the quest of the enemy. Washington, apprised, by Indians friendly to the British, of the advancing French, retreated to the Great Meadow, a short distance from the spot where he had assassinated Ensign Jumonville, a short time before. There he sought safety in Fort Necessity, a temporary defense of little strength, and awaited the avengers. He had not long to wait. De Villiers was soon upon him, and investing his entrenchments, poured in upon him a murderous fire from all sides. The engagement lasted nine hours. Washington seeing the futility of contending longer with such a superior and determined foe, after a short parlay, surrendered. The French, magnanimously permitted him to march out with side arms and camp equipage. In this affair Washington lost twelve killed and forty-three wounded. He returned to the east side of the Alleghanies, leaving not an Englishman or English flag on their western side. On leaving Fort Necessity, Washington's Indian allies killed all his horses and

12. "Judge it as we may, this obscure skirmish began the war that set the world on fire." *Montcalm and Wolfe.* By Francis Parkman. Vol. 1. p. 150.

cattle, plundered his baggage, knocked his medicine chest in pieces, and killed and scalped two of his wounded men. Left with no means of transportation his men were obliged to carry their sick and wounded on their backs.[13] He commenced his retreat on the fourth of July, a day afterward made glorious to a new born nation. The Fort Chartres contingent returned to the Mississippi flushed with victory, and without loss of a man.

They received a royal welcome from the garrison, and their successful humiliation of Mr. Washington and his loyal militia was celebrated in all the settlements around the Fort with prolonged festivities.

Not long after the return of this expedition a courier arrived at the Fort from Montreal with important despatches from the home government and from the Governor General of Canada. Among those papers were commissions of promotion, as rewards, for several of the officers and men who had faithfully discharged their duties in the erection of the new Fort. Of those thus rewarded by the King, Major Makarty was advanced to the rank of Colonel, and Lieutenant Saucier to that of Captain.

English emissaries were soon busy among the Indians all through the west attempting to win them over to their cause. And by liberal presents, more liberal promises, and misrepresentations, were successful in seducing several of the tribes from their allegiance to, and friendship for, the French. This change of policy by the savages caused much uneasiness and some trouble at Fort Chartres. A British invasion was among the possibilities expected; but no immediate danger of a general uprising of Illinois Indians was apprehended. Yet, the scattered settlements required protection, particularly from threatened inroads of the Chickasaws about the mouth of the Ohio river. Companies were detailed for police duty to different points, and frequent excursions were made in the interior of the country by detachments of soldiers to punish marauding bands of Indians. Chevalier de Volsci and his men having been ordered to Canada, Major Makarty sent Capt. Saucier to take command of the fort at Cahokia. This stockade was situated near the center of the village just across the road from the church, and was spacious enough to contain the entire population of the town in case resort to it for protection was at any time necessary.[14] Captain Saucier was quite a favorite

13. *Montcalm and Wolfe.* By Francis Parkman. Vol. 1. pp. 147–161.

14. In the course of certain improvements on the old Jarnot [Jarrot] place in Cahokia, made in 1890 by Nicholas McCracken, the proprietor, there was dug up part of a large mulberry post, much decayed, believed to have been one of the gate posts of the fort, planted there 150 years before.

among the Cahokians; and while commanding there was very successful, not in fighting the discontented Indians, but in pacifying them and regaining their friendship.

When spring returned peace prevailed throughout the Illinois, and the scattered soldiers were recalled to the Fort. The tribes in upper Louisiana; or, more properly, along the Mississippi river below the Ohio, however, were reported to have joined the English—as all the eastern colonists were called—, and were harassing the whites engaged in navigation of the river. One of the first pirogues enroute for New Orleans was captured by them, and its crew were all slain.

The time had again arrived for dispatching the boats to New Orleans for the garrison's annual supplies. In the then hostile attitude of the southern Indians, it was necessary to select for this service men of tried courage and endurance, and a commander of prudence, firmness and experience. Besides the supplies that might be drawn from the Quartermaster's and Commissary's departments in New Orleans, it would be necessary to purchase considerable quantities of stores there for the troops at the Fort. There were also expected at New Orleans important despatches, and a large sum of money, from France, for the Commandant, and Paymaster at the Fort; and it was very desirable that all these valuables should be brought up the river in safety.

After pondering the matter over for sometime, Col. Makarty sent for Captain Saucier, and asked him if he would undertake the management of the voyage, stating that he would not detail him for that service if he preferred not to go; but that he would regard it a personal favor if he would accept the perilous office. The Captain answered, without hesitation, that he was one of the King's soldiers, ready at any time to go wherever required, and this duty would suit him as well as any.

The late spring rains had long since ceased. The waters had receded from the low, overflowed lands, to the lowest level of their accustomed channels. The sandbars had reappeared with barren prominence above the river's surface, when Capt. Saucier repaired to Kaskaskia, and put his fleet of boats in readiness, as before. He was fortunate in finding the best men of his former crews, whom he engaged; and taking from the Fort a few of the most reliable enlisted men who were with him on his former voyage, he once more bid adieu to the Illinois, and set his flotilla in the current of the great river. He again took his departure when the young moon was a silvered

63

crescent about to drop into the dark western forest; choosing this phase of that orb for leaving, not from superstitious notions; but because he would have light at night for some time, enabling him to continue his course with the least possible delays.

At only two points on the river were hostile demonstrations made by the Indians, and these he repulsed without trouble, being constantly on his guard. By the exercise of cool judgment and careful management he reached his destination in comparatively a short time, without casualties, or encountering extraordinary hardships.

CHAPTER XI. *In New Orleans Again*

Thirty-seven years had passed since the first settlement was made at New Orleans by Bienville; and it was already a pretentious town,[15] the metropolis of all the vast territory claimed by the French Crown from the Gulf to the great northern lakes; and the commercial and military gateway to all that region. The primitive architecture of the place gave it the appearance of an irregular collection of huts with streaks of mud for streets. Yet, that early, much wealth was concentrated there, which—as in older communities—had the effect of creating social distinctions among its people. Squalor and poverty were conspicuous in some quarters of the place, while in others Parisian opulence and splendor, and Parisian styles and fashions were lavishly displayed. An aristocratic class had been fostered there by the late Governor of Louisiana, Pierre de Regaud, Marquis de Vaudreuil, who, a short time before, was transferred to Quebec as Governor General of Canada, superceding there M. de Gallisoniere. De Vaudreuil's pomp and state; his sumptuous style of living, punctilious etiquette and courtly manners, which found many servile imitators, caused his official residence, or chateau, on Rue Ponchartrain, to be named by the populace "Le Petite Versailles." The shipping interests of the town were represented by large and commodious warehouses, and the many gay shops and elegant stores gave evidence of commercial prosperity. The Jesuits were there, of course, since 1727; but the only edifices yet erected by the church were the Ursuline Convent, Hospital, and Chapel.

15. By the close of the year 1752, forty-five brick houses had been built in New Orleans. Gayarré's *History of Louisiana*. [II: 65; Gayarré was quoting a 1752 letter, which said that "in the last three years, forty-five brick houses were erected"—not that there were then forty-five brick houses in all.]

New Orleans was made the capital of Louisiana in 1721. On going ashore from his boat, near the spot where the Captain had met Monsieur Brusier when last here, the memory of that gentleman's doleful story was revived, with the wretched dispiriting effect he had experienced when listening to it. A feeling of extreme misery crept over him as he reviewed the cruel fate of those he loved, his blighted hopes, and lonely life. The vision of two angelic young creatures, now still in death, whose love had illumined his soul and lent a charm to existence, arising before him, with the shades of his revered father and foster parents beyond—all now gone forever—almost overpowered him with a sense of heart-rending despondency. Philosophy, however, came to his rescue. It argued to him that nothing could be gained by repining and brooding over ill-fortune. The dead were beyond his reach, the living had claims upon him, and he was yet young enough to dispel the incubus of grief, and to benefit humanity and his country. Rallying all the strength of his resolute mind, he determined to hide his sorrows in the recesses of his own thoughts, and act to the best of his abilities, the part assigned him in the world's affairs.

To further this resolve, he concluded no longer to mope in seclusion; but to reenter society, and seek forgetfulness in its pastimes and frivolities. This course, he correctly judged, would be the most effective to banish melancholy. Social gaieties and amusements in New Orleans were not, in that era, restricted to certain seasons. There was then no hegira of the favored class to northern watering places, or seaside resorts, during the heated term; but pleasure there, considered—next to obtaining the necessities of life—the chief duty of existence, its pursuit, in feasting, dancing and visiting, was always in order from one Christmas to another.

The Captain's presence in town was soon generally known, and but little time was left him to feel lonely. His military rank, his youth, manly figure and handsome features, with his gentlemanly bearing and manners, made him a desirable acquaintance; and the knowledge that he was an accredited government agent disbursing large sums of money for military supplies, gave him ready admission into the highest circles of society, in which he soon became conspicuous. He was lionized by the wealthy mercenary traders, by the educated and refined, and also by shrewd mothers having marriageable daughters. By accepting pressing invitations from all quarters, he was quickly inducted to the whirlpool of social entertainments, and was in a short time, one of society's chief attractions. He was a graceful dancer and interesting talker, and ever ready to take part in current amusements; but detested the coarse revelry and dissipation of the barracks and messroom.

Among the wholesale dealers and importers whose stocks of goods he inspected preliminary to making his purchases, was a merchant named Antoine Delorme, one of the wealthiest citizens of the town, a leader in its business circles, and an affable, hospitable gentleman. His residence on Rue Ponchartrain, in what was then known as the aristocratic quarter, was exteriorly plain, but large, roomy, and furnished interiorly with taste and munificence. Patterned after the gaudy mansion of the former Governor, the Marquis de Vaudreuil, it had all the appointments and accessories of luxurious comfort that wealth could provide, including a retinue of negro slaves perfectly trained for personal and domestic service.

Monsieur Delorme's family comprised only his wife and daughter, at home. Another daughter, who was married, resided in France, and a son, also married, was the principal merchant and shipowner in St. Pierre, on the island of Martinique. Madam Delorme was, in many respects, the antithesis of her husband. He had married her when both were young and poor, from a social stratum below that to which his parents belonged. She was a peasant's daughter, coarse, illiterate, and a stranger to the usages of refined society in which he had been nurtured. But she was a pretty girl, strong, healthy, industrious, and a shrewd, economical household manager. She had proven an efficient coadjutor in the accumulation of his large fortune, a true wife and exemplary mother. Advancing age had wrought serious changes in her girlish figure and rustic beauty; and her altered station in life had developed the, too common, arrogance and foolish vanity of riches displayed by vulgar people becoming wealthy. She was corpulent, florid and broad-faced, and spoke very ungrammatically; but dressed in fine, showy clothes made in the height of fashion, that illy became her rotund form, and wore a profusion of flashy, costly jewelry. Coming, as she had, from the mudsills of society, she seemed to have forgotten her early hardships and privations, and now looked down upon the plebeians with uncharitable contempt.

Her daughter, Mam'selle Rosealie, the youngest of her children, was reared in luxury and indolence, receiving considerable polish—if not much erudition—in a French convent in Paris. Her face was pretty but wanting in expression. With a tendency to obesity, she had inherited none of her mother's former energy and force, but all of her mother's later weakness for fine raiment and sparkling ornaments. She was blessed with an easy, good-natured disposition and pleasant voice; was a fair musician, a voluble talker and fine entertainer. To secure for this girl a husband of wealth, or rank—both preferably—was now the object for which Madame Delorme lived. No means were spared in making her salons attractive, and eclipsing all others in the sumptuousness and brilliancy of her entertainments, not excepting those of the late Governor De Vaudreuil. Her balls and dinners were grand, and her musicales and garden dejeuners superb.

Captain Saucier was not wealthy; but for business reasons, and because of his official position in the King's service, he soon became a frequent and welcome guest at the Delorme mansion. He was among the first invited to the Madame's fetes and parties, and was always graciously received when he dropped in, informally, to pass an hour in pleasant chat with Mlle. Rosealie.

CHAPTER XII. *The Mysterious Woman in Black*

A month had passed since the Captain's arrival at New Orleans, in which he had been busily employed every business hour each day. He had made all his purchases, but was still detained awaiting the expected despatches from France. Time however did not hang heavily on his hands. He had formed many agreeable acquaintances who extended to him the cordial hospitality of their homes, and vied with each other in their efforts to enhance the pleasures of his visit. He received flattering attentions in these charmed and charming circles, from the ladies particularly, who allowed him but little opportunity for serious retrospective reflection, and impressed upon him the axiom that life is for the living and should be enjoyed while it lasts.

Calling one morning before the sun's rays became oppressive, at the Delorme mansion, his knock at the door was answered, as usual, by a colored servant who ushered him into the small parlor, or drawing room, and then went to apprise her young mistress of his presence. As he entered the room he casually glanced through the open folding doors into the adjoining room and saw there a woman, apparently young, sitting in a large alcove engaged in sewing. Her hands, he saw, were white; but he did not see her face. She arose on his entrance into the parlor, and gathering up her work basket and the material upon which she was plying her needle, left the apartment with-

67

out so much as glancing in his direction. He saw, as she flitted out of the room like a shadow, that her tall, well-molded form was plainly but neatly dressed in black. As Mlle. Rosealie directly made her appearance, the woman in black passed out of his mind, and the pampered daughter of fortune amused and interested him for a time with her vivacious conversation and music.

The climate at New Orleans has not materially changed since the administration of affairs there by the "Grand Marquis" Vaudreuil, a century and a half ago. In the late summer the nights and mornings are pleasantly cool, with uncomfortable heat during the middle part of the day. In the olden days, however, the rush and bustle of business of the present time were unknown there, and through the heated hours business pursuits and pleasure-seeking were suspended until a fall of temperature in the evening.

A few days after the Captain's last morning call at the Delorme abode, he was again there one evening with a gay party of young gentlemen and ladies, who had met him on the street, and prevailed upon him to accompany them. Such impromptu gatherings of young society people were then of almost daily occurrence, and always highly enjoyed by hostess and guests alike. While the Captain was recounting to a group of girls some of his experiences in Kaskaskia and Cahokia society he chanced to look, from the piazza where he sat, towards the flower garden, and saw the same figure in black he had seen a few mornings before sewing in the alcove, enter the garden from the street, by a side gate, and passing through the shrubbery and flowers, disappear beyond the rear angle of the building. She wore, as before, a plain, neatly-fitting, black dress and her head was covered by a sunbonnet that concealed her face. He looked at the retreating woman as long as she was in view, though she seemed, from her garb, to occupy no higher station than that of an upper menial—a hired seamstress perhaps—and of no consequence. It may have been the striking contrast she presented to Mlle. Rosealie, in the perfect symmetry of her form and her graceful movements, that attracted his attention and curiously interested him. On two or three other occasions when at the Delorme mansion he again caught glimpses of that mysterious retiring young woman in the distance; and though he strove to dismiss her from his mind, as one in whom he was in no manner concerned, she strangely impressed him, and he found it difficult to suppress the desire to learn who she was.

The long looked for ship from France at length arrived, bringing the expected despatches and mails. The Captain, much relieved, now began earnestly to complete his final preparations for his long and trying return voyage. Early and late he was in the large Delorme warehouse, where his goods were stored, superintending and directing the assorting and transferring of bales, boxes, and casks to the boats, and seeing to arranging them there securely and compactly.

Coming into the spacious building on the first morning, to hurry forward this work, he was hailed by old Michael Mallait, the clerk and guardian genius of this department of the Delorme establishment who had been in the Delorme service since its commencement, with this cheery greeting:

"Ah! bon jour; bon jour; Monsieur le Capitaine. You are quite well, I am happy to see. And, so, you are going to leave us, eh?"

"Yes, Uncle Michael; I expect to bid New Orleans a long, and perhaps last, farewell, on next Monday morning, Dieu volante," said the Captain.

"Ah! mon cher fils," continued the old man, "we will all miss you very much when you are gone; and you don't know the devastation your departure will cause here."

"You are surely jesting, my friend; for what calamity can my leaving occasion?"

"Broken hearts among the demoiselles, of course," answered the old man, with a knowing smile; and then added; "I don't know how they will manage to get along without you in their fine balls and parties. And Mam'selle Rosealie, poor thing! will be inconsolable in your absence."

"Bah!" retorted the Captain, with some impatience, "she will very soon forget that I was ever here." This allusion to Rosealie reminded him of the plainly-attired young woman he had now and then seen about the Delorme premises, and seeing no impropriety in interrogating him about her, he asked, "Now that I think of it, mon oncle; can you tell me who that strange young woman is, of whom I have sometimes caught sight, up at the mansion?"

"No, I cannot; only this of her have I learned, that she has but recently arrived here—since you came—, from France, I think, and that she is a distant relative of Delorme's, an orphan, destitute, and trying to support herself with her needle. I have heard her name, but cannot now recall it. Of course she is not admitted into Mam'selle Rosealie's set."

Their conversation then turned on business affairs and each was soon engrossed in matters that concerned him most, and which gave them ample occupation for the balance of the day. This routine work continued until Saturday evening, when the Captain had everything in readiness to start away the next evening, or on Monday morning. His boats were all in first class condition, each with its cargo in place; his arms and ammunition carefully inspected; his bills all settled, and his men at their respective posts ready for duty. He would have given the order to shove off that evening, but for the conscientious scruples of the men, who could not agree to embark on such a perilous journey without first attending mass, and receiving absolution from the priest, on the Sabbath.

The Captain had a snug little cabin fitted up in his boat, walled around with bales and boxes, and covered with tarpaulin. At either end was a small window looking fore and aft, a carpet covered the floor, and a cosey bunk and a couple of chairs imparted to it an air of home-like comfort. The termination of his stay in New Orleans had arrived. He had paid all of his farewell visits, and bid adieu to all his social and business acquaintances including the Governor and military officers, then gladly left his quarters in the town, and took possession of his cabin and boat, prepared for the arduous task before him.

After retiring for the night he reviewed the time he had just passed in New Orleans; the mission he had successfully accomplished, interspersed and varied, as it had been, with many pleasant episodes, with courtesies, and the respect and kindness accorded him by his many new acquaintances, and many charming ladies. All this was gratifying to his self-esteem. He found that he had gained much of his former cheerfulness and interest in life, and ambition for an honorable career. He fell asleep congratulating himself that he had overcome the poignancy of grief without impairment of his loyalty to the memory of the dead, successfully resisting the arts and blandishments of the city beauties.

CHAPTER XIII. *A Miraculous Escape from Death*

The golden light of the Sabbath dawn shone resplendent in the east beyond Lake Borgne, and as the sun arose above the horizon, the curtain of fog, settled on the bosom of the great river during the night, was slowly furled and floated away.

From force of habit, observed in camp, at the Fort, and on the march, the Captain arose at the reveille hour. His daily practice while sojourning in the town was to be up before the rising of the sun, and take long walks before breakfast, for exercise. Sometimes he strolled along the levee above the river bank; or out to the lakes; then again, he walked through the noisy and odorous markets; or by the slumbering residences and perfume-ladened flower gardens in the opulent quarter; or among the lowly huts of the poor classes.

On this refreshing Sunday morning, seeing that everything about the boats was quiet and in order, he took his course to the old Place d' Armes, and then into the deserted streets, with no aim in view but to look for the last time on some of the objects and localities he had become familiar with. His unrestrained thoughts dwelled upon the possibilities and probabilities of his voyage; then wandered to the more serious problem of impending war with the English; mentally discussing its consequences in the Illinois, and its ultimate results, and how it would affect his individual plans and aspirations, and in what way he might best serve his King and country, and at the same time promote his own interests.

He walked on slowly, in deep reverie, heedless of his course; past the silent rows of closed shops and stores, and on through the little park, or commons, then towards the Ursuline Convent and Chapel, seeing no one astir but the devout few on their way to the Chapel to attend *la bas messe,* or matin services. Arousing himself from his meditations to take his bearings and see where he had wandered to, he noted that he was then passing the Chapel into which a few shuffling old people and young girls were noiselessly creeping, like straggling bees into a hive. He stopped, and concluded to retrace his steps, and regain the river and his boats by the most direct route. He walked back a short distance, but a sudden impulse caused him to again turn and continue in the direction he had been walking, as by that course he could, with a few detours, reach the boat landing without much loss of time or distance. Going on he passed by some of the better class residences where he had been, in the last few weeks, royally entertained; and, for a moment felt a pang of regret in exchanging those generous luxuries for the rough fare of the river and camp.

A little farther on he came in sight of the well-known gables and piazzas, and spacious grounds, of the Delorme mansion now wrapped in the stillness of profound repose. As he proceeded toward the house, along the apology for a sidewalk, the side gate of the flower garden next to the street suddenly opened, and the black-garbed figure of the young woman he had occasionally seen about the mansion, emerged, with rosary and prayer book in hand, and head bowed in devotional attitude, evidently on her way to matin worship at the Chapel. She came on toward him with downcast eyes, walking slowly, as though in deep thought, or burdened with some secret sorrow. Though penniless and alone in the world, and consigned by fate to a life of toil and obscurity, as old Michael Mallait represented her, she moved with grace and dignity strangely at variance with her lowly station.

As they approached each other on the narrow walk, she raised her eyes slightly as he was about to step aside to let her pass by. His gaze was fixed upon her, and as she momentarily looked up he saw her face for the first time. Starting back in bewildered amazement, he exclaimed "Merciful God! Can this be but a mocking dream! Pardon me, Madame, will you please tell me who you are?" She did not faint or scream; but stood—like a statue—transfixed with surprise. The color left her cheeks for a moment, but regaining her presence of mind she answered firmly, "My name is Adel Lepage."

"Adel Lepage!", he repeated, with agitation; "But Monsieur Brusier told me that my—that is—I mean—the Adel Lepage whom I knew in France, died of the plague aboard the ship, L'Etoile du Nord, at sea."

"I escaped death almost by a miracle," said she; "but, pray sir, who are you?"

"I am Jean Baptiste Saucier," answered the Captain, as he clasped the astonished girl in his arms.

"Oh! Jean Baptiste," she cried half incredulously, "can it be possible that it is really you? They told us you were killed by the savages, and my poor parents and myself mourned for you with bleeding hearts."

He turned and walked with her in the direction of the Chapel; but so intent were they with mutual explanations of causes why they were not dead, and accounts of events transpiring in their lives since they had seen each other last, they passed the Chapel without seeing it, and proceeding to the Convent lawn sat down on one of the rustic seats there, and continued their animated conversation perfectly oblivious to all surroundings.

"Did you," she asked, "receive my letter giving you an account of your father's death, and of my father's conclusion to emigrate to New France?"

72

"Yes," he answered sadly, "and that was the last letter I received from you. You perhaps forgot to write to me again."

"Oh! Jean Baptiste, how can you say that?", she said reproachfully, and her eyes became suffused with tears. "I will tell you why I did not write to you again" she continued: "You no doubt remember Jo. Michot?"

"I do, indeed," said the Captain; "and I will hardly ever forget—nor do I think he will—the thrashing I gave him, when we were at school at Lachappelle, one recess, for meanly kicking over our dinner basket."

"Well," continued Adel, "he annoyed me very much by his persistent attentions, after you left home, and asked me to marry him. I, of course, refused; for I always cordially detested him. It was just after your father's death—a few days after I had written to you of it—and we were preparing to start to America, that he brought the intelligence from Orleans that you had been slain in battle with the Indians. From the accounts you had written us of those terrible savages, I believed the sad news he brought was true. He then told me I need not go to America to look for you, as you were dead; and I might as well marry him and remain in France. This not only pained, but infuriated me, and I replied that I was anxious to go to New France, and would go there, or anywhere else, if for no other reason than that I might be where I would never see, or hear of him again."

"Mille Tonnerre!", interrupted the Captain vehemently, "I wish the lying poltroon was here now, so that I could show him whether I am dead, or not."

"So then," continued Adel, "Monsieur Isidore Brusier told you all about the awful misfortunes that befel us on the ocean. Oh! it was dreadful beyond any human power of description. In an hour or two after I was attacked by the plague I lost all consciousness, and only know what followed by having been told of it by others. All were satisfied I was dying when Monsieur Brusier was stricken down, and they made preparations to throw me into the sea to follow my poor father and mother and the others who had died. And two or three times again it was thought I had breathed my last; but when the unfortunate ship next morning, cast its anchor in the Bay of St. Pierre, in the island of Martinique, I was still alive. All on board, sick and well, were immediately sent ashore.

"Monsieur Brusier's brother, who escaped the scourge, and who had cared for him every moment of his sickness, employed natives at once to carry the sick man to the northern part of the island, so as to be near relatives of theirs at Fort Royale. The other sick persons, who had friends or relatives with them, were also carried away to the hills as soon as possible; but I, having no one left to care for me, was taken on shore and placed in a vacant native hut under the palms, with no thought that I could survive many hours— or minutes, perhaps. The arrival of our vessel, and its disastrous voyage, were soon known in St. Pierre, and the citizens there lost no time in offering such relief as was in their power.

"Augustine Delorme, son of M. Antoine Delorme of this place, the wealthiest merchant in St. Pierre, and himself a shipowner, and whose grandmother was a Lepage, on learning from our ship's register my name, and my parents' names, as passengers, from near Orleans, thought we might be relatives of his, and sent an agent to the ship right away to enquire about us. On learning the facts he came himself immediately with a lot of servants, and caused me to be placed in a covered litter, or palanquin, and conveyed, by relays of carriers, to his summer house upon the mountain side. There a corps of physicians and nurses, superintended by Monsieur Augustine's good wife, bravely contended with the horrid disease that was consuming me, for many days, and finally triumphed."

CHAPTER XIV. *Marriage of Captain Saucier*

"I told them my story," continued Adel, "when sufficiently recovered to be able to talk, and when able to sit up my newly found relatives removed me to their home in St. Pierre, and installed me there as one of their family. I there did all I could for them to repay their great benevolence, by such services as I could render; and, while there, learned to be quite an expert dressmaker. Though every comfort was at my command, and every want gratified, I could not avoid the feeling that I was a dependent and object of charity. I begged M. Augustine to permit me to come to this town on one of his ships, where I might find better opportunities to earn my support. They all tried to dissuade me from the view I had taken and the purpose I had formed, and implored me to remain with them. It must have been some destiny impelling me, for I could not resist the constant impulse to come here.

"With reluctance and regrets, they at length consented; but only on my promise to go directly to M. Antoine Delorme's house, and make it my future home, and if I was disappointed in my expectations here to return immediately to them.

"I arrived here four weeks ago, and found the Delorme mansion a very pleasant home, and have been treated very kindly. I soon discovered, however, that my place there was that of a poor, dependent relation, and that I was expected not to transgress its bounds by intruding myself into Mam'selle Rosealie's circle.

"This situation has its twinge of humiliation; but not of hardship; for society has no allurements for me, and I long only for the quietude of obscure retirement—that Madame Delorme and Mam'selle Rosealie seem quite willing for me to enjoy. I have though, without consulting them, made arrangements to leave the mansion tomorrow morning, and commence work in Madame Durand's dressmaking and millinery establishment, on Rue St. Charles, where I can earn good wages and be measurably independent."

The Captain listened to this recital with deep interest, and to some of its passages, with illy-suppressed emotions. He then told her of Fort de Chartres and the country in which it was located; of Kaskaskia, Cahokia, and of the people who lived there. He told her of his life at the Fort, and of his former voyage down the river, and the great joy he anticipated in meeting her and her parents in New Orleans, and of his plans for their future settlement in the colonies near the Fort. He recounted his eager watching for the arrival of their ship, and of his heart-rending disappointment and grief when he met Monsieur Brusier, and heard from him the terrible reality, with assurance of her death also. He then informed her of his present mission to New Orleans, its objects accomplished, and his arrangements all perfected for starting that evening, or early the next morning, on his return, not omitting a description of the perils and hardships of the voyage. Then taking her hand in both of his, he said, "Adel, will you be my wife, and go with me?"

She raised her eyes to his, beaming with joyous confidence, as she answered unhesitatingly; "Yes, Jean Baptiste, I will; and will go with you anywhere."

They again met early next morning at the Ursuline Chapel, and knelt together at the altar. The officiating priest, informed of the Captain's situation, dispensed with the Church's rule in ordinary marriages, of publishing the bans from the altar for three consecutive Sundays, and proceeded to solemnly pronounce the ceremony that made them man and wife.

The only witnesses present were old Michael Mallait and Monsieur

Delorme; Madame Delorme and Mam'selle Rosealie, if invited, did not deign to even send their regrets, much less to offer either reception or wedding feast for the young couple. An hour later the boats were moving up stream, with Adel as mistress of the Captain's cabin, enroute to a new, strange world to found a new home under novel auspices.

Their progress up the tortuous river was laborious, and not altogether free from exciting adventures and narrowly averted dangers; but in due time, all arrived safely at the Fort.

New Chartres, the town near the entrance to the Fort, so named in contradistinction to Old Chartres, near the gate of the old fort below, had grown to respectable dimensions. Commencing with temporary habitations of artisans and laborers, it had absorbed the population of the old town, and the greater part of that of St. Philip.[16] Several traders settled in it and some of the officers and soldiers of the garrison having families resided in the village in preference to the restricted limits within the walls. A beautiful lawnlike esplanade, or drill ground, of twenty acres, laid between the great gate and the town. We can well imagine the maneuvers here of grenadiers, in pleasant weather, viewed with patriotic pride, by the officers and their friends, from the large stone platform surmounting the carved arch of the principal gate. Captain Saucier's cottage was the newest and neatest in the village "officers row," its attractiveness and embellishments due to the taste and industry of his handsome wife. As a token of his special regard for the Captain, Chevalier Makarty transferred Lisette to Adel, for whom she formed an attachment at their first meeting; and the true, worthy servant remained in the Captain's household, through its fortunes, the rest of her days.

For several years after his marriage Capt. Saucier remained steadily on duty at the Fort superintending the work of the builders, until, at last, in 1763, the great structure was almost completed. The broad stone platform over the fine arch of the main gate was placed in position; and also the stone

16. "On the first-named grant, Renault established a little village, and as is the fashion in more modern times, honored it by his own baptismal name—St. Philip. It was on the rich alluvion and had its 'common field' there, the allotments made by himself and within five miles of Fort Chartre, then just erected on a small scale, and with no view to durability or strength; within its shade grew up 'Chartre Village,' as it was called, with its 'common field' also, and 'commons' embracing a large scope of the unappropriated domain, and with a chapel served by a Franciscan friar and dedicated to St. Anne. Not a vestige of these two villages now remain, save some asparagus yearly putting forth its slender stem upon the open prairie." —*The Early History of Illinois.* By Sidney Breese, Chicago, 1884, pp. 177–178. [Quotation corrected.]

stair case and balustrade leading up to it. The cannon,[17] bearing on their surface, the monogram and arms of Louis XIV, were mounted in the bastions, and the buildings and arched magazine within the huge walls were all nearly finished. On the low swampy bank of the Mississippi river, in the far western wilderness, it stood, a marvel of engineering skill and labor, the grandest and strongest fortress in America.

CHAPTER XV. *Surrender of Fort Chartres to the English*

Fort Chartres was the depot of arms and munitions, and the seat of military power for all the vast region from New Orleans to Montreal west of the Alleghenies, as France then claimed the entire Mississippi valley. England's rapidly increasing colonies on the Atlantic seaboard however passed the mountain barrier, and were overrunning the territory claimed by France north of the Ohio river. Their aggressions brought on local conflicts which, in 1755, resulted in war between the two nations. Braddock that year marched on Fort Du Quesne and was defeated. In 1756, the English General, Forbes, with 7,000 men, retrieved Braddock's disaster and compelled the French to evacuate Fort Du Quesne, where all the garrison of Fort Chartres, but one company, had been drawn. It was now plain that the empire of France in America was tottering to its fall. It was too extensive to be successfully defended at all points from onslaughts of such a foe. For three years more the unequal contest continued, when it was practically terminated by the English victory on the Plains of Abraham, and fall of Quebec, on the 13th of September, 1759. The boldness and sagacity of Pontiac, the friend and ally of the French, however, prevented the victorious English from taking possession of the Illinois until six years later.

17. The cannon, five in number, were taken from the ruins of Fort Chartres, in 1812, by Gov. Ninian Edwards and mounted on his Fort Russell, a mile and a half from the present city of Edwardsville. One of them was bursted when firing in celebration of Gen'l. Jackson's victory at New Orleans, in January, 1815. Of the other four no trace can be found. Of the aspect of Fort Chartres, when he visited it in 1802, Gov. Reynolds says; "It was an object of anti-quarian curiosity. The trees, undergrowth, and brush are mixed and interwoven with the old walls. It presented the most striking contrast between a savage wilderness; filled with wild beasts and reptiles, and the remains of one of the largest and strongest fortifications on the continent." He visited it again in 1854, and found "Fort Chartres a pile of mouldering ruins, and the walls torn away almost even with the surface." At present nothing of the great structure remains but one angle of the wall a few feet in height, and the magazine. [Cf. Reynolds' remarks in *My Own Times* (1855 ed.), 44, 52–53; about half of the words here attributed to Reynolds must be Snyder's own.]

The reverses of the French arms were severely felt at Fort Chartres, and throughout the settlements on the Mississippi, though they were not in the theatre of the war. The Fort had been rebuilt at immense expense of treasure and labor, designed to be a permanent bulwark for the French possessions in the Mississippi Valley. Yet, it was not completely finished when the fall of Canada clearly presaged its doom.

In 1761, Col. Makarty was, by his own request, ordered back to France, and Capt. Neyon de Villiers, who, of seven brothers in the military service of the King in America, was the only survivor, the other six having been killed in defense of Canada, succeeded him in command at the Fort. The retiring veteran, upon taking his departure, bid farewell, with touching sadness, to the officers and men, to the colonists who revered him, to the splendid citadel he erected, and to the grave of his idolized daughter. When he parted with Capt. Saucier, who accompanied him from France, and had for a decade been intimately associated with him in all the affairs of the Fort, and had shown his daughter such tender attentions, his iron firmness failed, and tears coursed down his bronzed cheeks as he flung himself into his boat and left the Illinois for ever.

When the weak and corrupt King of France, having secretly transferred Florida, New Orleans and all the territory west of the Mississippi, to Spain, purchased peace with England by ceding to her all the balance of his possessions in America, in 1763, the settlers in the Illinois district were overwhelmed with surprise and mortification. Disgusted and heart-broken, Captain de Villiers abandoned Fort Chartres and went to New Orleans. Captain Saucier, not wishing to return to France, and seeing his military career in America terminated, handed de Villiers his resignation from the army and took up his abode in Cahokia. The veteran Commandant, Louis St. Ange de Bellerive, who many years before commanded the old stockade Fort Chartres, now came from Vincennes, with forty men, and assumed command of the grand new Fort, only to formally surrender it, on the 10th of October, 1765, to Captain Sterling [Thomas Stirling], of the 42d Highlanders, much to the chagrin and deep disgust of Pontiac and his braves, and to all the French colonists. To the lasting disgrace and humiliation of France her lillies were hauled down from the bastion staff and replaced by the detested flag of Great Britain. Fort Chartres was the last place on the continent of North America to float the French flag. St. Ange de Bellerive, unwilling to live under English rule, after the surrender embarked with his handful of men, at the Fort landing and proceeded up the river to St. Louis, which he thought was yet in French territory, and assumed command of that post. New Chartres was speedily deserted; several of its inhabitants following St. Ange to St. Louis, and the balance scattering out in the neighboring settlements.

Captain Saucier and wife, enamored with the country and people, upon his resignation left New Chartres and purchased an elegant home in Cahokia, where they were accorded the highest respect and consideration by the entire community. The feeble exhibition of authority by the new rulers of the Illinois effected no perceptible change in the old regime, and the peaceful habitants were soon reconciled to the new dynasty. Cahokia continued to flourish and grow in importance. Captain Saucier engaged actively in business pursuits and prospered; and was a patriotic citizen of the United States for many years after George Rogers Clark, on the night of the 4th of July, 1778, tore down the odious banner of St. George at Kaskaskia, and planted in its stead— for all future time—the ensign of political freedom.

Owing to the loss of the Cahokia parish records—in the confusion of removing the Church property to a place of safety during the disastrous overflow of the Mississippi, in 1844—it is now not known when Capt. Saucier and his wife died. But it is known that they were buried, side by side, in the little graveyard adjoining the old Cahokia Church, and that their dust still reposes there with that of several generations of the early French pioneers of the Illinois.

GENEALOGICAL

The marriage of Capt. John B. Saucier and Adelaide Lepage was blessed by the advent of three children, in the following order: Baptiste Saucier, Matthieu Saucier, Francois Saucier.[18]

Baptiste Saucier and Marie Josephine Belcour were married, in Cahokia, in the year 1778. Of the three children born to them, Adelaide Saucier and Matthieu Saucier survived; a younger son, John Baptiste Saucier, died when a grown young man.

18. *Pioneer History of Illinois.* By John Reynolds. Second (or Fergus) edition, Chicago, 1887, pp. 286 to 291. See also *Adam W. Snyder and his Period in Illinois History, 1817–1842.* By Dr. J. F. Snyder, Virginia, Illinois, 1906.

The daughter, Adelaide, married, in 1799, a young Frenchman named Jean Francois Perry, from the vicinity of Lyons, in France; and of their four daughters, three survived, named Louise Perry, Adelaide Perry, Harriet Perry.

Adelaide Perry, married on the 18th of October, 1820, at Cahokia, a young man from Fayette County, Pennsylvania, named Adam Wilson Snyder; and of several children born to them, three sons survived, named William Henry Snyder, Frederick Adam Snyder, John Francis Snyder.

APPENDIX

Note A

During the early agitation for revision of the Dreyfus trial, in 1897, frequent mention was made in public prints of "General Saussier, Military Governor of Paris." In the press despatches from Paris there appeared this paragraph: "Paris, January 16, 1898. One hundred and twenty-six patriotic and military Societies held a demonstration today in the Place Vendome in honor of General Gustave Saussier, Commander-in-Chief of the French Army, and Military Governor of Paris, who now retires under the age limit."

The announcement of his death, in 1905, was cabled to this country as follows:

PARIS, Dec. 20.—General Felix Gustave Saussier, former commander-in-chief of the French army, died today. He was one of the best known and bravest officers in France. In the battles around Metz a quarter of a century ago he distinguished himself most signally. The famous infantry charge at St. Privat, which practically barred the progress of the Germans on that side, was led by him. Saussier was one of the officers who signed the protest against the surrender of Metz. General Saussier also served in Italy, Mexico and the Crimea. He was a deputy for some time and in 1873 distinguished himself in the discussions on the reorganization of the army.

Note B

In the confusion incident to removing the church property to a place of safety during the great overflow of the Mississippi in 1844, the parish records of Cahokia were lost. Fortunately, at some time prior to 1844, Mr. Oscar W. Collet, of St. Louis, copied the Cahokia register of marriages, which copy was discovered, nearly half a century later, in the St. Louis University. It is, however, quite defective, having many errors and omissions. The parochial records of Kaskaskia and St. Anne, still preserved, are also very defective, with errors, omissions, and important parts entirely missing. Hence the difficulty, or impossibility, of tracing the family history, or personal identity, of many citizens of French descent who were prominent in the first settling of Illinois. Tho some of them were well educated, they left no written records of themselves or their times. For these reasons there is today much uncertainty regarding the earlier members of the Saucier family in America, several of whom were noted among the pioneers from Canada to Louisiana.

The following brief references—comprising in great part the present knowledge of them—are copied, by permission, from the "Saucier Papers" of Judge Walter B. Douglas, of St. Louis:

Louis Saucier, (son of Charles Saucier and Charlotte Clairet, of St. Eustache, Paris), married, at Quebec, Canada, Margueritte Gailliard *dit* Duplessis, on the 12th of January, 1671. They had two children, Charles and Jean.

Charles, baptised Sept. 1st, 1672, married, 1st, Marie Anne Bisson, 2d, Marie Madeline St. Dennis, and, 3d, Marie Francois Lebel, and had four children.

Jean, baptised Dec. 4th, 1674,—further history not given.[19]

One Jean Saucier was an early inhabitant of Louisiana, as appears in the census of 1706, towit, "Jean Sossié, a wife and 2 children."[20] In Hamilton's *Colonial Mobile*, p. 80, his name is given as J. B. Saucier, his wife was Gabrielle Savary, and his occupation a "Marchand."

In the same book "Madame Socie" is mentioned, p. 151, as a land owner in Mobile in 1760. On page 192 it is stated, "of other officials, we know Fr. Saucier as sub-engineer in 1751." [Quotation corrected.]

When New Orleans was settled, in 1722, some of the family removed there, as in the list of first grantees of lots is the name "Sautier" as a grantee of lot 144.

"Le 24 x bre (24th of October), 1739, Mr. Sauzier, ingenieur, est party avec un detachment d' Arcanzas et quelques Canadiens a dessin de charcher le chemin par on Mr. d'Artaguet avoir este aux Chics."[21]

19. Tanguay's *Dictionnaire Généalogique des Familles Canadiennes*. [Spelling of title corrected.]
20. Fortier's *History of Louisiana*, p. 52 [53 of Vol. 1; quotation corrected].
21. Journal de la Guerre du Micissippi . . . en 1739 et finie en 1740, le Ier d'Avril. Par un Officier de l'Armée de M. de Nouaille. N.Y. Shea. 1859. [Spelling of title corrected. This is No. 10 of John D. G. Shea's Cramoisy Series of Jesuit Relations.]

The place from which he departed was Bienville's camp near the present site of Memphis.

In the Kaskaskia parochial register, "Saucier" signs as a witness to a marriage, on the 20th August, 1742. In same, under date of July, 1761, is this entry. "Marie Jeanne Fontaile, widow of Francois Saucier, lieutenant reformé (half pay) and ingineur pour le Roy at Fort Chartres, married Alexander du Clos. In March, 1788, she was married, for the third time, to Jean du Martin, a native of Ax, in Gascony. She is decribed in the last entry as "Marie Jeanne Saucier, widow of the deceased Alexander du Clos."

Jauvier 7, 1761, Monsieur Saucier fils signs as a marriage witness.

1759, Francois Saucier, cadet, is a godfather.

From the St. Anne parish register it is learned that "le Sieur Jean B. Sausie, ingenieur," was godfather at Fort Chartres on the 19th of February, 1752.

In the same register, 12 avriel, 1758, Sausier was witness at the marriage of Marie Anne Belcour.

1758, 30 Jullet, Saucier again signs as marriage witness.

1760, 10 Juin, Saucier again signs as marriage witness, and is designated in the entry as "Monsieur Saucier."

1760, 8 Janvier, a negro slave of Saucier was buried.

There was in early days, Billon says, in St. Louis, Marie Barbe Saucier, wife of Julien Le Roy. They were married at Mobile in 1755. One of their daughters married Jean Baptiste Frudeau, first school master in St. Louis. Joseph Francis Saucier was godfather of some of the Le Roy children in 1767.

Prof. Clarence W. Alvord, of the Illinois State University, found in the Canadian Archives, copied from Archives Coloniales a Paris, several legal documents emanating from "nous, Francois Saucier, Arpenteur, Soussigné, &c;" and states: "Saucier was still Arpenteur in 1737, beginning in 1707 (Archives C. F. 224, p. 24 and G. p. 80), most of the documents of the period in the volume were written by Saucier."

I am also indebted to Prof. Alvord for the following records copied from those of Kaskaskia and St. Anne, (translated):

Feb. 6, 1733. Village of M. Renault. Francois La Croix and his wife Barbe Meaumenier, sold to their son-in-law, Henry Saussier, a *terre* of three arpents front extending from the Mississippi to the bluffs, lying between land of M. Girardot and Francois La Croix, for three hundred minots of wheat, payable in yearly instalments of 10 minots. Furthermore, Saussier promises to maintain in repair the commune which crosses his land, and to pay the seignioral rights. Signed by cross for La Croix, and cross for his wife. Robbilhand witness. Jerome, Notary.

Sept. 22, 1737, Jean Baptiste Saucier acknowledges to have sold to Joseph Deruisseau and company a family of slaves, consisting of a negro, a negress, a negroit and negrillome, for 2000 livres payable in wheat, &c. Made in the house of J. Bte. Bauvais. Signed J. B. Saucier, J. Deruisseau, (and company), J. B. Beaulieu, Joseph Leduc, Barrois. Notary.

Sept. 17, 1758, at the request of Henry Saucier, and on the order of M. Buchet, judge in the jurisdiction, the Royal hussier (auctioneer), Louis Robinet, offers at auction before the door of the parish church of St. Anne, after mass, land of two and a half arpents front extending from the Mississippi to the bluffs, situated in the commons of the village of St. Philippe du Marais, belonging to the said Saucier. It is offered three times, and is finally sold for 305 livres to J. Belcour. Signed Robinet, Huissier. Belcour signed with a cross. Metius, Duchemin, witnesses.

April 19, 1763. In the house of M. Deselle at Prairie du Rocher an elaborate marriage contract was entered into by Sieur Antoine Duclos, Ecuyer, "natif de la paroise de St. Anne a la Nouvelle Chartres, aux Illinois, diocese de Quebec, fil de Sieur Alexandre Duclos, ancien officer des trouppes de sa majeste tres Christienne," on the one part, and "Demoiselle Marie Jeanne Saucier, fille d Sieur deffunct Francois Saucier, ingenieur pour le Roy," &c., of the second part, with consent of her mother, Sieur Pierre Girardot, her appointed guardian, of Dame Magdeliene Loiselle Girardot, her aunt, Demoiselle Felicite Saucier her sister, and Sieur Baptiste Saucier her brother. Parties and witnesses all signed in presence of Viault Lesperance, Notary.

In Collet's "Index" to the old Cahokia marriage register the following are the only Sauciers recorded:

Baptiste Saucier married Marie Josephine Belcour. Before 1784.
Francois Saucier married Angelique Roy *dit* Lapensee. Before 1787.
Matthieu Saucier married Catherine Godin, 1788.
Matthieu Saucier married Josette Chatillon, Sept. 8, 1812.
    fils du Baptiste   fille du Francois Chatillon
    Saucier et Marie   et Margaret Lachaine
    Josephine Belcour

And all of them enumerated in the census of Cahokia in 1787 are: Matthieu Saucier; Matthieu son fils; Francois Saucier pere; Charle son fils; Bte Saucier pere; Jean Baptiste son fils; Matthieu son fils.[22]

The three heads of families here named, brothers, Baptiste, Matthieu, and Francois Saucier, were quite prominent in the public affairs of Cahokia and vicinity during the latter part of the eighteenth century, all three serving for some time as Justices of the district court.[23] Matthieu and Francois Saucier "founded the village of Portage des Sioux in Upper Louisiana,"[24] and for many years were successful traders there.

The writer of this sketch was for many years intimately acquainted with Matthieu Saucier, (my mother's uncle), son of above named Baptiste Saucier. He was born at Cahokia in 1782, married Josette Chatillon *dit* Godin in 1812, and died at Prairie du Pont in 1863, at the age of 81. He was a very intelligent, quiet and unassuming gentleman, with but limited education, and only traditional knowledge of his ancestral genealogy. All that he knew of his grandfather was that he came from the Loir district in France, and had been an army officer at Fort Chartres. He believed him to have been the Francois Saucier mentioned—as quoted in this Note—in the *Journal de la Guerre du Mississippi en 1739*, etc., as the "ingeneur" who led a detachment of "Arcanzas" and a few Canadians on the route taken by d' Artaguiette against the Chickasaws in 1736; and, in Hamilton's *Colonial Mobile*, as a "sub-engineer in 1751;" and the inference of his death prior to 1760 from the registry of marriage of his widow, in July, 1761, to Alexandre du Clos, in which he is alluded to as a retired (reformé) lieutenant and engineer at Fort Chartres. That lieutenant Saucier evidently was in the King's military service on the Mississippi at quite an early day, and probably served as an engineer in the building of the first Fort Chartres, and perhaps of the second Fort also.

In 1737 there was a Jean Baptiste Saucier at Prairie du Rocher, of whom nothing is now known, and who is supposed to have come to America with Renault in 1721.

It is learned from the St. Anne parish records that "le Sieur Jean B. Saucier, ingenieur," was at Fort Chartres in February, 1752.

Reynolds says, "in 1756, Jean Baptiste Saucier, a French officer at Ft.

22. Collections of the Illinois State Historical Library. Vol. II. Cahokia Records. C. W. Alvord. 1907, p. 624 *et seq.*
23. Cahokia Records. Alvord, 1907.
24. Reynolds' *Pioneer History of Illinois*, p. 286.

84

Chartres, and married in that vicinity. After the country was ceded to Great Britain in 1763, he located himself and family in Cahokia, where he died. He had three sons: Jean B., Matthieu, and Francis Saucier, who were popular and conspicuous characters in early times in Illinois." [25]

Edward G. Mason states—in his *Kaskaskia and its Parish Records. Chicago, 1881. p. 18.*—"On May 22d, 1806, [occurred] the marriage of Pierre Menard, widower, and Angelique Saucier, granddaughter of Jean B. Saucier, once a French officer at Fort Chartres, who resigned and settled in the Illinois country."

25. Pioneer History of Illinois, 2d Ed., Chicago. 1887, p. 286. [Quotation corrected.]

THE OLD FRENCH TOWNS

OF ILLINOIS IN 1839

A Reminiscence

Reprinted from *Journal of the Illinois State Historical Society*, XXXVI (Dec., 1943): 345–67. All numbered footnotes except the one in quotes, No. 7, which was Dr. Snyder's, were added by the editor of that *Journal*.

IN THE EARLY AUTUMN OF 1839, I—then nine and a half years of age— accompanied my father and mother on a very pleasant excursion through parts of St. Clair, Monroe, and Randolph counties, of which I still retain a vivid recollection. In the family carriage drawn by two fine horses, we left our home in Belleville at sunrise one bright morning in the first week of September, taking our course due south through the town, across Richland Creek, and, passing the Ripley and West farms, were soon on the broad road in the high open prairie. Free from the sultry heat of August, but still delightfully mild and pleasant, the weather was simply perfect. Though the wild roses had shed their flowers, and the tall grass and rosin weeds that bordered the roadway were sere and yellow with the presage of maturity, the landscape was fresh and beautiful, enlivened at every step by the shrill song of the meadow lark, and the whirring flight of flocks of startled quails and prairie chickens.

My father, Adam W. Snyder, was at that time a prominent Democratic politician, having, on the previous 3d of March, completed a term as representative in Congress of the First Illinois district, which comprised the western half of southern Illinois, including Macoupin, Gallatin, Alexander and Madison counties.[1] My mother, a descendant of early French settlers of this state, was a native of Prairie du Pont, in St. Clair County, and in that vicinity were also born her mother and grandmother. Consequently her circle of relatives and acquaintances extended not only throughout the limits of the

---

1. Adam W. Snyder was a native of Pennsylvania who settled in St. Clair County, Illinois, a year or two before Illinois was admitted to the Union. He served three terms in the Illinois Senate and one in Congress. In 1842 he was his party's nominee for governor, but he died on May 14, less than three months before the election. The story of his life is told in *Adam W. Snyder and His Period in Illinois History, 1817–1842* (Virginia, Ill., 1906), by John F. Snyder.

American Bottom on this side of the Mississippi River, but from St. Charles down to Cape Girardeau on the other side.

Our destination that morning was Kaskaskia, and the object of our expedition presumably was social visiting and recreation. However, my observation of politicians in the years that have intervened since then leads me now to suspicion that my father's underlying motive in making that journey was to "feel the public pulse" in that part of the district in regard to his re-election to Congress. In those days, when state elections were held on the first Monday in August, political campaigns commenced the year before, and electioneering was perennial. He was then in the grasp of that merciless scourge of the human race, tubercular consumption; but during the past summer his health had apparently much improved, and he was buoyed up with the vain hope of ultimate recovery. Following the smooth road through High Prairie and on in a southwestern direction, we arrived about noon at Waterloo, the county seat of Monroe County. Founded by Daniel P. Cook and George Forquer in 1818, Waterloo in 1839 was quite a brisk little village, bearing a strong family resemblance to all the other "American" county seats of southern Illinois, having its public square and courthouse, its tavern, stores, groceries, and blacksmith shop, and full complement of idle men and boys whose sole aim and ambition in life was to continue their existence.

The tavern was a pioneer structure of logs, subsequently weatherboarded, with porches and other additions made to keep up with the progress and requirements of the times. It was owned and conducted by an early pioneer, David H. Ditch, a sturdy, quiet, slow-going man, perfectly contented with his condition and surroundings, and never in a hurry. He was a native of Fayette County, Pennsylvania, born there (about the year 1780) within less than a dozen miles of my father's birthplace. His wife was Hannah Forquer, sister of George Forquer and half sister of Gov. Thomas Ford. They were married where they were born, in Fayette County, Pennsylvania, and came to Illinois with Mrs. Ford and her other children in the fall of 1804. That log tavern was among the first houses built in Waterloo, the logs cut and in great part "notched" by Mr. Ditch, and there he and his wife entertained the traveling public for many years, and raised a highly respected family.

Driving up to the tavern Mr. Ditch, in shirt sleeves and straw hat, with bluff, cheerful salutation, invited us in, and relieved my father of further care of the horses. And Mrs. Ditch, answering to his call, took charge of my mother and myself, leading the way to her best room where her hearty welcome banished all restraint and caused us to feel very much at ease. We had not long to wait before the tinkling of the dinner bell announced the noonday meal was ready—for which I also was in readiness, my juvenile appetite being whetted by the invigorating ride of twenty miles. The dinner was not served "en course;" nor were there any printed bills of fare on the table, or waiters around in spiketail coats; but the platters and dishes were all there heaped high with the most savory, and well-cooked, products of the country from boiled roasting-ears to luscious apple pies, interspersed with chicken pie and roast beef; to all of which we did ample justice while Mrs. Ditch and one of her daughters kept the flies off with long, slender peach tree limbs.

The coming of my father to Waterloo that day must have been expected there, as in the course of the afternoon and evening many of the most prominent citizens and politicians of the town and county called to see him, and "pay him their respects;" and some of them no doubt to consult him concerning the program and "slate" of the Democratic Party for the very important elections to be held the next year. It seemed as if my father was in fact "in the hands of his friends," so numerous were they as to give the occasion the appearance of a public reception on his part. They were all strangers to me excepting a few I had seen as visitors at our house in Belleville; but with some who were there that day I became well acquainted in after years. I well remember John Morrison who was there, the youngest son of the pioneer, William Morrison of Kaskaskia,[2] the oldest of the seven brothers who came west in early days from the Morrison hive in Philadelphia. He, John Morrison, was the father of Col. William R. Morrison the distinguished soldier, statesman, and Democratic leader of our times.[3] I recall, too, Col. James B. Moore, a plain, but solid-looking man, who was then the state senator representing Monroe, St. Clair and Madison counties jointly with Senator George Churchill of Madison and Senator John Murray of St. Clair. As Col. Moore was a Whig it must be inferred that his call upon my father just then had no political significance, but was prompted altogether by personal friendship and courtesy.

2. William Morrison came to Kaskaskia from Philadelphia in 1790. He soon built up a thriving mercantile business, and was long the foremost merchant of early Illinois. He died at Kaskaskia in 1837.

3. Veteran of the Mexican and Civil wars, state legislator, member of Congress, member of the Interstate Commerce Commission, 1887–1897, and chairman of the commission after 1892.

Another plain, and pleasant-mannered person, still retained in my memory since that day, was Edward T. Morgan, at that time the Monroe County member of the state legislature, a fluent talker in conversation, and of social, friendly disposition. But the two men in that assemblage who more particularly attracted my attention—probably because I attracted theirs and they spoke very kindly to me—were Col. James A. James and Dr. William H. Bissell. Col. James, the son of Gen. Thomas James, one of the early pioneers of Monroe County, had the appearance of a substantial and prosperous farmer of more than average prominence in the community. The Democrats elected him the next year (1840) to succeed Col. Moore as state senator, and in 1847 he was elected a delegate to the constitutional convention. Col. James and his family were Catholics, by the influence of the Catholic lady he had married. His cousin, John James, a Protestant, was also a Monroe County farmer, residing not far from the Colonel, down in the American Bottom. Dr. Bissell, at that time, was practicing medicine in Waterloo in partnership with Dr. Harper. He left Painted Post, Steuben County, New York (where he had practiced his profession for three years after his graduation, in Philadelphia), in the spring of 1837 for Galesburg, Illinois. He came by the usual immigrant route from the East of those days, down the Ohio and up the Mississippi; but did not reach his intended destination, leaving his boat, for some unknown reason, at Harrisonville, in Monroe County, and soon began teaching a country school in the Bottom, and boarding with the family of Mr. John James. At the August election in 1840 his election by the Democrats (defeating Madison Miller, his Whig opponent), to represent Monroe County in the legislature, was the beginning of his brilliant public career.[4] In December, 1840, he was united in marriage to Miss Emily Susan, daughter of Mr. John James, in the house where she was born on the 14th of December, 1819. In 1841 they moved to Belleville, and there she died in 1844.

Another conspicuous and well-known Democratic politician at the Ditch tavern that day was Hon. John D. Whiteside, son of the noted Indian fighter, Col. Wm. Whiteside, and born at Whiteside Station, a few miles north of Waterloo, where he lived all his life, and died there in 1850. He was then

---

4. Bissell served in the Mexican War as colonel of the Second Illinois Volunteers. He was elected to Congress as a Democrat in 1849 and served three terms. He left his party on the Nebraska issue, and in 1856 was elected as the first Republican governor of Illinois. Bissell died in office in 1860.

state treasurer, forty-five years of age, ruddy-faced, square built, and a strikingly handsome man. He had served Monroe County as representative in the 7th, 8th, and 9th legislatures, and was elected to the state Senate in the 10th, which position he resigned to accept that of treasurer; was presidential elector in 1836, went to Europe as state fund commissioner, finally hypothecating the $804,000 state interest bonds with Macallister [Macalister] & Stebbins for $261,500 "contrary to law," as Ford says. He was a member of the constitutional convention of 1847, and, lastly, again represented Monroe County in the 14th General Assembly. As he was a warm personal friend of my father's, whom he frequently visited at our home, I was well acquainted with him, and admired him very much, especially when he had on his fine broadcloth cloak. Another distinction thrust upon John D. Whiteside was his selection, in September, 1842, by Gen. James Shields to act as his second in the duel he challenged Mr. Lincoln to fight; a duty Whiteside gallantly performed; but the intervention of mutual friends fortunately averted bloodshed.

I soon lost interest in the visiting statesmen, and wandered out into the public square to view the town. While looking around, a good deal of loud talking and swearing in a "grocery"—as dramshops were then called—on one side of the square attracted my attention, and, boylike, I cautiously approached the place to see what was going on. My curiosity was soon gratified when two drunken men came tumbling out of the door clenched in a desperate fight, and pounded each other, in the dirt and dust, to the great amusement of a crowd of idle spectators, until one of them "hollered enough," when they were separated.

The next morning we left Waterloo, after an early breakfast, taking the old pioneer road southward that led us to the picturesque bluffs and down into the broad American Bottom not far above Prairie du Rocher. We stopped at that old French village long enough to water the horses and allow them half an hour's rest, then trotted on over the smooth level road to Kaskaskia. As we went along my father pointed out to my mother the location of Elvirade, the first residence in Illinois of Gov. Ninian Edwards; also the place near it where Judge Jesse B. Thomas[5] had first settled when he came to the Territory in 1809; and across the Kaskaskia River the mill built by Gen. John

5. Illinois territorial judge, president of the first Illinois constitutional convention, and United States senator, 1818–1829.

Edgar.[6] But about that time I felt much more interested in the prospects of getting to the dinner table than I was in those old historic places.

It was a little past noon when we arrived at the old town and drove up to the broad front porch of the widow Short's tavern, the same tavern—then conducted by Col. Sweet—where Gen. Lafayette was entertained when he visited Kaskaskia in April, 1825. It was a long, one-story frame building with wide porches on each side, spacious fireplaces at each end, and roomy attic above, lighted and ventilated by dormer windows. Situated on the main street leading north from the ferry landing at the top of the slope from the river, it faced the east, and was but a short distance from the old church and cemetery. Mrs. Short, the landlady, was the daughter of Major Nicholas Jarrot distinguished in the annals of Cahokia as one of its early and most enterprising citizens. She was married in 1826, at Cahokia, to Thomas Short, son of the noted ranger and frontiersman, Capt. Jacob Short. They resided for awhile, from about 1830 to 1833, at Illinoistown (now East St. Louis), engaged there in tavern keeping, then moving to Kaskaskia took charge of the "Col. Sweet Hotel," the only tavern there. Tom Short died in 1837 leaving his widow with one child. Mrs. Short, a brisk, energetic woman, when thrown upon her own resources, continued in the tavern business with much success. She was a handsome, intelligent, and vivacious brunette, of gay, sunny disposition, very highly esteemed by a wide range of friends and acquaintances. In 1841 she married William Morrison, son of the first William Morrison of Kaskaskia, and with him moved to Belleville where they resided the rest of their lives. Mrs. Short and my mother, born within a mile of each other, and about the same age, grew up together, attending mass together at the old Cahokia church, and dancing at all the village balls, were close friends until separated by death. Mrs. Short's only child, a boy named Tom, a year or so older than myself, a merry, kindhearted, sportive fellow, was my constant companion during my stay at the Short tavern, and succeeded in making my visit interesting and exceedingly pleasant. From our first meeting we took quite a fancy to each other, that grew, with daily association after he came up to Belleville and was our nearest neighbor, to a firm friendship severed by his death in 1852.

Kaskaskia at that period, though past its political and commercial glory,

6. Landowner, merchant, and miller who settled in Kaskaskia in 1784 and lived there until his death in 1832. Edgar County was named in his honor.

was still a considerable town, and, socially, very lively. In almost every feature it bore the aspect of age, and in some were seen the ravages of decay. Many of the houses were decidedly antiquated, and some dilapidated; but the inhabitants, who were mainly of the primitive Canadian French stock, seemed to be well contented with their condition and surroundings. The town had no factory of any description, or other local industry to employ its people, as the community was agricultural and pastoral, deriving its support chiefly from its "commons," a magnificent tract of adjoining land, several thousands of acres in extent, level as a floor, and not surpassed in fertility by the famed valley of the Nile. Three general stores in which dry goods, hardware and groceries were sold supplied the wants of the villagers in those lines, and one "grocery"—not yet dignified by the title of saloon—not far from the tavern, I remember, had its full share of public patronage. The dwellings, with few exceptions, were of the ancient French pattern, made of wood, one story and attic, many with dormer windows in the roof, and all surrounded with porches, having around each ample, well-kept gardens with fruit trees, shrubbery, and profusion of flowers.

Homemade carts constructed altogether of wood, and drawn by one horse, or pony, were in general use by the French *habitants,* and their only means for transportation and travel. A few, very few of the most opulent citizens had eastern-made, or imported carriages. Occasionally a light one-horse "dearborn" wagon was seen, and now and then a covered two-wheel gig known there (improperly) as a *calèche*. The two-horse farm wagons that came to Edgar's mill, and into the town, with grain or other produce, invariably belonged to American settlers, and were an innovation that the French were very slow to adopt. The natives were very partial to horseback riding, and had a great number of ponies of degenerate Canadian stock, but few, if any, large or fine horses.

Tom Short, Jr., and myself were attracted to each other on my arrival at the tavern, becoming at once boon companions, much to the gratification no doubt of my parents who were thus measurably relieved of my care, enabling them to devote their time without hindrance to their many social engagements. Tom was familiar with every nook and corner, and with every inhabitant, of the place and vicinity, and was given the right of way wherever he chose to go. For five days we rambled at will about the town, along the river bank, and among the ancient gravestones in the little grass-grown cemetery, having with us at times, as companion and special guardian, a Negro boy, a few years older than either of us, who belonged to one of Mrs. Short's boarders. There was no order or regularity in arrangement of the tombs and gravestones in the cemetery, and the number of them was very small in proportion to the multitude of dead buried there. Some of the headstones had fallen down and lay half buried in the ground, and all were weather-beaten and lichen-stained. The surface level of the cemetery was elevated considerably above that of the surrounding streets and lots, raised by addition, through passing centuries, of human remains.

The old church, time-worn and dilapidated, was still there where it had stood in defiance of the winds and storms of a century and a quarter. I have no recollection of the plan or materials of its construction, and did not see its interior; but its peculiarities that particularly attracted my attention, and indelibly impressed my memory, were its wide projecting eaves, the heavy growth of moss covering its roof like a green velvet carpet, and the rickety old belfry on its front end surmounted by a cross.[7]

The population of Kaskaskia at that time could not have exceeded six hundred including, perhaps, from fifty to seventy-five Negro slaves. All of the native whites were of French descent, and, of course, Catholics. The language they spoke was the *patois* of Canada, a perversion of the French—with which I then was much more familiar than I was with the English.

---

7. "The statements of certain writers regard[ing] the church at Kaskaskia, though conflicting, plainly discredit what I have written about it here. In a paper read by Rev. David J. Doherty, on Feb. 15th, 1877, before the Missouri Historical Society, he said, in reference to the old church: 'It has this year, 1838, been pulled down, on account of its being too much injured by the weather, &c.' Edmund Flagg, author of *The Far West*, who visited Kaskaskia in the summer of 1836, after describing the old church there (Vol. II. pp. 172–173) added a footnote when his book was published, two years later, asserting in it that, 'The old building has been since dismantled, however; its bell removed from the tower, and the whole structure will soon, probably, be prostrated by "decay's effacing finger."' A letter appearing in one of the Chicago Sunday papers in Sept., 1898,—said to have been written by Judge H. W. Beckwith—mentions the demolishing and removal of the brick church building in Kaskaskia on account of the rapid encroachment of the Mississippi River on the remaining remnant of the old town, and adds in reference to that brick building, 'It was erected in 1831, sixty-seven years ago, &c.' The brick church was, in fact, not erected until the year 1841, and finished some years later.

"Though I was but nine and a half years old at the date of my first visit to Kaskaskia—as herein related, in September, 1839—I remember distinctly the old church, as described by Edmund Flagg, and am positively certain it was still standing there. Its broad eaves and moss covered roof made an impression on my youthful mind not effaced, or even dimmed, by the passing of sixty-nine years. That impression was strengthened, confirmed, and fixed by frequent allusions to the old church as we saw it, in conversations with my mother to the time of her death, in 1881. J.F.S."

There were, however, then residing there several "Americans," as all English-speaking persons were designated, but they had learned the native dialect and adopted the methods of life, customs and habits of the natives. One of that class was Doctor Swanwick, a permanent boarder at the Short tavern, and a very pleasant though somewhat eccentric gentleman, who won my respect and admiration by gathering up from the table after each meal scraps of food, as he said, "for his dear little children," as he styled the two kittens he kept at his bachelor quarters, or office.

Of the social life of Kaskaskia of that era I can recall but little, for, in fact, I had but little opportunity to observe it, as I was running at large every day with Tom Short, Jo. Chenon, and other boys, while my parents were receiving, or calling on, their friends; or attending society entertainments at which, then as now, the presence of children was not particularly desired. And after the strenuous exercise of the day I was usually more inclined to go up to my bed in the attic soon after supper, although sounds of merriment and strains of the fiddle from near-by points indicated that joy in the old town was still unconfined, than to lose sleep as a mere looker-on.

But one day as Tom and I were hurrying from the dinner table to go canoe riding on the river with our colored guardian, we were notified to be home early if we wished to go with our parents to a fine party that evening. The Okaw River was at a low stage, with sluggish current that offered no great resistance to the canoe's progress as paddled by our *garcon* who was an expert oarsman. We went up to the mill, and there fished awhile in fine luck, catching quite a string of fish notwithstanding the lateness of the season. Returning leisurely we reached the tavern in good time for supper and to dress for the expected entertainment. That noted event was a reception and ball at the residence of Judge Nathaniel Pope[8] in honor of my father. By seven o'clock we arrived at the Judge's mansion, where we found the greater number of his invited guests already assembled. It was a brilliant affair graced by the presence of all the elite and beauty of the town and vicinity, and also by a good many of the plain, common people. The reception proper occupied but a short time, and then dancing commenced. I can now see, in memory, the rotund figure of Judge Pope with my mother, and my father with Mrs. Pierre Menard, as partners, leading the dance in the first set.

8. Territorial secretary of Illinois, and the territorial delegate who obtained the admission of the state to the Union. Appointed United States district judge in 1819, he held that position until his death in 1850.

Tom Short and I were admitted as spectators in charge of a colored serv-ant girl of Mrs. Short's, who had strict instructions to see that we violated none of the proprieties, to take us home when we became sleepy, and see us safely in bed. Much to the gratification of our saddle-colored chaperon, we didn't get sleepy until sometime after the midnight banquet, nor at any time did we overtax her vigilance, as she passed the night in hilarious enjoyment with the other servants in the kitchen and dining room.

At that time Judge Pope was fifty-five years of age, in the vigorous prime of his life, his dark hair streaked with gray, yet firm of step, and activity un-impaired. He was not quite six feet tall, very slightly stoop-shouldered, and a little inclined to corpulency. He was a deliberate talker, dignified in bearing, and courtly in manners. His conversation, by no means devoid of humor, was cheerful and entertaining. When presented to him by my father he spoke to me very kindly, and on leaving him he expressed the hope that I would grow up to be of some service to my native state.

Col. Pierre Menard was there, then seventy years old, with all the ap-pearance of an old man.[9] He looked weak and careworn, perhaps from ill-health; but was mentally bright, and very talkative. Mrs. Menard, who was with him, was his second wife, and apparently several years his junior in age. She was yet a handsome woman, with tall, shapely figure, black eyes and black hair, dark complexioned, and animated in speech and manners. She was, before her marriage to Col. Menard, Angelique Saucier, a daughter of François Saucier, and cousin of my mother's mother—whose maiden name was Adelaide Saucier. In consequence of that distant relationship we received from her and Col. Menard very marked attention.

The rooms were well lighted by candles on the mantelpiece and in tin sconces on the wall; and the floors, well polished and waxed, were as smooth as glass. The reigning belle of Kaskaskia society was Miss Adeline Maxwell, a radiantly beautiful native of the place, who some years later married a steamboat captain, and lived to an old age. But all the ladies—more particu-larly the young and middle-aged—who participated in that dance, were a marvel of grace and finery, which was well worth a journey to the site of Kaskaskia to see. Their dresses, with very few exceptions, were of fine mate-rial, colored, figured and showy, cut very *décolleté,* with short and narrow

9. Menard died in 1844, at the age of seventy-eight. He was a prominent merchant of Kaskaskia, and the first lieutenant governor of Illinois.

skirts, extremely short-waisted, and only apologies for sleeves, or none at all. Some had their hair done up in curls, but the most of them confined their hair to the back of the head with high, broad, tortoise-shell combs. They were adorned with a profusion of jewelry, gold bracelets and rings, and necklaces of gold, pearl, and jet beads; and all had earrings, many of which were pendants of gold and gems that touched their bare shoulders. As dancing was a hereditary talent with those French natives, all danced elegantly, entering into it with keen enthusiasm. The parish priest was an interested guest until after refreshments were served, and certainly fully enjoyed the entertainment.

While I was entranced with every feature of the function—with the supper particularly—the one that most especially interested me, I think, was the music, or rather, the musicians. There were two of them, both fiddlers—not violinists—playing together, one a mulatto, the other a white native Creole. The latter wore a gaudy, red-figured calico shirt and buckskin breeches with a red sash around his waist and a bandana handkerchief tied around his head. They both played well, the Creole calling the figures in a loud clear voice, at the same time keeping perfect time by tapping the floor with his foot, his very soul enwrapped in the performance. For some time I sat near him in silent appreciation of his genius. I have since heard Ole Bull, and other world-famed violinists, but none of them ever held me so spellbound as did that Creole fiddler with the red shirt. An hour, or so, after supper the dusky damsel to whose care we had been consigned escorted us home; but the older members of our party did not return until very near, or quite, daylight.

A favorite place of rendezvous for the Kaskaskia boys, for playing, getting up fishing excursions, or other sports and pastimes, was a vacant lot near the center of the town, about a hundred yards west by south of the convent. It was sandy, and measurably free from weeds; but all through it were buried, or half-hidden, rocks the remains, beyond doubt, of a building, or buildings, that once stood there. The name by which it was known among the boys was "the old fort" (le vieux fort), a name unmeaning to them, as it was to myself; but many years later I recognized its historic significance as the surviving vestige of a tradition lost to all but a very few in that community. Upon that lot was situated the Jesuit establishment founded in 1720, and confiscated to the Crown (of France) in 1763 by the Superior Council of Louisiana, a year before the French parliament suppressed the Jesuit order. When the British were forced by overflow of the Mississippi in 1772 to evacuate Fort Chartres, they moved to Kaskaskia where they took possession of the vacant Jesuit buildings there, enclosed them with high pickets, and gave to their new station the name of Fort Gage, in honor of Gen. Gage, commander of the British forces in America. Six years later, on the night of July 4, 1778, sixty-one years before my visit there, that fort was captured by Col. Geo. Rogers Clark. It then passed into possession of the state of Virginia, and subsequently into that of the United States. After its abandonment by the Virginia garrison, in 1780, it gradually fell in ruins which were for a long time known locally as "the old fort."

My father and mother, Mrs. Short, Tom and myself leaving the tavern one morning, in our carriage, crossed the Kaskaskia River on the flatboat ferry and drove to Col. Menard's mansion to spend the day.[10] The hearty, cheerful hospitality of the Colonel and his family, the perfect weather and charming surroundings, made the visit an occasion of rare pleasure and enjoyment. While the grown folks spent the time in social converse and hilarity in the parlor and on the broad front porch, Tom and I rambled at will about the spacious premises, finding amusement and interest in all we saw. With abundance of peaches, apples and watermelons, and the kindest attention paid to us we had no reason to feel lonesome; yet, by the time dinner was over we were tired—perhaps weary of the restraint imposed by our clean clothes, and the special caution impressed upon us not to soil them. Early in the afternoon Col. Menard sent a Negro man, with a horse and cart, to Kaskaskia for a sack of salt he had there—a commodity in those days shipped from the Gallatin and Jackson County salines in sacks containing 200 pounds each. The novelty of a cart ride and our desire to get back to the tavern determined us to ask the colored man's permission to go with him, which he gladly granted, provided our mothers assented; and they did—gladly too, I think. Seated on clean straw he put into the cart for our accommodation, we had a jolly time getting to town though the traveling was not very speedy.

In the afternoon of the next day, again in our carriage with my parents and others, we crossed the broad, level commons dotted with hay and wheat stacks, and the pastures still green with grass and clover, to the bank of the Mississippi, three miles west, to pay our homage to the great river, and inci-

---

10. The Menard home, now a state memorial, is the only building of old Kaskaskia still standing. Located across the river and at some distance from the town, it escaped destruction when the Mississippi changed its course and obliterated the town proper.

dentally catch a glimpse of the old village of Ste. Genevieve on the western side, nine miles beyond at the bend of the stream. The water was very low, giving unusual prominence to its many snags and long, barren sandbars in midstream and stretching out from either bank. No steamboat was in sight, or other river craft, but the skiff and canoe of a Frenchman who occupied a cabin near by and eked out his living by fishing and rowing occasional passengers across the river. In returning we stopped at the old two-story brick mansion of Gov. Bond, then still in good condition,[11] and tenanted by acquaintances of some or all of our party, arriving at the tavern as the rays of the setting sun were gilding the crests of the bluffs beyond the historic Okaw [Kaskaskia River].

Much too soon to suit me our visit reached its limit. After the noonday meal of the fifth day of our sojourn there, we bid our friends farewell and took our departure from Kaskaskia. Passing out at the Cahokia gate we followed the well-beaten road leading north, in sight of the Kaskaskia River until we passed the point where it breaks through the range of bluffs in its course from the northeastern prairies to join the Mississippi, and continuing on the old trail along the foot of the bluffs, arrived at Prairie du Rocher early in the afternoon. Having several old-time acquaintances to visit there we remained overnight in that ancient hamlet, entertained at its only public house—or rather, at the private residence of Monsieur Antoine Barbeau, an old native of the place, who obligingly entertained the few travelers happening to come that way. The only indelible impression I have retained of Prairie du Rocher on that occasion is of the grand rocky cliff towering over a hundred feet perpendicularly above the village, and the great swarm of cliff swallows circling around, or clinging to their mud nests built on the face of the rock, keeping up in the meantime an incessant shrill chattering or discordant warbling. I also have a lively recollection of the mosquitoes there, more numerous, and more voracious than those of Kaskaskia. The Barbeaus, our host and hostess, were unalloyed specimens of the non-progressive exotic Creole race that originally settled in the American Bottom, dark-complexioned, black-haired and black-eyed, slow-motioned, contented, sociable, and very kind and hospitable.

11. Half a century or more ago the home of Governor Bond was taken down, removed to Kaskaskia Island—that paradoxical portion of Illinois which lies west of the Mississippi River—and there rebuilt. It is still standing.

Having a long journey before us next day we made preparations for an early start, and in the morning left Prairie du Rocher with the rising of the sun. Taking with us, as a guide, a Creole employe of Mr. Barbeau's mounted on a pony, we drove over a very dim, grass-grown road to the site of old Fort Chartres nearly four miles west. The long, dry summer had dried up the intervening sloughs leaving their beds solid enough to drive over without difficulty. What I most distinctly remember about the site of the great fortress were the tangled bushes and briars and tall trees that had overgrown the place. I then, of course, knew nothing of the history of Fort Chartres, but understood from my father's remarks as he pointed to the course of the stone walls, which in some places were still three or four feet high, that it was an old and very interesting ruin. We inspected the old magazine that to me appeared to have been built for an ice house, the thought suggested by the ice house at our home constructed of stone and partly below the surface of the ground. A well we saw before getting to the magazine was a conspicuous object, as its lining wall of neatly cut and accurately fitted stones, denuded, by action of water currents during an overflow of the Mississippi, of some of the surrounding earth, stood up about three feet high much resembling the top of a sunken chimney. Our guide led us out through bushes and tall prairie grass to the Cahokia road some distance above Prairie du Rocher, from whence, taking leave of us he returned to the village, and we continued our course northward. At midday we halted for an hour or more at a farm house by the roadside for refreshments for ourselves and horses, then resuming our journey we drove into Cahokia at dusk.

But a short time after our arrival a delegation of young folks came to request—and insist upon—the presence of my parents at a dancing party going on at the residence of an old friend near by. They would listen to no excuse, so, notwithstanding the fatigue of a fifty mile journey that day, my father and mother yielded to their persuasion and went with them. As I was given the option of going along with them, or going to bed I chose the latter without hesitation.

Cahokia in 1839—the same as Kaskaskia—was perceptibly in its decadence, but still retaining very much of its former importance and peculiar interest, with no appreciable contraction of its original limits. Nor had its people changed in type and characteristics since the village was founded in 1698. Their habits, customs, manners and dress were about the same as those of their peasant ancestry of the northern provinces of France in the 17th century. The early possessors of a virgin country of untold natural resources, and for half a century surrounded by the example and influence of an incoming progressive, enterprising and industrious race, they were stationary, or gradually retrograding. They were all Catholics, and, with very few exceptions, all illiterate; without aspirations, or impulse of ambition, they were perfectly contented, with never a thought or desire to better their condition. In my boyhood I was well acquainted with an old lady there, a native of the place and mother of a grown-up family, who had never been in St. Louis—simply because she had never desired to go there—although the distance was but seven miles, and ferriage of the Mississippi was free to all Cahokians in consideration of the ferry landing on the Illinois side being on part of the Cahokia Commons. In 1839, and until the great overflow of the Mississippi in 1844, there were quite a number of very neat, and some elegant, residences in Cahokia, surrounded by fine, well-kept gardens, fruit orchards, abundant flowers, and all the domestic conveniences of that day.

The few "American" citizens of the village, married to native Creoles, had adopted all the ways of life of the Creoles, spoke the Creole dialect, and were, in every essential respect, Creoles by naturalization. The most important resident of that class then there was Doctor Armstead O. Butler, a native of Virginia and graduate of a Philadelphia medical college, who located in Cahokia in 1824, and married Miss Jene Tournot, whose parents, as well as herself, were born in Cahokia. His son, John O. Butler, three years older than myself, was my companion while there, introducing me to the best melon patches and peach trees in the village, and managed his dugout canoe on the *rigole* in our daily excursions with the dexterity of an Indian. Another Cahokian by adoption of note was Doctor William Gale Goforth, a man of sense, but of peculiarly grotesque physiognomy, and many eccentricities of mind and habits. He came there from Cincinnati in 1825, soon learned the local language, was a successful practitioner of medicine, and married Miss Eulalie Hay, daughter of John Hay, the most popular, highly efficient, and best educated of the Creoleized Americans of the American Bottom. They were, however, divorced by act of the legislature in 1834 * because of incompatibility of temperament.

* According to Governor John Reynolds, Dr. Goforth settled in Illinois in 1815—*My Own Times* . . . (Chicago, 1879), 131. The divorce was granted on Feb. 17, 1823.

Among our entertainers was Mrs. Julia Jarrot, who was born there in 1780, widow of Major Nicholas Jarrot, still occupying the grand mansion, built by the Major in 1800 of brick brought from Pittsburgh. We were there shown—as all non-resident visitors were shown—the long vertical crack in the west wall of the fine old building caused by the memorable New Madrid earthquake of 1811. After 1844 it presented to curious visitors another point of historic interest in the discoloration of the interior walls marking to what depth—about seven feet—it was submerged during the unprecedented flood of that year.

We remained in Cahokia three days, in the meantime visiting Prairie du Pont, a mile south of it, my mother's birthplace, and mine, one afternoon, returning to the old town by moonlight. During the entire three days we received the kindest personal attentions and generous hospitality from the people who knew my parents so well, and among whom they had together commenced the earnest struggle of life; and on the morning of the fourth day, to my regret—for I knew on the next Monday I would have to again start to school—we took up our course homeward.

CHARLES DICKENS IN ILLINOIS

Reprinted from *Journal of the Illinois State Historical Society*, Vol. III, No. 3 (Oct., 1910), pp. 7–22. [The Dickens quotations have been corrected where necessary.]

A HIGHLY PRIZED VOLUME in my library is an old, stained copy of the first American edition of the *Pickwick Papers* (published by Carey, Lea & Blanchard, Philadelphia, 1838), which my father gave me in 1841. Reading and re-reading that book with boyish delight during the school vacation of that summer interested me in its author, known then as "Boz," a *nom de plume* he had adopted early in his literary career. He was already famous out here, so that when the eastern papers announced his contemplated visit to the United States the next year, I shared with our people generally the hope and expectancy that he would extend his tour as far west as the Mississippi, which he subsequently did. No railroad had then penetrated the wilderness as far as St. Louis, at that time the frontier city of the vast west, and steamboats and stage coaches were about the only means for public transportation west of the Allegheny mountains. Mr. Dickens, accompanied by his wife, came by the old emigrant route, in steamboats, down the Ohio river from Pittsburg, and up the Mississippi, arriving at St. Louis on the 11th of April, 1842.

The steamboat Fulton, upon which Mr. and Mrs. Dickens had taken passage at Louisville, Ky., arrived at St. Louis in the evening (of the 11th), but as it was not expected until the next day, no reception committee appeared to meet the distinguished tourists, and they made their way, in a hack, to the Planters House, then by far the finest hotel west of the Mississippi, where they were regally entertained. When their arrival became known, the citizens of St. Louis spared neither pains nor expense in pressing upon them every social attention and the most cordial hospitality during their stay.

Mr. Dickens having expressed—as he says in his *American Notes*—"a great desire to see a Prairie before turning back from the furthest point of my wanderings; and as some gentlemen of the town had, in their hospitable consideration, an equal desire to gratify me, a day was fixed, before my departure, for an expedition to the Looking-Glass Prairie, which is within thirty miles of the town." Friday, April 15,* was the day selected for the excursion, and the 13th chapter of his *Notes* is devoted to the description of that "Jaunt to the Looking-Glass Prairie and Back."

Besides Mr. Dickens and the drivers of the four teams, there were nine men—and no ladies—in the party, only two of whom I could identify and can now remember. These were John J. Anderson, a banker, and George Knapp, of the *Missouri Republican*. They were all young men connected with the newspapers and business interests of St. Louis, bent upon affording their famous guest a glimpse of the grandeur of Illinois, the "two large baskets and two large demi-johns," with ice and other extras, taken along, indicating the picnic aspect of the "jaunt," and intent to make it as pleasant for him as possible. Seated in the several conveyances with one of their number on horseback as guide, they crossed the Mississippi in the early morning on one of the Wiggins Company ferry boats. At that season of the year the miry road across the seven miles of soft loamy soil of the American Bottom, and the succeeding seven miles of sticky clay uplands to Belleville, usually rendered traveling over it slow and difficult, and was, in fact, at times almost impassable.

To make matters worse, a heavy rain had fallen the night before, filling the chuck-holes in the road full of water, and further diluting the already deep mud. "We had a pair of very strong horses," says Mr. Dickens in his *Notes*, "but travelled at the rate of little more than a couple of miles an hour, through one unbroken slough of black mud and water. It had no variety but in depth. Now it was only half over the wheels, now it hid the axletree, and now the coach sank down in it almost to the windows." This description of traveling over that part of the great National Road at that day is not greatly overdrawn. But Mr. Dickens failed to notice the topography of that region further on, or forgot it in the two years transpiring between his visit and the publication of his *American Notes*, as, after leaving the French Village at the foot of the bluffs where the road ascends to an elevation of a hundred feet, he says: "We went forward again, through mud and mire, and damp, and festering heat, and brake and bush, attended always by the music of the frogs and pigs, until nearly noon, when we halted at a place called Belleville, ... a small collection of wooden houses, huddled together in the

* On April 15 Dickens was aboard the steamship *Messenger* en route to Cincinnati from St. Louis; letter in John Forster's *Life of Charles Dickens* (rev. ed., New York, n.d.), I: 283. Dickens says there that he made the trip to Looking-Glass Prairie on Tuesday, April 12.

very heart of the bush and swamp." His memory of the continuation of *mud* all the way was certainly correct, but Belleville, situated on high rolling ground far removed from sloughs and swamps, was even then a flourishing, pretentious town containing quite a number of business houses and handsome residences substantially built of brick and stone. There was then no telegraph to apprise the Belleville people of the great novelist's coming, or of his arrival at St. Louis, and but few of them knew that he had honored our town by his presence until the next issue of the weekly paper. Two years later, 1844, the first telegraph line to reach St. Louis was constructed by the O'Reiley Company alongside of the old stage road from Vincennes, with the wire fastened by insulators to the trees where it passed through the timber, and crossed the Mississippi from the top of a tall mast at Illinoistown (now East St. Louis) to a similar one on Bloody Island, and from there to the top of the shot tower near the Belcher sugar refinery on the other side.

Returning home, at about eleven o'clock in the forenoon of that 15th day of April, from an errand upon which I had been sent to the eastern part of the village, I had reached the public square when the line of carriages came pulling through the mud up Main Street from the west. In doubt as to whether they formed a funeral procession, or transported some kind of show, I stopped to see them pass by. Just then Philip B. Fouke, editor of the *Belleville Advocate,* and in later years our Congressman, came down the street to the court house, and I asked him who those traveling strangers were. He had, a few minutes before, interviewed the horseman who had arrived in advance of them to have luncheon prepared for the party, and was hurrying into the court house—circuit court being in session—to inform the bench and bar the object and purpose of the novel expedition that had excited my curiosity. Startled by hearing that Boz, the author of the *Pickwick Papers,* was actually there, I turned about and, keeping abreast of the front carriage, followed it up the street until it stopped at the door of the Mansion House. On the way I was joined by several other boys, my daily associates, not one of whom perhaps had ever heard of Charles Dickens, but attracted by the unusual appearance of so many strange vehicles, went along gazing at them with open-mouthed wonder.

When the barouche conveying Mr. Dickens halted at the curbstone, he was the first of its four inmates to step from it to the sidewalk, and did so with a look of evident relief. It was a perfect day "overhead," warm for the middle of April, with clear sky and the refreshing air of early spring. The landlord, Mr. McBride, came bustling out, bareheaded, to receive the company, and was introduced to the famous writer by one of his traveling companions. The man introduced as "Mr. Dickens" was (to me) a disappointing surprise. In fact, my youthful ideal of the genius who created Mr. Pickwick, Sam Weller and the Widow Bardell, was badly shattered. It is natural for the average man—woman or boy—when hearing much about any noted individual, to form a definite idea of that person's appearance; or, upon reading an interesting book to draw an imaginary portrait of its author. Mr. Dickens was, on that day, a very ordinary looking man indeed, with no external indication of true greatness. In the estimation of "us boys" he compared very unfavorably with Col. Richard M. Johnson, of Kentucky, the slayer of Tecumseh, and late Vice President, who had, a short time before, visited Belleville, and had been given a grand reception with brass band accompaniment.

Mr. Dickens was at that time 30 years of age, of medium size—about 5 feet, 8 or 9 inches tall—square shouldered, erect, and well proportioned in figure, weighing (probably) 140 pounds. His complexion was not of the usual ruddy English cast; his eyes were brown, and dark, slightly curling hair surmounted a broad forehead and smoothly shaved face, then sunburned and mosquito bitten, but none too handsome at best. With the license of conscious superiority he dressed very carelessly, and on this occasion, incased in a common linen coat and coarse straw hat bound around with green ribbon, he attracted some public attention, but certainly ran no risk of being mistaken by strangers for either General Scott or Daniel Webster. He was not very talkative, but when he spoke his voice was soft and pleasant, with clear and distinct pronunciation of every word. He seldom laughed, but his frequent smile was expressive of his keen sense of humor, and appreciation of his novel surroundings. There was about his countenance a cynical expression; but no affectation perceptible in his speech or manners, yet every movement and gesture plainly indicated that he regarded the homage paid him by our simple people as justly his due, and that any courteous acknowledgment of it on his part would be an unwarranted condescension.

On this part of his American tour the memoranda he jotted down, from day to day, of transpiring events and objects and persons that interested him, must have been brief and disconnected, as his published *Notes* bear internal evidence of having been written out some time after his return to England, with many passages supplied by memory. And his memory of many things he tells of, unaided by his notes made at the time, was often at fault and much confused.

His description of Belleville, as being "in the very heart of the bush and swamp," is an instance of this. Of the Belleville houses he further says, "Many of them had singularly bright doors of red and yellow; for the place had been lately visited by a travelling painter, 'who got along,' as I was told, by 'eating his way.'" When this was written he drew upon his memory alone, it having retained an indistinct impression of the sloughs and lakes of the American Bottom, and the French Village, through which he passed, and of Belleville, all mixed up together. The old French Village, at the foot of the bluffs, it is true, had recently been visited by a tramping painter who left the impress of his art on several gaudily colored doors in that vicinity, but he had not yet "eaten his way" through, or to, our town.

The sarcasm in Mr. Dickens' account of his "Jaunt to the Looking-Glass Prairie," though pungent and stinging, is, in the main, amusing, in some instances just, but as often totally devoid of wit or humor, amounting simply to willful malignant misrepresentation, actuated by an animus difficult to comprehend. At the time of his arrival in Belleville, he says, "The criminal court was sitting, and was at that moment trying some criminals for horse-stealing. . . . The horses belonging to the bar, the judge, and witnesses, were tied to temporary racks set up roughly in the road; by which it is to be understood, a forest path, nearly knee-deep in mud and slime." True the circuit court was then in session, with Sidney Breese on the bench, Wm. H. Underwood, the prosecuting attorney, Wm. C. Kinney, the circuit clerk and Sam. B. Chandler, sheriff. The bar attending that court comprised Lyman Trumbull, Gustavus Koerner, James Shields, Joseph Gillespie, U. F. Linder, N. Niles, Wm. H. Bissell, P. B. Fouke and [former] Governor John Reynolds.

His "forest path" was the public square in the middle of the town, just as it now is, excepting the paving and buildings it then contained. Northeast of its center was the fine old brick court house, and across the street, to the west, the two-story brick offices of the county officials. Fronting that on the south was the new market, also of brick, and on the opposite corner, facing the court house, was the public well. There *were* hitch racks on the east and north of the court house, and—we may as well admit also—some mud in the streets, as usual in the spring months.

The "Mansion House," on the northeast corner of Main and High streets, is still there. Solid and substantial, tho a dingy-looking relic of a past age in the midst of modern progress, it is yet (1910) serviceable as a business house, and, with pride, is pointed out to strangers, by the older residents as the hostelry where Mr. Dickens was entertained in 1842. Of it he says, "There was an hotel in this place, ... an odd, shambling, low-roofed out-house, half-cowshed and half-kitchen, with a coarse brown canvas table-cloth, and tin sconces stuck against the walls, to hold candles at suppertime." The Mansion House was really a large, roomy brick building, fully up to date in all respects, two stories high, with long two-story frame addition, erected only three years before, by Rev. Thomas Harrison, and was well arranged, well furnished and conducted in first-class style by his daughter and her husband, Mr. and Mrs. Wm. J. McBride.

Mr. Dickens and companions on arrival were escorted by the landlord up stairs to rooms provided with water, towels, etc., where they might perform their ablutions and "dress for dinner," and the carriages, from which the horses were unhitched and taken to the stable, were left standing in front of the hotel.

Court having adjourned for the noon recess, Colonel Niles, Governor Koerner,* Phil Fouke and two or three other members of the bar, with several citizens, came up to the Mansion House to pay their respects to the famous guest. Judge Breese and Jo. Gillespie declined to accompany them.

With boyish curiosity and eagerness to see all that was going on, I followed Mr. Dickens—unasked and no doubt unwanted—to the foot of the stairs, and waited there until he came down and was introduced to the lawyers and some of the other visitors. I was in close proximity to his coat tail when he was presented to "Dr. Crocus," and was an interested witness to that interview, which, as narrated in the XIII chapter of the *American Notes*, is substantially correct, with the exception that the landlord, Mr. McBride, was not addressed as "Colonel." He was a quiet, unobtrusive, upright man, an exemplary citizen and rigid Methodist, but not a colonel. The man portrayed as "Dr. Crocus" was an adventurer calling himself Dr. Angus Melrose—perhaps an assumed name—who had, a few months before, alighted in Belleville as a lecturer on phrenology, then a very popular fad, and incidentally offering his professional services for the healing of all known diseases.

* Gustavus Koerner was lieutenant governor of Illinois, 1853–1857.

To Mr. Dickens' question, "Do you think of soon returning to the old country?" Dr. Melrose answered, "Not yet awhile, sir, not yet. You won't catch me at that just yet, sir. I am a little too fond of freedom for *that*, sir. Ha, ha! It's not so easy for a man to tear himself from a free country such as this is, sir. Ha, ha! No, no! Ha, ha! None of that till one's obliged to do it, sir. No, no!" In this grandiloquent declaration the Doctor was very evidently—as Mr. Dickens intimated—"playing to the galleries," but he also intended Mr. Dickens to understand that he was speaking ironically and, by innuendo, expressing his contempt for American institutions. With proverbial English obtuseness of perception, however, Mr. Dickens failed to catch the Doctor's covert meaning.

Dr. Melrose was over six feet in height, and robust in proportion, with florid face and long nose. Of friendly, social disposition he was a fluent talker, speaking correct English with broad Scotch accent. To Mr. McBride he stated that he had recently graduated in medicine at the Edinburgh University, and having but limited means, to gratify his desire to see America, he had recourse to the lecture platform, phrenology, and the practice of medicine to defray expenses of touring the country. He remained in Belleville several months, but tho immortalized as "Dr. Crocus" by the *American Notes,* very few persons now living retain the slightest recollection of him.

For half an hour or more Mr. Dickens was surrounded by a throng of citizens, to several of whom he was formally introduced, but to none of whom he addressed anything more than curt, commonplace remarks. It was plain that he was both bored and amused by the curiosity and evident disappointment of the crowd inspecting him, and seemed glad when the dinner bell ended the impromptu reception. The glimpse obtained of him from the open dining room door, when all were seated at the long table, left no doubt as to the ample justice he was doing to the "chicken fixings" specially prepared for him. Dinner over he strolled out on the sidewalk in front of the hotel, viewing the part of town in the range of his vision, while conversing with his St. Louis friends until the horses were brought from the stable and all was ready to move on again.

"From Belleville," says Mr. Dickens, "we went on, through the same desolate kind of waste, and constantly attended, without the interval of a moment, by the same music" (the croaking of bullfrogs). Here again, with the American Bottom vaguely in mind, he drew upon his memory and it failed him. The road from Belleville to Lebanon—then almost the entire twelve miles through dense woods, broken here and there by the farms of Governor Kinney * and other old settlers—is over high, undulating and beautiful country, remote from sloughs or swamps or other habitats of the festive mosquito or musical frog.

The hotel at Lebanon was more fortunate than the one in our town in catching the fancy of the great novelist, and he accorded it this dubious praise, "In point of cleanliness and comfort it would have suffered by no comparison with any English alehouse, of a homely kind, in England." It was a large barn-like frame building, called the Mermaid Hotel, with a large square sign on a tall post, in front, on which was painted a full-sized mermaid standing on her tail on the waves, holding a looking glass before her with one hand, and combing her long golden tresses with the other. The house was owned and conducted as an inn and stage stand by Capt. Lyman Adams, a retired New England sea captain, of kind and genial disposition, who ended his days there, highly respected and esteemed by all who knew him.

The interest of Mr. Dickens' visit to Illinois culminates in his impressions and description of the prairie, the objective point of his "jaunt," thus recounted in his *Notes,* "It would be difficult to say why, or how—though it was possibly from having heard and read so much about it—but the effect on me was disappointment. Looking towards the setting sun, there lay, stretched out before my view, a vast expanse of level ground; unbroken, save by one thin line of trees, which scarcely amounted to a scratch upon the great blank; until it met the glowing sky, wherein it seemed to dip: mingling with its rich colours, and mellowing in its distant blue. There it lay, a tranquil sea or lake without water, if such a simile be admissible, with the day going down upon it: a few birds wheeling here and there: and solitude and silence reigning paramount around. But the grass was not yet high; there were bare, black patches on the ground; and the few wild flowers that the eye could see, were poor and scanty. Great as the picture was, its very flatness and extent, which left nothing to the imagination, tamed it down and cramped its interest. I felt little of that sense of freedom and exhilaration which a Scottish heath inspires, or even our English downs awaken. It was lonely and wild, but oppressive in its barren monotony. I felt that in traversing the Prairies, I could never abandon myself to the scene, forgetful of all else; as I should do in-

* William Kinney was lieutenant governor of Illinois, 1826–1830.

stinctively, were the heather underneath my feet, or an iron-bound coast beyond; but should often glance towards the distant and frequently-receding line of the horizon, and wish it gained and passed. It is not a scene to be forgotten, but it is scarcely one, I think (at all events, as I saw it), to remember with much pleasure, or to covet the looking-on again, in after-life."

Immediately following this is his account of the sunset lunch that was eaten, which the great writer seems to have enjoyed much more and remembered better than his view of the prairie. "We encamped," he goes on to say, "near a solitary log-house, for the sake of its water, and dined upon the plain. The baskets contained roast fowls, buffalo's tongue (an exquisite dainty, by the way), ham, bread, cheese, and butter; biscuits, champagne, sherry; lemons and sugar for punch; and abundance of rough ice. The meal was delicious, and the entertainers were the soul of kindness and good humour. I have often recalled that cheerful party to my pleasant recollection since, and shall not easily forget, in junketings nearer home with friends of older date, my boon companions on the Prairie."

There is a discrepancy in the prairie scene drawn by Mr. Dickens difficult to reconcile, excepting upon the grave suspicion that the "champagne, sherry; lemons and sugar for punch" must have operated as a disturbing element in his vision and memory. "Looking towards the setting sun," he says, "there lay, stretched out before my view, a vast expanse of level ground . . . with the day going down upon it." Now, from Lebanon Mr. Dickens and party traveled almost directly east, a mile through the timber, and about a mile into the prairie to that "solitary cabin." They were then on the *western* border of the prairie. From that point, therefore, in looking over that "vast expanse of level ground," the setting sun was behind them. The time was sunset, and had Mr. Dickens been "looking towards the setting sun," as he says, he would have seen no "vast expanse of level ground," but instead only a half-mile slope down to the rivulet and a corresponding half-mile ascent on the other side up to the Silver creek timber surrounding Lebanon. In looking over the prairie his face was turned to the *east,* and the sun was sinking in the forest behind him. Nor is there any expanse of *level* land there, no prairie in Illinois having more perfect natural drainage than Looking Glass.

A few years later, when a student at McKendree College, I paid several visits to that "solitary cabin," made historic by Mr. Dickens' champagne dinner, and his first and only view of our prairies. The cabin long since disappeared, and its site, made memorable by the pen and presence of the author of *Pickwick* and *David Copperfield*, is lost in the mazes of endless corn fields.

Mr. Dickens perhaps wrote his candid impression of the prairie as it appeared to him; but his disparaging description of "a level plain," with the sun setting in the east, written many months later, warrants the belief that in that sketch he again relied altogether upon his capricious memory.

Looking Glass Prairie, in fact, at that time presented as charming a landscape as could be found in the prairie region of Illinois. It was merely one of the many prolongations, or offsets, of the grand treeless plain extending north and east beyond the limits of the State. Framed around, on the west and north, by the wooded hills of Silver Creek, and by the timbered line of Sugar Creek to the east and south, eight miles away, it presented to the eye, from the site of that "solitary log cabin," a magnificent panorama of undulating plain diversified with isolated groves and brush-fringed rivulets. Seen as Mr. Dickens saw it—and as I first saw it—in its virgin freshness, undefiled by the plow, or yet marred by the embellishments of civilization, it was one of nature's finest rural gems, fascinating in interest and wild sublimity.

After dining on the prairie, Mr. Dickens and party returned to Lebanon and passed the night at the Mermaid Hotel. The next morning he arose at 5:00 o'clock and, after a short walk about the village, returned to the tavern and amused himself for some time in the inspection of its public rooms and back yard, which seems to have afforded him more genuine enjoyment than his view of the prairie.

In his narrative of the "jaunt to Looking Glass Prairie and back," he only mentions the topography of the country he saw to misrepresent and vilify it, and is silent regarding its productions, resources and future possibilities. But he describes in detail an old whisky-soaked settler of the backwoods type, and devotes an entire page to his interview with the tramping Scotch doctor, and more space to a pen picture of the Lebanon tavern and its stable yard than to the prairie he came specially to see. He was much impressed by the sight of a tailor's shop on wheels, and brightly painted front doors, and the moving of a small frame house down the street from one locality to another, but makes no mention of those noted pioneer institutions of learning, McKendree College, at Lebanon, and Rev. John M. Peck's Rock Spring Seminary, three miles west of Lebanon, both very conspicuous objects by the roadside along which he journeyed.

In full sight of the spot where the party dined on the plain, and less than a mile away, stands Emerald Mound, the most prominent landmark of the prairie, one of the finest and most perfect of all the earthen monuments of the aborigines in the State. This remarkable vestige of a vanished prehistoric people is well calculated to attract the attention and interest of any intelligent foreign (or native) tourist; but not a word did Mr. Dickens write about it. He could not well have failed to see it, and that he did see it is confirmed by his trivial notice of its more majestic contemporaneous structure, the great Cahokia mound, near which he passed when returning to St. Louis by the upper, or more direct, road.

Of that wonderful work he merely says, "Looming in the distance, as we rode along, was another of the ancient Indian burial-places, called The Monks' Mound; in memory of a body of fanatics of the order of La Trappe, who founded a desolate convent there, many years ago, when there were no settlers within a thousand miles, and were all swept off by the pernicious climate: in which lamentable fatality, few rational people will suppose, perhaps, that society experienced any very severe deprivation."

Mr. Dickens does not mention, in his *Notes*, the name of any one of the young men who took him over to Illinois to see the prairie; nor did he write one word expressive of gratitude for their generosity in leaving their business and providing lavishly, free of all expense to him, everything necessary to conduce to his pleasure and satisfaction in that excursion. It seems that a sense of ordinary courtesy would have prompted him to at least return some slight public acknowledgment of that obligation.

Cairo was the only other locality in Illinois visited by Mr. Dickens. To see Cairo was really the main object of his journey to America. In 1837 one Darius B. Holbrook, a shrewd Boston Yankee, organized the Cairo City and Canal Company, a scheme as audaciously illusive as John Law's Mississippi Bubble of 1718; and going to Europe he plastered the walls everywhere there with flaming lithographs of a grand city at the junction of the Mississippi and Ohio rivers—in fact as mythical as the fabled Quivira of Coronado's search. In London was the banking house of John Wright & Co.—the same that, in 1839, confidenced the Illinois Fund Commissioners, Governor Reynolds, Senator Young, General Rawlings and Colonel Oakley, into depositing with them $1,000,000 of Illinois bonds, resulting in a loss to the State of half their value. Through John Wright & Co., Holbrook actually sold bonds of his

Cairo company to the amount of $2,000,000. Among his numerous victims was Mr. Dickens, who, it is asserted, invested in those bonds a large part of his slender means.

A few years later, becoming, with other investors, suspicious of the flaunted magnificence of the American Cairo, Mr. Dickens concluded to satisfy himself by a personal inspection of it. He came, and thus described what he saw: "At length, upon the morning of the third day, we arrived at a spot so much more desolate than any we had yet beheld, that the forelornest places we have passed, were, in comparison with it, full of interest. At the junction of the two rivers, on ground so flat and low and marshy, that at certain seasons of the year it is inundated to the house-tops, lies a breeding-place of fever, ague, and death; vaunted in England as a mine of Golden Hope, and speculated in, on the faith of monstrous representations, to many people's ruin. A dismal swamp, on which the half-built houses rot away: cleared here and there for the space of a few yards; and teeming, then, with rank unwholesome vegetation, in whose baleful shade the wretched wanderers who are tempted hither, droop, and die, and lay their bones; the hateful Mississippi circling and eddying before it, and turning off upon its southern course a slimy monster hideous to behold; a hotbed of disease, an ugly sepulchre, a grave uncheered by any gleam of promise: a place without one single quality, in earth or air or water, to commend it: such is this dismal Cairo."

This crushing disappointment and shocking dissipation of his cherished dreams of golden profits accounts for Mr. Dickens' malignant defamation of everything he saw west of Louisville, and explains the venom in his satirical novel that soon followed, entitled *Martin Chuzzlewit,* in which he wreaks his vengeance upon the United States generally, and upon Cairo particularly under the pseudonym of "Eden."

FORGOTTEN STATESMEN OF ILLINOIS

James Harvey Ralston

Reprinted from *Transactions of the Illinois State Historical Society*, XIII (1908): 215–32.

EARLY in the eighteenth century the Ralston and Neely families emigrated to the United States from Londonderry, one of the nine counties constituting the province of Ulster, in the northern part of Ireland. They stopped temporarily in the state of New York; then moving to the western wilderness settled permanently in the region now known as Bourbon county in Kentucky. They were the progeny of intermingled Scotch and Irish—the Ralstons tracing their descent, according to their family records, "from Ralph, son of MacDuff who slew Macbeth and restored the rightful monarch to the throne of Scotland," while the Neely's "sprung from the Clan MacNeil, known in Scottish history and romance as the 'Lords of the Isles,' the histories of these families filling a large space in the annals of Scotland. Many marriages have occurred between them in succeeding generations, and their kinship and clanship are marked by strong physical resemblances, and similar traits of character." Among the products of the American interblending of those families in our recent history were Gen. John J. Neely, Judge James H. Ralston, J. Neely Johnson who was elected Governor of California in 1854 [1855], and others who served their country with distinction both in civil and military life.

One of the several intermarriages mentioned of members of those noted families was that of John Ralston, a young Kentucky farmer and Miss Elizabeth Neely, who were united in wedlock, in Bourbon county, near the close of the eighteenth century. Though environed from their birth by the institution of slavery, young Ralston and wife were not of the patrician class, or included in the blue-grass aristocracy, as they owned no slaves, or possessed, besides their farm, little more than sound health, industry, and contentment. From their prolific union were born, as the years went by, fourteen children— four sons and ten daughters—an exuberant fulfillment of their sole mission of life. To rear and properly train that swarm severely taxed the resources of the parents; but the youngsters, as they grew up, scattered away to search out for themselves their destined spheres in the world wherein to achieve their individual fortunes. Occupying no higher station himself than that of an ordinary farmer, John Ralston seems to have been ambitious that his sons should rise to a higher intellectual level than mere tillers of the soil. Or, it may be that he perceived in them indications of superior talents that he considered it his duty to develop at the cost of any reasonable sacrifice to himself it might involve. Possibly, and very probably, he may have been influenced in so doing by the boys giving free expression to their aspirations to higher mental culture, and more refined vocations than his. At any rate, after duly discussing the matter with his wife, he determined to give his son, Thomas Neely Ralston, a thorough education which would prepare him for the ministry. In that course he was doubtless guided by the boy's natural predilection for the church, inherited from some far-back Scotch Presbyterian ancestor. In his limited financial circumstances, with a rapidly increasing family, principally of girls, to give the boy a collegiate education was really a grave undertaking for John Ralston. However, by diligent labor, economy and frugality, he accomplished it. Thomas graduated at Transylvania, was ordained, attained the degree of Doctor of Divinity, and for many years was a famous pulpit orator and divine of Lexington, Kentucky. Another son, Joseph Neely Ralston, born January 25th, 1801, was also educated at Transylvania University, choosing for his calling in life the profession of medicine. He left Kentucky in 1832 and located in Quincy, Illinois, where he continued the practice of medicine until his death, in June, 1876. Of Dr. Ralston, Hon. Wm. A. Richardson says, "He was one of my patron saints, a fine gentleman and noble man, respected and loved by every one." He is thus mentioned in the *History of Adams County, Illinois,* published in 1876, "Of his eminence in the profession it is sufficient to say that for more than forty years he held a leading position among the physicians of Quincy and Adams county. He was one of the founders, and the first president of the Adams County Medical Society, and was at several subsequent periods re-elected to that position. Weighed down through his long life with the cares and anxieties of the most exacting of professions he never forgot the duties of a citizen, maintaining to the last his interest in public affairs. Identified with every movement promising to promote the public welfare, he was keenly alive to the educational interests of his adopted home, enjoying a leading social position, and maintaining always a large practice. He was rather tall and spare in figure, dignified in carriage, courteous almost to punctiliousness in manner, clean and precise in speech, self-poised, quick in his perceptions, steadfast in his convictions, sagacious in counsel—the sturdy virtues which commanded for him universal respect and confidence." *

William H. Ralston, a third, and younger son of John and Elizabeth (Neely) Ralston, was a lawyer, who also resided for awhile in Quincy, then moved to Leavenworth, in Kansas, where he became quite eminent in his profession, and was a very prominent citizen.

James Harvey Ralston, the subject of this sketch, was born in Bourbon county, Kentucky, on the 12th of October, 1807. His boyhood years were passed on his father's farm, not in luxury and idleness; but, early initiated in the arts and toil of agriculture, he grew up to manhood as an ordinary farm laborer, industrious, energetic and self-reliant. A prominent trait of his youth was pride of character, inciting a desire to learn, in order to improve his mental and social condition. But he could only occasionally be spared from his post on the farm for a few weeks in the winter time to attend the country schools in his neighborhood, where little more than the simplest rudimentary branches were taught. What he acquired there increased his yearning for more learning; but he understood his father's situation well enough to know that the paternal resources would be totally exhausted by the heavy expenses incurred in educating his brothers, Thomas and Joseph, so that no assistance for himself could be expected from that quarter, or cessation of his farm work be permitted, to advance his own schooling. Driven, therefore, to depend upon his own efforts, he resolutely applied himself to study at home, taking advantage of every spare moment—by fire-light at early dawn, and aid of the grease lamp, or tallow dip, at night when the day's drudgery was ended—to enlarge his store of knowledge from the few books within his reach. With such restricted opportunities, and no systematic instruction, his education was necessarily very defective. That drawback, however, occasioned no depression of his ambition, or of faith in his own abilities. Having one brother in the ministry and another in the medical profession, neither of whom, in his estimation, was his superior, notwithstanding their higher education, and unwilling that he should in any way cast discredit upon the family, he aspired to rank with them in literary and social position. Thereupon, without

* The quotation is from p. 680 of *The History of Adams County, Illinois* . . ., published by Murray, Williamson & Phelps of Chicago, in 1879, not 1876. Snyder rearranged several phrases of the quotation and failed to indicate omissions, but since none of these changes alters the meaning, the transcription has been left as Snyder presented it.

the essential foundation of scholastic training he embarked in the study of law.

Arriving at the age of legal emancipation from servitude to his father, he left Kentucky in the fall of 1828, and made his way to Quincy, Illinois to begin there the shaping and upbuilding of his own career. One of his sisters, married to a Kentuckian named Stamper, who had preceded him to Quincy, was probably the influence that induced him to settle in that frontier village. History is silent regarding the occupation he engaged in for the first two years after getting there—if in any; but that during that time he steadfastly kept his high aims in view, and persistently continued his legal studies there, must be inferred from the following record in Vol. B. of the Law, Chancery and People's Records in the circuit clerk's office of Adams county, Illinois; "At a circuit court begun and held at the court house in Quincy for the county of Adams and State of Illinois on Thursday, the twenty-first day of October in the year of our Lord, one thousand, eight hundred and thirty. Present, the Hon. Richard M. Young, judge of the fifth judicial circuit of the State of Illinois. On motion of George Logan, Esq., an attorney of this court, James H. Ralston, Esq., appeared and was sworn as an attorney and counsellor at law, he having presented a license according to law, signed by two of the judges of the Supreme Court."

A short time before his admission to the bar, Mr. Ralston was elected a justice of the peace in and for the county of Adams, and served in that capacity for three or four years, or until he became well established as a lawyer in the higher courts. Responding, in the spring of 1832, to the call of Gov. Reynolds for a force of armed men to repel the hostile incursion of Black Hawk and his band, Mr. Ralston at once volunteered and was enrolled, along with Orville H. Browning, a brother attorney of Quincy, as a private in Captain Wm. G. Flood's company of mounted riflemen, which subsequently was incorporated in the second brigade commanded by Brigadier General Sam. Whiteside. On the company's roster he is reported, "Absent on duty," and was honorably mustered out of service, at the mouth of Fox river, on the 28th of May, 1832. His career as an Indian fighter was brief and not very eventful, but from another record at Quincy it is learned that a few months later he again enlisted, in a more peaceful cause and for a longer period of service. That record states that on the 11th day of October, 1832, James H. Ralston was united in marriage with Miss Jane Alexander, daughter of Col. Sam.

Alexander, a well known substantial citizen of Adams county. She was born on the 6th day of October, 1811, and was at the time of her marriage, a sprightly, intelligent, and very attractive girl. Before the approaching winter had set in, Attorney Ralston and bride were settled down to housekeeping on their own account in a modest home near the northeast corner of Eighth and Hampshire streets, in Quincy, where the residence of Mr. Nehemiah Bushnell now stands, adjacent to the post office. They were, for the following fourteen years among the most conspicuous and highly esteemed members of Quincy's best society, taking a leading part in all social gaieties and entertainments, as well as in every public movement for the improvement of the town and welfare of its citizens.

Esq. Ralston began the practice of law in the courts presided over by Judge Richard M. Young, whose circuit originally embraced all the territory between the Mississippi and Illinois rivers from the mouth of the latter to Lake Michigan. Of that bar he was for many years, excepting when in public office, one of its busiest and most successful practitioners. For some time he was in partnership with Almeron Wheat, and later with Joseph Warren, Quincy lawyers of marked ability. In the terrible epidemic of Asiatic cholera brought west by General Winfield Scott's troops about the close of the Black Hawk war, which visited Quincy as it spread swiftly down the Mississippi the next year (1833) with appalling fatality, about its first victim in that village was Mrs. Sarah Stamper, sister of Dr. Joseph and J. H. Ralston.

In August, 1836, James H. Ralston and George Galbraith * were elected to represent Adams county in the lower house of the tenth General Assembly—that historic legislature made famous by its enactment of the wild system of internal improvements that proved such a disastrous failure. Mr. Galbraith died during the first session, (which convened at Vandalia on December 5, 1836, and adjourned March 6, 1837), and his vacancy was supplied by election of Archibald Williams at a special election in the spring. That legislature is also famous for the number of its talented members who later achieved high distinction in the public affairs of Illinois and of the nation. In the senate were Orville H. Browning, Cyrus Edwards, Wm. J. Gatewood, Archer G. Herndon, Henry I. Mills, William Thomas, John D. Whiteside

---

* His name appears in the election returns as "Galbreath." See Theodore C. Pease, *Illinois Election Returns, 1818–1848* (*Collections of the Illinois State Historical Library*, XVIII, Springfield, 1923), 300, 306n.

and John D. Wood. With Mr. Ralston in the house were James Semple, James Shields, Robert Smith, Edward D. Baker, Milton Carpenter, Newton Cloud, Richard M. Cullom,* John Dougherty, Stephen A. Douglas, Jesse K. Dubois, Ninian W. Edwards, Abraham Lincoln, Augustus C. French, Wm. L. D. Ewing, Wm. A. Richardson, John A. McClernand, Usher F. Linder and John Moore; names interwoven everlastingly in the fabric of our State and national history, an aggregation of intellectual strength seldom, if ever, equalled and never surpassed, in any other legislative assembly of Illinois. And yet, the State, with all its immense resources, was forty years in recovering from results of the stupendous folly of their legislation in that one session.

Mr. Ralston, of course, voted for the internal improvement measures. He would have been ostracized by his party and by the community he represented had he opposed them. As was the result with all his eminent associates in that legislature who voted, as he did, for the crazy scheme, its total and disastrous failure subjected him to no public censure or loss of popularity. On the 14th of December, 1836, the tenth General Assembly in joint session elected Hon. Richard M. Young U.S. Senator for the full term of six years to succeed Hon. W. L. D. Ewing who was elected by the preceding legislature for the unexpired term of Hon. Elias K. Kane deceased. Up to the time of his promotion to the national senate Judge Young had presided over the old fifth, or Quincy, judicial circuit since his election to that position in 1828. His resignation immediately after the senatorial election left the Judgeship vacant, which the Legislature proceeded to supply, by ballot, in joint session on the 14th of January, 1837, with the following result: Sixty-three ballots were cast for James H. Ralston, forty-two for Wm. A. Minshall, and nineteen for George P. W. Maxwell. The commission for Judge Ralston's new office, the duties of which he at once entered upon, was dated February 4, 1837. If he resigned his seat in the legislature when elevated to the circuit bench no record of that fact can be found; no one was elected to succeed him in that General Assembly, and his name does not appear in the house journal of its second session, held for the purpose of legalizing suspension by the banks of specie payments, which met at Vandalia on the 10th and adjourned on the 22d of July, 1837.

---

* Cullom's middle initial was N (for Northcraft), not M, as Snyder consistently gives it. He was the father of Shelby Moore Cullom.

Judge Ralston was but twenty-nine years and three months old when elected to the Judgeship—a young man of striking personality, six feet tall, straight and well-formed, with auburn hair, blue eyes and faultless features. Polite and agreeable in address, he was as courtly and dignified in bearing and manners as the Virginia gentleman of colonial days. In disposition he was sociable, kind and generous, though impulsive, spirited and ambitious. Strictly honest in personal affairs and the discharge of public duties, actuated in every relation of life by a high sense of honor, he was an eminently respectable citizen, moral, sober, and of unblemished character. In some instances, no doubt, his judgment was at fault, but in the main his motives were pure, and he perhaps never wilfully violated his conceptions of right and justice. He was a plausible, showy, man in public, entertaining in conversation, and a fluent, impressive speaker, though not invariably grammatical in his language, or exactly correct in his logic or rhetoric. As before stated, his early education was only rudimentary, and tho greatly improved in after years by promiscuous reading and desultory study, he probably never was a student of close, systematic application, consequently his learning in some directions had advanced little beyond general principles and common-sense deductions. A prominent characteristic of Judge Ralston is said to have been his firmness and determination of purpose; yet, he was weak in resisting flattery and blandishments; and was easily influenced by those in whom he had implicit confidence.

He was a member of the Masonic Order, but not attached to any church, having very liberal views on the subject of man's so-called spiritual nature and future responsibilities. He was fond of music, of gay, lively society, and had quite a taste for literature; poetry particularly, which he often quoted. One of his favorite quotations, consonant with his own sentiments, from the tragedy entitled "Pizarro," was this:

"Should the scales of justice poise doubtfully, let mercy touch the beam and turn the balance to the gentler side."

As all contemporaries of Judge Ralston of that period have long since gone to their final rest, the only means accessible for forming an estimate of his ability as a jurist are the records of his court. The unavoidable inference to be drawn from them, notwithstanding the scurrilous criticism of Gov. Ford,[1] is that he acquitted himself as a judge with credit and honor. During

1. Ford's History of Illinois, p. 307.

the two and a half years he presided over the Quincy circuit very few of his decisions were taken to the Supreme Court on error or appeal and of those few, only two were reversed.[2] He may in some instances have erred [in] too inflexible adherence to forms and technicalities; but certainly nothing can now be found in the history of the old fifth judicial circuit to sustain the malignant strictures of Gov. Ford. The annual salary of circuit judges at that time was seven hundred dollars, a sum less than the wages received by some of the skilled mechanics. Dissatisfied with that meagre pay, and assuming that he could earn a larger revenue by the practice of his profession, Judge Ralston resigned his position on the bench, on the 31st of August, 1839, and resumed his place at the bar.

Gov. Ford's vilification of Judge Ralston evidently did not express the estimate placed upon him, at the time, by the people of Adams county. His judicial services, instead of disparaging him in public opinion, seem to have increased his popularity in that community. In 1838 a majority of Whigs were elected in both branches of the Illinois Legislature, and that party came nearer electing its State ticket than it ever did before or afterwards, Thomas Carlin, the candidate of the Democrats for Governor, being elected over Cyrus Edwards the Whig, by the majority of only 996.* Two years later, in 1840, the Whigs made stupendous efforts to retain their ascendency gained in 1838, and also to carry the State for their national ticket, Harrison and Tyler. The Democrats were as equally determined to regain their lost supremacy in the Legislature and to secure the electoral vote of the State for their presidential candidate, VanBuren. In order to sway the people in their favor both parties presented their strongest and most available men for local candidates in each of the several counties. In Adams county the Whigs brought out Archibald Williams to head their county ticket as their candidate for State Senator. He was an able man, well known all over the Military Tract; was a volunteer in the Black Hawk war, stood high in the esteem and confidence of the people of Adams county whom he had served well as Senator in the eighth and ninth General Assemblies and as a member of the House in the tenth General Assembly in which he received a respectable vote for U.S. Senator, but was defeated by Hon. Richard M. Young.

2. First and Second Scammon Reports.
* More reliable election return figures than those given by Snyder can be found in Pease, *Illinois Election Returns, passim.* In this case, for example, Pease shows that Carlin's majority was 926, not 996.

After mature deliberation the Democrats of Adams county selected Judge Ralston to oppose him. The political campaign of 1840 far surpassed any in the previous history of the State for strenuous exertions and excitement, for expensive and spectacular displays, and impassioned oratory, particularly by the Whigs. In Adams county the fury of the contest centered in the race for State Senator. In their eagerness to elect Williams the Whigs exceeded all bounds of legitimate party contention, carrying their opposition to Judge Ralston to the extreme of personal enmity. He was invulnerable however, to all their attacks, and at the election, on Aug. 3, 1840, was elected, receiving 1,546 votes to 1,447 cast for Williams, a clear majority of 99. At the November election of that year he was also elected presidential Elector for that district.

The first, or called, session of the twelfth General Assembly convened at Springfield on the 23d of November, and adjourned December 5th. The second, or regular session commenced on the following Monday, December 7th, and adjourned March 1, 1841. Judge Ralston was there again in company with many of the leading politicians and statesmen of the State, some of whom, as himself, had been promoted since their service in the House, four years before, to seats in the upper chamber. With him in the Senate were Edward D. Baker, Richard M. Cullom, Wm. J. Gatewood, John Moore, Archer G. Herndon, Wm. A. Richardson, Adam W. Snyder and John D. Wood. Among the great commoners in the House were Wm. H. Bissell, John J. Hardin, John Dougherty, Cyrus Edwards, Joseph Gillespie, W. L. D. Ewing, Wickliffe Kitchell, Abraham Lincoln, John A. McClernand, Lewis W. Ross, Lyman Trumbull and David M. Woodson. There was in each branch of the Legislature a decided majority of Democrats. The Governor, Thomas Carlin, and Lieutenant Governor, Stinson H. Anderson, were Democrats, and of that party General W. L. D. Ewing was elected Speaker of the House defeating Abraham Lincoln the Whig candidate. Three of the justices of the Supreme Court, however, were Whigs, and but one a Democrat.

In the seventy working days of that regular session of the twelfth General Assembly a surprising amount of legislation was enacted, which comprised some measures of weighty importance to the public, and others of questionable policy. Political parties at that time were divided chiefly upon the bank question. As a part of the great internal improvement scheme of 1836 the

State was made a stock holder in the State bank to the amount of $3,100,000.[3] The banks were prohibited by law from issuing notes of less denomination than five dollars; and the law of 1838 provided that any bank having suspended specie payments, and failed to resume such payments before adjournment of the next session of the Legislature thereafter, would forfeit its charter and close its doors unless that session of the Legislature sanctioned the suspension and permitted it to continue. All the banks had suspended specie payments, and had not resumed the paying of specie when the twelfth Legislature came together. The Democrats, supreme in that body, were divided on the State banking system. The radicals among them favored enforcing the forfeiture penalty and closing up the banks at once; but the other faction, known by the radicals as the "week-kneed" voted with the Whigs, not only to legalize suspension of the banks, but to permit them to issue bills of less denomination than five dollars. Judge Ralston was one of the "week-kneed" and in that matter voted with the Whigs.

Though really hostile to the banks, and loyal to all the main principles of the party, Judge Ralston and the other "bolting" Democrats very plausibly justified their course by the reason that the woeful depression of business, extreme scarcity of money, and unprecedented hard times generally, rendered the leniency they extended to the banks absolutely necessary for relief of the commercial interests of the country, and for averting further hardships to the people. And the end, in that emergency, certainly did justify the means.

Party lines were not observed in much that was accomplished by the Legislature at that session. The members of both parties voted together in desperate attempts to provide ways and means for paying the semi-annual interest on the enormous State debt, and for trying to devise plans to extricate the State from its crushing embarrassments. They were also united, actively or passively, in granting the infamous Mormon charters, neither party daring, by its opposition, to offend that new powerful voting element.[4] The crucial test of party fealty, however, was presented in support of the bill concocted by Democratic leaders for "Reorganizing the judiciary," an audacious scheme for converting the Supreme Court from a Whig to a Democratic tribunal by an addition to it of five Democratic justices, and legislating the

3. Ford's History of Illinois, p. 299 *et seq.*
4. Adam W. Snyder, and his Period in Illinois History. 1906. Pp. 406–408 *et seq.*

circuit judges out of office, which was passed by a constitutional majority of both houses, and passed again over the Council of Revision's veto. There is no better proof of Judge Ralston's fidelity to his party than the fact that he voted with it throughout for that high-handed revolutionary measure. He was an active, vigilant and influential senator, a member of the judiciary committee and chairman of the Committee on Public Accounts and Expenditures, on all occasions watchful of his constituents['] interests as well as those of the public.

At that time the State was apportioned into three Congressional districts, the first comprising the western half, and the second the eastern half, of southern Illinois, the third embracing the balance of the State north of Greene county, from the Mississippi to the Wabash. In the third district the numerical strength of the parties was very nearly equal, Major John T. Stuart, the Whig candidate, having defeated Stephen A. Douglas for Congress at the August, 1838, election by only thirty-five majority, receiving 18,248 votes to 18,213 for Douglas. The act of February 15, 1839, changed the date of the next Congressional election from its regular biennial time in 1840 to August 2, 1841, and biennially thereafter. It was known that Major Stuart would be a candidate for re-election. Douglas could not again be his competitor, having been elevated by the "Reorganization of the judiciary" to the Supreme Court bench. Upon consultation, the Democrats chose Judge Ralston for their candidate to oppose Stuart. He made the race, and was defeated by the surprising plurality of 2,164, with 19,562 votes for him in the district, 21,726 for Stuart, 507 for Frederick Collins (Abolitionist), and twenty-six scattering.*

Governor Ford attributes that overwhelming defeat of Ralston to his course in ignoring the Democratic policy regarding banks, and voting in the Senate with the Whigs to legalize the bank suspensions.[5] That explanation is in part correct, but only in part. Opposition to banks was a Democratic article of faith, fixed and sacred as the dogma of a high protective tariff is with the Republican party of today. But there was another, and far more potent, factor responsible for the failure of Ralston's election, overlooked, or purposely ignored by Governor Ford. That was the votes of the Mormons

---

* The more accurate figures in Pease, *Illinois Election Returns,* show minor variations from those given here.

5. Ford's History of Illinois, p. 308.

given as a unit for the Whig ticket. In the three years, from 1838, when a total of 36,461 votes were polled in the district, to 1841, when the number of votes was 41,821, an increase of 5,360—there had been an astonishing influx of Mormons into Hancock and adjoining counties of the district. They had been driven out of Missouri by the Democrats in power, and on coming to Illinois voted solidly for the Whigs in retaliation. All white males among them, over the age of 21, voted (constitutionally) after a residence here of six months, and many voted in less than six weeks after their arrival, as none were challenged, and all voted for Major Stuart. Hence Judge Ralston's Waterloo.

At the general election in August, 1842, the Democrats, aided by the Mormons who then had turned against the Whigs, swept the State, electing the Governor, Thomas Ford, with a plurality of 8,317, the entire State ticket, and a large majority in both houses of the Legislature. In the thirteenth General Assembly, that met at Springfield on December 6th, Judge Ralston, not having resigned to run [for] Congress, was, with E. D. Baker, Richard M. Cullom and others, one of [the] hold-over senators industriously attentive to his duties, as before. The earnest work of that session, proving of inestimable value to the people, marked the beginning of a new era for Illinois.

The law-makers had recovered from their lunacy of 1836, and returned to methods of sanity and sound common sense. Getting together, regardless of party differences, they passed a bank adjustment bill, a bill for completion of the canal, one for securing the State's portion of proceeds of public lands sales, another for redemption of outstanding Macallister [Macalister] and Stebbins bonds; they appointed the Governor the State Fund Commissioner, and, as a crowning act of wisdom, provided a "two mill" tax (20 cents on the $100.00) on all property, which ensured the prompt payment of maturing interest, and placed the gigantic State debt in process of ultimate honorable extinction. The bank adjustment bill was a "compromise" entered into by Gov. Ford and the bank directors, whereby the banks agreed to go into liquidation, call in their circulating "shin plasters" and surrender to the State their bonds to the amount of $2,050,000.00 in exchange for an equal amount of bank stock held by the State. That was Gov. Ford's pet measure. He claimed that he wrote the bill, and that it was passed by his personal influence.

Although it was adopted by the Legislature almost unanimously, for some reason not now apparent, Judge Ralston opposed it. Lyman Trumbull, then

Secretary of State, did all he could to defeat it, and Stephen A. Douglas, Supreme Court Justice, as one of the Council of Revision, voted to veto it after it had passed both houses.

Governor Ford was one of the ablest jurists in the State, a man of singularly clear, philosophical mind, largely endowed by nature with vigorous, comprehensive intellect which was reinforced by a fair education and much study. In stature he was small with thin, homely features, deep-set gray eyes, and long, sharp nose turned slightly at the point to one side. Well supplied with vanity and self-esteem, his prejudices were invincible, and his arrogance at times, intolerable and ludicrous. As insignificant in body and soul as he was admirable in mental power, lacking in physical and moral courage, vindictive, obstinate and spiteful, he hated those whom he could not control, and, when opportunity offered, caused them to feel the sting of his resentment. His spirit of vengeance outlived the lapse of time. He might forget a benefaction, but never forgave an injury. Of those who opposed his bank compromise bill, Douglas was beyond his reach, but Trumbull who was at his mercy, was immediately dismissed from the office of Secretary of State and replaced by Thompson Campbell. Having no chance to punish Judge Ralston he "nursed his wrath to keep it warm" until he wrote his *History of Illinois* several years later, in which he fully vented his pent-up malice. However, expecting to publish the book soon, and knowing that Judge Ralston was still living, he was too cowardly to designate him by name in his contemptible villification.[6] When General Shields published Ford's *History* in 1854, Ralston was on the Pacific slope, and probably never saw in what terms his fellow Democrat, whom he had helped to make Governor of Illinois, had so meanly maligned him.

When the Legislature adjourned Judge Ralston again took his accustomed place at the Quincy bar, giving to his profession his undivided attention. It is not to be presumed, however, that he abjured further interest in politics, or renounced all political ambition. Few, indeed, in this great Democratic republic who have once enjoyed the subtle charm of office-holding voluntarily relinquish it, or lose the ardent desire to regain it. The Judge was doubtless at all times, as all politicians are, in a receptive mood, willing to "make the sacrifice for the public good," but was not openly a candidate for any position. Yet, he was accused in 1845 of coquetting with the

6. Ford's History of Illinois, pp. 307–308.

Mormons, his erstwhile foes, who still voted the Democratic ticket, and held the balance of power in that district, but he stoutly denied the (Whig) impeachment.[7] It is though, altogether probable that his hold on popular favor had waned, and the fickle public was fawning upon new idols, as it often does.

To the class of "has been," or of "would like to be," politicians, the war with Mexico in 1846 opened up grand vistas of glowing opportunities. It also stirred the martial spirit of thousands of worthy citizens who only saw that their country's honor was at stake. Of that multitude Judge Ralston's patriotism was so aroused that he offered his services to the Polk administration, which were accepted by his appointment, June 26, 1846, to the position of Assistant Quartermaster General for the Illinois Volunteers, with the rank of Captain, and he was ordered to San Antonio, Texas. Closing up his business at Quincy, he left Illinois and arrived at his destination on the 13th of October. After resting a few days he started for the seat of war in Mexico, but his train was overtaken before it had gone far by an order from headquarters, at Washington, assigning him to duty at San Antonio. Returning there he relieved Captain Wall, the officer in charge, and remained there until the war closed. Though never within three hundred miles of the fighting line, the work Captain Ralston did was of more value to the army, and the cause it was engaged in, than the services of many officers in the field of higher rank. Vast quantities of supplies obtained upon his requisitions from New Orleans and elsewhere, droves of beef cattle, hundreds of horses, mules and oxen, wagons, harness, and other property necessary for the subsistence and transportation of the northern division of our army in Mexico, purchased by his disbursement of many thousands of dollars, were forwarded from his post and distributed to the soldiers beyond the Rio Grande.

He employed for his chief clerk Mr. Edward Everett, a young man of education and very superior business qualifications, a nephew of the distinguished Massachusetts statesman of the same name, and at the time a sergeant in Captain Morgan's Quincy riflemen in Colonel Hardin's regiment, who was then incapacitated from active military service by a severe wound in the knee inflicted by a drunken Texan ruffian. Quartermaster Ralston took possession of the historic Alamo buildings, then in a ruinous condition, and converted them into a depot for supplies, storehouses, quarters for his men,

7. Quincy Whig of Sept. 24th, 1845.

and offices for himself and clerks. Assuming that he would probably be stationed at that post for some time, he sent for his wife who joined him there early in March, 1847. Not of robust constitution, her health failed as the heat of summer advanced, and she soon fell a victim of that enervating climate. She died on the 3rd of July, 1847, at the age of 35 years, eight months and twenty-seven days, and was buried there. She had lost four children in their infancy, there remaining but one left to her, a daughter named Elizabeth, who subsequently married Marcellus Tilden, a lawyer of Sacramento, California.

Captain Ralston's clerk, Mr. Everett, was, in politics, as his illustrious uncle, a staunch Whig, passing in later years by easy transition into the ranks of Illinois Republicans. In his highly interesting *"Military Experience"*— donated by him to the Quincy (Illinois) Historical Society, he says of his superior, "Captain James H. Ralston was a Kentuckian who had settled in Illinois—tall in person, and sallow complexion, with that formality of address, and assumed dignity so often seen in the western lawyer. In politics he was a Democrat, and as he termed it 'a strict constructionist' though moderate and non-partisan in his views. He was mild and pleasant in his intercourse, and was quite popular with the citizens of the place; and no unkind word ever passed between us—though on occasion, as a delinquent once observed after a reprimand, 'he could use a fellow up in very few words.'" From this last sentence it must be inferred that the Captain when provoked employed harsh expletives to emphasize his utterances; yet, he was not usually profane in conversation. He was addicted to the use of tobacco, as all Kentuckians are; but, though a native of Bourbon county, very seldom tasted liquor of any description. Mr. Everett adds, "He was occasionally called on to make speeches on public occasions, as his delivery was good and his manner impressive, but as his early education had been very deficient, he would make out a rough draft of what he had to say, and then hand it to me to improve the language, and write it out clearly. His letters and reports to the heads of the departments at Washington were gotten up in the same manner."[8]

In November, 1848,[9] Captain Ralston was relieved of his duties as Assistant Quartermaster at San Antonio by Captain M. Morris, A.Q.M., U.S.A.

---

8. 1905—Transactions of the Illinois State Historical Society, p. 216. [Punctuation corrected to conform to that of source.]

9. Ibid., p. 228. [The quotation which follows has also been corrected.]

Then followed for several weeks the work incident to turning over to the new officer the military stores, and settling up the business of the post. That transfer and settlements completed, Captain Ralston, with Mr. Everett, departed for Port Lavacca; thence took steamer to New Orleans, from there up the Mississippi and Ohio rivers to Wheeling, Virginia, and on to Washington. "Here," says Mr. Everett, "we made our final accounts, and explained such points as were objected to by the auditors. The sum of public money expended by Captain Ralston while in Texas was a very large one, besides which the property, mostly means of transportation, passing through our hands, not included in the above, was very considerable. The accounts passed a very rigid examination, and everything was finally allowed and Captain Ralston and myself were honorably discharged." In the meantime the gold discovered by Jim Marshall in the tail-race of Capt. Sutter's mill at Coloma, California, Jan. 4, 1848, had frenzied the nation with the lust for riches. Captain Ralston received his discharge from military service on the 3d of March, 1849, and hastened back to Quincy. He was much disheartened by the changes time had wrought there in his former domestic and social surroundings during his absence of almost three years. His wife dead, his home desolate, his law business gone, many old and cherished friends passed away and replaced by strangers, saddened and discouraged, he concluded to join the mad rush of argonauts for the New Eldorado, and there commence life anew. Quickly disposing of his property, and making provision for his daughter, he set out on the long and unknown journey. Arriving there at the age of forty-two, in the prime and vigor of manhood, he found himself in a strange world of infinite possibilities, teeming with people of all races and stations, wildly scrambling for sudden wealth. Shunning the gold mines, so attractive to the multitude of immigrants, the Judge located at Sacramento City, where, in partnership with Thomas Sunderland, he engaged in the practice of such law as was then recognized to be in force. Making a specialty of protecting and defending the rights of miners and squatters against those who claimed titles to their properties by virtue of Spanish grants, he gained wide popularity and prospered.

The civil government of California was at that period in chaotic condition, with no one in authority, and without so much as territorial organization. Its American population [10] was daily increasing by thousands, and al-

10. Citizens of the United States, in contradistinction to the natives of Spanish descent.

ready a horde of hungry politicians were clamoring for its admission as a state into the union. In pursuance of a call issued, they selected delegates who met in convention in Colton hall at Monterey, on Sept. 1, 1849, and framed a State constitution which expressly excluded the institution of slavery. By its provision a legislature was elected which convened at San Jose on December 15th, and petitioned Congress for a State government. In response to their appeal Mr. Clay, early in that winter, introduced in the U.S. Senate his celebrated omnibus bill, or "Compromise," by the terms of which California was admitted as a state, and New Mexico and Utah were organized as territories. That measure passed the lower house of Congress on the 7th, and was approved by President Fillmore on the 9th of September, 1850.

The political turmoil preceding and attending the birth of the new state (Sept. 9, 1850), awakened in Judge Ralston the old office-seeking instinct that for a few years past had been semi-quiescent. He was again an active politician, keenly interested in watching the machinery of the young state set in motion, and also watching incidentally for his opportunity. It came in 1852, when he was nominated and elected by the Democrats to represent Sacramento county in the State Senate, that county constituting a senatorial district. The legislature of California then met annually. Representatives were elected for one year, and senators for two. The state's capitol had not yet been located, the several towns were making strenuous efforts to secure it, occasioning much jealousy and ill-feeling, with some scandal. The third General Assembly, to which Judge Ralston was elected, convened at Vallejo on the 5th of January, 1852, and on the 12th of that month moved to Sacramento, remaining there until it adjourned on the 4th of May. Senator Ralston was made chairman of the Standing Committee on Corporations, and a member of the Committees on State Library and Enrolled Bills.

In its then formative stage the infant state required much careful legislation to regulate its many diversified interests, define its land tenures, and establish constitutional government in place of the capricious exercise of authority by Alcaldés and priests to which as a province of Mexico it had long been subjected. Judge Ralston was one of the most attentive members of the Senate, taking an active and conspicuous part in all the important work of the session. The estimate in which he was held by that body may be inferred by the fact that in the election by joint ballot of a U.S. Senator, though not a candidate for the position, he received eight votes on the first and second ballots, and nine votes on the third, when he withdrew his name. The contest then narrowed down to David C. Broderick and John B. Weller, with selection of the latter on the eighth ballot.

The extraordinary amount of rain that fell in upper California during the winter of 1851–52, by raising the Sacramento river over its banks, inundated a large area of its valley. No levee having then been thrown up to protect Sacramento City from the annual overflows of the river, it was for several weeks another Venice, its traffic and business carried on by boats over the streets covered with water from two to six feet deep. The writer of this sketch went down to Sacramento from the mines in March, 1852, and while there visited the legislature on several occasions in a canoe or skiff, the means of transportation employed by the legislators, state officials, and others, from their hotels or residences to the building used temporarily for a state house.

The fourth general assembly of California was convoked at Vallejo on the 3d of January, 1853, and moved from that place to Benecia [Benicia] on the 4th of February, continuing there its deliberations until it adjourned on the 19th of May. Those towns, built on low sand flats on Napa Bay, are six miles apart, and twenty-three miles northeast of San Francisco. Each town was in succession made the State capital, General Vallejo's offering to the state a large quantity of land and $350,000.00 in money as an inducement to locate it in his town, Vallejo; but, [as] it was totally unsuitable and without houses or other requisites in either town for a state capitol, the seat of government was, in 1854, permanently fixed at Sacramento, a more central point, seventy-five miles in direct line east of San Francisco. Upon organization of the legislature, in recognition of Senator Ralston's ability and party leadership, he was given the post of highest honor and responsibility, that of Chairman of the Judiciary Committee. He was also placed on the important committees on Finance and Corporations. For fidelity to his duties, for industry, capability, and influence, during that session he was not surpassed by any member of either branch of that assembly.

He was not an applicant for office that year having in consideration a matter of much weightier concern to engage his personal attention. For seven years he was a widower, solaced in a measure for his great loss by the care and affection of his only child, his daughter Elizabeth. But the inevitable occurred. A rising young lawyer of Sacramento found favor in her eyes, married her, and took her to a new home. Realizing then the dreary loneliness of his situation, he decided that the wisest course to pursue would be to look around for another life companion to replace the one taken from him by death in Texas. With that view he went to New York City, having doubtless arranged all necessary preliminaries by correspondence, and there, on the 20th of October, 1853, was united in marriage with Miss Harriet N. Jackson, daughter of Rev. Aaron Jackson, a Baptist minister of that city, who several years before had been stationed in charge of a church at Quincy, Illinois.

Returning with his bride to Sacramento he applied himself with renewed diligence to his profession, having apparently exorcised for all time the *ignis fatuus* of political ambition he had so long been chasing. Its fascination was, however, too strongly intrenched in his nature to be permanently shaken off by such a trivial affair as marriage. Yielding to the persuasion of friends, he again entered the arena in 1856 as a candidate for chief justice of the Supreme Court on the Democratic ticket. Up to that time the old-line Democrats had dominated California politically; but the disaffection, and disintegration, of the party in the eastern states, owing to repeal of the Missouri Compromise and its consequences, in 1854, had spread to the Pacific slope with the result of arraying against it the united elements of all opposition, including the Whigs, Free-Soilers and Know-Nothings. Still, the Democrats carried the state for Buchanan in 1856 though routed in many of the counties and for most of the state offices. Judge Ralston was one of the victims of the Douglas heresies, and went down in defeat before the forces of the political revolution that, rapidly gaining strength, in a few years swept the country. In 1860 and 1864 California gave its electoral vote to Lincoln, and assumed its place in the column of Republican states.

That disaster to his party was intolerable to Judge Ralston. On receiving the official returns of the 1860 election he immediately settled up his business and left the state, going over the mountains to Virginia City in Nevada, where he once more established himself in the practice of law. Nevada then had a population of about 15,000, which, upon development of the amazing deposits of silver and gold in the Comstock and other mines, quickly grew to nearly 50,000. Politicians were there early and in force, having some time before begun, and continued, agitation for territorial organization, which Congress granted in March, 1861. That act, instead of allaying political ebulition, stimulated it to increased activity in the direction of a demand for admission of the territory into the union as a state. In furtherance of that object a call was issued in 1863 for a convention to frame a state constitution. In that call was presented to Judge Ralston a tempting opportunity he could not resist. Offering his services to the people he was elected a delegate to represent Storey county, of which Virginia City is the county seat, in that convention. In a private letter received from Mr. Wm. Epler, at present a citizen of Jacksonville, Illinois, he says, "During the fall of 1863 it was my good fortune to become intimately acquainted with Judge James H. Ralston. We first met as members of the first constitutional convention of Nevada, he a delegate from Storey county, and I a delegate from Humboldt county. For the forty days of the convention we occupied seats and desks within arms length of each other.

"The fact that he formerly resided in Quincy, Illinois, and I in Jacksonville, brought us in close touch at once. In that convention Judge Ralston won the respect and esteem of the entire body by his dignified, modest and gentlemanly manners, his evident ability, and close attention to business. He came over to Nevada territory from California, as did nearly all the other members, my own case being an exception, as I never lived in California before becoming a citizen of Nevada. Not long after adjournment of the convention, early in 1864, he moved from Virginia City to Austin, in Lander county, near the center of the territory, and there resumed his practice of law; but, which was destined not to continue long."

At that period Judge Ralston was physically and mentally vigorous and active, with every prospect of many years of exertion and usefulness in store for him. Of optimistic temperament he looked forward with cheerful expectancy to the admission of Nevada into the Union in the near future, and perhaps was planning to play an important part in the political affairs of the new state. The human family surely has few greater blessings than that impenetrable veil excluding the future from its vision. Nevada was made a state by Act of Congress in October of that year (1864); but five months before that event the public was shocked and saddened by the melancholy death of Judge Ralston. The mournful story of its occurrence, learned from various sources, was published in full in the *Quincy Whig* (Illinois) of June 26 [28], 1864, and is in substance as follows:

"About the 1st of May (1864) the Judge, with another man, left Austin on horseback to visit his ranch in Smoky Valley, thirty miles distant. They soon separated, his companion going to some other point, and he went on alone. Mrs.

Ralston says 'he was caught in a blinding snow storm on the desert,' and no doubt lost his way. When he did not return after the lapse of two or three days, his family and friends, apprehensive that he may have met with some accident, organized a party to go in search of him, but without success, having ascertained at his ranch that he had not been there. A number of experienced plainsmen then, with a skillful Indian guide, starting from Austin, upon going some distance 'struck his trail, and followed it in the direction of San Antonio for a distance of ninety miles, then crossing Smoky Valley at the Indian Wells opposite Coyote Springs, keeping a southern course, passing Link Barnes' ranch, a few miles farther fell in with some Indians who told them that Judge Ralston was dead, and directed them to his body which they found but eight miles northeast of San Antonio, and five miles from the Barnes' ranch.' Lost and bewildered he traveled for days without food or water until finally he fell from his horse exhausted, and there expired. From all the 'signs' and circumstances observed it was concluded that his tragic death occurred on the 8th of May (1864), when 56 years, 6 months and 26 days of age.

"Some Shoshone Indians (Root Diggers) were the first to discover the dead body, which was considerably mutilated by the coyotes. To prevent its further mutilation by those little wolves, the Indians in accordance with their tribal custom of cremating their dead, piled dry sage brush over the remains and burned them. The searching party gathered up all that remained of the dead statesman and jurist, placing them in a sack for transportation on horseback, and conveyed them to his home in Austin. With his remains were found some gold coins he had in his pockets, together with his spectacles and watch, the latter ruined, of course, by the fire, 'but valuable as melancholy relics of his sad fate.'

"His body upon its arrival in town was taken in charge by his brother Masons, of which order he had attained the rank of Knight Templar. At an early hour yesterday, the members of the legal fraternity met at the court house and resolved to attend in a body the funeral of the honored deceased. The procession formed in front of the court house at one o'clock and, headed by the Austin brass band, followed by the Masons in regalia, members of the bar, firemen, hearse, the family of the deceased, citizens on horseback and in carriages, the cortege marched to the cemetery. This was the most imposing funeral that has yet occurred in Austin. The worth, position and high esteem, the melancholy circumstances attending the death of Judge Ralston, gave a solemn and universal interest to the occasion. After the interment the procession returned, marching to a lively tune, to the court house, and dispersed." [11]

In publishing the foregoing account, the *Quincy Herald* of June 29, 1864, said: "The old settlers of this part of the State, and, indeed, of the whole State, will regret to learn of the death of Judge Ralston. The particu-

11. Austin [Nev.] Star, May 12th, 1864.

lars concerning his death we give in this article below, copied from the *Whig*. He was one of the early settlers of this part of the State, where he earned a high reputation as a lawyer, and achieved distinction as a leading politician. He was universally respected for his integrity and candor, both as a public man and private citizen, and was sincerely beloved as a citizen and neighbor." The dreary, sandy waste in which Judge Ralston so wretchedly died was then named "Ralston's Desert," a name it still bears, and is so designated on the government maps.

From the marriage of Judge Ralston and Miss Jackson two children were born, a daughter, Mary Aurora Ralston, who died in early life, and a son, Jackson H. Ralston, now and for several years past, an eminent attorney of Washington, D. C., "who was counsel representing the United States in the Pious Fund case, the first tried before the Hague tribunal. He was also the umpire between Italy and Venezuela in the Court of Arbitration at Caracas a few years ago." Mrs. Harriet N. Ralston, the Judge's widow, is also at present (1908) a resident of Washington.

It is not certain that any relationship existed between Judge Ralston and William Chapman Ralston of San Francisco, though Mrs. Harriet N. Ralston asserts they were second cousins. Wm. C. Ralston, a native of Plymouth, Ohio, and a "Napoleon of Finance," it may be remembered, was for three years president of the great Bank of California at San Francisco, until deposed from that position by the directors, and the bank closed its doors about noon on the 26th of August, 1875. That afternoon the dethroned president took his customary bath in the Bay at North Beach. Swimming far out from shore he "seemed to be taken with a fit" and drowned before a boat could reach him. The cause of the bank's suspension, it was soon known, was the abstraction of four and a half millions of its funds by President Ralston, which he converted to his own use and lost it all in wild speculation.[12]

[To Mrs. Harriet N. Ralston of Washington, Hon. Wm. A. Richardson of Quincy, Illinois, and Hon. James A. Johnson of Oakland, California, I am greatly indebted for special information, without which the foregoing biographical sketch of Judge Ralston could not have been written—J. F. S.]

12. History of San Francisco. By John S. Hittell. 1877, pp. 407–408.

FORGOTTEN STATESMEN OF ILLINOIS

Richard M. Young

Reprinted from *Transactions of the Illinois State Historical Society*, XI (1906): 302–27.

Preceding the text of the article is the following note by Dr. Snyder:

NOTE—Though but forty-five years have elapsed since the death of Judge Young, so evanescent is human fame that, apart from the records of his public acts, an extensive correspondence for a long time failed to discover anything of his personality, or domestic life, or even the locality of his place of residence. By suggestion of Col. Wm. R. Morrison I wrote to Hon. J. C. Allen of Olney, Ill., who answered that he had no personal knowledge of Judge Young, but remembered when in Congress, in 1853–55, a daughter of the Judge was a frequent caller upon Mrs. Richardson, wife of Hon. Wm. A. Richardson then representative of the Quincy district in Congress. Inferring from this that Quincy was probably the former home of Judge Young, I wrote for information to Hon. Wm. Collins of that city, who kindly had my letter inserted in the Quincy Daily Herald where it was noticed by Hon. Wm. A. Richardson, Jr., to whom I am indebted for the results of his elaborate search of all accessible facts in the history of Judge Young. This led to my communication with Mrs. Matthews, of Talbotton, Georgia, widow of Major Robert A. Matthews, (whose first wife was a daughter of Judge Young,) and to her I am under great obligations for much important material bearing upon this investigation. With these valuable and much appreciated aids I am enabled to present the following biographical sketch.   J.F.S.

RICHARD MONTGOMERY YOUNG was born in the southern part of Fayette county, since then organized as Jessamine county, on a farm near East Hickman creek about ten miles southeast of Lexington, Kentucky, on February 20, 1798. His parents, Scotch-English descent, were early settlers in that part of Kentucky, having migrated there from Virginia, their native state. His early boyhood was passed on the farm and in the country schools of that neighborhood until when about twelve or thirteen years of age, he was sent to a select school or academy in Jessamine county, known as Forest Hill, and conducted by Prof. Samuel Wilson.* He there acquired some knowledge of the higher branches at that time taught in the colleges of Kentucky, including Latin, algebra, geometry and the natural sciences. He was there associated

* A famous academy and college in Washington County, St. Thomas's, was operated by a Dominican priest, Father Samuel Thomas Wilson. Nothing is known about Forest Hill.

with the sons of the first families of Kentucky and some of the adjoining states, as the school was patronized chiefly by the wealthy slave-holding class.

In 1814, then sixteen years of age, he completed his studies at Forest Hill and commenced the study of law with Col. James Clark, a leading lawyer of Nicholasville, the county seat of Jessamine county. After two years of diligent application the Jessamine county court, at its November, 1816 term, gave him a certificate of moral character and permission to be examined in his legal studies. In accordance therewith he was duly examined by Judge Wm. T. Barry of Lexington, and Judge Benjamin Johnson of Georgetown, then Justices of the General Court of Kentucky and of the circuits in which they resided. Passing a highly creditable examination he received a license dated November 22, 1816, to practice law in his native state, and forthwith opened an office for business under the auspices of his preceptor in Nicholasville. About the same time he joined the state militia, and was elected cornet, or ensign, of a troop of light horse cavalry.

It required but a short time to convince him that competition in his profession in that old and wealthy community was too strong and active to permit his speedy promotion, and he was too impatient and impulsive to wait and bide his time. The territory of Illinois, then agitating the question of admission into the Union, offered a tempting field to aspiring Kentuckians, many of whom, already there—including the Territorial Governor and delegate to Congress—had gained high distinction. The young lawyer could not resist the opportunities presented there for early rewards of energy, industry and genius, and in the spring of the next year, 1817, left the blue grass paradise of Kentucky for the post oak hills of Southern Illinois. He located at Jonesboro in the western part of Johnson county, assured that that town would soon become the seat of justice of a proposed new county to be named Union; which was so organized on the Second of January of the following year, 1818, and he was then enrolled as a member of its bar. At that time he was a tall, handsome stripling, straight as a ramrod, with piercing hazel eyes and brown hair slightly inclined to curl. Social and friendly in disposition, with the polished manners of a Chesterfield, he was an interesting talker, a good speaker and full of life and energy. His fine figure and soldier-like bearing attracted the attention of Gen. James M. Duncan (formerly from Bourbon county, Kentucky) commander of the Second Brigade, Western Division of the Illinois militia, who appointed him his Aid-de-Camp with the rank of

Captain, and he was so commissioned by Gov. Shadrach Bond on June 20, 1820.*

From Mr. Young's first appearance as a citizen of Jonesboro the pioneer backwoodsmen of that region recognized his sprightly intellect, and his manly deportment won their esteem and confidence. As a lawyer he was successful. His practice was not long confined to the meagre litigation of Union county, but speedily extended to the courts of the several counties between Shawneetown to the east and Kaskaskia on the north, and to Missouri Territory beyond the Mississippi. He was a close and interested observer of the transition of Illinois in 1818, from a territorial form of government to that of a state, and actively participated in its embryo politics as a supporter of John McLean for Congress and Thomas Cox for the State Senate.[1] He was fascinated by public life as he then saw it, and it inspired him with aspirations in that line that influenced and shaped his subsequent career.

As time passed, Mr. Young's friends observed with pleasant surprise—as an evidence of increasing prosperity—the frequent calls for his presence at the courts over in Missouri Territory. They discovered later, however, that courting of another kind was the chief trans-Mississippi attraction for the young lawyer. In his earlier professional visits over there he had met, and fallen in love with, Miss Matilda James, second daughter of Judge William James, of St. Genevieve county, a beautiful girl, tall and graceful, and—for those days—highly educated and accomplished. She fully reciprocated his attachment, and accepted his proposal of marriage, but her parents positively refused their consent because of incompatibility of religious faith. They were devout Catholics, and were opposed to the marriage of their daughter to a heretic. Young, however, was not the sort of a man to permit such nonsense as that to wreck his visions of happiness, or frustrate any course he had determined to pursue; and the brave girl, wholly devoted to him, was willing to defy parental objections and authority of the church to share his fortunes. By preconserted agreement she eluded the family espionage and joined him at the tavern in St. Genevieve, and there, in the presence of a few friends, they were married, on June 25, 1820, by Rev. Justinian Williams, a Methodist preacher, and immediately left for their future home in Jonesboro.

---

* The Executive Record, 1818–1832 (MS in Illinois Archives), shows that the commission was issued June 22.

1. For a sketch of Colonel Thomas Cox see *Annals of Iowa*. Third series, Vol. VII, No. 4, January, 1906.

The high merit and ability of Mr. Young, and his rising prominence in public esteem in a few years reconciled Judge James and his wife to the union of their daughter with him though an unbeliever, and they became very proud of their unshrived son-in-law. To quiet their qualms of conscience, and ensure perfect domestic harmony, a special dispensation was obtained from Right Rev. Bishop Rosatti [Joseph Rosati], and in the month of August, 1827, Mr. and Mrs. Young were again married, by the Bishop himself in the old church at Kaskaskia, with the prescribed Catholic ceremony.

In the year 1820 Mr. Young's star was decidedly in the ascendent, and honors crowded upon him in quick succession. On the twentieth of June in that year he was commissioned a military captain; on the twenty-fifth he was married, and thirteen [forty-three] days later, at the general State election, on August 7, he was elected to represent Union county in the lower house of the Legislature by a much larger majority than was given any other candidate on the ticket.

The second General Assembly—to which Mr. Young was elected—was the first held at Vandalia, the new capital, and convened there on December 4, 1820. Vandalia, surveyed and platted but a few months before, was a dismal, muddy, collection of a dozen rude houses around a two-story frame building hastily erected for a State House, on a heavily timbered bluff of the Kaskaskia river. It was situated on the north side of that stream in a forest of trees and stumps through which a few roads had been cut in lieu of streets. Elias K. Kane was Secretary of State, and had a short time before the Legislature met, caused the State records to be brought there, from Kaskaskia, by Sidney Breese, his chief (and only) clerk, in a two-horse wagon. Pierre Menard, the Lieutenant-Governor, presided over the Senate of fourteen members, and the House, comprising twenty-nine members, was organized by choosing for Speaker, John McLean, who had been defeated in his second race with Daniel P. Cook for re-election to Congress, and was elected to the Legislature by the people of Gallatin county, and Thomas Reynolds, who was some years later Governor of Missouri, was elected clerk.

The message of Governor Bond to the Legislature was brief and sensible. Among other recommendations, he advised the law makers to establish "a seminary of learning," and to locate it with the Supreme Court, at the State Capital (where in after years our State University should have been placed), "because," he argued, "by an occasional visit at the Houses of the General

Assembly, and the courts of justice, the student will find the best specimens of oratory the State can produce, imbibe the principles of legal science and political knowledge, and by an intercourse with good society his habits of life would be chastened, and his manners improved." In the standing committees assignments Mr. Young was placed in the committee on Judiciary.

The most important legislation of the Second General Assembly was the chartering of a State bank, with branch banks at Shawneetown, Edwardsville and Brownsville, founded wholly on the State's credit without a dollar of cash capital. The banks thus created were authorized to issue notes of various denominations bearing two per cent interest, redeemable by the State in ten years, and were empowered to loan those notes to the people on personal security to the amount of $100,000.00, and to a greater amount on real estate mortgages. The originators and supporters of that "wild cat" scheme believed it would fill a long-felt want by relieving existing restrictions on business arising from the great scarcity of money, and would be received by the people generally with unbounded approval. But to their surprise it met very decided opposition by a strong minority in the House, led by Speaker McLean, the ablest debater and orator in that body. The rules of the House, however, precluded the Speaker from participation in discussions or debates on the floor excepting when in committee of the whole, and fearing the influence of McLean's overpowering eloquence the majority would not permit the bill to be referred to a committee of the whole House. Not willing to be silenced by such pusillanimous tactics McLean resigned the Speakership, and taking the floor, with his usual matchless force and power, denounced the bank project as unconstitutional, wrong in principle, and a pernicious folly, and predicted its speedy failure if enacted.

Richard M. Young, then but twenty-two years of age, as leader of the majority in defense of the bill, met McLean's objections, if not with equal oratory, with arguments more convincing to the friends of the measure. It was a contest of intellectual gladiators who had few equals in the State, and victory was won by Young. The bill passed both Houses, but was returned by the Board of Revision on the ground that it was unconstitutional and inexpedient. Both Houses immediately overrode that veto by again passing the bill with the constitutional two-thirds majority; and then the House, in a spirit of conciliation, re-elected McLean Speaker. Considerable time of the session was wasted in a foolish wrangle between the House and Senate; certain stay laws that time proved to be wholly ineffective, if not detrimental, were enacted, with other legislation of minor value, and the Assembly adjourned on February 15, 1821.

The State bank and its branches were immediately put in operation, and their utter failure within four years, with loss to the State of $300,000.00, verified McLean's prediction, and convinced Mr. Young that he had made a grave mistake in favoring such an absurd system. Governor Ford, commenting on this bank legislation twenty-seven years later, said: "The most distinguished advocate for the creation of this bank, amongst the members of the House of Representatives, was Judge Richard M. Young, who has since been so prominent in Illinois; and who is one of the very many examples in our history of the forgiving disposition of the people, to such of their public servants as have been so unfortunate as to be in favor of bad measures, or opposed to good ones." [2] Governor Ford was perhaps not entirely correct in attributing the "forgiving disposition" to the people instead of to the Legislature. There is every reason to believe that Mr. Young's constituents did not approve of, or forgive him for, his aid in establishing that State bank. That he voluntarily declined political promotion and sought retirement after his brilliant triumph over ex-Congressman McLean is scarcely credible of one possessing his vaulting ambition. But, certain it is, he was not endorsed or vindicated by re-election to the Legislature, and was never afterward elected to a public position by popular vote, excepting that of Presidential elector in 1828. However, in August, 1821, he was elected by the militia of Union county colonel of the Tenth regiment of Illinois militia, and was commissioned as such by Governor Bond on the tenth of the following September, when but twenty-three years old.

Colonel Young's military duties were limited to occasional dress parades and the annual "corn-stalk" musters of his regiment, as required by law—a burlesque military drill affording the enrolled militia a day each year of patriotic ebulition and convivial amusement. Laying aside, for a while, further political aspirations, he applied himself studiously to his books and profession to such profit that in two or three years his reputation as a learned and able jurist was heralded throughout the State and beyond its borders. As widespread also was his personal acquaintance with the leading men of the day, particularly those of the legal fraternity and prominent politicians. He was

2. Ford's History of Illinois, p. 46. [Quotation corrected.]

well informed on all questions of public policy before the people, and seldom hesitated to express his opinions concerning them in unmistakable terms. Born and reared in the South, Colonel Young was educated to regard the institution of slavery—which was sanctioned and upheld by the national constitution and State laws—as right in principle and practice, and steadfastly adhered to that view through life. Upon that issue he opposed the election of Edward Coles for Governor in 1822, and voted for Judge Thomas C. Browne, one of his pro-slavery opponents. He favored the convention scheme of 1823 for establishing slavery in Illinois, and voted for its adoption in August, 1824.

The atrocious attempt by the third General Assembly to fasten slavery upon Illinois was followed for eighteen months by a canvass of the utmost bitterness and malignity. It sundered old friendships and family ties, divided neighbors and kinsmen, and arrayed them against each other. Personal collisions and personal violence were of common occurrence, and the struggle increased in wild excitement and violence until the State seemed on the verge of civil war. But from that protracted and vigorous discussion of the question came a reaction—or, more properly, an awakening—of public opinion that resulted in defeat of the proposed convention by a large majority, and of the election, on August 2, 1824, of the fourth Legislature, which was more decidedly anti-slavery in complexion than that of 1822 was in favor of slavery. Supreme in its control of legislation it should, consistently and logically, have rewarded, with public positions at its disposal, the faithful leaders of the Free Soil party in the fierce conflict just past for rescuing Illinois from the impending curse of slavery. Instead of so doing, however, it surprisingly and inexplicably displayed that "forgiving disposition" mentioned by Governor Ford, by electing to the United States Senate John McLean and Elias Kent Kane, two of the ablest and most active supporters of the slavery convention in the State. And in its reorganization of the judiciary it elected (for life) William Wilson Chief Justice and Samuel D. Lockwood, Thomas C. Browne and Theophilus W. Smith Associate Justices of the Supreme Court, the two last named conspicuous leaders of the slavery party. It also chose for Judges of the five Circuit Courts created John W [Y]. Sawyer, Samuel McRoberts, Richard M. Young, James Hall and James O. Wattles, all of whom had voted for the convention to perpetuate slavery in the State.

Thus, on December 30, 1824, Richard M. Young, at the age of twenty-six was elevated to the bench and commissioned a Circuit Court Judge by Governor Coles on January 19, 1825. On receiving his commission he changed his residence from Jonesboro to Kaskaskia, the most central point of the third judicial circuit, over which he was to preside. He thereupon entered upon the discharge of his new duties with enthusiasm, apparently quite elated by the unexpected honor conferred upon him. On Saturday, April 30, 1825, the steamboat Natchez, from St. Louis, rounded to and tied up at the Kaskaskia landing, amid the roar of cannon and strains of martial music and shouts of an assembled multitude of people, having aboard the distinguished guest of the nation, the Marquis de Lafayette, who came to visit Illinois in response to an invitation extended to him by the Legislature. Judge Young was one of the officials specially appointed to welcome the illustrious visitor, and, with Governor Coles and others, escorted him to Colonel Sweet's old tavern, and then to the grand reception at the home of General John Edgar, and afterward to the brilliant ball at the Morrison mansion, where, of all the youth and beauty gathered there, no couple shone more resplendent than Judge and Mrs. Young. General Lafayette was escorted by Governor Coles and a few other State dignitaries to Vandalia,[3] then to Shawneetown, and from there by chartered steamboat to Nashville, Tenn. Returning to Shawneetown he took his departure to the east, accompanied by Governor Coles.

The law creating the new circuit courts provided that the judges should each receive an annual salary of $600; the Supreme Court judges were paid $800 per annum.

Any prosperous lawyer would have hesitated to relinquish his paying practice for such a beggarly salary and those of that class who did so accepted the judgeships merely as stepping stones to something better. Consequently the judges, with very few exceptions, were active politicians, constantly scheming and electioneering for promotion to higher or more lucrative positions. Judge Young was not one of those few exceptions. He conducted his courts with dignity and conscientious rectitude, but neglected no opportunity to keep himself in the limelight of popular favor. An illustration of this is seen in a letter he wrote to Governor Edwards from Kaskaskia on July 8, 1825, urging Edwards to be a candidate for governor the next year to succeed Governor Coles. "There seems at this time," he said, "to be an almost unanimous

---

3. The visit of General Lafayette to Vandalia is stated upon the authority of Governor Reynolds in his *Life and Times*, first edition, p. 258.

acclamation in your favor against the pretensions of any other person that might offer against you, in all the Southern Counties and such is the state of feeling towards you that your most inveterate enemies below (who are very few), are compelled to admit that in the Counties of Union, Alexander, Johnson, and Pope, you would get five Votes to one against any Candidate that could be brought out against you." [4] At the time Judge Young wrote this he was not one of Governor Edwards' political followers, but belonged to the Bond-Thomas-McLean faction that opposed him. He was, no doubt, sincere in the belief expressed that Edwards could, and would, be easily elected in 1826, and thought it prudent to "cast an anchor to the windward" in time.

Edwards was elected governor, though in the four counties named by Judge Young he received but 424 votes to 404 for Thomas Sloo, the opposing candidate. Of the 12,579 votes polled in the State at that election, 6,043 were given to Edwards and 5,973 to Sloo; a majority of 70 for Edwards. [5]

Judge Young gained nothing by "bending the pregnant hinges of the knee" to Governor Edwards, as the result of the election showed that he knew nothing of the public sentiment in his district, or misrepresented it if he did, apparently with the transparent object of currying favor. After his election Governor Edwards, who was one of the directors *ex-officio* of the old State bank at Edwardsville—the branch banks having failed and suspended some time before—found time to maintain a vigilant supervision of the bank's affairs, as is seen in the following letter he wrote to Richard J. Hamilton, the cashier, dated, Belleville, Oct. 11, 1828:

DEAR SIR:—Your letter of the 26th ult. is just received, in which, after representing how, and on what security the loan to Judge Young was made, you state that by an order of the Board of Directors, on the same day, he was appointed attorney for the bank; that he was to retain the money of the bank to the amount of his loan whenever he collected that much as its attorney; but, that shortly afterwards he informed you that he wished to withdraw his paper, and not to consider the loan as an accommodation to him, from which the most natural inference would seem to be that he had no loan at all, which is directly contrary to the statement in your letter of the 15th October last, in which, after reciting the order for his loan, you say: "on this order the money was afterwards paid out of the bank, and shortly afterwards again repaid to the bank by Young."

As this apparent discrepancy, though doubtless susceptible of explanation by you, leaves me altogether in the dark as to the actual state of this case, and as it is

4. Edwards Papers, p. 237–238. [Quotation corrected.]
5. Ibid, p. 251.

as necessary and proper that I should understand *it* correctly, as that of any other Director, I have to request you to furnish me with a copy of all charges and credits on your books against and for Judge Young, with their respective dates; such information as you may possess as to any collections made by him for the bank; when respectively made; whether the quarter-section of land mortgaged by him was patented at the time; whether it was valued, and if so, by whom.[6]

Unfortunately, the cashier's answer to this demand for information is lost, but the tone and purport of the letter plainly imply that Judge Young had the confidence of the "bank ring" that defied executive control, and that he was himself, not an especial favorite of the Governor.

The legislature of 1824–25 required the supreme court justices to prepare a revision of the Statutes of the State and report the same to the next session of 1826–27, which was done and the result of their labors was then adopted. Governor Ford said, "the laws then presented by them, have been standard laws in every revision since." The work was mainly done by Justices Lockwood and Smith, with some aid by two or three of the circuit judges. "Judge McRoberts prepared the act concerning frauds and perjuries; Judge Sawyer, the act concerning insolvent debtors; Judge Young, the act concerning wills and testaments. . . ."[7]

The expenses for entertaining General Lafayette, paid by the State amounted to $6,473. That amount, together with the expenses of the adjourned session, the cost of taking the late State census, and the salaries of the five new circuit court judges, not only drained the treasury, but caused a deficit of $40,000. A State debt of that magnitude alarmed the people. With but insignificant sources of revenue, and only depreciated paper currency in circulation, there seemed to them no possibility for averting either grinding taxation or bankruptcy. Then was raised from all quarters a demand for retrenchment of public expenses. "A great outcry was raised against extravagance of the judiciary system, the prodigal waste of public money to pension unnecessary life officers upon the people; and a talented young lawyer, of stirring eloquence in the southern part of the State, a man possessing many qualities which admirably fitted him for a demagogue of the highest order (A. P. Field?), mounted the hobby, and rode it in a storm of passion through several counties in the south."[8] Principally upon that issue the legislature of

6. Edwards Papers, p. 375–376. [Quotation corrected.]
7. Ford's History of Illinois, p. 60. [Quotation corrected.]
8. Ford's History of Illinois, p. 57. [The parenthetical query is Snyder's; the quotation, corrected here, is one of the few in Snyder's work that has a serious copying error. Snyder's

1826–27 was elected, and one of its first acts, on January 12, 1827, was to repeal the circuit court system, thereby turning the five new circuit judges out of office, and requiring the four supreme court justices to hold the circuit courts as before, thus effecting an annual saving for the State of $3,000!

Judge Young wasted no time in repining for his lost office, but immediately resumed the practice of law at Kaskaskia in partnership with Hon. Elias K. Kane, at that time United States Senator. About that time, 1827, an Illinois State Historical Society was organized at Vandalia with Judge James Hall as its president. Among its active members was Judge Young, with Sidney Breese, John M. Peck, Chief Justice Wilson, Governor Coles, Governor Reynolds, and other distinguished jurists, scholars and statesmen of literary tastes, interested in preserving the State's History. For a few years the Society continued its valuable labors, but was finally abandoned owing to the political and financial vicissitudes of its members, and for want of aid and encouragement from the State, and its empty treasury.

The election of John Quincy Adams to the Presidency by the lower house of Congress, in 1825, had the effect of marvelously increasing the popularity of General Jackson, and of sharply defining political party lines. The nomination of Jackson for President 1828 by the Republican Democrats—as his party was styled—in opposition to Adams, the candidate for re-election, of the Federalists, or Whigs, was productive of boisterous excitement in Illinois. An interesting relic of the party spirit and organization of those days, now preserved in the State Historical Library, is the proceedings—in the handwriting of Charles Slade—of a "Jackson convention" held at Kaskaskia, on Monday, June 9, 1828, for selecting a candidate for Presidential Elector for that district. John S. Hacker was called to the chair and Charles Slade and James Jones elected Secretaries. On roll call of counties the following delegates answered:

From the county of St. Clair, Danl. Stookey and John Middlecoff; from the county of Monroe, Dr. William G. Goforth and Isaac W. Starr; from the county of Clinton, Charles Slade and Caton Usher; from the county of Randolph, Richd. M. Young and Saml. Crawford; from the county of Jackson, Geo. Butcher and Saml. Atherton; from the county of Johnson, James Jones and Jos. Kuykendall; from the county of Union, Alex. P. Field and John S. Hacker.*

transcription had the young lawyer's oratory "stinging," not "stirring."]
  * This transcription is not literal; others from the convention proceedings have been corrected.

A committee of seven was provided, on motion of A. P. Field, to draft resolutions expressive of the sense of the convention, and the chair appointed Field, Middlecoff, Goforth, Usher, Young, Butcher and Kuykendall, said committee. The first resolution of their report declared a total want of confidence in the political integrity and principles of John Quincy Adams, but that we "have unshaken confidence in the integrity, firmness, patriotism, and ability of General Andrew Jackson." The fourth resolution

Resolved That having entire confidence in the character and unshaken political entegrity and republican principles of our fellow citizen, Richd M Young Esq of Randolph County, we hereby nominate him as a suitable candidate to be supported as one of the Electors, on the Jackson Electoral Ticket of this State, in conjunction with Conl. John Huston of Crawford County, and Conl. John Taylor of Sangamon County of whose nominations, by the friends of Genl. Jackson we most cordially approve, and the undivided support of every friend of Republican Government, and the preservation of Free principles in this State, ought to be given to their election.

"Mr. Field then arose and in an appropriate and eloquent address assigned the reasons of the committee for preferring the claims of Genl. Andrew Jackson over those of John Quincy Adams for the next presidency and concluded by recommending the adoption of the resolutions as they had been reported" by the committee, which was done by a unanimous vote of the convention. And yet, that same Colonel A. P. Field, upon his appointment by Governor Edwards to the office of Secretary of State, on December 31st of that year, 1828, joined the Whig party, and was thenceforth an inveterate enemy of the Jackson Democracy. It is needless to add that Judge Young and the entire Jackson ticket carried Illinois at the November election by an overwhelming majority.

Defeat of the convention scheme in 1824, and the assurance thereby given that Illinois was irrevocably a free State, greatly augmented the stream of emigration that for some years had been pouring into it. The "Military Tract" between the Illinois and Mississippi rivers seemed to offer special inducements to the newcomers to locate there, and was rapidly dotted over with pioneer settlements. In order to extend the protection, and restraints, of civil law over that influx of population it was necessary to organize the territory west and north of the Illinois river into counties, though some of them, still occupied by Indians, would contain less than 400 white people. Pike county had been organized in 1821, and Fulton in 1823. The Fifth General Assembly then created, in 1825, the counties of Adams, Schuyler, Peoria, Hancock, Henry, Knox, Mercer and Warren. McDonough was added in 1826, and Jo Daviess in 1827. That multiplication of counties over-taxed the four Supreme Court Justices whose duty it was to hold circuit courts in all the counties of the State. The Sixth Legislature, that convened at Vandalia on December 1, 1828, came to their relief by passing an Act on January 8, 1829, forming a fifth judicial district comprising all the territory, west and north of the Illinois river within the State's limits. The Legislature then elected Richard M. Young judge of that circuit with a salary of $700 a year to be paid in quarterly installments; and fifteen days later, January 23rd, he received his commission from Governor Edwards, who probably experienced no sorrow in thus committing him to exile.

For the next six years Judge Young was the only circuit judge—elected and commissioned as such—in Illinois.* With his usual energy and enthusiasm he immediately commenced the work of his new office with William Thomas, of Morgan county, as State's Attorney, who was commissioned on the same day as himself. Mr. Thomas was succeeded as State's Attorney of that fifth district by Thomas Ford, on March 15, 1830, who was again appointed on February 15, 1831. Ford was succeeded by Wm. A. Richardson, on February 13, 1835, who served until February 25, 1839, when he was followed by Wm. Elliott, Jr. In the autumn of 1829 Judge Young left Kaskaskia and located in Galena, then at the zenith of its lead mining industry, and the most populous and busiest town in the State. Judge Samuel D. Lockwood, of the Supreme Court, who resided at Jacksonville, had held court at Galena, Quincy, Peoria and Lewisto[w]n, but gladly relinquished that part of his circuit to the newly elected judge.

A search of the records at Galena[9] failed to reveal any evidence that Judge Young at any time purchased real estate there; from which fact it may be inferred that he regarded his residence in Galena as only temporary. That he purchased certain personal property there, however, is shown by the following significant bill of sale recorded July 24, 1830, on page 108 of Record "A" of Deeds:

---

* The Supreme Court judges presided over the circuit courts in other circuits.
9. By Hon. William Spensley, the well-known Galena attorney, to whom I am indebted for many personal courtesies and valuable information.

"Wharton R. Barton
  to
R. M. Young.

Know all men by these presents that I, Wharton R. Barton, for and in consideration of the sum of seventy-five dollars to me in hand paid, the receipt whereof is
hereby acknowledged, have this day bargained, sold and delivered, and by these
presents do bargain, sell and deliver unto Richard M. Young of the town of
Galena, County of Jo Daviess, and State of Illinois, a negro girl of a black color,
named Mary, five years of age the 14th of March last, and the daughter of a
registered negro woman now in the care of John V. Miller in the said town of
Galena; to have and to hold the said negro girl Mary unto the said Richard M.
Young, his heirs and assigns, together with the benefit of her services, until she
shall arrive at the age of eighteen years, at which time by the constitution and
laws of Illinois she is entitled to her freedom. Witness my hand and seal at Galena
this 17th day of May, 1830.

Signed, Wharton R. Barton   [Seal.]

Witness, John Foley.
Acknowledged before James Nagle, Justice of the Peace.
Recorded July 24, 1830.

James W. Stephenson,
Recorder."

After Judge Young was elected judge of the new fifth district, in 1829,
he was strongly urged by his numerous friends to enter the race for Governor
with John Reynolds and Wm. Kinney, and was much tempted to do so. For
some time he seriously considered the matter, and finally, concluding that a
bird in the hand was worth more than two in the bush, declined becoming
a candidate.[10]

In 1831 the Seventh General Assembly organized and added to Judge
Young's circuit the counties of Cook, Rock Island and La Salle, completing
the area of his jurisdiction from Galena to Lake Michigan, thence down the
Illinois river to its confluence with the Mississippi.

Desiring a quieter place of residence for his family than Galena then on
the extreme frontier, and little more than a large mining camp infested with
speculators, gamblers, and every variety of social outcasts who respected
neither moral or civil law, Judge Young moved to Quincy in the spring of
1831. On the thirteenth of June following he entered the north half of the
N. W. qr. of Sec. 4. 2S. 8W; eighty acres, to which he added, by entry, on

10. Edwards Papers, p. 426.

Dec. 26, 1832, the N. W. qr. of the N. E. qr. of the same section, forty acres, in Adams county. On that 120 acre farm he built a substantial two-story frame dwelling, a barn and other necessary out-houses, and moved there, from the village, as soon as the buildings were completed. Mr. Wm. A. Richardson writing of that farm house, in the Quincy Herald, Dec. [Oct.] 19, 1905, said it was situated "on the east side of the country lane between Broadway road and State street road, and sometimes called 'Forty-eighth street,' then some three miles and a half due east of the village of Quincy. This old white house, with its green blinds, was a home of genuine hospitality—the politicians and men of affairs going out to see Judge Young, and the society people going out to see Mrs. Young. Mrs. Young was particularly fond of young people, and generally tried to have some young lady stay with her when the judge was away 'riding the circuit.' Doubtless, these brought other maidens and their beaus and other swains, and the old farm house was full of life and innocent gayety." *

During the greater part of each year, for the eight years Judge Young presided over that circuit, he traveled to hold his courts in the scattered settlements generally on horseback and often alone, following dim Indian and buffalo trails, through trackless prairies and pathless woods and across unbridged streams, not unfrequently camping by the wayside when night overtook him.

Ballance, writing of him said: "In May, 1833, he made his appearance in the Village of Peoria, and announced that he was on his way to Chicago to hold court. He had traveled about 130 miles from Quincy, where he lived, and had to travel, as the trail then run, not less than 170 miles further, to hold the first court on his circuit. Just think of a horseback ride of at least 300 miles to hold a three days' court!" [11]

Judge Young was not deterred from his circuit riding by the turmoil and dangers of the Black Hawk War in 1832, but rode fearlessly without escort from one county seat to another and held his courts while the volunteers were chasing the Indians out of the State. On the twentieth of May of that year occurred the heartrending murder of fifteen settlers by a party of Black Hawk's Indians at the house of Wm. Davis on Indian creek, twelve miles north of Ottawa, in LaSalle county; and the only two then there whose lives

* Quotation corrected.

11. History of Peoria, by C. Ballance, Peoria, 1870, p. 63.

were spared, Rachael and Silvia Hall, were carried away by the savages. *
Two of the Indians implicated in that massacre and abduction, To-qua-mee
and Co-mee, were afterwards apprehended and indicted by the grand jury of
LaSalle county (instead of being summarily lynched) and after long delay
were tried before Judge Young and a jury at Ottawa. Thomas Ford was the
prosecuting attorney and the Indians were defended by Hamilton and Bige-
low. For want of certain identification the culprits were acquitted, and afterwards boasted of their guilt.

About a year after Judge Young's location at Quincy, he established and
conducted a Democratic newspaper there, entitled the "Illinois Bounty Land
Register," edited by himself and published by C. M. Woods. It was the first
newspaper published north of the Illinois river, with the exception of the two
papers at Galena established there a short time before. Nothing is now known
of the paper's subsequent history. †

Though almost constantly engaged on his extensive circuit, Judge Young
managed to attend all terms of the Supreme Court at Vandalia, and also to
visit the State Capital at every session of the Legislature. He was personally
known to all the officials and politicians in the State, and was himself one of
the most popular and highly esteemed of the State's public men. When the
lower house of the Eighth General Assembly preferred charges, in 1833,
against Justice Theophilus W. Smith of the Supreme Court, and placed him
on trial for impeachment before the Senate as a jury, he selected as attorneys
to defend him, Sidney Breese, Richard M. Young and Thomas Ford. The
managers on the part of the House, who prosecuted him, were Benjamin
Mills, John T. Stuart, James Semple, Murray McConnel and John Dougherty, an array of talented, learned men on both sides—not surpassed in the
legal profession of the State. The trial lasted from January 9th to February
7th, resulting in a negative acquittal. The speech of Judge Young on that
occasion, January 29th [28th] was one of the best efforts of his life. It was
listened to with intense interest by the entire Legislature, and all others who

---

* Snyder's account of the Indian Creek Massacre is the traditional one, but it contains
numerous errors. The massacre took place on May 21; although Rachel and Sylvia Hall were
the only survivors among those in the house, several men and boys in the nearby fields and
shop escaped; the exact composition of the attacking Indian band is unknown: some of Black
Hawk's warriors were certainly in the party, but the ringleaders were Potawatomi from villages
not far distant.

† This paper became the *Quincy Herald* (1842–1926), merging into the present *Herald-
Whig.*

could crowd into the room, and added new laurels to his already high reputation for forensic ability.

The Ninth General Assembly began its first session at Vandalia December 1, 1834. One of its first duties was the election of a United States Senator to succeed Hon. John M. Robinson, who was a candidate for election to succeed himself. General Robinson had served in the Senate very acceptably since he was elected in 1830, to fill the vacancy occasioned by the death of John McLean; but objection was raised to his re-election, by some, on the score of his personal habits and by others because of his Southern location, White county, claiming that as all the Senators had been chosen from the Southern counties since the admission of the State into the Union, simple justice would demand the next Senator be taken from one of the Northern counties. When, therefore, the two houses met in joint session for the election on the thirteenth of December, Judge Young was presented as a candidate by one of his friends, and, considering all things, developed surprising strength. However, General Robinson was elected, receiving 47 votes to 30 for Judge Young, and 4 for Wm. B. Archer.

Having disposed of the Senatorial election the Legislature took up the serious consideration of other important matters before them. The population of the State was increasing rapidly, and litigation in the courts correspondingly increasing to such an extent that the four Supreme Court justices were no longer able to hold all the courts in their respective circuits and satisfactorily discharge the functions of a Supreme Court. Ballance says: "In those days there were but few roads and bridges in the northern half of the State. No road of any kind had then (1833) been opened from Peoria to Chicago. In fact, the most essential requisites of a good judge for this circuit were to own a good horse and be a good rider. These two requisites Judge Young possessed in a high degree. He was a fine looking, complaisant Kentuckian, who possessed a fine, high-blooded Kentucky horse, and knew well how to ride him." [12] Yet, notwithstanding those valuable requisites, the legal business of Judge Young's immense district was growing beyond his capacity to properly manage it. The Legislature, convinced that something must be done to relieve the overworked judiciary, accordingly passed, on January 7, 1835, an act providing for the election of five additional Circuit Judges, and exempting the Supreme Court justices from further Circuit Court duty. By

12. *"History of Peoria,"* by C. Ballance, 1870, p. 63.

that act Judge Young was retained judge of the fifth district, as before; and on the seventeenth of January another act was passed curtailing that district to Pike, Adams, Hancock, McDonough, Knox, Warren, Fulton and Schuyler counties, which territory included the counties of Calhoun, Brown and Henderson, subsequently organized.

That change affording Judge Young some leisure for social and domestic enjoyment, he concluded to leave his farm and move into the village of Quincy. Whereupon he sold, on June 25, 1835, to John Cleveland, for the sum of $2,500, his farm of 150 acres, reserving possession until the first of the next March. On the twenty-sixth of the following September he purchased of Thomas Carlin and wife, for $500, lot six in block ten "of the original town of Quincy, fronting on Hampshire street 99 feet and running back at right angles 198 feet." On December 8 he sold to Samuel Jackson, for $300, twenty-five feet off the west side of that lot, and on the remaining seventy-three feet he built a fine brick mansion two stories high, with a hall running through the middle." Mr. John Wheeler, a nonagenarian, remembers hearing Judge Young say that he had moved to town to please his wife, but that he himself would prefer to live in the country. Mr. Wheeler says Mrs. Young was regarded by people of those early times as a fashionable society woman, and that her home was a center of social gayety. He says further that they were "a very good looking couple, the Judge tall and straight, and his wife above medium height and beautiful." [13]

"Judge Young, in 1835, bought the land where the Tremont House, the barber shop and cigar store now stand on Hampshire street, and built him a home thereon. Many of our citizens remember the old Young mansion, and some of the older ones remember grand parties given there by Judge and Mrs. Young. Some remember one of their daughters, and some remember two." [14]

As before stated, Judge Young sold to Samuel Jackson, on December 8, 1835, twenty-five feet off the west side of lot six—where the cigar store now stands—for $300. After having built his mansion he, and wife Matilda, executed a mortgage deed of the property to Edgcombe H. Blatchford, on February 26, 1848, to secure a debt of $3,397.71. On August 17, 1849, the Judge and wife sold to Hiram Rogers another part of lot six—where the barber shop is—for $1,000. March 13, 1852, the judge and wife executed, at Washington

13. From Mr. William A. Richardson's notes.
14. Quincy "Daily Herald," October 19, 1905. [Most of this quoted paragraph is not in the paper cited.]

city, a power of attorney to Harrison Dills, of Quincy, "to sell remaining right and title, interest and claim of, in and to, lots six and seven, in block ten, as designated on the original plat of the city of Quincy." Mr. Dills sold the premises, on April 8, 1852, to Mrs. Rebecca Carlin for $3,500, and she conveyed the same to John Schell, who lived there several years, and sold it to Mr. Cather. That gentleman tore the old "Young mansion" away in 1856 or 1857 and built on its site the hotel which was first called the Cather House, and afterwards, in other hands, the St. Charles, and afterwards again, and still in other hands, the Tremont.

The second session of the ninth legislature was commenced at Vandalia on December 7, 1835. On the twenty-ninth of that month a special message from Governor Duncan to the two houses conveyed the sad intelligence of the death of Senator Elias K. Kane, and advised that an election to fill his vacancy be held "during the present session." By agreement the two houses met in joint session on the afternoon of that day and proceeded with the election. The principal candidates were James Semple, Speaker of the House, and General W. L. D. Ewing. The friends of Judge Young and of Lieutenant Governor Alexander M. Jenkins among the members placed them in nomination also. The first ballot stood, 25 votes for Semple, 19 for Young, 18 for Ewing and 15 for Jenkins. Eleven ballots were taken when Ewing was elected, "by the aid of Lincoln and the anti-Jackson men," [15] receiving 40 votes to 37 for Semple. Judge Young's name was withdrawn after the eighth ballot. Senator Ewing served until March 4, 1836, sixty-three days. It is hardly probable that Judge Young would have sought to be a candidate for a brief term of sixty-three days in the United States Senate, or made any effort to secure it. That he was placed in nomination for the place and voted for through eight ballots while he was busily engaged on his wilderness circuit was no doubt due to the partiality of his friends in the legislature, and must be regarded as evidence of his popularity, and the appreciation of his worth and talents. However, at the next Senatorial election for a full term successor to General Ewing, in which Young and Ewing were again candidates, the tables were turned, the Judge retrieving his defeat by a decided victory over the General.

Judge Young had been twice presented by his friends to the legislature as a candidate for the Senate, whether with his consent or connivance, or not, is now immaterial; but when the legislature again met at Vandalia, on De-

15. Moses' History of Illinois, vol. I. p. 405. [This is not a verbatim quotation.]

cember 5, 1836, he was there and announced himself again a candidate for the Senate to succeed General Ewing. That [tenth] general assembly "was one of the most remarkable bodies of law-makers which ever assembled in the legislative halls of Illinois or of any other state." [16] "No legislature of our State before, and very few since, have comprised such an array of brainy, talented men; or as many who subsequently gained such eminence in the annals of the State and nation. In the Senate were Orville H. Browning, Cyrus Edwards, Wm. J. Gatewood, John S. Hacker, Robert K. McLaughlin, Henry I. Mills, Wm. Thomas, John D. Whiteside and John D. Wood. And in the House were Edward D. Baker, John Hogan, Milton Carpenter, Newton Cloud, Richard N. Cullom (father of Senator Shelby M. Cullom), John Dement, John Dougherty, Stephen A. Douglas, Jesse K. Dubois, Ninian W. Edwards, Abraham Lincoln, Wm. L. D. Ewing, Augustus C. French, John J. Hardin, Usher F. Linder, Dr. John Logan (father of General John A. Logan), John A. McClernand, James Semple, John Moore, Wm. A. Richardson, James H. Ralston, and Robert Smith. In this list are found one President of the United States, six who have occupied seats in the United States Senate, eight Congressmen, three Governors, three Lieutenant Governors, two attorney Generals, five State Treasurers, two State Auditors, one State Superintendent of Schools and several Judges." [17]

The two houses met in joint session on the fourteenth of December and proceeded at once with the Senatorial election. Neither of the candidates voted for received a majority of all the votes cast on either the first or second ballot. On the third ballot 62 legislators voted for Richard M. Young, 24 for Samuel McRoberts, 17 for Archibald Williams, 12 for Wm. L. D. Ewing, 7 for Judge Thomas C. Browne, and 1 for Chief Justice Wm. Wilson. Elected United States Senator for the term of six years by that famous assembly, by a majority of 7 votes over the combined vote of all his distinguished opponents, was an honor of which Judge Young might well be proud. Yet, it was that same assembly—that body of collective wisdom—that, later in the session, enacted the wild Internal Improvement folly which brought the State so nearly to the verge of ruin and bankruptcy.

16. Moses' History of Illinois, vol. I. p. 406–407. [Punctuation and capitalization corrected.]

17. Adam W. Snyder, and His Period in Illinois History, 1906, p. 214. [Snyder did not quote from himself accurately; the source has numerous variations in punctuation, abbreviation, and word order.]

On January 2, 1837, Senator Young resigned his judgeship preparatory to entering upon the duties of the higher position to which he was elevated, commencing on the fourth of the following March. Proceeding to Washington in November he took his seat in the Twenty-fifth Congress, as the junior Illinois Senator, with his collegue, Hon. John M. Robinson. Illinois was then represented in the lower house of Congress by Adam W. Snyder, Zadok Casey and Wm. L. May. Martin Van Buren was President and Richard M. Johnson Vice-President. During Judge Young's term in the Senate the deliberations and legislation of Congress were uneventful. Our country was prosperous and at peace with all the world—excepting the Seminole Indians of Florida. The main issues dividing the political parties were, the financial policy, internal improvements by the general government, and, incidentally, some phases of the slavery question. The Whigs favored a U. S. bank, and national roads made by the government. The Democrats were opposed to both, and contended for hard money and the sub-treasury system. Much time was consumed in both houses of Congress in efforts to establish a fixed plan for disposition of the public lands, and adjustment of pre-emption laws. Then later, recognition of the independence of Texas by the United States, and the proposed annexation of that lone star republic to the Union as a slave state, and the introduction of a bill providing for a national bankrupt law, were productive of long acrimonious debates and much ill-feeling.

Senator Young was not remarkable as a parliamentarian or orator, but was admittedly a dignified, able and clear-headed statesman. His speech in the Senate on January 8, 1839, in reply to Senator Crittenden, of Kentucky, on the bill to graduate and reduce the price of public lands; and that on February 1, 1841, on the prospective pre-emption bill and Senator Calhoun's proposition to dispose of public lands in the new states, were efforts of surprising strength. Among his best political productions was a circular letter he addressed to the people of Illinois, from Washington, on June 30, 1842, defining in masterly style the leading principles of the Democratic party. That address was published in all the Democratic papers of the State coincident with the selection of Judge Ford as the candidate of that party for Governor, and contributed largely to the decided success of the Democratic ticket at that election. A noted episode of Judge Young's Senatorial term was his mission to England, in 1839, to negotiate a loan for the State of Illinois.

The Eleventh General Assembly authorized the State to borrow, upon its credit, an additional sum of $4,000,000 for the completion of the Illinois and Michigan Canal. It also elected Thomas Mather, Charles Oakley and M. M. Rawlings, Fund Commissioners, to negotiate all loans, and sell all bonds for said loans. John Reynolds was elected to Congress in August, 1838, at the same time Thomas Carlin was elected Governor, but would not take his seat in the House until sixteen months later, December 2, 1839. He had long desired to visit Europe, and now saw his opportunity to do so at public expense. Reynolds and Carlin were old friends; both were of Irish descent, and early pioneers of Illinois; they had served together as rangers in the war of 1812, and were together in the Black Hawk war. Governor Reynolds visited Vandalia to see his friend Carlin inaugurated in the executive chair, and remained, almost as long as the Legislature did. As the State's credit was nearly exhausted here, he had no difficulty in persuading Governor Carlin that it would be better to send a special commissioner of national reputation to negotiate the new $4,000,000 loan in foreign money markets. Though three Fund commissioners were provided for that purpose by the legislature, Reynolds easily wheedled the Governor into making him that special commissioner. Then after securing his free junket, aware of his incapacity for such a responsible task he begged Carlin to appoint another special commissioner to accompany him. To this the Governor acceded, and chose his friend and neighbor in Quincy, Senator Young, for the second commissioner.

It is doubtful if two other men so conspicuous in public life at that time as Governor Reynolds and Senator Young, could have been found, so little qualified—so destitute of financial tact and skill, for such a difficult and important mission as they. When Governor Carlin was made aware of that fact by friends in whom he confided, he sent two of the Fund commissioners along, Colonel Oakley and General Rawlings, to manage the business. Governor Reynolds and wife left at once for New York. There the Governor met Oakley and Rawlings, and the three sold to Thos. Dunlap, a broker, 1,000 State bonds of $1,000 each, and to one Delafield 300 bonds of the same denomination, on such conditions as to result in ultimate loss to the State of over $150,000. They then proceeded to London where they were joined by Senator Young and wife. There the four commissioners sold and deposited with John Wright & Co., a firm of English sharpers, another million dollars of Illinois bonds, with no regard to security, or specific provisions of the law from which they derived their authority. The brilliant financiering of the four commissioners resulted in clear loss to the State of over half a million of dollars. While Oakley and Rawlings remained in London arranging details of their negotiations, one of the special commissioners with his wife rambled around to see the sights in England, then crossed the channel to the continent and visited Paris, Brussels, and other points of interest.[18]

The reports of Reynolds and Young were received by the called session of the eleventh assembly, convened on December 9, 1839, and referred, in the House, to a special committee, which, after careful consideration of all official acts of the junketers, submitted, on January 29, 1840, majority and minority reports. The majority report—adopted by a large majority of the House— "highly disapproved" of all the transactions of the commissioners; declared they "transcended the powers vested in them by the State;" also declared their "negotiation with John Wright & Co., of London, to be and is, void," and demanded return of the State bonds the junketers deposited with that firm for sale. In the preceeding pages of this sketch Governor Ford is quoted when citing Judge Richard M. Young, as "one of the many examples in our history of the forgiving disposition of the people" to their erring public servants. But the people of Illinois never forgave Reynolds and Young for their bungling failure as special fiscal agents of the State. From that ill-judged junket of the two statesmen dated the decline of their popularity. Occurring before the introduction of telegraphs, railroads and modern daily newspapers that now thoroughly ventilate such jobs. Governor Reynolds was reelected to Congress in the following August, and then permanently retired from further participation in national affairs.

Before the close of Judge Young's senatorial term the Democratic party had adopted the convention and caucus system for selection of candidates for office. When the time arrived for the thirteenth general assembly to choose a successor to Senator Young, the Democratic members met in caucus on December 9, 1842. Four candidates were presented for nomination, Young, Breese, Douglas and McClernand. "After a stormy session, lasting from seven o'clock p. m. until one o'clock a. m., Judge Breese was successful on the nine-

18. Only Governor Reynolds and wife went over to the continent. Senator Young remained in London until he concluded the negotiations with Wright & Co., about the last days of October, (1839), when he and his wife took passage for New York on the English ship British Queen commanded by Captain Roberts, who later was lost with all on board when crossing the Atlantic on the new ship President, in 1841.

teenth ballot, by the narrow margin of one majority, he receiving 56 votes, Douglas 52, and McClernand 3." [19]

After several ballots, with but little prospect for securing the nomination, Judge Young was induced to withdraw from the contest by promise of a place on the supreme bench. Governor Ford, upon his election, had resigned his judgeship; so also had Judge Theophilus W. Smith because of failing health, and Judge Breese also resigned immediately after his elevation to the Senate. Three associate justices of the Supreme court were then to be chosen by the legislature to supply vacancies. The two houses together proceeded with that election on January 14, 1843. General James Semple was elected to succeed Breese, Hon. John M. Robinson in place of Ford, and Richard M. Young to succeed Judge Smith, receiving 122 votes; 12 ballots were cast blank, and 8 scattering. He received his commission on the twenty-fifth of February, and at the expiration of his Senatorial term, on March 3, returned to Illinois to reenter the judiciary. Resuming the ermine he was assigned to the seventh judicial district which included Chicago.

Judge Young acquitted himself on the supreme bench with much credit. A critical comparison of his written opinions with those of the other distinguished Supreme court justices with whom he was associated while a member of that august tribunal proves him to have been a superior lawyer and judge. In 1843 he delivered four decisions of the court and one dissenting opinion; [20] in 1844 he wrote six decisions, one separate, and one dissenting opinions, [21] and in 1845 he delivered ten decisions, two separate, and two dissenting opinions. [22] Well and concisely written, they are all clear and accurate judicial statements supported by ample references and sound reasoning. His separate opinion, of twenty pages, in the celebrated case of Jarrott vs. Jarrott, delivered at the December 1845, term, [23] is remarkable for profound, far-reaching knowledge of the law, and of history involved in the questions before the court. The action, of assumpsit, was brought by Pete Jarrott, a French negro slave, against Mrs. Julia Jarrott of Cahokia, who owned him, for services rendered. It was tried at the October 1843, term of the St. Clair county

---

19. Moses' History of Illinois, vol. I. p. 455. [Quotation corrected.]
20. 4th Scammon Reports. [A cursory check of the *Reports* shows that Young delivered five decisions in 1843; legal scholars would be well advised to double-check Snyder's statistics.]
21. 1st Gilman Reports.
22. 2d Gilman Reports.
23. 2d Gilman, p. 12 *et seq.* [Wilson and Caton also concurred.]

circuit court before Judge James Shields, and a jury that rendered a verdict for defendant, and was taken up to the supreme court on appeal by Lyman Trumbull and Wm. H. Underwood, plaintiff's attorneys. There the decision of the lower court was reversed. The court's opinion was delivered by Justice Walter B. Scates, with which Judge Young coincided, Justices Thomas, Treat and Shields dissenting. The case attracted wide spread attention and unusual public interest, as the decision of the Supreme court gave Pete Jarrott his freedom, and practically removed from the statutes the last vestige of authority for slavery in Illinois.

At the same term of the court, in the case of Rhinehart vs. Schuyler *et al.*,[24] brought from Adams county on appeal, Justice Young delivered the opinion of the court, covering 36 pages, in which his able review of the case tried in the lower court before Justice Thomas, in October, 1843, his familiarity with the law governing the points in controversy, and precedents cited, and the strong, clear arguments sustaining his conclusions, are not surpassed by any opinion emanating from that court.

In the month of July, 1845, he was chosen by Governor Ford an arbitrator on the part of the State, under an act of the Legislature, to settle a matter of difficulty between the State and the State Bank of Illinois; Judge Stephen T. Logan having been selected by the Bank, and succeeded in adjusting the matter in a manner entirely satisfactory to the Governor.

No opinion by Judge Young appears in the Reports for 1846, and by the records of the court it is seen that he was absent from several of its sessions that year. The truth is, he had become tired of judicial work. On failing to be reelected to the U. S. Senate he accepted the Supreme court Judgeship because nothing better was then accessible, and found its laborious obscurity in too marked contrast with the dazzling eminence of the Senate. He craved a public station of political prominence and conspicuous authority. When the term of Governor Ford was about to expire the Democrats held a convention, at Springfield, on February 10, 1846, to nominate a candidate of the party to succeed him. The aspirants before that convention for the nomination were two of the Supreme court Justices, R. M. Young and Walter B. Scates, Lyman Trumbull, John Calhoun, Augustus C. French and Alfred W. Cavarly. Upon the first ballot Trumbull led with 56 votes, to 45 for French, 44 for Calhoun, 35 for Young, 35 for Scates and 20 for Cavarly. On the third ballot

24. 2d Gilman, p. 493 *et seq.*

"the choice—in accordance with a line of precedents, which seemed almost to indicate a settled policy—fell upon him who had achieved least prominence as a party leader, and whose record as a public man had been least conspicuous,"[25] Augustus C. French.

When a member of the Senate a mutual friendship existed between Judge Young and Hon. James K. Polk, then Speaker of the House of Representatives, who was elected president in 1844. Having failed to secure the Democratic nomination for Governor, the Judge visited Washington later in 1846, when Congress was in session, presumably, to ascertain what might turn up there to his advantage. Hostilities with Mexico having commenced, he, no doubt, could—with the prestige of his early military experience as Ensign, Aide and Colonel of militia, and his fine soldierly figure and martial bearing—have obtained from the president a commanding position in the volunteer contingent of Illinois. But his aspirations were evidently not in that direction. In 1845 President Polk appointed James Shields, of Illinois, Commissioner of the General Land office, which he resigned in 1846 to accept a Brigadier General's commission in the Mexican war. The supplying of that vacancy was perhaps the only civil position, allotted to Illinois, the president then had at his disposal. It was offered to Judge Young, and by accepting it he committed the gravest mistake of his life. He was appointed Commissioner of the General Land office, to succeed General Shields, on January 6, 1847, and resigned his seat as one of the associate justices of the Illinois Supreme Court on the twenty-fifth of the same month, and immediately set out for Washington to enter upon the duties of his new office. Two days later, the twenty-seventh his vacancy on the supreme bench was supplied by election of Jesse B. Thomas, Jr.

Judge Young was a citizen of Quincy until late in 1849 when he moved his family to Washington, and never returned to reside in Illinois. The General Land office was at that time an integrant part of the Treasury department and one of the largest, and most arduous bureaus to manage in the government. The Judge seemed to have a natural predilection for that kind of work, and took its administration in hand with zeal and earnestness, giving to every detail of the business, and to the sixty clerks employed, his constant personal supervision. His annual report, submitted at the beginning of the year 1849, was evidence of the ability and thoroughness of his management of the gov-

25. Moses' History of Illinois, Vol. 1. p. 505.

ernment's land interests. It was a lengthy and elaborate document, characterized by unusual clearness in arrangement of details, remarkable for the sound sense and modesty of its author and valuable for its tabular statements of all public lands sold and in market, of land and coast surveys, population, representation in Congress and other highly useful information, illustrated with numerous maps and diagrams. That report attracted much attention throughout the country, and received the flattering commendation of newspapers and public men of both parties.

In 1848 the Democratic party lost control of the government by the election of a Whig, General Zachary Taylor, to the presidency. In free and enlightened America no statutory mandate has greater force than that unwritten law of political parties, "to the victors belong the spoils." A change of administration necessarily implies a change of office holders, excepting now, the Civil Service class. In obedience to that law a sense of honor compels higher officials of the defeated party to present their resignations to the victors. But, Judge Young was so infatuated with the "pomp and panoply" of official position he not only did not resign, but—although a lifelong radical democrat—he made a strong effort to be retained as Commissioner of the General Land offices by a Whig president. He had some Whig support, as against Mr. Lincoln who was a candidate for the position, and who was generally endorsed by the Whig members of Congress. Young would have been reappointed but for the fact that during the campaign he wrote a very severe article against General Taylor and sent it to all the newspapers in Illinois, and on the copy he sent to Quincy he stated at the bottom of the article in large letters, "I wrote this, R. M. Y." Browning got hold of the article and sent it to Lincoln, who showed it to General Taylor, that settled the pretentions of the Judge in that direction. Through the influence of Daniel Webster the land office was given to Justin Butterfield of Chicago. (Mss. of John Wentworth.)[26]

The mania for office-holding is one of the most deplorable and pitiable forms of mental degeneracy. There are in Washington city at all times a number of political wrecks and derelicts—gray-haired, broken-down men, who once held high and responsible positions there, then dropped by the everchanging caprice of party favoritism, remained there in enchanted helplessness, reveling in memories of their former grandeur, or vainly hoping that

26. Foot note on page 511, Vol. 1. Moses' History of Illinois.

another turn of the wheel of fortune may again restore them to public notice. Judge Young was unfortunately a victim of that mania. Otherwise he would have pursued the course of his successor in the Senate, Judge Sidney Breese. Stepping down from the Senate upon the Supreme Court bench of his State, he should have made a virtue of necessity, and remained there—a highly honorable station for which he was, by natural endowment and acquirements, eminently well fitted. Had he done so, in all probability he could have retained it—as Breese did—the balance of his life. Fascinated, however, by the illusory glitter and charm of life at the national capital, he descended from the bench a long step lower to the superintendency of a department bureau. Deposed from that transitory haven, he further descended to the clerkship of the thirty-first Congress, to which he was elected by the House of Representatives in December, 1849. Adjournment of the session in 1851 terminated his long and highly creditable official career. With no longer a salary to rely upon for subsistence, and having accumulated no productive property, he reached the bottom where necessity forced him to resume the struggle as he had commenced it in Johnson county, Illinois, thirty-four years before, by the practice of law. Combining with his profession a general claim agency, by diligence, aided by the prestige of his distinguished antecedents, he was fairly successful.

On February 26, 1842, he had been admitted to practice as an attorney and counsellor at law in the United States Supreme Court, having been presented to that high tribunal and recommended by Hon. Robert J. Walker, of Mississippi, Secretary of the Treasury.

In stature Judge Young was six feet two inches in height, erect and well proportioned, weighing usually about 170 pounds. His forehead, high and broad, was surmounted by dark brown hair, and his large hazel-colored eyes were over-arched by heavy, dark eyebrows. With florid complexion, his features were prominent, regular and prepossessing, indicative of great good nature, absence of malice, matured judgment and perfect self-confidence. In disposition he was social, affable, and one of the kindest and most genial of men. Without the gift of flowery oratory, he was a strong, forcible speaker, and as a conversationalist could not be surpassed, having an exceedingly entertaining style of expression and a limitless store of anecdotes and apt illustrations always at his command. Though very friendly and easily approached by all, he could not tolerate undue familiarity, adhering all his life to the stately politeness and courtly manners of the old Virginia type of gentleman.

It is related that in the early days of Quincy Orville H. Browning, then a budding young lawyer, had as a member of his household a younger brother, full of fun and boyish mischief, who answered to the name of "Milt." On one occasion Milt knocked on the cabin door, and when Mrs. Browning opened it to welcome a supposed visitor, Milt, with his right hand over his heart, bowed low, in imitation of Judge Young, and then ran away. A few days later Mrs. Browning again heard a knock at the door, and thinking she recognized Milt's rap, not to be fooled again by him, cried out, "you go around to the back door; there is where you belong." Then, it occurring to her that she might be mistaken, opened the door, and to her surprise and confusion found the caller (in quest of Mr. Browning) to be Judge Young, who was very indignant at her reception, and with considerable hesitation accepted the profuse apologies and explanation she offered.

As a politician Judge Young was aggressive, fearless and honorable; always ready to contend for the policies and principles he believed to be right; never arrogant or personally abusive, and invariably extended to his opponents the respect and liberality he exacted for his views. As a judge he was dignified, self-possessed, patient and very courteous to the members of the bar, as also to the jurors, witnesses and litigants. Always punctual in attendance to public business, he never lost sight of the fact that he was the people's servant, and never slighted or neglected the trust they reposed in him. His judgments, emanating from much legal learning, good sense and sound reasoning, bore well the test of time and the closest scrutiny. His courts were always models of decorum and order. Very seldom he found it necessary to inflict penalties for contempt or misdemeanors in court. When he did the fine was usually remitted when the offender admitted his error and promised not to be guilty of it again. When compelled to enforce punishments he inquired into the standing and pecuniary circumstances of the culprit in order that the sentence he imposed might not be unjust or too oppressive.

In regard to personal habits the judge was temperate and moral, never indulging in the vices too common among his contemporaries and political associates. Of domestic tastes he was much attached to his home and his family, and enjoyed entertaining his friends, his house being famed for its frequent gay and festive social gatherings. For general literature, arts and poetry he had special fondness, and was very partial to music—boasting of some musical talent himself—occasionally producing some fine strains from an old fiddle he highly prized, which he bought in 1816 when a law student in Kentucky.

His views of the abstract principle of slavery can be inferred from the fact that all his early associations and impressions were formed amidst and influenced by the institution of slavery and that he was himself a slave holder so long as slavery was tolerated in Illinois. He never outgrew the strong, mutual attachment that existed in his boyhood days between the members of his father's household and their slaves, as is evidenced by the entry in his family record of the death of two faithful negro servants of his father's, known as "Uncle Ned" and "Aunt Dinah," both of whom were emancipated long before the Civil War. They both came to Illinois, but in 1850 Uncle Ned returned to the old homestead in Kentucky and died there. Judge Young never joined any church, and left no statement of his religious belief. He was, however, a member of the Masonic order, having been initiated on April 20, 1829, into "Union Lodge No. 8," of that ancient fraternity.

From memoranda of his cases and clients, found among his papers, it is inferred the judge received liberal patronage from 1851 to 1859,* and must have done a thriving business; for during that period he had employment, which probably was no doubt satisfactory in respect to remuneration. While so engaged, however, he was rapidly passing out of public notice. In the ever recurring mutations of public affairs in Illinois new men were crowding to the front, while Judge Young—for thirty years a conspicuous factor in its political life—no longer in view, was then simply a historic figure. The passing of his prominence and importance was galling to one of his sensitive nature and self-esteem. He knew the fate of politicians when their course is run, and well knew his inability to perform the miracle necessary to restore his lost prestige and power. Brooding over his blighted ambition and lost opportunities, his business troubles and unpromising future preyed upon his mind and nervous system until finally his health failed and his bright mental faculties became clouded. In the fall of 1858, when perplexed and overtaxed by a case involving peculiarly intricate legal questions, his reason tottered and he was forced to retire from further activity. With the best medical skill at hand and the constant kind attention of his family—particularly the faithful care of his son-in-law, Robert A. Matthews, the year 1859 passed without perceptible improvement in his condition. By advice of his physician, he was taken on

* Snyder says below that Young was forced to retire in the fall of 1858.

April 17, 1860 to the Government Hospital for the Insane, in Washington, for treatment. He had passed so completely out of public thought and public observation that nothing was known in Illinois, and nothing was recorded at Washington, of the closing days of his life. The published histories of our State contain but brief and unsatisfactory biographical sketches of Judge Young and his public career, vaguely mentioning his death occurring "in an insane asylum in 1853." [27] Newspaper writers have stated that "he was confined in the dungeon of a Washington insane asylum, a raving maniac, part of the time restrained by chains and manacles." Balance says: "But for some time before his death he was confined in an asylum for maniacs. Of his last days I will not speak, because of them I know nothing, only as I have been informed by a brother of his, since he has passed away. If his story is true, Judge Young, who was once one of the most popular men in Illinois, passed many a day and night in a dungeon, under the torturing hands of fiends in human shape, in the great capital of the nation; and yet for a long time so secretly that a brother, living in that city, had no suspicion of it." [28]

Ascertaining that Dr. W. A. White is the present superintendent of the Government Hospital for the Insane at Washington, a letter of inquiry regarding the truth of above statements, addressed to him last winter, by the writer, was courteously answered by him as follows:

"DEAR SIR—I beg to inform you, in response to your letter of the 12th inst., that the records of the hospital show that Hon. Richard M. Young was under medical treatment for a mental affection from April 17, 1860, to October 15, 1860. Having recovered he was discharged from treatment upon the date last mentioned. The records are silent as to the existence of violent mental disturbance; and it can be taken for granted that the rumor that he was "confined in chains in a dungeon" was without foundation in fact—the hospital being without either of those accessories. I have no knowledge of Judge Young's career subsequent to his discharge from the hospital. Your letter states that it was understood that he "died in the Government Hospital for the Insane at Washington in 1853." As mentioned above he was discharged—cured—in 1860; and as a matter of fact, no patients were received into the hospital prior to 1855.

"Very respectfully, etc.,

"Wm. A. White, Superintendent."

27. Moses' History of Illinois, vol. I, footnote on page 511.
28. History of Peoria by C. Balance [Ballance], pp. 64, 65.

Rest and medical treatment at the hospital for six months restored the quietude of Judge Young's mind and nervous system, but he never regained his former spirits and animation. He was, in fact, a mental and physical wreck. At his home he remained secluded during the winter of 1860–61, a semi-invalid incapable of much exertion either of mind or body. The stirring events of 1861 excited his interest, at times arousing his patriotic devotion to the land of his birth and the cause for which it was contending. But the fires of youth were burned out, and only the smouldering embers remained to be momentarily and feebly rekindled. With advance of summer and advent of autumn his vitality continued to fail; he grew weaker until finally he died from exhaustion on November 28, 1861, at the age of 63 years, 9 months and 8 days. He was buried in the Congressional cemetery at Washington.

Judge Young's thoughts were never centered for any length of time on money making. Not a financier, and content with the salary he drew, or ordinary pay received for his legal services, he expended it all for the comfort and well-being of his family, and entertainment of his friends, neglecting many favorable opportunities for accumulating riches. Balance,* who knew him well, says: "He lived and died poor; but had he lived until now [1870], and held on to certain property which has been sold by his wife since his death, he would be rich. One piece of property, which he obtained in Omaha as a fee, is said to be worth many thousand dollars." [29]

By his last will and testament Judge Young devised "all of his property, real, personal and mixed, wheresoever situated," to his wife, Matilda. They had but two children, both daughters; one named Matilda James, and the other Berenice Adelaide, whose date of birth and place where born cannot now be ascertained. Matilda James Young was married to Robert A. Matthews at Washington, D.C., on June 29, 1852, and died without issue at Talbotton, in Talbott [Talbot] county, Georgia, on September 24, 1872.

Berenice Adelaide Young was married to John A. Crawford, at Washington, D.C., in 1857, and died at Richmond, Virginia, on January 19, 1862, leaving but one child that also died within two months thereafter. Mrs. Matilda, widow of Judge Young, departed this life at Washington, D.C., on January 31, 1871, and was buried by the side of her deceased husband, in the

---

* The misspelling of Ballance's name here and in n. 28 was probably a typographical error, for it was spelled correctly earlier. The bracketed date in the quotation was in parentheses in Snyder's transcription.

29. History of Peoria, by C. Ballance, 1870, p. 65.

Congressional Cemetery there. She left a will bequeathing all her property to her son-in-law, Robert A. Matthews, who during the Civil war was a major in the Confederate service. The name of Robert A. Matthews appears on the roll of attorneys practicing in the Supreme Court of Illinois in 1845.

DOCTOR JAMES D. ROBINSON

Reprinted from *Journal of the Illinois State Historical Society*, IV (Jan., 1912):
446–58.

ONE DAY in the early spring of 1840 the daily four-horse stage coach, carrying
the mail on the route from St. Louis to Vincennes, drew up, as usual, at the
hotel on the public square in Belleville, Ill.; and of the several passengers who
alighted from it, one was a young man, a total stranger, who seemed glad
that he had reached his journey's end. On the hotel register he wrote, in a
free, business-like hand, "Charles Mount, New York City," as his name and
address. Telling Jake Knoebel, the landlord, that he would probably remain
there some time, he asked for a comfortable room, well lighted and heated,
and not higher up than the second floor, which was assigned to him, and into
it his capacious trunk and other baggage were soon snugly stowed. Having
the evident faculty for accommodating himself to his environment, he seemed
at once to feel quite at home in his new quarters, and very favorably disposed
to the town and its people. He was not bothered with excessive diffidence or
bashfulness; neither was he morose, exclusive, or tongue-tied; but, being what
is now known as a "good mixer," it was not long before he was on the best of
terms with the most prominent men of the place.

Concerning himself, he told his newly-found acquaintances that he was
born and raised in a town (which he was careful not to name) in western
Massachusetts; and having recently graduated at Yale College—a fact verified
by the diploma he exhibited from that institution—he had concluded to
gratify a keen desire, long entertained, to visit the great West, of which he
had heard and read so much, before selecting a profession or settling down in
any permanent business occupation. He was, therefore, here merely to see the
country. Apparently well supplied with money, he paid cash for all that he
bought or received, was liberal in his expenditures, but not profligate or extravagant.

Charley Mount, then 23 years old, was, in every respect, a remarkably
prepossessing young man. He was 5 feet, 7 inches in height, perfectly proportioned, weighing perhaps 140 pounds, and his black, wavy hair sur-

mounted a handsome beardless face to which the sparkling, dark eyes gave an expression of intelligent animation. His hands and feet were small and well-shaped—a feminine feature that gave rise, in certain quarters, to the suspicion that he was a girl masquerading in male attire. That notion was strengthened by his exceptional habits—abstaining totally from the use of liquor, tobacco, and vulgar or profane language. He was a Chesterfield in manners and deportment, affable and friendly in disposition and refined and cultured in conversation. His clothes, of fine texture, fitted perfectly, and he was invariably neat and clean; yet there was about him no affectation of the fop or dandy, but the easy bearing of the well-bred gentleman.

Among the guests of the Belleville House at the time Charley Mount arrived there, was an Irish lawyer, a generous, big-hearted bachelor 30 years of age, who had recently changed his place of residence from Kaskaskia to become a member of the Belleville bar. His name was James Shields—the same who in later years was a general in two wars, and had the unique distinction of representing three different states in the United States Senate. Notwithstanding the disparity of seven years in their ages, and also some disparity in their personal habits, a mutual attraction at once drew the lawyer and the young stranger together in bonds of warm friendship. In a brief space of time they both enjoyed immense popularity, particularly in the younger stratum of Belleville society; were much admired by the young ladies, and became conspicuous figures in all their dancing parties and other social gatherings.

In the northwest corner of the public square was a small two-room brick house—one room behind the other—built there in 1835 by Adam W. Snyder for a law office; and after him it continued for many years to serve that purpose for several other lawyers who gained high prominence in the legal and political annals of the state. Col. Snyder, in failing health, had retired from the practice of law, but still retained that building as his political headquarters, passing some time there daily when the weather permitted. When abandoning the active work of his profession, he installed there Gustavus Koerner (his late partner) and James Shields, who had entered into partnership, as his successors. And that law office was the haunt where Charley Mount whiled away many of his leisure hours, though he frequently visited the offices of the other town lawyers, and also of the doctors. When he came to Belleville the memorable "coonskin and hard cider" political campaign had commenced and was rapidly gaining momentum in popular interest and excitement. On the 4th of December, 1839, the national Whig convention at Harrisburg, Pa., had chosen Wm. Henry Harrison as the candidate of that party for the presidency, and John Tyler for vice president. Martin Van Buren, then president, was the candidate of the Democrats, though not until the 5th of May, 1840, was he unanimously nominated to succeed himself by his party's convention at Baltimore. State and all local issues were ignored, and the fierce contest was waged altogether on national and personal questions.

Since 1834 the population of St. Clair county had annually gained large accessions from the incoming German immigration. And all of that "element" who acquired the right of suffrage in six months' time or less, guided by Koerner and Snyder, voted the Democratic ticket as a unit. Hence, St. Clair county was one of the most important Democratic strongholds in the State, and one the Whigs especially desired to overcome. As the campaign progressed the enthusiasm of both parties became a wild frenzy. The Whigs particularly, who had never yet elected a president, and who had at the last general election run the Democrats so closely in Illinois, brought every agency to bear that ingenuity could suggest and money provide to carry this State. In Belleville, as everywhere else throughout the country, their almost continuous succession of the most extravagant pageants, parades and mass meetings kept up the turmoil at fever heat for months, answered, in some measure, with as noisy and absurd demonstrations by the Democrats.

In the Whig parades the predominant emblems, intended to represent the pioneer life and career of their candidate, Gen. Harrison, were canoes, yawls, skiffs, scows and log cabins, mounted on wheels, embellished with coon and deer skins—live coons, also, in many instances—barrels of hard cider, gourds, camping outfits, and profusion of flags and banners. Fortunately the torchlight accompaniment had not been invented. Brass bands were scarce, and in their stead fifes, drums, fiddles, with an occasional French horn, or trumpet, provided the music. Campaign songs, in every key and note, in all places and at all times, fretted the air and made life a prolonged misery. As a sample, a favorite ode of the Whigs commenced thus:

> "We do not wish Van Buren dead,
> Nor wish he had a broken head;
> But if he once were dead and gone
> We should not wish him to return.

> In Abraham's bosom may he lie,
> And over hell may Abraham fly;
> Then open wide his roundabout
> And let Van Buren tumble out."

The Democrats retaliated with melodies reciting how Tecumseh was killed by Col. Dick Johnson, of Kentucky, a Democrat; and how Gen. Harrison hid under a big soap kettle during the battle of Tippecanoe. At Belleville, all through the months of June and July, mass meetings, now called "rallies," were held by both parties, with all sensational accompaniments, every few days. The few daily newspapers then published had not learned the knack, possessed by the press of today, of reporting speeches in full, thereby dispensing political knowledge and wisdom to the people. Consequently, the people depended for knowledge of public affairs upon the party orators, which insured to every advertised speaker a satisfactory and attentive audience. Both parties called to their aid their best local debaters and such of wider fame that could be secured. The rostrums of the Democrats were supplied by Governor Reynolds, candidate for Congress; Col. Snyder, candidate for the State Senate and presidential elector; Lyman Trumbull, candidate for the Legislature; Koerner, Shields and other local lawyers, with the occasional addition of Dr. Bissell of Monroe county, candidate there for the Legislature; Judge Breese, Sam McRoberts, John Wentworth, Stephen A. Douglas, Senator Thos. H. Benton of Missouri, and other "foreign" party leaders of more or less note.

Bob Smith, of Alton, came down one day and addressed the Belleville multitude. He had twice represented Madison county in the Legislature, was a rattling, strong stump orator, and had Congressional aspirations, justly claiming that as St. Clair county had had the Congressman of that (the First) district continuously since Joe Duncan's last term, it would be no more than fair to let Madison, the next strongest Democratic county in the district, have it a while. His speech was boisterously applauded by the large concourse of people who listened to him.

While Smith was making "the boys" cheer and yell, Gov. Reynolds stood on the outskirts of the crowd in scowling mood, "viewing with alarm" Bob's rising popularity, apprehensive that it would seal his official doom—as it did; for the first Democratic Congressional convention held in that district, in 1842, nominated Bob Smith for the next term and thereby relegated the Old

Ranger to private life. While the governor was standing there listening, with illy-disguised disgust, to Smith, a teacher of the county schools, named Tam— a loud-talking, brazen fellow, who in conversation made use of the biggest words in the dictionary, generally inappropriately, and who had ambition to run for office—approached him and said: "Governor, I would like mighty well to discourse to these people on the magnitudinous questions of the day. Do you think if I announced an appointment to speak here on a specific date they would come to hear me?" "Of course they would," answered Reynolds, "they would turn out to a man; for, as a rule, the d——der the fool to listen to the bigger the crowd." Mr. Tam didn't speak, but after the election moved to Arkansas where he later attained considerable prominence.

The Belleville Whigs also enlisted a strong contingent of speakers to advocate their cause and give aid and comfort to their local candidates. Among the most able and effective of them were A. P. Field, then Secretary of State; E. D. Baker, Cyrus Edwards, Ex-Gov. Duncan, U. F. Linder, John J. Hardin, John Hogan, Jos. Gillespie, and last, but not the least, Abraham Lincoln, a candidate for the Legislature in Sangamon county. Even then Lincoln was known as the "Rail Splitter," and he certainly looked it. Gov. Koerner, writing of that period, says: "In point of melody of voice and graceful delivery, though not in argument, most all the other speakers surpassed him. It was the first time I saw Mr. Lincoln. It must be said that his appearance was not very prepossessing. His exceedingly tall and very angular form made his movements rather awkward. Nor were his features, when he was not animated, pleasant, owing principally to his high cheek-bones. His complexion had no roseate hue of health, but was then rather bilious, and, when not speaking, his face seemed to be overshadowed by melancholy thoughts. I observed him closely, thought I saw a good deal of intellect in him, while his looks were genial and kind. I did not believe, however, that he had much reserve will-power. No one in the crowd would have dreamed that he was one day to be their President, and finally lead his people through the greatest crisis it had seen since the Revolutionary War."[1]

When the exercises were over on the day Mr. Lincoln spoke, he and Joseph Gillespie boldly invaded the enemy's camp. That is, they called on Col. Snyder at his home. Lincoln and Snyder were together as captains in the

1. *Memoirs of Gustave Koerner, 1809–1890.* Vol. I, pp. 443–444. Pub. Cedar Rapids, Iowa, 1909. [Quotation corrected.]

Black Hawk war, and Judge Gillespie was a private in Captain Snyder's company. Their visit was exceedingly pleasant to all. After a little jocular allusion to the existing political situation, their conversation was altogether reminiscent, and in the spirit of cordial familiar friendship.

Charley Mount had perhaps never given the subject of politics a serious thought before coming to Illinois. Influenced by his associates here, however, he was soon a rampant "Locofoco," as the Whigs, in derision, termed the Democrats. He was not a speaker, but accompanied Shields, Koerner, and others, on their precinct appointments, applauded them vociferously, joined in singing the campaign songs and wrote flaming reports of their meetings to the party newspapers.

At the election only six states cast their electoral votes for Van Buren, one of which was Illinois. Harrison and Tyler were elected, but it proved to be a barren victory. In this State the Democrats made almost a clean sweep, securing two of the three Congressmen and both houses of the Legislature; but the Whigs elected Gillespie in Madison, and Lincoln in Sangamon, to the Legislature, and John T. Stuart to Congress in the third district.

In the intervals of political engagements at Belleville, both Charley Mount and Shields found time to fall in love with their landlord's charming daughter. Charley, the most sentimental of the two, raved about her, styling her "angelic," etc., and wrote verses about her, which she probably never saw. Mr. Knoebel, a very quiet man of few words, but much strong, practical common sense, would, of course, never have permitted his daughter to marry either of them, regarding them as mere adventurers having no fixed place of abode or visible property assets. The girl seems to have shared her father's views in that matter, and abruptly ended their romance by marrying Mr. Neuhoff, a wealthy German a few years older than herself, and not quite the Adonis in personal graces that Charley Mount was, but one of Belleville's most enterprising and substantial citizens.

The newly elected Twelfth General Assembly, largely Democratic in both houses, early in the session elected James Shields to the position of State Auditor. Going to Springfield to enter upon the duties of his office, he took Charley Mount along and installed him as his chief clerk. In a social point of view Belleville's loss in that move was the State capital's gain. In the second year of the new auditor's incumbency, 1842, occurred the famous Shields-Lincoln embroilment wherein the former challenged the latter to mortal combat. Shields selected John D. Whiteside, late State Treasurer, for his second, because of that gentleman's political prominence and the martial prestige of his name. But Charley Mount pluckily stood by him in that fearful ordeal, stating afterwards that he had determined to avenge the death of his Hibernian friend in case he fell, perforated by the broad sword of the future immortal Emancipator. Fortunately for the nation the ludicrous affair was adjusted without bloodshed, and shortly thereafter Charley Mount abruptly resigned his clerkship and returned to the East.

Nothing more was heard of him until early in 1847, the second year of the Mexican war, when he again suddenly appeared in Belleville, the same jovial, genial fellow, only looking more manly and mature, his handsome face adorned with an elegant black mustache. But he had undergone a strange transformation. He was no longer Charles Mount, but Dr. James D. Robinson, the name he inscribed on the hotel register. In explanation of that surprising metamorphosis he said an old bachelor uncle, named James D. Robinson, who many years before had migrated from Scotland to New England, and there accumulated a large fortune, learning of his (Charley's) purposeless stay in the West, wrote to him to return to his eastern home and study for a profession, promising, if he would do so, to defray all his expenses; and further proposed, if he would legally assume his name—James D. Robinson—he would constitute him his heir. He said he gladly accepted that offer, immediately went back to his home, had his name changed by the court, chose the medical profession, and his uncle liberally supplied him with funds until his graduation at the best medical college in New York. But unfortunately about that time the old gentleman suddenly died without having executed a last will and testament, and the law distributed his wealth among his nearest of kin; and he, Dr. Jas. D. Robinson, the heir presumptive, was left to continue the inevitable struggle.

After a brief visit he returned to the East. He had come, it was learned, to secure the recommendations of influential friends in Illinois in support of his application for a federal appointment in the medical staff of the volunteer army. In that he was successful, receiving from President Polk the position of assistant surgeon of Col. E. W. B. Newby's regiment, mustered into the service at Alton, June 8, 1847. In that regiment was a company from Belleville, of which Wash Hook was captain, Wm. H. Snyder first lieutenant and regimental adjutant, and Enoch Luckey second lieutenant, with all of whom the doctor was previously well acquainted; and he shared with them the hardships and glory(?) of their campaign in New Mexico and the Navajo country. He was highly esteemed by all the command, proving to be a skillful surgeon and able physician, invariably attentive, kind and sympathetic in the discharge of his duties. Before the regiment's term of service expired he was ordered to New York City for service in a government hospital there.

Lost then to his Illinois friends, he was no more heard of until one day in the spring of 1856 he unexpectedly again alighted from the stage coach in Belleville. To those interested in his history he told that when relieved from hospital duty, after the war closed, he practiced medicine awhile in New York City. Then he had accepted the position of physician on the vessels of the Cunard line of steamships, and in that capacity, with ample salary, had crossed and recrossed the Atlantic for some years, passing his vacations in England, Scotland, and various parts of the continent. Tiring of that service, and longing for the freedom and charm of the West, he relinquished his post on the briny deep, and came to settle down permanently in Illinois. He had intended to locate in Belleville, but the profession there being then, as now, so wretchedly overcrowded, he went to Illinoistown (now East St. Louis) and established himself. From the start he was successful. Though the country was in a ferment of excitement about the repeal of the Missouri Compromise, he paid no attention to politics, devoting the little leisure he had to the pursuits of literature. In an old scrap book here is a "Carrier's New Year's Address" of the *Belleville Advocate's* "Printer's Devil," of Jan. 1, 1857, inserted in the paper with this comment by the editor: "*New Year's Address.—* The address of our carrier is of such poetic merit that we are induced to give it to all our readers. We are indebted for it to the skillful and accomplished pen of Dr. James D. Robinson of Illinois town."

As a place for residence in those days Illinoistown was not altogether an Elysium, but a decidedly "hard" town. That fact, and his increasing acquaintance and business on the other side of the river, prompted Dr. Robinson to move over to St. Louis in the early days of 1858, and there establish his office a few blocks west of the Planters' House. Another inducement for him to change his location was his marriage, about that time, to Miss Rachael Addis, a young lady of striking beauty of form and features, said, by gossips, to be a Jewess who had renounced her faith for a career on the stage. Rumors were whispered that her reputation was not altogether unclouded, and, later, vague reports of infelicity in their domestic life were heard.

The success of Dr. Robinson was marvelous. Devoting but a few hours daily to office practice, he was a familiar figure on the streets of the city, seated in his fine buggy, driving a spirited horse, in serving a constantly widening circle of resident patrons. One day in the autumn of 1858, the doctor's equipage came down the street, and the horse, as long accustomed, stopped at his post in front of the office door. Directly some passerby noticed that the horse was not hitched to his post as usual, and the doctor, pale and motionless, retained his seat in the buggy. Closer inspection revealed the startling fact that he was dead, and, on further investigation, a small empty vial emitting the unmistakable odor of prussic acid, found on the floor of the buggy at his feet, conclusively indicated that he had deliberately committed suicide.

Early the next morning a stranger arrived in St. Louis from the East, in search of Dr. Robinson, and from him the true history of the doctor's life was learned. His name from his birth, was James D. Robinson, as was also that of his father. The rich Scotch uncle, who promised to make him his heir on condition that he would change his name, was a myth of his own creation, and never existed. In his childhood both his parents died, leaving him an orphan with but a limited patrimony. Precocious, studious, and bent on acquiring a classical education, he had exhausted all his means at the beginning of his senior year at Yale, and, it seemed, would be compelled to abandon the object of his ambition. But a wealthy maiden lady of his native village, several years older than himself, captivated by his handsome face and figure and polished manners, had fallen violently in love with him. He reciprocated her passion, or pretended to, and they were married. She gave him all the funds necessary to complete his course at the university, then installed him in luxuriant ease in her elegant home.

There could be but little harmony in a pair who differed so radically in every respect as they did. He was not wayward, ill-natured, or inclined to dissipation, but fond of adventure, amusements, gay, jovial society, and rather skeptical regarding some of the sublime truths of the sacred scriptures. She was staid and sedate in disposition, of serious, ascetic temperament, rigidly pious, and an orthodox Christian in mortal dread of sin and Satan. Nevertheless she adored him, and undertook to convert him to her puritanical notions.

177

But the task was hopeless. Impatient of restraint, and longing to see the great west, he forged her name to a check for quite a sum of her money; then, as Charley Mount, came to Belleville. He was there, in the frontier settlements, before the introduction of railroads and telegraphs, as safe from detection as fugitive criminals were in Texas.

Clerical work in the auditor's office failed to satisfy his aspirations, as he had arrived at the age when, he thought, he should have a higher and more stable life vocation. He desired to enter the medical profession, and saw but one way to compass that end. That way he at once adopted by returning to his wife, meek and repentant, and throwing himself upon her mercy. Woman-like, she forgave the wrong he had committed, and defrayed all his expenses through a full course of study at a New York medical college. Graduated there, he commenced the practice of his new profession at his boyhood home. For a while all went well, but again his wife's strict discipline grew very irksome. He was meditating schemes for escaping from it when, fortunately, the Mexican war presented the opportunity. It was some time before he could convince his wife that patriotism and honor demanded he should obey his country's call in its hour of peril. Gaining her consent at length, he joyfully went with Col. Newby's regiment over the old Santa Fe trail.

When relieved of hospital service at New York he made a brief tour of Europe, and, returning to the New England village, resumed his professional work, which he very probably continued until 1856, when he again escaped from his connubial thralldom and came west.

The stranger from the East who came in quest of him was a civil officer and also a relative of his wife. He was provided with a requisition from the Governor of Massachusetts for the doctor's arrest and extradition; but, finding him dead, declined to make any explanation of the offense he had committed. It was presumably a felony, perhaps another forgery. By some means the doctor learned that a minion of the law was coming for him. Rather than be taken back to his birthplace a prisoner, and face the disgrace of prosecution for bigamy and a yet graver criminal charge, and, it may be, unhappy in his second marital relations, he sought relief in self-imposed death. The officer executed his writ by taking his prisoner's dead body back to the old Bay state and laying it in a grave in the village cemetery alongside those of his parents.

PART III

Pioneer Illinois Archaeologist
John Francis Snyder

AN APPRAISAL

By Melvin L. Fowler

ARCHAEOLOGY as a science dealing with the cultures of prehistoric man is comparatively new, having been taught in the universities of this country only since the late years of the nineteenth century. Classical archaeology, the study of the remains, art work, and ancient cities of the more advanced civilizations (such as the Greek and Roman), is an older discipline.

Although the universities generally neglected prehistoric archaeology as a formal discipline, there were earlier nineteenth-century students who sought out knowledge of the prehistoric inhabitants of North America. Their efforts centered primarily in the Bureau of American Ethnology in Washington, D.C. In Illinois there was no such center of research until the 1920's when the University of Chicago established a Department of Anthropology and the University of Illinois initiated a program of field work. Prior to that time, the pioneering efforts of some very competent amateur archaeologists had indicated the importance of such research in the state. Most outstanding among these pioneers was John Francis Snyder, a physician who lived in Virginia, Illinois.

The contributions of these pioneers has been of inestimable value to modern studies of archaeology.

We who are familiar with modern archaeological techniques must give proper credit to these early pioneers of the nineteenth century. They were explorers in a new subject field of science. . . . Their objective statements concerning archaeological conditions and objects which they found are still an integral part of the modern archaeologist's fund of knowledge. Great credit is due these serious students of eastern United States archaeology who laid the foundations upon which our modern studies are built.[1]

Dr. Snyder was early acquainted with reminders of Illinois' prehistoric past. The house in which he was born was at the edge of a large pyramid-shaped Indian mound near East St. Louis, Illinois. He spent most of his childhood in the vicinity of Cahokia and Monks' Mound, the largest man-

1. Carl E. Guthe, "Twenty-five Years of Archeology in the Eastern United States," in J. B. Griffin, ed., *Archeology of Eastern United States* (Chicago, 1952), 1–12.

made structure in North America. On a trip to California as a young man he observed Indians at first hand. The interest thus stimulated became a dominant concern of his life, and at every opportunity he was digging into Indian mounds and studying the remains recovered.

He once confided in a letter to a friend:

I have, thank God!, reached that financial condition that I longed for, for many years, when I could be enabled to lay aside a distasteful occupation—for which I had no natural adaption—and, though late, enjoy in the evening of life such studies, or mental recreation, as are genial and pleasant to me. I always detested the profession into which I was ensnared when young—and ignorant—and which I was compelled, through years of drudgery and untold mental wretchedness, to pursue for support of my family. But, through that drudgery, and sacrifice of everything that life is worth living for, and prudent economy and judicious investments, I am now emancipated; and am doing my best to be classed strictly with the laity. The upshot of this preamble is, that I never look at Medical Journals, or any other class of medical literature; and feel no more interest in it than I do in reports of Methodist Conferences or Sunday School Conventions. My mind is now in different, and far more pleasant channels of thought.[2]

Despite his busy schedule Snyder soon became a well-rounded archaeologist. He studied every published source on the subject, but was more than just an armchair archaeologist, for he did much actual excavation of sites, located many new and previously unknown sites, and checked in the field the work of other people. The results of his study, field work, and reading were reported in more than thirty published articles between 1877 and 1917. His reputation was widespread, and he corresponded with all of the leading archaeologists of his time in America.[3] Many of them called upon him for advice and asked him to compare his finds with their own. Finally, in an effort to bring archaeology to the public and to other students, Snyder edited an archaeological journal.

To appraise Snyder's contributions one must turn to his many published articles. These can be divided into four major groups. The first is the site reports, or reports of field investigations. In the second category are articles which present large interpretive pictures of Illinois' prehistory based on compilations and syntheses of data. A third group deals with historic Indian tribes

2. Dr. J. F. Snyder to Dr. Carl E. Black, Nov. 5, 1900, Personal Correspondence, Black Letters and Papers, Illinois State Historical Library, Springfield.
3. Robert E. Elkin, "John Francis Snyder and Illinois Archaeology" (Master's thesis, University of Illinois, 1949), *passim*.

and consists of their identifications, migrations, and so forth. This field he delved into only lightly, preferring the study of actual archaeological remains. The final category, represented by only a few articles, though it was one of Snyder's most consuming interests, deals with the need for the conservation of prehistoric remains and for their proper scientific study. The following appraisal of Snyder's archaeological works is made on the basis of these apparent divisions.

THE EARLIEST of Snyder's published articles as well as several later ones dealt with his discovery of discs of chipped flint ("hornstone") in an Indian mound near Beardstown.[4] These were not finished implements but percussion-chipped oval-shaped objects that were buried in the mound in large numbers either as a type of paving or as caches of raw materials. He compared these with the finds of Squier and Davis[5] at Clark's Works (later known as the Hopewell Group[6]) in Ohio, thus early recognizing the relationships between Illinois cultural groups and those in Ohio now called the Hopewellian.

Easily the most significant today of his numerous field explorations was his work at the Baehr site in Brown County, Illinois.[7] There he utilized excavation techniques (such as cross-trenching and sectioning of mounds) that were in advance of his time. Snyder's report on the Baehr site was the basis for the identification of a particular pottery style significant in the analysis of change in the Hopewellian culture in Illinois.[8] Among his other field explorations are the Hemplull site[9] and the Brown County ossuary.[10]

Snyder's many articles, including the site reports, reflect his ability to synthesize his finds and compare them with other finds in interpreting the

4. "Deposits of Flint Implements," *Annual Report of the . . . Smithsonian Institution, 1876* (Washington, 1877), 433–41.

5. E. G. Squier and E. H. Davis, *Ancient Monuments of the Mississippi Valley: Comprising the Results of Extensive Original Surveys and Explorations* (Smithsonian Contributions to Knowledge, I, Washington, 1848).

6. Warren King Moorehead, *The Hopewell Mound Group of Ohio* (Field Museum of Natural History Publication 211, Anthropological Series, Vol. VI, No. 5, Chicago, 1922).

7. John Francis Snyder, "An Illinois 'Teocalli,'" *The Archaeologist*, II (Sept., 1894): 259–64.

8. James B. Griffin, *Additional Hopewell Material from Illinois* (Indiana Historical Society Prehistory Research Series, Vol. II, No. 3, Indianapolis, Dec., 1941) and "Some Early and Middle Woodland Pottery Types in Illinois," in Thorne Deuel, ed., *Hopewellian Communities in Illinois* (Illinois State Museum Scientific Papers, V, Springfield, 1952), 93–129.

9. Sometimes called Hemphill in the literature. Griffin, *Additional Hopewell Material;* Byron Knoblock, *Banner-Stones of the North American Indian* (LaGrange, Ill., 1939).

10. John Francis Snyder, "Prehistoric Illinois: The Brown County Ossuary"; see pp. 216–29 below.

broader aspects of Illinois prehistory. Indicative of his broad insight was his prediction or recognition of the prehistoric cultural relationships and sequence in Illinois. He early recognized that the material he obtained from "memorial" mounds in Illinois, such as the Baehr site, was related to similar material in Ohio. He first studied these relationships in 1876.[11] He also suggested that tomb-mounds, such as those at the Baehr site, were of an earlier time period than the truncated platform mounds of the Cahokia area; this insight has since been confirmed by scientific stratigraphic excavations of University of Chicago archaeologists in Fulton County, Illinois.[12] He suggested, further, that the stone-lined graves common to southern and western Illinois bluff areas were of a later period than the flat-topped "domiciliary" mounds.[13] Of these proposals Griffin and Morgan said:

It was Dr. J. F. Snyder . . . who seems to have done the best work in Illinois during the nineteenth century, and who clearly predicted the cultural sequence now firmly established in the state. Snyder recognized the relationship of the Middle Mississippi material in the Illinois Valley to that found in the Missouri-Arkansas area and suggested that it was certainly later than the Hopewellian sites found during his own excavations and that of the related mound group near Montezuma.[14]

One of the major contributions of Snyder's articles is that they report on sites long since destroyed by "the gnawing tooth of time."[15] He records, for example, what appears to have been one of the largest burial mounds ever known to have existed in the Illinois area.[16] By checking the site itself, interviewing eyewitnesses, and having the strata then present analyzed chemically, Dr. Snyder was able to present a reconstruction of the Beardstown mound and its contents as it had been before it was completely destroyed in

---

11. "Deposits of Flint Implements"; he later proposed, in "An Illinois 'Teocalli,'" 263–64, that such a relationship would be established, and he referred on other occasions to the relationship—see, for example, "Prehistoric Illinois: Certain Indian Mounds Technically Considered; Part Second: Sepulchral and Memorial Mounds"; see pp. 245, 255 below.

12. Fay-Cooper Cole and Thorne Deuel, *Rediscovering Illinois: Archaeological Explorations in and around Fulton County* (The University of Chicago Publications in Anthropology, Archaeological Series, Chicago, 1937).

13. "Prehistoric Illinois: Certain Indian Mounds Technically Considered; Part Third: Temple or Domiciliary Mounds"; see p. 273 below.

14. James B. Griffin and Richard G. Morgan, eds., *Contributions to the Archaeology of the Illinois River Valley* (Transactions of the American Philosophical Society, Vol. XXXII, Pt. 1, new series, 1941), 47.

15. "Sepulchral and Memorial Mounds," p. 247 below.

16. *Ibid.*, p. 251 ff. below.

1865. Another unusual site, also now destroyed, was the charnel house mound near East St. Louis. Inside the mound was a

"bone-house" . . . twelve feet square and seven feet high. The corner posts, of cedar, were still in place; the other uprights and roof timbers, of softer wood, were reduced to dust. The side walls of the house, constructed of poles planted perpendicularly and interlaced with long slender willow sprouts, or reeds, had disappeared, leaving only here and there their impression in the adjacent dry clay. In that charnel-house had been gathered from the scaffolds and stored the remains of all members of the tribe who died within a certain period. . . .[17]

After this charnel structure was filled with bones, it was covered with a mound some thirty-five feet in height.

Viewed as a record of such sites now obliterated or lost to record by cultivation and destruction, Snyder's writings are invaluable.

There are phases of Snyder's work which are not acceptable today, but in light of the times in which he wrote he should not be criticized for these. He seemed convinced, for instance, that the aboriginal Illinoisans belonged to a race low on the scale of human evolution. This conclusion was based upon "the ape-like prognathism, the flattened tibiae, perforated humerus, retreating forehead and prominent supraorbital ridges." [18] "In life," he states, "they must have been as hideous as the gorilla." [19] The skeletal remains he illustrates, however, are of modern man, and the appearance of the sloping forehead comes from the faulty alignment of the skull fragments.[20] His conclusion was no doubt also attributable to a common pursuit and intellectual interest of the late nineteenth century: seeking the so-called missing links of evolution.

Snyder approached much of his writing with preconceived ideas of the nature of the American Indians and their works. Thus he reports that Monks' Mound was never finished, as evidenced by the fact that it was not all of one level. For it was Snyder's concept that all such mounds should be symmetrical and level on top. The reason this mound was left incomplete, he said, was that

the tribe became demoralized and abandoned the work. The arrest of their labors may have resulted from one of two causes. They were, perhaps, overwhelmed and

17. *Ibid.*, p. 250 below.
18. *Ibid.*, p. 256 below.
19. "Brown County Ossuary," p. 218 below.
20. *Ibid.*; see below, Figs. 1 and 2, Pl. 23 and Fig. 2, Pl. 24.

dispersed by an incursion of wild savages; or, owing to the incoming herds of buffalo, they relapsed from their higher development of semi-sedentary life and agricultural pursuits back into nomadic savagery and subsistence by the chase.[21]

On the other hand, Dr. Snyder's keen insight often pervaded the cloudy thinking of specialists. At a time when geological experts were claiming that the Cahokia mounds were merely a natural formation,[22] Snyder presented very lucid and straightforward reasoning to refute this idea and to show that the mounds were indeed primarily man-made structures.[23] This view was completely vindicated by the later position of Crook[24] and the thorough geological studies of Leighton.[25]

Another good example of Snyder's logical and perceptive thinking in the light of counter trends was his criticism of the then-popular concept that the "mound builders" represented a race of people, now extinct, who preceded the American Indians in North America. In 1882 he postulated correctly that the "mound builders" were the ancestors of the American Indians who were in eastern North America at the time of European discovery.

As both archaeologist and historian, Snyder was interested in the history and customs of the Indians inhabiting Illinois and surrounding areas in historic times. In his brief studies of these peoples he demonstrated his skill as a documentary researcher. It appears that there were few source materials available in his time which he did not utilize. One of his more interesting papers of this type deals with the subject "Were the Osages Mound-Builders?"[26] In this article he discussed a supposed instance of Osage mound-building and the concurrent legend that these Indians had originally come from the upper Ohio Valley, an area abounding in mounds. This latter assertion he dismisses:

The Osages, it is well known, are a branch of the Dakotas, and migrated to Missouri from the north, or northwest; and perhaps the only members of that

21. "Temple or Domiciliary Mounds," p. 270 below.
22. See, for example, N. M. Fenneman, *Geology and Mineral Resources of the St. Louis Quadrangle, Missouri-Illinois* (*United States Geological Survey Bulletin 438*, Washington, 1911) and A. R. Crook, "Origin of Monk's Mound," *Bulletin, Geological Society of America,* XXVI (1915): 74, 75, "Additional Note on Monk's Mound," in *ibid.,* XXIX (1918): 80–81, and "The Composition and Origin of Monk's Mound," *Transactions of the Illinois Academy of Science,* IX (1916): 82–84.
23. John Francis Snyder, "The Great Cahokia Mound," *Journal of the Illinois State Historical Society,* X (July, 1917): 256–59.
24. A. R. Crook, *The Origin of the Cahokia Mounds* (*Bulletin of the Illinois State Museum,* Springfield, 1922).
25. M. M. Leighton, "The Geological Aspects of Some of the Cahokia (Illinois) Mounds," *University of Illinois Bulletin,* Vol. XXVI, No. 4, Pt. 2 (1928), pp. 109–43.
26. *Annual Report of the . . . Smithsonian Institution, 1888* (Washington, 1890), 587–96.

tribe who have at any time visited the headwaters of the Ohio were the few who joined the force that defeated General Braddock in 1755, and the peaceful delegations that have since visited Washington City.[27]

The first assertion he discusses in great detail, marshaling evidence from geological writings, historical documents, and personal observation. The so-called mound, it turns out, was but a large hill, or erosional remnant, left standing when the glaciers planed down the surrounding area. He concludes:

Systematic investigation by adepts may yet discover the mortuary customs of the Osages. Their cemeteries have perhaps not yet been found. They died, of course, but as yet we are ignorant of the disposition of their corpses.[28]

One of the greatest problems facing modern archaeologists is the fact that archaeological sites are daily being destroyed by vandalism, expansion of cities, industrial growth, and farming operations. Snyder was faced with the same problems and with apathy on the part of the public toward saving these resources. In his lifetime he had seen the great Beardstown mound leveled to obtain fill for the village streets.[29] He had witnessed the destruction of unusual mounds at Mitchell Station to make way for railroad construction. These and many other similar happenings aroused his intense concern. His greatest contribution to Illinois archaeology was his work for conservation of prehistoric remains and his attempts to stimulate state-sponsored professional study of Illinois' prehistory.

In this field he was particularly active in the effort to make Monks' Mound into a state park. He was a founder of a group called the "Monks of Cahokia" whose main purpose was to encourage the preservation of Monks' Mound as a park. For them he wrote a pamphlet, "The Prehistoric Mounds of Illinois," which was "respectfully submitted to call to the attention of the public a project, now before the General Assembly of Illinois, to make of these prehistoric mounds a State Park." This effort was not successful, but the movement was underway, and in 1933 the state of Illinois purchased Monks' Mound and the surrounding land for a state park. Recently the park has been expanded by further action of the Illinois Division of Parks and Memorials.

Along with conservation Snyder saw the need for greatly expanded scien-

27. *Ibid.*, 588.
28. *Ibid.*, 594.
29. "Sepulchral and Memorial Mounds," pp. 252–53 below.

tific work. In his time he was a "lone wolf" in scientific archaeological field work in the Midwest. He saw many people who operated as curio collectors and who looted sites only for individual gain and in complete disregard for the scientific value of the materials. He deplored the trend of archaeological journals in advertising Indian artifacts for sale since he recognized that this encouraged the looter.[30] The remedy for this piecemeal looting, he felt, was state sponsorship of careful and thorough field work by professional archaeologists. At the first meeting of the Illinois State Historical Society he presented these views in a paper, "The Field for Archaeological Research in Illinois."[31] Again he met with no immediate response, and it was not until twenty years later that any state agency sponsored archaeological work in Illinois.

TODAY THERE ARE many institutions conducting archaeological research within the state of Illinois, but we still face the same problems of conservation and research that troubled John Francis Snyder at the turn of the century. These problems are aggravated now by the great increase in population, the rapid industrial expansion of the last decades, the new farming techniques of plowing the soil deeper than ever before, and lack of concern on the part of the public for this heritage. National growth and development cannot be halted to preserve all archaeological sites, but public-spirited individuals, as Dr. Snyder was, can be aroused to see that provisions are made to salvage as much as possible of these remains. The present federal highway program has wisely provided for such situations, and many industries are recognizing the value of archaeological remains. But untrained and selfish vandals still dig—without making adequate records of that which they destroy—for the sole purpose of building up private collections and selling them at a profit. They are not interested in the study of the people who made these specimens. The words of Dr. Snyder written fifty years ago are still urgent and timely.

But some light may yet be shed . . . by persistent, systematic and intelligent study of the broad and inviting archaeological field our State presents. With some highly creditable exceptions, antiquarian research in Illinois has heretofore been conducted principally by curiosity mongers and mercenary vandals for selfish gain only. It demands and should receive, before it is too late, the earnest attention of active, scholarly workers in the interest of science.[32]

30. Elkin, "Snyder and Illinois Archaeology," 75.
31. *Transactions of the Illinois State Historical Society*, IV (1900): 21–29.
32. "Sepulchral and Memorial Mounds," p. 256 below.

In field work, in published articles, in insight, in conservation, and in promoting scientific investigation, Snyder was well ahead of his time. He was a voice "crying in the wilderness" and should be remembered today as "the ranking pioneer in archaeology of the state of Illinois." [33]

33. Warren King Moorehead, "John Francis Snyder," *Dictionary of American Biography,* XVII: 389.

PART IV

Selected Archaeological Writings

A GROUP OF ILLINOIS MOUNDS

THESE ARTICLES were first published by J. F. Snyder in *The Archaeologist* and *The American Archaeologist*. Reprinted here as examples of his work as a field archaeologist, they illustrate his careful recording of the materials he found. Since he utilized the data from these sites in his later writings, they can be considered fundamental reports. Much of the material Snyder obtained from the Baehr and Hemplull sites was purchased by the American Museum of Natural History. James B. Griffin has reported on this data, and his additional observations are reprinted following Snyder's own articles. The American Museum of Natural History has kindly supplied photographs of the Snyder material, and, together with Snyder's and Griffin's articles, they comprise a fairly complete site report on materials excavated by John Francis Snyder over sixty years ago. This is a fitting tribute to a man who lived before the advent of prehistoric archaeology as a science and yet had developed the ethics and precision of that discipline. Griffin's work provides evidence of the validity of Snyder's strong feeling of the necessity for recording the finds so that they might be utilized by others. Of all the moral responsibilities that stand out as cardinal for modern archaeology this is foremost. As examples of such reports, if for no other reason, these articles represent a significant aspect of Snyder's work as an archaeologist. M.L.F.

SECTIONS I AND 2 [*]

The five mounds represented in the diagram (Pl. 6) are on the west side of the Illinois River, thirteen miles below the city of Beardstown, and opposite the mouth of Indian Creek. When I first saw them, twenty-five years ago, they were covered, as were the surrounding bottom and bluffs, with a dense growth of timber and underbrush. At that time they were considerably higher than now, and large trees were growing upon them. Fifteen years ago, the land including them was purchased by Mr. Paul Baehr, who cleared it up and put it in cultivation; and the plow and rains have since then materially reduced their altitude. They are situated on the alluvial river bottom, above the highest line of overflow, and the three largest are so near each other that the margins of their bases are contiguous. When constructed, they were, at the nearest point, 200 yards from the river which has since receded half a

[*] Reprinted from *The Archaeologist*, III (March, April, 1895): 77-81, 109-13; both parts of the article bore the title "A Group of Illinois Mounds."

mile or more to the east, leaving a broad, shallow slough to mark its ancient channel. The long axis of the largest of the group, No. 1, coincides very nearly with the anticlinal line of a high ridge of the bluffs, 90 yards west of it. In a ravine on the South side of this isolated ridge is a spring of pure water; and on its northern slope, for the space of two or three acres, can be seen where the drift clay, constituting, in main, the material of the five mounds was dug or scraped out.

The circle in the diagram, designated by the letter A is a platform mound of clay, 98 feet in diameter, with level top, originally eight feet high, but now reduced by the plow and elements to half that height. On its western side there yet remains the vestige of a graded way from the surrounding level to its top. At C, and indeed all around this flat mound are scattered in great profusion flint chips, pot sherds and other debris, indicating the site of extensive primitive workshops.

The first attempt to explore these great mounds was made in the summer of 1890, by sinking a pit, 14 feet square, a little south of the center of the largest one, No. 1. The result of this investigation I embodied in a paper, read before Section H of the American Association for the Advancement of Science at its Madison, Wis., meeting in 1893, and subsequently published in the October, 1893, number of *The Archaeologist*. Last November the work of investigation was resumed. The excavation made in Mound No. 1, in 1890, was enlarged by taking out a cross section, 20 feet in width, and extending the opening to the west, as is indicated by the dotted lines in the figure. By this means, a more comprehensive view of the structure was obtained, and mistakes of my first imperfect observations in several important particulars were corrected. My recent work discovered no additional relics but 91 more black flints and one circular disc, three inches in diameter, of milk-white flint—the only disc of white flint found; and also, two extramural—that is, outside of the enclosure of logs—skeletons, totally decayed.

The initial step in rearing this stupendous monument—comprising not less than 30,000 cubic yards of earth—was laying down on the alluvial soil an oval-shaped layer of clay, ten feet in width by eighteen feet in length, and less than a foot in thickness. Over this, and extending beyond the limits of our excavation, the surface had been covered with sand, and the whole area burnt by a long continued fire, in which many human bones were incinerated. On the center of the clay oval were then laid three large hornstone nodules close together, and around and over these, as far as the clay oval extended, was a mass of black hornstone implements, that apparently had been thrown down in lots of from 6 to 20, with sand over and between each lot, as though to isolate them from each other. This deposit of 6,199 flints was covered with a stratum of clay, 10 inches in thickness; and on this another fire had been maintained for some time, in which a few bodies, or skeletons, had been cremated. Associated with these charred remains were found several large sea shells, some of them converted into drinking cups; sheets of mica, beads of shell and bone, stone celts, flint arrow and spear points, many bone awls, several bears' tusks perforated and partially drilled for the insertion of stone settings (Fig. 1, Pl. 7), pipes of stone (Fig. 2, Pl. 7), and of clay (Fig. 3, Pl. 7), a thin hammered, plume-shaped copper ornament (Fig. 4, Pl. 7), two spool-shaped ear-ornaments of copper (Fig. 5, Pl. 7) and many other objects, but all more or less destroyed by fire and natural decay. Then, all of this had been covered several feet in height with clay, and the whole enclosed with heavy logs from 12 to 20 inches in diameter (Fig. 5, Pl. 8), and the interstices between them "chinked" with large, rough stones. Finally, over all, the immense mass of clay was carried from the bluffs, at B, and heaped up to form this gigantic tumulus.

The material of this mound, No. 1, is altogether drift clay (loëss) homogeneous throughout, without admixture of sand or loam. For 22 feet down, nothing was encountered to distinguish it from a natural outlier of the bluff, or denote its artificial construction but occasional chips of flint, a few pottery fragments, and now and then a rude arrow-point or muscle shell. The few pot sherds seen in the clay exhibited good workmanship, some having the usual exterior lines and cord impressions; but those found within the log vault were exceedingly coarse and heavy. Fig. 6, Pl. 7, represents the only vessel found entire with the flints; its capacity is a pint and a half; its bottom is three-fourths of an inch thick, and the few knobs on its rough sides its only ornamentation.

The flints forming the nucleus of this mound are also very rudely fashioned; some are quite neatly finished, but the greater part of them are only slightly chipped and ill-shaped. The pattern to which they were aimed to conform is the mulberry leaf, pointed at one end and round at the other, as shown by Fig. 4, Pl. 10. The material from which they were wrought is glossy, black hornstone, occurring in nodules, not yet found anywhere in this state; [1] and in dimensions they will average seven inches in length by four in width; nearly an inch thick in the middle and chipped to an edge all around.

Mound No. 2 was opened in the same manner as was the first, by cutting transversely through its middle a trench 20 feet wide down to the bottom, as indicated by the dotted lines (Pl. 6). Before this was done, Mr. Baehr's sons had undertaken to remove the entire western end of the mound, but soon abandoned the work. Eighteen inches below the surface (c) was unearthed a skeleton that crumbled to the touch; and with it a fine copper axe nine inches in length, four inches broad at the cutting edge, and weighing three pounds. It bore no traces of wrappings of any kind. A little south of that point a shaft, 4 by 6 feet, was sunk down to the bottom level revealing nothing of interest. At *d,* near the lower, eastern edge of the mound, the plow turned out the skeleton of an Indian, an intrusvie burial, much decayed, and though the bones fell apart on handling them I succeeded in saving and preserving the skull.

On removing the section between the dotted lines, Pl. 6, from the second mound, its structure and buried contents were fully exposed. And it was plainly apparent that the *motive* for its erection was identical with that of No. 1. As in the inception of the first mound, the soil had been burnt and covered with sand. On the floor thus prepared had been laid eight large hornstone nodules, similar to the three in the first mound, arranged in pairs a foot apart, and the pairs eighteen inches from each other on a line east and west, or nearly so. On and around these nodules, covering an ovoid area 8 feet wide and 14 long, were deposited 5,300 hornstone implements, placed in four layers with a stratum of yellow sand between each layer. Flints of the largest size placed on edge, or verticle, encircled the entire deposit, and the whole mass was enclosed in a cribwork of large timbers and covered with logs and large flat stones. Immediately upon the upper layer of flints sand had been spread, and that was covered with clay several inches in depth. On this, five feet north-west of the center, was the skeleton of a middle aged person almost totally decayed; and, near it were nine large marine shells, and several awls, or pointed instruments, made of the fibulae of the deer; also 175 canine teeth of the coon perforated at the base, Fig. 1, Pl. 8, that had no doubt formed a necklace; and in one of the large sea shells were 75 small ones, (*Marginella*),

1. In a very interesting paper on "Material for Aboriginal Stone Implements," in the November, 1894, number of *The Archaeologist*, Mr. Gerard Fowke states that he has discovered nodules of this stone, in clay matrix, in Southern Indiana.

each ground through at the shoulder for the purpose of stringing them together to be worn as ornaments. With these were 80 shell beads, some
cylindrical, others almost spherical, and four small shark's teeth, triangular
with serrated edges, and also, pierced at the base to be worn as beads. A few
feet south of the first skeleton was another, even more decayed than the first,
with the head resting on a large sheet of mica. In proximity to it were the
jaws of a beaver, decomposed almost beyond recognition, resting on a small
copper axe [2] that had been wrapped in some sort of fabric, the oxide coating
of the metal still retaining a few shreds of it as well as the distinct impression
of a feather. Half way between the center and eastern border of the flint bed
was the "mound" pipe represented by Fig. 2, Pl. 8, drawn one-fourth of actual
size, and several more bone awls; and nearby, the "banner" stone of transparent, pink jasper, Fig. 3, Pl. 8.

The composition of this mound differed materially from that of No. 1.
From the log-encased sacrificial, or commemorative deposit, up to a few feet
of the outward surface, this massive sepulchre was a mottled mixture of
earths taken from different localities. Here a batch of bluff clay, about the
quantity an individual could conveniently carry in a basket or deer's skin;
next to it the same quantity of black loam from the bottom; and adjoining
these a similar lot of sandy mud interspersed with pebbles and muscle shells
from the margin of the river. And all through were innumerable muscle
shells, of which I identified seventeen species now living in the Illinois river;
and pot sherds, flint chips, and occasional arrow points. And throughout this
heterogeneous admixture there occurred, from the bottom to five feet of the
top, remains of numerous camp-fires, such as beds of ashes and charcoal,
burnt stones, pottery—fragments, and bones of various mammals and birds,
among which I recognized those of the buffalo, deer, coon, otter, beaver,
wolf, wild turkey, ducks and geese; while many others were undeterminable
on account of extreme decay. With these I found also human bones, singly
and in numbers, but so decomposed as to offer no support to any vague suspicion of cannibalism. The exterior of the mound, to the depth of four to six
feet, was of drift clay altogether, with no foreign objects but muscle shells,
that may have done service in scraping it up, for portage, into baskets or sacks.

Considering the rough, unfinished state of the greater part of the 6199

2. The proportions of this axe are: length 5¾ inches; width at edge 3 inches, at other end
1¾ inches; weight 17 ounces; thickness ⅝ths of an inch.

flints in the first mound, had they been discovered at shallow depth below the surface of the ground, unprotected by vault or mound, as many small deposits of unfinished flints are found in all parts of the country, we could not well have escaped the inference that they were a stock of raw material stored there for safety until convenient to work them up into finished implements. The testimony of their environment however is fatal to this supposition, and proof that final, permanent, deposition was the specific motive of their burial.

Further proof of this—if any is required—was revealed by the deposit at the base of mound No. 2. Here, laid down with the same ceremoneous observances, and with the same protection of large timbers and stones enveloped in many thousands of cubic yards of earth, associated with human remains and art relics, were the amazing number of *fifty-three hundred* finely proportioned, smoothly chipped, and artistically finished, flint implements. The material of all is black hornstone, and they range, in form, from that of Fig. 8 * to Fig. 4, Pl. 10; and, in size, from three to eight inches in length by from two to five inches in width. Many of them seem to have never been used, but a large proportion bear the marks of long-continued service.

Mound No. 3 has not yet been explored.

The small conical mound, No. 4, was almost entirely removed without disclosing much of importance. Its composition was very similar to that of mound No. 2, a mixture of different soils and clay; in places very hard and compact, and quite loose in others; with ash-heaps, charcoal, burnt stones, muscle shells, and bones of animals and birds scattered about all through it. Its exterior coating, for two feet in depth, was unmixed bluff clay. A foot and a half below the surface, near its apex, were found two skeletons, probably of recent Indians, much decayed; and at its base, resting on the alluvial soil, were two other human skeletons so nearly crumbled to dust that it was impossible to ascertain the relative positions they occupied. The inhumation of these two, at the mound's base, seems to have been effected with no unusual arrangement or care, and the only product of their arts buried with them was a necklace of eighty bone beads remarkably well preserved. A view of the interior structure of these great mounds cannot fail to produce the impression that they are very old. All the intrinsic evidence observed—the complete

* Snyder mentioned another Fig. 8 in the text but reproduced only one figure—the copper ax that appears here as Fig. 7, Pl. 7. He did not illustrate the flint implement mentioned above.

decay of enclosed osseous remains and large timbers; the disintegration of associated mica plates and marine shells; and the heavy incrustation and cementing together of the buried flints with *patina*, or ferruginous carbonates of lime, considered with the recession of the river from its ancient course, at the period when these strange monuments were commenced, to its present distant channel—fully attest their vast antiquity. They were probably not raised to their present proportions by single continued efforts, but by periodical additions of materials after long intervals of rest, or absence of their builders. Dark lines of demarkation, conforming to the outward contour of the tumulus, shown in the cross section of No. 1 at its center, Fig. 5, Pl. 8, (too distinct and too numerous in the cut), can only be interpreted by this suggestion.

The most remarkable feature of the relics found entombed at the bases of these interesting monuments is the peculiar type of the human crania. Owing to the destructive agencies of time, fire, and crushing of superincumbent earth, no entire skull could be secured; but enough fragments were obtained to enable me to form a correct estimate of the characteristics of all. They were short, or *brachycephalic*; with unusual thickness of parietal tables; high, heavy malar bones, and very prognathous jaws. Figs. 1 and 2, Pl. 9, faithfully portray the enormous development of supraorbital ridges and well-nigh total absence of forehead exhibited in *all* the specimens recovered. This form of crania has occasionally been noticed in some of the most ancient mounds of the Mississippi valley. Col. J. W. Foster figures one from the Kennicott mound;[3] and Prof. A. J. Conant[4] gives an account of two obtained in a burial mound in Southeast Missouri, identical in conformation, and apparently of as great antiquity, as those buried in these mounds on the Illinois river. The cuts given by those authors to represent the skulls they describe are fair reproductions of *all* the crania I found here. The numbers of individuals interred in this group of mounds, presenting similar cranial and facial types, though large, are yet probably too limited to justify the conclusion that the development constituted the *race* type of the people inhabiting this region at the beginning of the mound-building era. An ideal restoration of them, based upon the few bones exhumed, not yet quite reverted to dust, depicts figures compactly and strongly built, not above the average American Indian

3. "Pre-Historic Races." By J. W. Foster, LL.D., Chicago, 1873, *pp.* 278–80. On the latter page is also figured an equally remarkable skull from a mound in Haas's Park.
4. "Foot-prints of Vanished Races." By A. J. Conant, A.M., St. Louis, 1879, *pp.* 106–7.

in stature, with protruding jaws, fierce black eyes, and retreating foreheads covered with a mass of coarse, black hair that joined enormous, shaggy eyebrows; hideous in features as the gorilla.

In former papers [5] I have expressed my views regarding the *incentive* prompting these surprising deposits of flint implements. With no desire to invite discussion of this question at present, I cannot avoid noticing the persistency of the belief—confined however, in general, to those having no personal knowledge of them—that they are only *cachés* of raw material, temporarily stored for security, with the view of being withdrawn when wanted and rechipped into finished weapons and tools. I confess that I cannot quite comprehend how the *caché* theory can be satisfactorily harmonized with the ceremonies evidently practiced when the flints were laid down; with their associated human remains and art relics; and with the idea of permanent and final interment plainly conveyed by their enclosure in vaults of ponderous logs and stones, reinforced by not less than twenty-five feet of earth over and on all sides of them.

In this connection the significant fact must be stated that in all the mass of "shop refuse" around the "temple mound" A, I did not find a dozen chips or splinters of hornstone, or black flint.

These recent investigations have removed from my mind all doubts—if any existed—of the sacred, or religious, character of these singular flint deposits; and fully confirmed the correctness of the axiom I heretofore formulated, *i.e.* "that *all* original mound interments were, by the mound makers, considered sacred, and intended to be complete and final, never again to be disturbed."

SECTION 3 [*]

In the periodical that preceded this magazine, The Archaeologist, for March and April, 1895, was published the report of my partial exploration of a group of large mounds situated on the alluvial bottom of the Illinois river, in Brown county, Illinois, thirteen miles below the city of Beardstown.

---

5. Smithsonian Annual Report for 1876, *pp.* 433 *et seq.* Proceedings of the American Association for the Advancement of Science, Vol. XLII, 1894. Also, *The Archaeologist,* Vol. I, No. 10, pp. 181–186.

* Although this section originally appeared in another magazine, it is a continuation of the earlier report; reprinted from *The American Archaeologist,* II (Jan., 1898): 16–23.

As many readers of this new "Archaeologist" may not have seen that report; and for a clearer understanding of the results of my later investigations in the same field, I will briefly summarize the account then given of my observations there. In the accompanying diagram, Pl. 6, the circle A, is a platform mound of clay, 98 feet in diameter, with level top, originally eight feet high, but now reduced by the plow and rains to half that height. On this western side may still be seen the vestige of a graded way, ascending from the surrounding plain to its top. Fifty yards north of this is the mound, marked 1 in the plat, 180 feet in length, 100 feet wide, and 30 feet high; at the base of which, at its center, we found 6199 rudely-chipped discs of glossy, black flint, known as hornstone, resting on a low platform of hard-burned clay, in or upon a bed of ashes containing innumerable fragments of charred human bones. The flints, averaging six inches in diameter and an inch in thickness, were covered with a stratum of clay a foot in thickness, upon which another fire had been maintained for some time, incinerating a few more human bodies, or skeletons, together with many large marine shells, sheets of mica, stone implements and various ornaments of bone, shell and stone, that no doubt had been cast into the flames as votive offerings, and were more or less destroyed by the fierce heat. All this had been enclosed in a cribwork of large logs and rough rocks brought from the hills near by, and in time covered by the immense heap of bluff clay without admixture of other materials. The only objects of copper discovered in this mound were a thin, plume-like head-piece, Fig. 4, Pl. 7, and a pair of spool-shaped ear rings, Fig. 5, Pl. 7, that evidently had embellished the same head. The only pottery associated with the fire-scarred deposits, and, indeed, all that was seen in the entire mound, from a foot or two below its outer surface, was a small vase, Fig. 6, Pl. 7, and a few sherds of similar composition. This vessel, of a little over a pint capacity, is made of red clay, not of this locality, and coarse gravel or crushed rock, thick and uneven, and was rudely molded in the hands of the potter.

Mound No. 2 is contiguous to the first, of the same oblong form, but not quite so large. It was concluded to commence its examination by cutting down the western end with plow and scrapers; but this was abandoned after having reduced the altitude of that portion a little less than two feet. In the progress of this work a decayed skeleton was unearthed at C, eighteen inches below the surface. With it were a few shell beads and a fine copper axe, of the flat, hammer-marked variety, nine inches in length, four inches wide at the edge, and weighing three pounds. A cross trench was then commenced, and finally a large pit was sunk down to the base, where, some distance from the center of the structure, was found, in a bed of yellow sand, the surprising number of 5300 neatly-finished, leaf-shaped implements, of the uniform type represented by Fig. 4, Pl. 10, ranging in size from two to seven inches in length, by from one and a half to three inches in width, and chipped from black flint almost identical with that found in the form of discs in the first mound. No signs of fire were discovered about this deposit. Like that of the first mound, it was enclosed in a crib of ponderous logs, and resting on the clay-covered flints were several human skeletons with bone and stone implements, mica plates, marine shells and other relics of personal adornment. Among these remains was a small copper axe, lying on the lower jaw of a beaver; and nearby, among decayed bones of a middle-aged individual, was recovered a large platform pipe made of white marble, Fig. 2, Pl. 8.

The composition of this mound was totally different from that of the first. No. 1 was a compact mass of drift clay (Loess) with nothing to distinguish it from a natural outlier of the bluffs; but No. 2, above and around the clay covering of the primal deposits, at its base, was built up of varied ingredients in separate quantities, that could be conveniently carried at once in baskets or deer skins, and dumped together; sand, black muck, clay and gravel, in mottled confusion; and interspersed all through with beds of ashes and charcoal, burnt stones, mussel shells and bones of birds, fishes, turtles and several species of wild animals, the familiar debris of camp fires; plainly indicating that some of the builders, as was the case with shell-heap makers, dwelt upon the mound while increasing its dimensions.

Work was resumed on mound No. 1 in September last by cutting a trench twenty feet wide from the center to the western extremity, as shown in diagram, Fig. 1, Pl. 12. Previous to this, intrusive burials of single bodies had been exhumed, from a foot beneath the surface, at K, and A[a] on the eastern end. Twenty inches below the original upper surface—at B, was brought to light a few crumbling bones and a beautiful copper axe with curved edge, Fig. 7, Pl. 7, five inches long and three wide at the broadest place, weighing 40 ounces. Six feet southeast of this point, at C, was found the little headless image, Fig. 2, Pl. 12, shown in front and rear view, of actual size, resting on a sheet of mica badly broken, with several flint chips; and nearby, where a skeleton's head had been, were two ear rings of bone, once polished, and yet in a fair state of preservation, Fig. 4, Pl. 8, full size. These exquisite ornaments were made from cross-sections of the long bones of some large animal, cut from the solid, articular ends. Fifteen feet west of B was the artistic vase, Fig. 2, Pl. 13, very symmetrical in form, made of dark clay, thin and hard, and neatly decorated with indentations around the neck, and thumb nail impressions lower down. Nearby, at H, was another skeleton in the last stages of decay, holding in the right hand (apparently) the small, polished and partially drilled stone, Fig. 3, Pl. 13. Over the breast were several flat, ovoid beads, made of shell, Fig. 3, Pl. 9, full size, perforated through the long diameter for fastening to the sash or garment, and each having on one side two holes drilled an eighth of an inch deep to receive brilliant stone or jewel settings. (Among the propitiatory sacrifices offered up, on the pyre over the mass of flint discs, in this mound I rescued, in fair condition, a few, of many, large teeth of the grizzly bear that had formed the necklace, or adorned the girdle, of some swarthy brave. Each one was perforated at the maxillary end for the purpose of suspension, and on one side two shallow holes were drilled, as are the beads just described, in one of which, Fig. 1, Pl. 7, a small ruby was still intact.) On each side of this ancient native's head was an ear ring, Fig. 4, Pl. 9, actual size, of fine-grained, polished wood, black and solid as ebony, and wonderfully well-preserved.

In close proximity to this burial were lying nearby the half of each of two different earthen vases, six inches in diameter, of fine, dark material, and elegant forms. And only a few feet in another direction, and a little higher up at I [Fig. 1, Pl. 12], I was much surprised to discover another small vase of red clay, nearly entire, and almost identical in size, texture, material and coarseness with the one found some time before near the base of this mound, Fig. 6, Pl. 7. Mr. Clarence B. Moore found pottery of this description in some of the sand mounds of Florida, and similar vases from Alabama have come under my notice. Associated here with fictile ware of much lighter type, suggests its importation and precludes any theory of evolution of the ceramic art at this locality.

At G, unconnected with any other object, the ornament of sheet copper, Fig. 1, Pl. 13, full size, was turned up. It is very smooth and as accurately corrugated as though pressed by machinery. It seems to have been with those old savages a favorite form of decoration, as several of the same type have been found in Ohio, Florida, Georgia and other states.

At D the spade turned out another fine copper axe of the gouge style, the exact counterpart of Fig. 7, Pl. 7, so nearly resembling it that the two can scarcely be distinguished from each other, and look as though they may have been cast in the same mold. On the flat side of this one was the canine tooth of a wolf, probably buried in the same bark or skin envelope with it.

So far in our exploration of this portion of the mound, all the remains mentioned occupied positions on the same general horizon, twenty inches, more or less, beneath the original upper surface. Continuing the excavation sixteen inches deeper we encountered, at E, another surprise. As though carefully wrapped together when buried, in a woven fabric of vegetable fiber, that left its impress on the oxidized metal, were a copper axe, of the thin, hammer-marked kind, Fig. 1, Pl. 10, six inches long by three wide, and weighing one and a half pounds; the terra cotta image, Fig. 2, Pl. 10, drawn full size, and the small vase, Fig. 3, Pl. 10, also of actual size. The tiny vase—of about an ounce capacity—is a curious anomaly, having but few, if any, counterparts in the whole range of prehistoric pottery of the Mississippi Valley. It is of the same color and material as the little images, perfectly proportioned, hard-burned and polished. Its convoluted base is the quarter of an inch thick, gradually thinning to an edge at the rim.

The terra cotta images are as foreign to this region as is the diminutive vase. Col. C. C. Jones (Antiquities of the Southern Indians, pp. 430–31), says in treating of this class of art remains in the South: "Next in order of durability are small images formed of burnt clay and modeled after the similitude of birds and animals and of man. These occur in various parts of the State, and vary in height from three to seven inches. Those which represent the human figures are little more than rude, terra-cotta dolls, clumsily fashioned." This description accords well with the specimens he figures and with those in his collection. The two found here, though not anatomically accurate, are far superior, both in conception and execution, to those Colonel Jones describes, and, as art creations, will rank well with the best prehistoric sculptures occurring north of Mexico. They are hard-burned and smoothly finished. Both are nude; the smaller one wearing a small, pointed apron, held in place by a belt around the loins; the other having only an elaborate head covering, bearing some resemblance to the Roman helmet, and pully-shaped ear rings in its disproportioned ears. The appearance of the fractures indicate that they were purposely mutilated before burial.

Scarcely a mile north of this lowland group of mounds, on one of the highest points of the bluffs that bound the immediate valley of the Illinois river on the west, is another majestic, earthen monument of the same class, and beyond doubt of the same age and erected by the same people. The view obtained from its summit is truly magnificent. The winding river far below, here and there hidden by dense forests, is seen for miles in either direction; its broad expanse of wooded bottoms diversified on either hand by small, sunny prairies and miniature lakes, with a grand background of picturesque bluffs in the distant east, presents a landscape of rare beauty.

There was surely a tinge of refined sentiment in the savage that responded to the esthetic and sublime in Nature, and moved him to seek such charming spots as this for the last resting places of his cherished dead.

This mound, on the very crest of the bluff, is 125 feet in length and 80 feet in width, and 15 feet high at either end with a slight saddle-like depression in the middle, shown in Fig. 1, Pl. 11. Its composition is unmixed clay identical with that of the bluff upon which it rests. Its exploration was commenced last fall and prosecuted for some time with discouraging results. The plow and scraper were put into operation to excavate a cross section near its middle, but soon discontinued as impracticable because of the steep grade on the southern side. The plan then adopted as more feasible was to remove the entire eastern end; and this has not yet been accomplished. At D, on the surface projection of the mound, Fig. 2, Pl. 11, a very chalky, intrusive skeleton was reposing, scarcely a foot beneath the sod. The skull of this individual was remarkably thick, with very receding forehead and an abnormal vertical depression in the mid-line of the occiput, three-eighths of an inch deep. Two feet below the surface, at E, were laid, with some degree of order, a cart load of rough stones in a pile nearly four feet in diameter. Carefully removing them, they were found to cover nothing artificial but five small beads, each the quarter of an inch in diameter; three were made of copper, one of bone and one of pearl; the latter considerably decayed, but still preserving its natural luster. At the depth of two and a half feet, at C, lying close together, were disclosed three plummet-shaped pendants, almost exactly alike, wrought from a marble-like, compact, silicious stone, dark-colored and finely polished. Their form is well represented in Fig. 3, Pl. 11, drawn one-third of their actual size. At about the same depth, at B, the plow struck another mass of rough stones that covered the partly-cremated remains of a human skeleton. A quantity of ashes and charcoal, the fire-stained earth and burnt bones, were proof that when the mound had attained half its present height at this point a shallow pit was sunk in it, and in that the fire was kindled, and the body, or dry skeleton, consumed by its heat and then covered over with a few inches of clay, on which the rocks were heaped. The only relic that, with a small portion of the skeleton, escaped destruction by this fire, was that shown by Fig. 4, Pl. 11, known by the absurd and meaningless name of "banner-stone" —when made of stone. This one, however, was cut out of the thick part of some large marine shell, and is a little over three inches in length, an inch wide and almost as much in thickness, and highly polished.

No additional burials or deposits were met in the great mass of earth re-moved from that point down to the bottom, where the spades exposed the original surface of the bluff to the fresh air and sunlight for the first time in centuries past. Only half a dozen fragments of (recent) pottery were seen in all this work—and they occurred near the top surface of the mound—and several single valves of the Unio, that had served as clay scrapers, and a few broken flints. The absence of pottery here, however, must not be accepted as conclusive that the builders of this mound were ignorant of the art of manu-facturing it. They may have used earthenware at their camps about the fine springs at the foot of the bluffs and dispensed with it in their labors at the summit.

The bluff top having been denuded of its mound covering for a space, it was noticed that, at A, in an elliptical area of eight by seven feet, the ground was soft and yielding, as though it had, at some former time, been disturbed. This supposition was soon verified on digging into it. The looser dirt, though identical with the balance, contained streaks of darker earth, occasional flint chips, numerous shells, and at the depth of five feet, the broken horn of a deer was thrown out. As the spading progressed the walls of this well, or pit, became fully defined, firm and solid and still retaining in places the marks or cuts made by flint or copper tools used in its first excavation. The pit, A, Fig. 1, Pl. 11, was found to be very nearly twelve feet deep, eight feet across in its long diameter, east and west, and seven feet wide. Down ten and a half feet the spades grated against a layer of rough stones, that had been carried up from the carboniferous outcrops in the lower ravines, similar to those seen before at B and E. Each rock was carefully removed and the loose dirt all cleaned out, disclosing the totally decayed skeletons of eight persons, so crushed and shattered by the superincumbent stone and earth covering as to be scarcely recognizable, rendering it impossible to make out the relative positions they occupied when placed there. There were no ashes or fire stains, but instead, a coating of black loam on the floor of the pit, the residium from decomposition of the bed prepared for the dead, presumably of bark, skins, and perhaps fine furs. With only one of the entombed bodies had been interred worldly possessions of a kind that survived the lapse of ages. We are at liberty to imagine that this one was a distinguished personage, and the other seven, his wives or slaves, slain at his death to attend him in the other world. Let that be as it may; if in his day the finances were based upon a single copper standard, he was reasonably well fixed. Near his head was a nodular nugget of pure, native copper—unwrought raw material—weighing 24 pounds; and along his sides were ranged ten copper axes. Around his neck were three necklaces; one of oblong, large beads, made from the columella of marine shells, perforated longitudinally; another of over 200 incisor teeth of the squirrel bored at the root, shown, with one of the beads, in Fig. 1, Pl. 8, and the third was composed of 283 globular, copper beads, solid, and smooth as if moulded and then polished. The largest ones, in the middle of the neck-lace, are half an inch in diameter, and they gradually decrease in size at the ends to the quarter of an inch. The cord that suspended them, a two-strand, twisted twine, apparently of hemp, was still in place, but crumbled at the touch. Across his breast, and following each other an inch apart, were five plates cut out of fluor spar, each six inches in length, two and [one] half inches wide, square-cornered, and the fourth of an inch in thickness, as smooth as glass, and in the sunlight as resplendent as burnished silver. Each was per-forated with two holes, one two inches from either end, for attachment to the dress. The copper axes are of three types, three of them of the thin, hammer-marked sort, Fig. 1, Pl. 10, three inches wide and seven, nine and ten inches long respectively. Three are of the celt shape, Fig. 5, Pl. 11, com-pact, very smooth and sharp-edged; and three, four and four and a quarter inches long. The other four are flaring at the edge, Fig. 6, Pl. 11, heavy, with even, well-finished surfaces, weighing from two to four pounds each, and are ornamented by cuts a line in depth and an inch to an inch and a half in length, on both sides, at irregular intervals of half an inch or more, seemingly made with a cold chisel or other edged tool.

SECTION 4 [*]

The specimens from the Baehr component now in the American Museum include a good cross section of the articles described by Snyder. There is no record of the mound from which the various specimens came, but, since the entire group is undoubtedly of Hopewellian character, this lack of information is not of great importance.

The flint specimens mentioned by Snyder are represented by 4 nodules of flint, 4,742 flint blades, and 94 blue flint blades.

The bone artifacts include 3 copper-stained beaver jaws, a number of loose canine teeth, 5 antler arrow points, and 10 deer or elk split metatarsal awls or skewers. The longest of these awls measures 32 cm., and the shortest 20 cm. (Pl. 14). On five of them the articular surface forms a handle. One of them is partially copper-stained and has a handle which, on its rounded end, has five deeply incised notches converging on the center. Animal canine teeth perforated for a necklace number 141 whole pieces and 20 loose and broken ones.

The shell pieces include beads, ornaments, and containers. One string of beads consists of 72 short cylindrical shells ranging from 7 mm. to 2 cm. in length. A string of 165 small perforated shells include Marginella, Campeloma, Goniobasis, and Helisoma shells (Pl. 15, Fig. 2). There are 26 miscellaneous shell beads preserved from the two mounds of cylindrical, disk, and small globular shapes. A small flat ovoid shell ornament with two holes bored at each end and two bored from the base, so that it could be sewed flat onto a skin or cloth, is shown in Pl. 15, Fig. 1. There are whole and broken portions of 16 Busycon shells, two of which are perforated, and two "conch" shells. Two perforated vessels of Cypraea and two portions of Triton shell vessels complete the list of shell artifacts in the collection.

Four sheets of mica and a piece of galena mentioned by Snyder are in the collection. The largest copper ax which he mentions is also there. It is ovate oblong with bit excurvate, and measures 23.1 cm. long, 11 cm. wide at the

---

[*] This section is extracted from the chapter entitled "The Baehr and Hemplull Components," in James B. Griffin, *Additional Hopewell Material from Illinois* (*Indiana Historical Society Prehistory Research Series*, Vol. II, No. 3, Indianapolis, Dec., 1941), 184–95, 204–6. Griffin's discussion of the Baehr and Hemplull components included extensive quotations from the three Snyder articles reprinted here.

bit, and 7 cm. wide at the poll. The thickness in the center line from bit to poll varies 6 mm., 1.1 cm., and 5 mm.

The pottery collection from this mound group is of particular interest and helps to provide valuable cultural correlations. Unfortunately none of the vessels are whole, but, from a knowledge of similar vessels, it can be definitely stated that there are two general types of pottery represented.

The first type, represented mainly by body sherds, is characterized by grit tempering, medium to medium-coarse texture, a hardness of 2–2.5 to 2.5, and a thickness of from 5 to 9 mm. Most of the sherds have smooth to smoothed outer surfaces—a characteristic of a majority of the Hopewellian pottery from Fulton County, Illinois, sites (Pl. 17, Figs. 8 and 10). Four sherds have surfaces marked by cord-wrapped-paddle impressions (Pl. 17, Figs. 6 and 9; Pl. 16, Fig. 8).

One basal sherd of this group is from a flat-bottomed jar whose side walls rise vertically from the base (Pl. 16, Fig. 10). Its exterior surface is smoothed over cord markings. The base is 7 mm. thick, and the side wall 1.3 cm. thick. One rim sherd shows a smoothed surface and a rounded slightly everted lip (Pl. 16, Fig. 7).

Closely connected with this type, if not of it, are three rim sherds with punched-out nodes arranged in a horizontal row and placed in a smooth horizontal band (Pl. 17, Figs. 2, 4, and 5). Both above and below this horizontal band are horizontal rows of vertical or oblique stamp impressions. On one (Fig. 2) the lower rows are of the rocked-dentate-stamp type. The lips of these sherds are flattened and slope inward. The rim thickness is 8 mm., and two of the lips are also 8 mm., while the third has a width of 1.2 cm. The rims are straight.

The majority of the sherds of the second type are limestone tempered; their texture is medium fine, and their hardness is practically the same as that of the first type. One of the characteristic features is a straight vertical rim, the upper segment of which projects slightly from the rim wall and bears a band decorated in some manner, usually with incising (Pl. 16, Figs. 2–5; Pl. 17, Figs. 1 and 3). The major portion of the rim is smoothed to burnished and is not often decorated. Three of these rim sherds which conform to the generalized type in the absence of decoration of the lower rim have interesting rim bands. One (Pl. 16, Fig. 5) has a crosshatched rim band with a horizontal row of hemiconical punctates made from the left directly below. Another (Pl. 16, Fig. 3) has a series of right-to-left slanting, closely spaced, narrow, shallow incised lines above a horizontal row of hemiconical punctates made from the left. The third (Pl. 16, Fig. 4) has a smoothed upper rim band above a horizontal row of small punctates made from the right.

A specialized variant of this type found at the site has narrow, shallow horizontal lines on the rim and a horizontal row of small closely spaced punctate impressions directly beneath it (Pl. 17, Fig. 1). The lower rim is marked by the points of a series of open base triangles extending up from the body. The areas between the triangles are smoothed, while the areas within are decorated with closely spaced, narrow, vertical, shallow incised lines. There are four rim sherds from vessels of this variant type, and two of them, at least, show that their bodies had four lobes.

The lips on all but two of the seven rim sherds of the second type are narrowed and rounded (Fig. 4, Pl. 13). They measure 3 mm. in thickness and the rims 5 mm. in thickness. One sherd with a narrow and flattened lip has the same dimensions as the prevailing type. The rim bearing the crosshatched band, mentioned above, has a flattened lip 7 mm. wide; the rim is 5.5 mm. thick. One rim (Pl. 16, Fig. 1) has a diameter at the lip of 9.4 cm. and at the lower rim of 8.3 cm.; another (Pl. 16, Fig. 2) measures 9.4 cm. and 8 cm. at the same points respectively.

One limestone-tempered rim sherd is from a bowl (Pl. 16, Fig. 6). It has a smooth upper rim band 1 cm. wide, terminated by a medium-wide, medium-deep horizontal incised line. Between this line and another one of similar character is an area 1 cm. wide, decorated with closely spaced, horizontal dentate stamp impressions. The limestone-tempered body sherd, shown in Pl. 16, Fig. 9, probably belongs to this second type. It has a smooth surface marked by two parallel, curvilinear, medium-wide, deep incised lines.

The pottery types can be briefly described as follows. Type names have been given to them which may or may not prove satisfactory. Only the characteristics actually present at this site for each type have been listed.

NAPLES STAMPED POTTERY

Texture	grit
Temper	varies from medium fine to medium coarse, predominantly medium
Hardness	2–2.5 and 2.5
Color	various shades of brown to gray; considerable blackening on some sherds
Surface finish	cord-wrapped-paddle impressions on entire outer surface or smoothed over cord markings
Decoration	
Technique	dentate stamp
	rocked dentate stamp
	punching to form horizontal row of nodes
Design	horizontal rows of vertical or obliquely placed dentate stamp impressions on rim
	horizontal row of nodes on rim a short distance below the lip
Rim	straight and vertical, or slightly flared
	diameter at base of rim somewhat less than lip or body
Lip	flattened – slopes inward
Body	one flattened base; one conoidal base
Thickness	lips 8 mm.; rim and body 5 to 12 mm.; base, 1 specimen, 7 mm.

HOPEWELL ZONED INCISED

Temper	limestone – which sometimes has leached out leaving holes
Texture	medium fine to medium
Hardness	2–2.5 and 2.5
Color	exterior, dark to reddish brown or gray; paste, gray; evidence of smoke discoloration on all sherds
Surface finish	interior smooth; exterior smooth to polished
Decoration	
Technique	incising by narrow, shallow lines or medium-wide, medium-deep lines
	punctating by small hollow cylinder at an angle to rim surface
	dentate stamping
Design	crosshatched incised lines on cambered rim
	parallel horizontal or oblique lines on cambered rim
	horizontal row of punctate impressions at base of cambered rim (Punctates on majority of vessels appear to have been made from the left.)
	parallel incised lines within outlined areas set off from plain areas

	dentate stamp impressions in bands set off from plain areas
	curvilinear plain bands outlined by paralleling incised lines
Rim	straight, vertical
	upper segment cambered and decorated
Lip	narrowed and rounded
	narrowed and flattened
Body	lobed at shoulder level
Thickness	lip 3 to 7 mm.; rim 5 to 7 mm.

In addition to the above-listed pottery traits, the following culture traits from the Baehr component were obtained from Snyder's reports and from the collection in the American Museum.

Topographical position, structural and burial traits:

1. Mounds in river valley
2. Mounds of various sizes in close proximity
3. Ovate and circular mounds
4. Basket-load structure in mounds
5. Village refuse in mounds
6. Ash beds in mounds
7. Prepared clay floor at base of mounds
8. Clay floor covered with sand layer
9. Prepared mound floor used for cremation
10. Large deposit of flint disks arranged in small groups, with groups separated by sand
11. Log structure chinked with stone covering ceremonial cremation platform
12. Burials on original ground surface
13. Cremation on prepared platform
14. Artifacts of special excellence placed with burials
15. Large amount of artifacts with some burials
16. Ceremonial destruction of artifacts
17. Extended burials (?)
18. Burials distributed throughout mound
19. Pottery vessels with burials
20. Burials in poor state of preservation
21. Skull of burial placed on mica sheet
22. Intrusive (?) burials in mound

Stone artifacts:

1. Large ceremonial cache of flint disks
2. Flint nodules ceremonially placed

3. Celts
4. Flint arrow points
5. Flint spear points
6. Mica sheets
7. Shark-tooth pendant (petrified?)
8. Banner stone of "pink jasper"
9. Galena

Bone artifacts:

1. Beads
2. Bear canines perforated for insertion (of pearls?)
3. Bear canine pendants
4. Awls
5. Ear spool, peripheral groove perforated
6. Perforated raccoon teeth
7. Long deer or elk split metatarsal skewers
8. Antler arrow points
9. Antler handle

Shell artifacts:

1. Large marine shell containers
2. Marine shells – Busycon, Triton, and Cypraea
3. Marginella beads
4. Campeloma beads
5. Goniobasis beads
6. Helisoma beads
7. Cylindrical beads
8. Disk beads
9. Spherical or globular beads
10. Ovoid beads
11. Flattened ovoid shell ornament with diagonal perforations at two ends

Copper artifacts:

1. Ear spools of "Hopewell" type
2. "Plume"
3. Conjoined tube
4. Axes, ovate oblong, bit excurvate
5. Gouge or adze

Pipes:

1. Stone platform pipe, convex base, spool-shaped bowl centrally placed
2. Stemless clay pipe with incised human effigy face

Miscellaneous traits:

1. Fabric impressions on copper ax
2. Feather impressions on copper ax
3. Pottery figurines
4. Ear spool (of wood?), peripheral groove perforated

There are few types of artifacts from the Hemplull site and no pottery at all in the collection in the American Museum. Its most interesting feature is worked copper, particularly copper axes. The axes are illustrated on Plates 20 and 21. Three of them are rather small (Pl. 20, Figs. 4–6) with an ovate-oblong shape, and one of this group (Fig. 4) has a slightly flaring bit. Three of the large axes (Pl. 20, Figs. 1–3) are ovate oblong, with a narrow straight poll, and an excurvate, slightly flaring bit. The remaining four (Pl. 21) have the same basic shape as the others, but are distinguished by a sharply flaring, excurvate bit, and on each of the two flat sides they have irregularly placed, short horizontal gashes. The size of each of these axes is given below in centimeters.[6]

Plate No.	Length	Width at poll	Width at bit	Center thickness at bit	Thickness at center	Thickness at poll
Pl. 20, Fig. 5 ......10.1		3.8	5.8	.4	.5	.6
Pl. 20, Fig. 4 ......11.1		4.8	8.3	.9	1.1	.8
Pl. 20, Fig. 6 ......14.2		5.5	6.9	.9	1.1	1.0
Pl. 20, Fig. 2 ......21.7		4.5	10.1	.6	1.4	.8
Pl. 20, Fig. 3 ......25.7		5.1	10.8	1.1	1.3	.9
Pl. 20, Fig. 1 ......26.5		4.6	10.4	.6	.7	.5
Pl. 21, Fig. 2 ......19.1		5.5	11.9	.6	.7	1.0
Pl. 21, Fig. 1 ......21.4		6.8	13.3	1.1	1.5	1.4
Pl. 21, Fig. 4 ......21.7		6.7	12.1	.7	1.2	1.0
Pl. 21, Fig. 3 ......22.6		5.7	11.4	1.0	1.2	1.2

Two strings of small copper beads from this mound are now in the American Museum. One of these has 134 flattened, spherical beads that average 1.1 cm. in diameter and are 8 mm. thick (Pl. 18). The other string is of 43 double-conical beads which have a diameter of 1.35 cm. and a thickness of 1.1 cm. (Pl. 19). There are also three strings of shell beads with a total of 88 beads. A representative string is shown on Pl. 19. A typical bead is 2 cm. long and 1.7 cm. in diameter. They were in all probability made from the

6. These axes are catalogued in the American Museum, nos. 20/6651–6660.

columella of large marine univalves such as *Busycon perversum*. Some fifty
or more fragmentary, small mammal canine teeth had been perforated near
the root for suspension.

Three plummets (Pl. 22, Figs. 4–6) with grooves around the narrow end
have the following lengths and greatest diameters: 8.2 by 3.7 cm.; 7 by 3.6
cm.; and 6.2 by 3.6 cm. A limestone plano-convex bar gorget or boat stone
with two perforations is 9.9 cm. long, 2.9 cm. high, and 3.1 cm. wide (Pl. 22,
Fig. 8).

Of special interest in this mound was the finding of five rectanguloid fluor
spar gorgets of exceptional workmanship (Pl. 22, Figs. 1–3, 7, 9). They are
all very nearly the same size, and each has two centrally placed perforations
drilled from one side only.[7]

Plate	No.	Length	Width	Edge Thickness	Center Thickness
22	1.........16.6		7.8	.5	.8
22	9.........17.1		7.8	.6	.7
22	7.........16.3		7.6	.5	.75
22	2.........14.5		7.7	.5	.7
22	3.........15.4		7.8	.6	.8

7. These gorgets are catalogued in the American Museum, nos. 20/6671–6675.

PREHISTORIC ILLINOIS

The Brown County Ossuary

This article, reprinted from the *Journal of the Illinois State Historical Society*, Vol. I, Nos. 2–3 (double number, July–Oct., 1908), pp. 33–43, is another excellent example of John Francis Snyder's site reports. It is particularly illustrative of his thorough analysis of material from a site. In the report he brings to bear a great deal of documentary evidence in interpreting the material recovered from the site. Thus he cites Catlin, Bartram, the Romans, the Jesuit priests, Thomas Jefferson, and early explorers of the American continent, as well as many of his contemporaries, in his interpretation of the burial customs that are illustrated by the finds in the Brown County ossuary. He suggests that his finds at the Baehr and Hemplull sites were of an earlier period than the ossuary, and this insight has since been abundantly verified.   M.L.F.

WITH EXCEPTION, perhaps, of the American bottom, no section of the State surpasses that portion of the Illinois river valley from the Sangamon down to the Mississippi in such profuse evidences of its early and long-continued occupancy by various tribes of Indians. It was the resort of mound building aborigines from the remote past up to the post-Columbian period, marked by intrusion of European art products among their sepulchred remains. In the mounds there, and the relics they inclose, can be discerned interesting and instructive differences, not only in the customs and degree of culture of the most ancient and more recent denizens of that region, but also in their physical and ethnological characteristics. The practice of mound building was carried to its highest perfection in that valley by its primitive prehistoric inhabitants. The oldest mounds are the largest and most complex in structure, and from that class of imposing earthen monuments can be traced in that locality the decadence of the custom of mound building with passing ages, down to the slight elevations of individual grave mounds of recent Indians perched upon almost every eminence of the landscape. They are all burial mounds. Artificial mounds built for signal stations, quite common on the Mississippi bluffs, and purely defensive earthworks, are very rare, if not wholly absent, in the Illinois river valley. In the older sepulchral mounds the usual Indian custom of burying all the property of the deceased with his dead body was generally observed, but in the later mounds it was measurably, and in many totally, ignored. Vessels or vases of burnt clay are almost entirely wanting in the older class of mounds as well as in the most recent, and are not abundant in any of them; nor are potsherds seen about old Indian camp and village sites here in such profusion and variety as in some other localities. None of the Illinois river tribes seems to have attained high proficiency in the fictile art; the few fine specimens of pottery occasionally exhumed in this territory being undoubtedly exotics, obtained perhaps by barter from the expert artisans in that line farther south.

Here, as elsewhere, throughout the continent, the mortuary customs of the successive occupants were not uniform. It is well known that some of them disposed of their dead by cremation, but by far the greater number buried theirs either in the ground or in mounds. No extensive prehistoric cemeteries have yet been discovered in Illinois north of the American bottom, but such may yet be disclosed by future systematic investigation. To what extent cremation was practiced by any one tribe can only be conjectured, as we are at present in possession of insufficient data upon which to base a satisfactory conclusion. The bodies that we know were burned may have been only those of prisoners captured in war; or may have comprised all those of the tribe who died within certain periods and were temporarily deposited in trees or on scaffolds. Our limited observations, however, warrant the belief that only the earliest and most degraded savages who peopled this valley employed the agency of fire in their final funeral rites. The results yielded by my exploration of the Baehr mounds, two miles below La Grange, in Brown county, in 1893, may be cited in support of this hypothesis.[1] At the base of the largest mound in that group—judged by every internal and external indication to be the most ancient in this part of the State—a fierce fire had raged for some time, and while burning was covered with a stratum of clay. From the mass of ashes and charcoal remaining were recovered, with other objects, many fragments of charred human bones, sufficient to reconstruct with considerable accuracy the anatomical characteristics of the bodies there cremated. Their crania were brachycephalic—as are those of all Illinois Indians—but with unusual thickness of the parietal tables, high, prominent malar bones, extraordinary development of the supraorbital ridges, and low

1. *Buried deposits of Hornstone Disks,* by Dr. J. F. Snyder, in Proceedings of the American Association for the Advancement of Science, at Madison, Wis., August, 1893, p. 318 *et seq.* Also, *A Group of Illinois Mounds,* by Dr. J. F. Snyder, in The Archaeologist, Columbus, O., Vol. III, 1895, pp. 77 and 109 *et seq.* [See pp. 193–200 above.]

retreating foreheads, as represented in Figs. 1 and 2, Pl. 23. In addition to decidedly prognathous features and low facial angle, perforation of the ulnar extremity of the humerus and platycnemism of the tibia clearly fixed their status as far down in the scale of human beings. These peculiarities of physical organization were by no means exceptional but apparently the race type of all. In life they must have been as hideous as the gorilla, and yet the implements and ornaments wrought of stone, copper, shell and bone, buried with them displayed mechanical skill of high order. In the art of making pottery, however, they were very deficient; the few vessels of burnt clay recovered were extremely coarse, rudimentary in design, and devoid of ornamentation.

Assuming that the bodies, or skeletons, there reduced to ashes were those of deceased members of the tribe that paid royal tribute to their memory by rearing over them that majestic tumulus, with its deeply buried votive offerings, it must be inferred that the remains of the dead had been carefully preserved from year to year to await the time fixed upon for the periodical tribal cremation. For it is hardly probable that the large number of dead Indians, of both sexes and all ages, constituting that funeral pyre could have perished at once either in battle, by epidemics or by any sudden catastrophe. Among a large proportion of the American Indians from the Atlantic seaboard to the Rocky Mountains, an old and widespread usage was to temporarily dispose of their dead by storing them in branches of trees, in "bone houses," or upon scaffolds erected for that purpose. But there was no uniformity of custom in the manner of their ultimate disposition.

We have the accounts of intelligent observers who witnessed, in the eighteenth century, this method of sepulture by tribes of the Iroquoian and Muskhogean families of Indians who then held the whole Appalachian region from Virginia to Florida, and by many tribes inhabiting the gulf states. As seen in 1776 by Wm. Bartram in his southern botanical tour, in each principal village of the semi-sedentary Carolina Indians, there was provided a "bone house" in which the dead bodies of the tribe, properly prepared and encased in coffins of cane basketry, were deposited and securely guarded until the house was filled. Then, he says, "The nearest kindred or friends of the deceased, on a day appointed, repair to the bone house, take up the respective coffins and following one another in the order of seniority—the nearest relations and connections attending their respective corpse, and the multitude

218

following after them—all as one family, with united voice of alternate alle-
lujah and lamentation, slowly proceed to the place of general interment,
where they place the coffins in order, forming a pyramid; and lastly cover all
over with earth which raises a conical hill or mount." [2] Corroborative observations of this custom with certain modifications, are related by Capt. Romans,
Adair, Capt. Bossu and several others. [3] Of the mounds in Virginia Mr. Jefferson said: "That they were repositories of the dead, has been obvious to
all. . . . Some ascribe them to the custom, said to prevail among the Indians,
of collecting at certain periods, the bones of all their dead wheresoever deposited at the time of death," and forming mounds by covering them with
earth. The mound forty feet in diameter at the base and seven and a half feet
high, "on the low grounds of the Rivanna" river, explored by him, contained
according to his estimate a thousand skeletons. [4]

Brebeuf says it was the custom also among the Indians of the lake region
to remove at certain periods the bodies and skeletons of a district from the
trees, scaffolds, and other temporary resting places, and deposit them with
much ceremony, in a single large pit. [5] "The Indians of Southern Georgia
frequently burnt their dead. This custom, however, was not universal, and
it obtained to a very limited extent among the tribes resident in the middle
and upper portions of the State. The practice of reserving the skeletons until
they had multiplied sufficiently to warrant a general cremation or inhumation
seems to have been adopted." [6] Preserving the dead bodies of their relatives
in coffins stored in bone houses was a refinement of obsequies confined to
the more sedentary Creeks, Choctaws, Cherokees and cognate tribes, that
were the most advanced in the arts of civilization. Other Indians were content to deposit their dead, well shrouded in deer and buffalo skins, in trees
or upon scaffolds; but with all tribes east of the Mississippi that was only preliminary to their final disposal by cremation, or inhumation either in pits or

2. *Travels through North and South Carolina, Georgia, East and West Florida, etc.*, by
William Bartram, London, 1792, pp. 495–496. [Quotation from pp. 514–15 of 1793 edition.
Since both editions have the same number of pages, Snyder's citation is apparently in error.]

3. *A concise natural history of East and West Florida, etc.*, by Capt. Bernard Romans, New
York, 1775, pp. 89–90. *Travels through that part of North America formerly called Louisiana,
etc.*, by Captain Bossu, London, 1771, Vol. 1, pp. 198–208 [298–99]. *History of the American
Indians*, by James Adair, London, 1775, p. 183 et seq.

4. *Notes on the State of Virginia*, by Thomas Jefferson. Trenton, 1803, p. 230 et seq.

5. *Jesuit Relations* for 1636, pp. 128–139. [See Chap. VIII, Vol. X of the Thwaites edition.]

6. *Antiquities of the Southern Indians*, by Charles C. Jones, Jr., New York. D. Appleton &
Co., 1873, pp. 189–190.

in mounds. West of the Mississippi "aerial sepulture"—as tree and scaffold deposits of dead Indians is termed by Dr. Yarrow [7]—was generally observed; but there the Indians having adopted nomadic life, without a semblance of fixed habitations, abandoned the further and essential part of the custom—that of periodically collecting and burying or burning the remains of their dead—and left them in their aerial perches to be decomposed and scattered by the elements.

In his description of the Mandan Indians, on the upper Missouri, Catlin says: "These people never bury the dead, but place the bodies on slight scaffolds just above the reach of human hands, and out of the way of wolves and dogs; and they are there left to moulder and decay. . . . Whenever a person dies in the Mandan village, and the customary honours and condolence are paid to his remains, and the body dressed in its best attire, painted, oiled, feasted, and supplied with bow and quiver, shield, pipe and tobacco—knife, flint and steel, and provisions enough to last him a few days on the journey which he is to perform; a fresh buffalo's skin, just taken from the animal's back, is wrapped around the body, and tightly bound and wound with thongs of raw hide from head to foot. Then other robes are soaked in water, till they are quite soft and elastic, which are also bandaged around the body in the same manner, and tied fast with thongs, which are wound with great care and exactness, so as to exclude the action of the air from all parts of the body" [8]—which is then placed upon a scaffold made of poles, erected on the open plain. The Sioux, Dakotas, Chippewas, Arapahoes and other Indians of the northwest, make that same disposition of their dead as a finality. [9]

There is every probability—in fact, positive evidence—that all prehistoric Indians of Illinois adhered, in a greater or less degree, to the custom of retaining for a time the remains of their dead before consigning them to final interment. But until very recently no instance had been reported of the discovery in this State, north of Union county, of a "dry bone" mound burial

7. *A study of mortuary customs among North American Indians*, by Dr. H. C. Yarrow, U.S.A. government press, Washington, 1880, p. 66.

8. *Letters and Notes on the Manners, Customs, and condition of the North American Indians*, by George Catlin. London, 1841, Vol. 1, p. 89. [Quotation corrected.]

9. *Handbook of American Indians*, by Bureau of Ethnology. Government press, Washington, 1907, part 1, p. 946. The writer of this paper was guilty of despoiling—in the interest of science, of course—a few aerial burials of dead Pawnees and Blackfeet when passing through their country enroute to California across the plains many years ago.

containing *all* the dead of a tribe which had been in "aerial sepulture" for a protracted period. Such an instance was discovered on the 7th of October, 1906, in Brown county. It was a remarkable ossuary, or Indian communal mound burial, of a type strange in that locality but not uncommon in the southern and southeastern states, and occasionally met with in the extreme southern portion of the State. The discoverer of it, Mr. W. W. Nash, of Ottawa, La Salle county, a gentleman of literary tastes, and quite an amateur archaeologist, on one of his usual outings on the river with some members of his family, in his steam boat, on that day tied at La Grange on the west bank of the Illinois river for a short prospecting excursion to the bluffs in quest of Indian relics. Following the Versailles road two and a quarter miles he arrived at Camp creek where it emerges from the hills on its course to the river, and is overlooked by ranges of picturesque bluffs a hundred feet or more in height, having almost every peak and crest crowned with the small burial mounds of recent Indians. Near that point his attention was attracted by a mound differing from those, in size and shape, forming an artificial ridge on the verge of a high, steep prominence of the bluff, and extending, saddle-like, some distance down the incline on either side.

Clambering to the top for a closer inspection he there found beyond the mound, a considerable area of comparatively level land, corresponding with the general surface level of that part of the State, on which is a five-acre farm, including the long mound, belonging to Mrs. Margaret Crabtree, whose residence is represented by Fig. 1, Pl. 24, showing the mound in the background. By the Brown county records it is seen that this farm is situated in the northeastern corner of the N.E. ¼ of the S.E. ¼ of section 1, in township 2, range 4; eight miles northeast of Mt. Sterling, the county seat.

In the little cultivated field between the house and mound were noticed many fragments of broken bones and pottery, ashes and bits of charcoal, the usual debris indicating a long-used Indian camping ground, or village site; but when the whites first took possession of that region it was all covered with a heavy growth of timber including large oak and hickory trees of undoubted great age. Excepting the removal of that timber growing upon it, the mound had never been disturbed, and, composed as it was of clay, it had apparently suffered but little erosion by the rains and frosts of past centuries. In height above the natural surface of the sharp point upon which it was built, it was a little over five feet; its average width at the base forty-five feet, and its extreme length ninety-five feet. Its construction had evidently been commenced on the highest elevation of the point of bluff, and extended as the ghastly work progressed some twenty-five or thirty feet down the southeastern slope of the hill, and forty feet or more down the northwestern slope.

Though it was Sunday, the request of Mr. Nash for permission to dig into the mound for Indian relics was readily granted by Mrs. Crabtree, without protest against such desecration of that day, or for profaning the sacred repository of the dead. Commencing his excavation three or four feet above the lower margin of the mound, Mr. Nash had not proceeded far when his spade brought to light a mass of human bones. Then prosecuting the search with care, in a short time he unearthed several perfect skulls, together with eight burial vases of neat form and finish, a number of mussel shell spoons, a few *Marginella* beads, a small arrow point of flint, and a number of pieces of chipped chert. As night was approaching he suspended further exploration and returned to his boat, not visiting the Crabtree farm again for two weeks.

The results of his prospecting experiment were soon known throughout the neighborhood, and attracted to the place many curious visitors. The extraordinary yield of relics from so limited a space in the mound, excited among those who came—as usual in such cases—a spirit of vandalism and cupidity. Among those earliest on the ground was Mr. Henry Clay Ren, son-in-law of Mrs. Crabtree, and at that time postmaster at Cooperstown, a small village in Brown county, five and a quarter miles northwest of the Crabtree farm. Believing the mound contained a vast store of relics similar to those taken out by Mr. Nash, having in market great commercial value, Mr. Ren abandoned his postoffice, and purchased from his mother-in-law, for the sum of five hundred dollars, the exclusive right to every thing remaining in the long mound, and also all that might be found in the few small grave mounds on the place. He thereupon set to work, with his hired help, to demolish that large mound as expeditiously as possible. Mr. Ren, a man of intelligence and keen observation, carefully noted everything of interest presented as the work progressed, and afforded to others the opportunity to scrutinize the mound's structure, and every detail of the relative positions and arrangement of its contents. There was but little indication of preliminary preparation of the ground upon which the human remains were to be deposited, and none of any ceremony involving the employment of fire attending the burial. If a layer of bark was placed there to receive them—as is very probable—it had totally disappeared.

There is every reason to believe that the ossuary was commenced by laying down, on the highest point of that bluff peak, a number of adult skeletons, or bodies, lying flat on the back, in a circle with their feet to the center. Two similar circles were added, on the declining surface of the ground, on either side of the central circle, separated from each other by a space of eighteen or twenty inches. Upon these prostrate skeletons were placed or thrown many others, without apparent order or arrangement. Among these were remains of young infants, and of children of various ages. Here and there skulls were found without any of the bones of the system to which they had belonged. Many "bundled skeletons" occurred; that is, bones of an individual, often without the skull, that had been gathered and tied together in a compact bundle, or originally wrapped in a deer's skin. In other places were masses of loose bones, parts of many skeletons, which seem to have been collected promiscuously and dumped down on the general heap. It is impossible to compute approximately the number of skeletons comprised in that stratum of bones a foot in thickness by eighty feet in length and twenty-five feet in width. Three hundred and fifty was the most conservative guess of those who saw it, but that probably fell short of the actual number.

When all had been brought in from their aerial burials there was spread over the whole osseous deposit a layer, eight or ten inches in thickness, of sharp, coarse gravel, brought from a gravel bed some distance away, which seems to have been mixed with some substance forming a mortar impervious when dry to moisture. By the protection thus afforded the bones and other objects covered by it were found in remarkable state of preservation; but such about the borders beyond the gravel covering crumbled to pieces upon exposure to the air. An analogous, but no doubt more elaborate preparation for preservation of entombed remains of the dead in mounds of this character was noticed in several localities by the employés of the U.S. Bureau of Ethnology. Prof. Cyrus Thomas, of that bureau, in his report of its *"Explorations of the Mounds of the United States,"* says: "In numerous mounds the skeletons were found closely packed side by side immediately beneath a layer of hard, mortar-like substance" that "had been placed over them while in a plastic condition, and as it must soon have hardened and assumed the condition in which it was found, it is evident the skeletons had been buried after the removal of the flesh." [10]

The ossuary mounds of Indians practicing this mortuary custom, who *permanently* camped and hunted in certain other localities, often contain several stratas of skeletons, as did the one described by Mr. Jefferson. A first stratum of skeletons was laid down by them—as was done in Brown county—and covered with sufficient earth for the safekeeping of that grewsome deposit. Then when the next period arrived for again collecting the aerial burials of the tribe, the mound was leveled down to receive the second stratum of remains, and was again rebuilt; and so on, until no more could be added, when another bone mound was started. From the fact that the Brown county charnel mound enclosed but one basal stratum of skeletons, and that it is the only ossuary of the kind yet discovered in the Illinois river valley, may be deduced the conclusion that it contained *all* members of the tribe that erected it who had died during their stay in this region; and that they who survived, after having thus paid their last obligations to their deceased kinsmen, left the country, either returning to the place from whence they came, or migrating elsewhere. They completed the final inhumation of their dead, after spreading the gravel layer over them, by heaping upon it the clay mound as their imperishable monument.

By some, who have given no attention to the study of American archaeology, two theories are advanced in explanation of the Brown county ossuary. The one is that all the bodies buried there were those of Indian warriors slain in some great battle; the other, that it was simply an old Indian burying ground lengthened by gradual accretion of corpses supplied in the course of years by the ordinary death rate of the tribe, with perhaps a few killed in wars. That it contained the remains of both sexes of all ages from infancy to extreme senility, effectually refutes the first supposition. The improbability of the second was shown by the systematic arrangement of adult skeletons first laid down; by the equal state of preservation of all; by the undisturbed continuity of the gravel layer, and the uniform homogeneous composition of the mound.

The total collection of relics secured from the ossuary comprised a quan-

---

10. *Twelfth annual Report of the U.S. Bureau of Ethnology*, Washington, 1894, p. 673. [Quotation corrected; the title of the paper is "Report on the Mound Explorations of the Bureau of Ethnology."]

tity of human bones, including a number of crania with jaws complete; over a hundred unbroken pieces of pottery, and many more crushed by the weight of superincumbent earth, hundreds of small marine shells (*Marginella*), perforated at the shoulder by grinding to serve as beads for necklaces and wristlets; several small flat rings, or perforated shell disks; two carved gorgets cut from large sea shells; a dozen or more long bone awls and needles made of the fibulae of deer and elks; mussel shells fashioned into spoons; one bead of fluor spar; several quartz crystals; one small, thin piece of hammered copper and fourteen small flint arrow points.

One of the skeletons lying at full length on the ground was surrounded and almost covered with mussel shells, and all through the clay of the mound were scattered river shells—valves of *Unio Multiplicata* predominating—the discarded or lost digging implements of the mound builders. No signs of fire were encountered excepting at the end of the mound nearest the spring far down the ravine, where mingled refuse of potsherds, ashes, charcoal, burnt stones and bones, evidenced the last camping place of the dusky funeral directors.

There was nothing about the mound, or the objects it covered, to sustain for it the claim of high antiquity. Possibly some of the noble red men whose bones reposed there were chasing the buffalo and deer when Columbus was studying astronomy at the great school of Pavia; or later. Bones of adults under the gravel envelope were comparatively sound, and even infants' bones not fully ossified had decayed but little. Still, that state of preservation is not reliable as a criterion of the age of such burials, as bone and shell imbedded in impervious clay having the perfect drainage of the bluff mounds, may resist disintegration for vast periods of time. All the skulls recovered were well formed, of the brachycephalic, or short head class—the true Indian type—with average proportion in parietal width to length of 84 to 100, Fig. 2, Pl. 24. The skeletons, as far as observed, indicated the historical American Indian in stature and figure; and not a perforated humerus or abnormally flattened tibiae was noticed among them.

The most notable feature of this ossuary mound was the distinctive character of the artifacts associated with its human remains. Burying all the personal effects of the deceased with his, or her, corpse was not a universal Indian custom. Some tribes observed it, and added also all the property of the nearest relatives; others, particularly the later Indians, seldom buried anything with their dead. The tribe that built this Brown county mound permitted the defunct squaws and children to retain their shell beads when placed in their rawhide winding sheets upon the desiccating scaffolds; but the men, though no doubt warriors, were denied their bows and arrows, stone tomahawks, belts, grooved axes, and even their pipes, as not one of those articles was obtained in the most searching exploration. The few flint arrow points secured were very probably fatally imbedded by enemies in the bodies of those in whose remains they were found. One was between two dorsal vertebrae of a skeleton; one in the pelvis of another; one skull had an arrow point in its mouth, and another small one alongside its lower jaw, while a flint weapon large enough to be classed as a spear head had penetrated another skull over the left eye.

The objects in the mound of greatest interest to archaeologists were the two spider gorgets represented by Figs. 1 and 2, Pl. 26, drawn two-thirds of actual size. Each one was on the breast of an adult skeleton in the position where they were worn in life by the medicine men or most distinguished chiefs as totems, or tribal symbols, of the spider gens to which they belonged. The gorgets are disks cut from large sea shells—the *Bucyon Perversum,* or *Strombus Accipitinus*—with the convex side smoothly polished and the figure carved on the natural glossy concave surface. Near the margin two small holes were drilled for a suspending cord around the neck, or for fastening to the garment. Of works of Indian art shell gorgets are most uncommon; but those bearing the effigy of the spider are very rare. There are probably not more than a dozen of them known in all the archaeological collections of the United States. Gen. Thruston figures one in his grand work on the *Antiquities of Tennessee,* that was found in a mound on Fain's Island in that state, and says: "It is an unusual type. Specimens upon which this curious figure is more naturally and elaborately represented have been discovered in the mounds at New Madrid, Missouri, and near East St. Louis, in Illinois. . . . The remarkable uniformity of design is also a characteristic of these spider gorgets. It seems strange that they should be discovered in mound districts so widely separated as east Tennessee, western Illinois and Missouri; yet we already have learned that both of these [latter] sections were once probably occupied by the tribes, or kindred, of the Stone Grave race of Tennessee." [11]

11. *Antiquities of Tennessee,* by Gates P. Thruston, second edition. Robert Clarke & Co., Cincinnati, O., 1897, pp. 335–336. [See also pp. 335–36 of the 1890 ed.; the quotation as given by Snyder varies only in punctuation.]

Professor Holmes commenting upon this class of strange emblematical carvings, says: "The spider occurs but rarely in aboriginal American art, occasionally it seems, however, to have reached the dignity of religious consideration and to have been adopted as a totemic device. Had a single example only been found we would not be warranted in giving it a place among religious symbols. Four examples have come to my notice; these are all engraved on shell gorgets." [12] One of those four was from a mound at New Madrid, Mo., two were from the American Bottom, and the fourth, the one mentioned by Gen. Thruston, from Tennessee.

One shell gorget with denticulated edge, and two or three smaller ones, all plain, were also found in the ossuary mound, together with several plain, flat rings of shell of various sizes having large central openings (Fig. 2, Pl. 25), obviously having served as ornaments. Shell spoons were modified bivalve mussel shells (Fig. 1, Pl. 25), most commonly *Unio Occidentalis*, or *U. Rectus*. They were generally within the pottery vessels, occasionally with bones of birds and small animals, all that was left of the food with which they were filled, when buried, for the dead on their journey to the unknown, but which had disappeared by absorption and decay. Of the shell spoons collected in the Cumberland valley Gen. Thruston remarks: "It will be observed, from the side of the bivalve selected, that the spoons were made for the *right hand,* showing that the mound builder, like his white successor, was right handed." [13] The pottery vessels were placed, as usual in Indian burials, on either side of the corpse's head, a water bottle on one side and a dish or bowl containing food on the other. Some of the deceased were provided with three or four such vessels, but many had none at all.

This pottery has many features in common with that recovered from the old Indian cemeteries and mounds of southeastern Missouri and northeastern Arkansas. Examples of that from the latter locality (in the writer's collection) represented by Pl. 27, are here introduced for the purpose of comparing them with some of those taken out of the ossuary by Mr. Nash on the day of his discovery, (Fig. 1, Pl. 25), and also with a few selected specimens secured by Mr. Ren. (Pl. 28.) Not only in grace of form and artistic design, but in material of composition and excellence of finish, the similarity is well sustained. Some pieces of this Brown county pottery seem to have been simply

12. *Second annual Report of the Bureau of Ethnology.* Washington, 1883, p. 289. [Quotation, corrected here, is from p. 286.]
13. *Antiquities of Tennessee,* p. 312.

sun dried, but the greater part of it was certainly fire baked. The prehistoric Indians had not attained the art of glazing their earthenware, and, of course, none of this was glazed, but in solidity and strength it would not be excelled by unglazed pottery of the same proportions and thickness made by expert potters of the present day.

The extraordinary number of skeletons and profusion of pottery interred in that elongated mound on Mrs. Crabtree's farm place it, among our local antiquities, in a class of itself without a parallel in central Illinois. In the great mound on the Baehr place, before referred to, about two miles distant, probably an equal number of desiccated Indians, at a much earlier period, had been cremated; and into the fierce fire that consumed them a multitude of finely wrought implements and ornaments of stone, shell and bone had been thrown as votive offerings, by their frenzied tribesmen. But in the remains of that weird holocaust not a fragment of pottery was discovered. And in all that huge mound but two clay vessels were seen, one of which near the base of the mound, an art product of its builders, was a small, coarse, heavy vase of brick red color; the other, a neat specimen of aboriginal art neatly decorated, situated in the mound structure a few feet below the top, had accompanied a much later intrusive burial. No pottery was encountered in either of the other four, almost contiguous, mounds. In the large mound on the bluff a mile north of the Baehr group—and of contemporaneous age— where the remains of only eight bodies (one of which was bedecked with a 24-pound nugget of native copper, ten copper axes, 283 solid copper beads, and several fine stone artifacts) were found beneath the mound's base at the bottom of a pit twelve feet deep, not a fragment of pottery was seen.[14]

In regard to products of the ceramic art, similar negative results were obtained by Gerard Fowke in his exploration—under the auspices of the Missouri Historical Society—of the eight mounds near Montezuma, in Pike county (Ill.), in 1905. Though potsherds occurred in the clay substance of the mounds, and were abundant on their surfaces, nothing approaching an entire pottery vase or vessel was met with. Many of the human bones in those mounds were "bunched" or "bundled," and all had been brought there from tree scaffolds. Neither weapons nor objects of utility or ornaments accompanied them, excepting a few pearl and shell beads, bone awls, a pair of "pulley" ear plugs, and a large sea shell (*Casis Flammea*), which had been

14. *The American Archaeologist.* Columbus, O., 1898, pp. 21–22. [See pp. 206–7 above.]

converted into a drinking cup. In the principal mound of the group (No. 1) "almost the entire bottom of the cist was covered with human bones, mostly in very poor preservation; they generally indicated skeleton burials, being deposited promiscuously." But no estimate of their probable number is given. The "cist or crib" at the bottom of the mound, 15 feet long by 7 in width, was built of logs. Beneath the skeletons, on a floor of decayed bark, "covering nearly the entire space enclosed, rested 1,197 chipped leaf-shaped blades [of variegated chert], three and one-half to six inches long, three to four and one-half inches in breadth"[15]—placed there as a propitiatory offering to the mythical spirits controlling their destinies.

To what extent the later Indians of the Illinois river valley made use of pottery can now be only conjectured; but the ever present potsherds about all their old haunts are proof that vessels of clay were their chief, and perhaps, only domestic utensils. It follows then that they must have lost, or never adopted the mortuary custom of supplying their dead with post mortem food and water to subsist them while awaiting their reincarnation; for, as before stated, their multitude of small mounds here are practically destitute of such food and water receptacles.

All facts connected with the Brown county ossuary considered—its exceptional quantity of "dry bone" deposits, the surprising amount and peculiar character of its pottery, its spider gorgets, and overlying stratum of gravel— seem to justify the tentative supposition that it was the sepulcher of a tribe, or part of a tribe, that wandered from the lower Mississippi up into the Illinois river valley to that vicinity, and after dwelling there for a period disappeared. Further search may discover in that region other identical bone and pottery mounds of the same people, or of others, making a revision of this hypothesis necessary, or wholly confuting it. Anthropologists, ethnologists and archaeologists must continue to grope in the dark with the limited knowledge we now possess of the primitive peoples who ruled over this fair domain prior to its invasion by the Gaul and Anglo-Saxon.

15. *The Montezuma Mounds.* Pamphlet, St. Louis, Mo., 1905. [The pamphlet was No. 5 of Vol. II of the Missouri Historical Society's *Collections;* quotations, corrected here, are from pp. 7, 5.]

CERTAIN INDIAN MOUNDS
TECHNICALLY CONSIDERED

Originally published as three separate articles by the Illinois State Historical Society, these papers are perhaps most illustrative of Snyder's ability to synthesize his vast knowledge of Illinois prehistory. They summarize all of his views and interpretations, and record the many sites which he dug, visited, or studied throughout his long lifetime of research. They represent Snyder the archaeologist at the peak of his career and are a fitting climax to his intellectual life (although he died some twelve years after they were published and later wrote several other papers). In these articles he lists the successive cultures that occupied Illinois. Another, and perhaps the most significant, contribution of these papers is that they list and describe many sites that have long since been destroyed. The Beardstown mound, the finds at Mitchell Station, and the East St. Louis charnel house would be unknown to archaeologists today except for Snyder's conscientious reporting. M.L.F.

PART FIRST: THE EFFIGY MOUNDS *

The custom of mound building by the North American Aborigines, coextensive with the limits of the United States from ocean to ocean, reached its highest perfection and longest duration on the eastern watershed of the Mississippi Valley, between the Great northern lakes and the Gulf of Mexico. And nowhere in that specified region were the earthen monuments of our Indian predecessors more numerous or more diversified than in the portion of it now comprised within the boundaries of Illinois. In this State occur every known type of prehistoric artificial mounds—the majestic sepulchral and memorial tumuli of high antiquity; the peculiar rock-lined graves and mounds

* Each of the three articles in this series bore the main title "Prehistoric Illinois: Certain Indian Mounds Technically Considered." Part I is reprinted from *Journal of the Illinois State Historical Society,* Vol. I, No. 4 (Jan., 1909), pp. 31–40.

Immediately preceding the text of Part I is the following note by Dr. Snyder:

"To adapt this paper to the limited space of the *Journal,* it has been divided into three parts, namely: The Effigy Mounds, Sepulchral and Memorial Mounds, and Temple or Domiciliary Mounds, which will appear in the order named, in three consecutive numbers of this publication. As a contribution to Illinois archaeology an example of each class of these local antiquities, not before figured or described in any public print, will be presented. But the main object of the paper is to attract attention of students to the rapidly disappearing remains of prehistoric Indian life and arts in Illinois, and aid (though feebly) in stimulating their interest in this sadly neglected substratum of Illinois history.—J.F.S."

of the "Stone Grave Indians"; the tribal ossuaries; the domiciliary, or temple, teocalli; signal, or observatory stations; elongate embankments, and the innumerable conical burial mounds of comparatively recent date.

Added to these, there are in four or five of the extreme northern counties of the State, a few of those strange earthen structures known as "effigy" mounds—the frontier outliers of the only area in the world where this class of imitative earthworks was so generally adopted for distinctive tribal symbols by a savage people. The geographical extent of that area is confined to the southern half of Wisconsin and the immediately adjoining portions of Iowa and Illinois.[1] The Wisconsin effigy mounds were designed to represent birds, reptiles, various local quadrupeds, and nondescript objects impossible to identify. They are often arranged in groups and generally associated with other mounds of the ordinary shapes and dimensions. Occasionally a solitary effigy mound is seen distant from any other, or among a number of common burial mounds; and in rare instances one of unusual figure is found alone on an elevated ridge or prominent bluff. They range in length from less than 50 to over 500 feet, and in height above the surface of the ground, from 1 to 6, or more, feet. Of the ordinary mounds that almost invariably accompany the effigies there is one more elevated than the others, and so situated relatively that from its summit is obtained a full perspective view of the image mound, or mounds, below, including every detail of proportion.

The first published mention of ancient earthworks in Wisconsin Territory, is found in the "Narrative of an Expedition to the Source of the St. Peter's River, etc., by Major Stephen H. Long, U.S.A., Philadelphia, 1824." But though Major Long gives interesting accounts of many Indian mounds he saw there in 1823, he strangely failed to observe that any of them were of unusual configuration and intended to resemble animated objects. That class of mounds were first brought to public notice in 1836 by Mr. I. A. Lapham in communications to newspapers descriptive of the "turtle mound" near Milwaukee, where he resided. Subsequently, in 1853–54, provided with the means by the American Antiquarian Society, he systematically surveyed almost the entire portion of Wisconsin containing the imitative earthworks. Mr. Lapham's report was published in 1855 by the Smithsonian Institution

1. Isolated effigy mounds elsewhere, as the great serpent mound in Adams county, Ohio, the two eagle mounds in Eastern Georgia, and some others, are well known, and are regarded as the sporadic work of different Indians actuated in their erection by different incentives.

as one of its "Contributions to Knowledge." At that time the extension of those anomalous earthen effigies into Illinois had not been detected. And to this day—notwithstanding the proximity of several great institutions of learning to the limited number of those unique antiquities, long since discovered south of the Wisconsin line—no survey or exploration of them has yet been made, or comprehensive description of them written.

Cursory notices of some one of them occasionally appeared in newspapers, devoid, however, of information of value to the archaeologist or antiquarian. The first published reference to them to attract the attention of scientists was the postscript to his geological survey of Winnebago county by the late Hon. James Shaw of Mt. Carroll, Carroll county, then Assistant State Geologist. He was intensely interested in all relics of the primitive American race, and a close observer of their numerous remains he found in the course of his field work, particularly in the valley of Rock river. In Winnebago county he "noticed and examined these classes of mounds," the prevailing type being round at base and conical in form. "The oblong-shaped mound," he says, "is of much rarer occurrence. At the locality in Rockford already alluded to there is a very remarkable one. It is one hundred and thirty feet long, about twelve feet wide at the base and three or four feet high. Near by this one is a mound of the third class, or those having a fanciful resemblance to some form of animal life. In Rockford it is known as the 'Turtle mound.' But it resembles an alligator with his head cut off more than it does a turtle. We give its dimensions: Whole length, 150 feet; width, opposite fore legs, 50 feet; width, opposite hind legs, 39 feet; length of tail, from a point opposite hind legs to end of tail, 102 feet; length, from a point opposite hind to a point opposite fore legs, 33 feet; distance from opposite fore legs to where the neck should begin, 15 feet.

"These measurements were not made with exactness, but are simply paced-off guesses. The figure lies up and down the river, on a line about north and south, the tail extending northward. The body rises to a mound as high as a standing man. The feet and tail gradually extend into the greensward, growing less distinct and indefinable, until they cannot be distinguished from the surrounding sod. The measurements across the body at the legs include those appendages, which are only a few feet long.

"The effigy, whether of alligator, lizard, or turtle, seems to be headless, and no depression in the surrounding soil would indicate that the materials out of which it is constructed were obtained in its immediate vicinity."[2]

The image mound thus described by Judge Shaw is shown in outline on Pl. 29, marked A. Two similar structures in the same county, represented and numbered 1 and 2 on Pl. 29, were reported and figured in The Antiquarian, in 1897, by George Stevens, and described as follows: They are situated "on the sandy, loam soil of the Rock river bottom . . . five miles south of the city of Rockford. . . . No. 2 . . . is 192 feet long, the body being 77 feet, and the tail 115 feet. . . . From one fore foot to the other, is 62 feet; and the hind feet stretch from each other a distance of 60 feet." The greater width of body, just below the front legs, is 60 feet . . . No. 1 is 110 feet in length and 30 feet wide at the broadest part of the body. No depression in the surface of the ground near these figures could be observed denoting from whence the material of which they are made was taken.[3]

In shape and general appearance these two effigies, identical in contour with the "lizard mound" in Rockford, are five feet high at the shoulders, and their tails point to the north. Near by them, as shown on the plate, are four ordinary mounds, two circular in form and two oblong.

At the time of their discovery these two "lizards" on the Rock river bottom were regarded as the extreme southern limit of the effigy mound system of Wisconsin. But two additional groups of them, farther east and fifty miles south of the Wisconsin state line, were found by Mr. T. H. Lewis, the well known archaeologist of St. Paul, Minn.—situated near the city of Aurora, in Kane county, on the eastern sloping terrace of Fox river, in latitude slightly lower than the mouth of the Chicago river, and but thirty-five miles west of it. They were 150 yards from the stream; and, as usual with the ancient works of that class, there were several mounds near them of the ordinary sort, as represented in outline on Pl. 30. The image figures are presumed to portray birds flying south—one of which is thought, by some strain of the imagination, to be the horned owl.

By carefully surveying the "bird" in group No. 2, Mr. Lewis ascertained its exact length to be 32 feet, and width, from tip to tip of its wings, 36 feet.

2. Geological Survey of Illinois. A. H. Worthen, Director, 1873. Vol. V, page 94. [Quotation corrected.]

3. The Antiquarian, Columbus, Ohio, 1897. Vol. 1, page 176. [Quotation corrected; the two sentences preceding the note number Snyder also included within the quotation, although Stevens does not say that the "greater width of the body" is 60 feet; all he says of the width is that "across the body, just behind the front legs, the effigy is 30 feet wide and 25 feet in width at the attachment of the hind legs."]

Its elevation above the surface of the terrace was 18 inches. There was formerly another image of similar design and dimensions—a bird, also—a few yards in advance and a little east of it, which the white man's aggressive and destructive progress had almost completely obliterated. The bird figures in group No. 1 were also raised above the general surface level about a foot and a half; and in length and breadth were somewhat in excess of that in the second group.[4]

In a recent popular work on Illinois history it is stated that "A singular monument of this latter race [Mound Builders] is found in the lead region, situated at the summit of a ridge, near the east bank of Sinsinawa Creek. It has the appearance of a huge animal, the head, ears, nose, legs, and tail, as well as the general outlines, being as perfectly conceived as if made by men versed in modern art. The ridge upon which it has been upbuilt tops an open prairie and stands three hundred feet wide, one hundred feet in height, and rounded off at the top by a thick deposit of clay. Centrally, along the line of the summit, is an embankment, three feet high, forming the outline of a quadruped measuring two hundred and fifty feet from the tip of the nose to end of the tail, and having, at the centre, a width of body of eighteen feet. The head was thirty-five feet long, the ears ten, legs sixty, and tail seventy-five. The curvature of the limbs was natural to an animal lying upon its side. In general, the figure resembles the now extinct quadruped known to science as the megatherium. Many scientists believe this animal actually lived in and roamed over the Illinois plains when these ancient Mound-builders first entered the valley of the Mississippi, and that this outline was later drawn from memory."[5]

Though very desirous to obtain an accurate drawing of this monument, I unfortunately utterly failed, after the most diligent inquiry, to discover its location. Several intelligent citizens of Jo Daviess county, on being interviewed—some of whom were born and raised on the banks of Sinsinawa creek—said they had never before heard of such a mound, and, of course, knew nothing about it. But there is, four miles east of Galena, the strangest and best defined effigy mound in Illinois, which has to the present escaped the attention of all antiquarian writers, and which in scarcely any particular corresponds with the one above described. It is on the farm of Mr. J. F.

4. The Archaeologist, Waterloo, Indiana, 1894. Vol. II, pages 85–89.
5. Historic Illinois. By Randall Parish. Chicago, A. C. McClurg & Co., 1906, pp. 20–21. [Quotation corrected.]

Leekley, occupying a level space on the top of a ridge rising 300 feet above the waters of Fever river. In configuration it bears some resemblance to a horse, Pl. 32, and for that reason is known locally as the "Horse mound." Its total length, from the forehead to the end of the tail, is 195 feet, the body is 116 feet, the tail 50 feet long and 14 feet wide at its broadest part, the head is 25 feet and the neck 29 feet long, measured from the breast of the figure to its lower jaw. The hind legs are 45 and the front legs 42 feet in length, the distance from the one to the other being 75 feet. The widest part of the body is 30 feet and its elevation at the shoulders 6 feet. The material of which it is composed is arenaceous clay, the drift, or subsoil of all that region.

This wonderful work of the aborigines is near the center of the level area on the ridge, which for many years has been in cultivation and was last season (1908) covered with a heavy growth of corn. And though worn down somewhat by the plow, it still stands in bold relief with all marginal lines sharply defined.

There may yet be more of the effigiated mounds of this type—that in the political division of the northwest into states have fallen within the confines of Illinois—than those described in the preceding pages. Raised but slightly above the surface, and in some instances overgrown with trees and bushes, their artificial contour and elevation have perhaps escaped detection. And no doubt there have been others within the same territory entirely destroyed by the rapacious encroachments of civilization. With one or two exceptions, no efforts have been made to preserve those now well known; nor has any intelligent investigation of them for the benefit of science been undertaken.

Earthen mounds, undoubtedly artificial, projected on huge scales and plainly imitative of common indigenous animals, are well calculated to incite surprise and profound interest. Their inspection irresistibly suggests the inquiries: What was their purpose? Who made them? The candid answer to which must be, we do not know. Until a few decades ago they were attributed to a mysterious, mythical people, styled Mound Builders, that long since mysteriously and unaccountably disappeared. It is now known that the Mound Builders were simply American Indians. But with our present limited knowledge—or, rather, absolute ignorance—of the habits, customs and methods of life of the primitive race of Indians, any attempt to specify what particular tribe of them built certain kinds of mounds, and the specific purpose for which they built them, obviously must be largely a matter of conjecture.

Yet, reasoning by analogy from what we do know of the tribal institutions and culture of modern Indians, rational conclusions may be deduced in some degree explanatory of the meaning of those earthworks in eccentric forms, which otherwise would appear to be aimless and purposeless freaks. Assuming that that class of mounds were intended by their projectors to portray birds and other animate objects, the legitimate and unavoidable inference is that their design was to represent the various totems of a tribe.

As is well known, the social organization of the American Indians, with some exceptions, was founded, not upon the family, but upon the gens, totem or clan, as the tribal unit. "The gens," says Major Powell, "is an organized body of consanguineal kindred," or kinfolk, that elect their own sub-chief and decide "all questions of property and especially of blood-revenge, within its own limits." Several gentes may, and often do, unite in phrates, or brotherhoods, within the tribe.[6] Each gens was designated by the name of a familiar object, usually that of some species of bird, quadruped or reptile; as, the wolf gens, or that of the turtle, bear, eagle, lizard, etc. Without graphic characters to express or record their language, each gens adopted the picture or image of the animal chosen for its emblem as its distinct designation. Consequently, as many of the customs and tribal regulations of recent Indians are derived, and were perpetuated, from their ancient ancestors, it is a reasonable presumption that the builders of the effigy mounds made them for symbols to mark the range or location, or to commemorate noted achievements of their respective gens; or, in many instances, as specialized monuments to the memory of their gentile dead interred in nearby sepulchral mounds.

It must be admitted, however, that no one of these hypotheses—or all together—furnish an infallible keynote to the intent of all the earthen images in question. The many lengthy linear mounds; the multitude of uncouth, anomalous structures resembling no known animate or inanimate object; the mysterious figures in intaglio (sunk in the ground, instead of being raised above it); the headless reptilian forms, are wholly inscrutable enigmas. I have heretofore offered tentatively the suggestion that the latter class were originally supplied with heads made of perishable materials;[7] but their great numbers militate against that supposition. It may not be improbable, however, that a decapitated alligator, or iguana, was adopted as the

6. The American Race. Daniel S[G]. Brinton, A.M., M.D., New York, 1891. Page 46. [Quotation corrected.]
7. Transactions of the Illinois State Historical Society, 1900. Page 25.

clan's escutcheon because of some incident occurring in its early history.

Mr. R. C. Taylor, who was among the first reliable observers to bring the Wisconsin animal mounds into public notice, in 1838, suggested "that their forms were intended to designate the cemeteries of the respective tribes or families (of Indians) to which they belonged; thus, the tribe, clan or family possessing as its characteristic totem, blazon or emblem, the bear, constructed the burial place of its members in the form of that animal; the clans having the panther, turtle, eagle or other animal or object for their totems, respectively, conforming to the same practice." [8] Mr. Taylor, as has since been proven, was in error in his belief that the adumbrant figures were themselves the cemeteries. They were but the indices thereto. It is true that human remains have been found in some of the Wisconsin effigy mounds. A large proportion of them were undoubtedly intrusive burials by later Indians; but many of them were surely primal deposits of bodies, or bundled skeletons, on the original surface of the ground. Those later burials, it may be, were at first in the conventional conical mounds, which subsequently were, by addition of more drift clay, enlarged into the form of the totemic effigy. Mr. Lapham says: "Indeed, the animal-shaped mounds have never been found productive in ancient relics or works of art. It was probably for purposes other than the burial of the dead that these structures were made." [9]

Of all the mounds in the United States of Indian architecture, comparatively few are constructed of the surface soil upon which they stand, excepting when built upon clay formations, such as the river bluffs, or upon sand, as in Florida and other localities. Clay was almost invariably selected for mound structure by the aborigines, and in many instances was conveyed long distances for that purpose. Some of the effigy mounds in southwestern Wisconsin are made of sand, and an exceptional number of them of river bottom loam; but by far the greater number—as well as those in Illinois—are composed of the drift clay subsoil. [10] This feature of mound building will be again adverted to in the parts of this paper that are to follow.

All known effigy mounds in Illinois are so projected as to appear traveling southward. There can be no doubt that they were so placed intentionally,

8. Silliman's Journal of Science and Art, 1838. Vol. XXXIV, page 91 [100; except for a few phrases, the words quoted are not Taylor's but Snyder's.]
9. Antiquities of Wisconsin. By. I. A. Lapham. Smithsonian Contribution to Knowledge, Washington, 1855. [Article 4, Volume VII.] Page 16.
10. Ibid. Page 92.

and not simply to conform with topical surroundings; but with what significance, if any, is impossible to determine. In the great mass of analogous works in Wisconsin no attention was paid to orientation of the raised images, as the heads and tails of those having such appendages point indiscriminately to various points of the compass. Pl. 31, a modified copy of the fifty-first plate of Mr. Lapham's treatise, illustrates a group of animal mounds on a ridge dividing the Kickapoo and Mississippi rivers, in southwestern Wisconsin.

It cannot be claimed that the builders of the effigy mounds were gifted in very high degree with what Ruskin styles the "art instinct." The technique of their work is crude, coarse and clumsy, with no regularity or order and little regard for relative proportion or accuracy of detail. There is manifest design in the earthen images, but not one of them is so artistically perfect that the bird, quadruped or reptile intended to be imitated can be recognized with certainty, and many of them are but caricatures that bear no likeness to any living thing now known in that region. It is strange that savages evincing such admirable mechanical skill in manufacturing pottery and stone implements should display so little fidelity to nature in their efforts to copy the forms of animals they were daily associated with and knew so well. Time and investigation have dispelled much of the glamour that, a generation or two ago, lent to those curious Indian mounds of Wisconsin a magnified import. The colossal "signs of the cross," in conspicuous relief on the sloping ridges there, gazed upon with reverent amazement as indisputable evidence of the pre-Columbian introduction of Christianity on this continent, are now known—as are also the famous man-shaped mounds—to be but awkward attempts to portray birds in flight. The marvelous "Elephant mound" in Grant county, cited by embryo scientists as proof positive of the contemporaneous existence here of man and the mastodon, is now conceded to be only a rude image of the bear, the wind having accidentally drifted loose sand so as to lengthen its nose into the semblance of a proboscis. But yet, with their many imperfections and defects, the effigy mounds are among the most extraordinary and interesting of American antiquities.

Their age is still a question in controversy, and perhaps will always be. The origin of artificial mounds in America, shrouded in fascinating mystery, was accorded remote antiquity as long as the "Mound Builders" were generally believed to have been an occult, semi-civilized race, distinct from, and far superior to, the invading Indians, by whom they were supposedly vanquished and exterminated. But since the researches of archaeologists have positively demonstrated that the Indians here when America was discovered, and the immediate ancestors of those Indians were, in fact, the builders of the mounds and artisans of the Stone Age, not only has American archaeology lost much of its olden charm, but the chronology of mound building has experienced a surprising revision, the age pendulum swinging from the dim past to the verge of the present era. Recognized authorities in the science of ethnology now teach that the historic Cherokees built all the mounds, the Shawnees made all the stone-lined graves, and the Winnebagos were the authors of the effigy mounds of Wisconsin! It will not be surprising to be next informed that the Apaches carved the Calendar stone and the Yaquis erected the Reotihuacan pyramids of the Sun and the Moon!

This statement, however, is not intended to intimate that the early Cherokees did *not* build mounds or the primitive Shawnees bury their dead in stone-lined graves. They, as well as other Indians, no doubt did, having inherited those customs from their ancestors. But very little evidence has yet been adduced in support of the assumption that the Winnebagos fashioned the effigy mounds, or knew anything of the Indians who did make them. When the Winnebagos were asked by the first white settlers in Wisconsin who made the effigy mounds, they answered: "We do not know. They have always been here." When the same question was asked by the Jesuit missionaries of the Indians then in that locality, they answered: "The Great Manitou made them as a sign to His children that this region abounded with game."

An argument of the "modernists" is that Siouan Indians—inferentially the Winnebagos—in recent times constructed, out on the northwestern plains, of loose boulders, effigies similar to those in lower Wisconsin. The Sioux and Dakotas, it is true, often designed, on the prairies, with small contiguous boulders, various odd figures in outline, having, however, not the slightest resemblance or affinity to the Wisconsin effigies. They were, as shown by T. H. Lewis and others, simply graphic characters conveying information of the moving party to others of the tribe who were to follow or who chanced to pass that way. Again, it is asserted the Winnebagos reproduced, with paint, the effigy mound figures on dressed buffalo skins. This is a mistake. The paintings on their buffalo robes were of the same import as those of all other hunter Indians of the west, pictographs recounting the prowess and great achievements of the robe's owner in war and the chase, with occasionally a tribal emblem for personal identification.

Obviously the "Horse mound" on the Leekley farm is of importance in this discussion; for if it is absolutely certain the structure was intended to represent the horse, it must be conceded a modern production, as the horse was not known here prior to 1536. It follows, then, that if that horse mound has no higher antiquity than three and a half centuries, the other effigy mounds of the Wisconsin system are little, if any, older. Therefore, if the Winnebagos were in that region that long ago, the contention that they were the effigy builders, and that the horse was one of their gentile symbols, must be materially strengthened. But was the so-called horse mound designed for an image of the horse? As before remarked, those effigy makers, as artists or molders in clay, were egregious bunglers. None of their earthen images can with certainty be identified. Mr. Lapham was unable to determine whether one of their commonest figures was that of a lizard or a war club. Considering the absence of ears and the broad, trowel-like tail of the mound image on the Leekley farm, notwithstanding its disproportionate length of legs and neck, it was doubtless devised for a totem of the beaver gens, and is therefore of the same unknown age of the other works.

With exception of the Eskimos, a recent intrusive people, both American continents when discovered were populated by only one race, the American race, since known as Indians. There is no evidence whatever that any other human race had previously existed here. There is, therefore, no proof required to maintain the Indian authorship of the mounds and other art remains of prehistoric times in America. The age, or ages, of those remains is altogether conjectural. But the oldest will probably not exceed eight or ten centuries prior to the landing of Columbus on San Salvador; the greater number of them, perhaps not the half of that period. The degree of cultural advancement of the American race from the beginning of the mound building epoch to its close can only be surmised; but there is little reason to believe that the builders of the most ancient mounds in the United States were physically or mentally far different from the Indians found here by DeSoto and other early European explorers. Some of them had then become somewhat sedentary, depending as much on agriculture for subsistence as upon the chase; but war was the principal pursuit of all. Wars of extermination, the absorption of weak tribes by the strong, frequent changing of tribal names and locations, was their life history. Mr. Lapham says: "Since the red men have become known to us, numerous tribes have been extinguished, with all their peculiar customs and institutions; yet, as a whole, the Indian remains. Many tribes have been overrun by others, and have united with them as one people. Migrations have taken place; one tribe acquiring sufficient power has taken possession of the lands belonging to another, and maintained its possession. In the course of these revolutions it is not strange that habits and practices, once prevalent in certain places, with certain tribes, should become extinct and forgotten."[11]

The Winnebagos were first seen by the Jesuit fathers near the mouth of the Fox river of Green Bay, and were then known as Ouimpegonec, or Ouimibegoutz. They were of the Sioux or Dakota stock, and called themselves Ho-chun-ga-ra, or the "trout nation," and had come from the western ocean, or salt water. Moving southward down Rock river, they came upon the territory of the Illini, who strenuously resented their encroachment, and after years of warfare, finally checked their further advance.[12] They, however, held possession of the Rock river valley as far down as within forty miles of its junction with the Mississippi until the Black Hawk war in 1832.

Neither space nor the scope of this paper permit prolonged discussion of the very little that is known concerning the origin of the effigy mounds. Within the historic era the territory they occupy has been alternately in the possession—in whole or in part—of the Mascoutins, Kickapoos, Sauks and Foxes, Chippewas and Winnebagos,[13] all of whom enclosed their dead in conical mounds, until they learned by contact with the whites to dig graves; and they all believed the effigy mounds to be natural elevations that had "always been there."

The most reasonable conclusion warranted by the meagre data obtainable is that the building of effigy mounds in Wisconsin and Illinois was a custom of indigenous inception and growth—for it cannot be traced to an extraneous source—of a small tribe of Indians enjoying a century or more of comparative quietude, then finally overrun, partially exterminated, and the survivors absorbed by a predatory incoming branch of the "Siouan" stock, the building of earthen images abruptly ceased and identity of their builders was soon lost.

11. Antiquities of Wisconsin. Pages 29–30. [Quotation corrected.]
12. The Illinois and Indiana Indians. By Hiram W. Beckwith, Chicago. Fergus Printing Co., 1884. Page 138.
13. Antiquities of Wisconsin. I. A. Lapham. Page 61[–62].

PART SECOND: SEPULCHRAL AND MEMORIAL MOUNDS [*]

Of all the artificial mounds in Illinois, made by Indians, at least 75 per cent were constructed for the final disposition of their dead. Not until they had been for some time in contact with the white people did the Indians here learn to dig graves and bury their dead beneath the surface of the ground. And after having adopted that method of inhumation they often modified it with the traditional practices of their mound-building ancestors. That tendency for adhering to primitive customs was well illustrated in the burial of Black Hawk, as late as seventy years ago. That renowned Indian warrior died on October 3, 1838, at his home near Eldon, on the Des Moines river, in Iowa, and was buried the next day by the members of his band and kinsmen. He was dressed in the uniform of a colonel in the U.S. army, with a cap on his head elaborately ornamented with feathers in Indian style. At his left side was a sword, on the right were two canes presented to him in Washington, and on his breast and about his neck, were medals and other presents, and trophies of his valor that in life he valued highly. Then, wrapped in four fine new blankets, his body was laid on a broad board which, taken to the place of burial, was placed in a slanting position, his feet in a shallow trench about fifteen inches lower than the general level of the ground, and his head raised a foot or more above it.

A forked post was planted at his head and another at his feet, each three feet in height, across which, from one to the other, a ridge pole was laid. Split puncheons fitted closely side by side, with one end resting on the ridge pole and the other on the ground on either side of the corpse, formed a strong roof over him, having its gable ends securely closed with puncheons set upright. That roof was then covered with earth to the thickness of a foot, and the whole sodded with turf to protect it from the erosive effect of rains and storms. In a circle, thirty feet in diameter, around that rustic tomb sharppointed pickets twelve feet high were planted and firmly retained in place by an earthen embankment three feet in depth thrown up against them on either side at the bottom.[14]

Here was seen all the essential conditions of ancient mound building but slightly modified by the influence of civilization: the innovations upon an-

[*] Reprinted from *Journal of the Illinois State Historical Society,* Vol. II, No. 1 (April, 1909), pp. 47–65.
14. Magazine of American History. New York, 1886. Vol. XV, p. 496.

cestral custom being the clothing of the defunct warrior in the white man's military garb instead of dressed deer skins, the substitution of blankets for buffalo robes, and the ridge pole and puncheons for the cribwork of logs to protect the remains from the ravages of wild beasts. But for the swarm of white pioneers then spreading over Iowa territory, a further observance of primeval Indian customs would doubtless have occurred. The loyal followers of the dead chief would, in all probability, have manifested their homage to his memory at each recurrent annual visit to his grave by piling upon it more earth until the memorial mound thus made had attained the magnitude commensurate with his fame and distinction in life. As it was, the remnant of Black Hawk's band removed after his death to the Sac reservation on the Kansas river and never returned. Long after his grave had been rifled of its contents by white vandals, the ridge pole and roof placed over his remains decayed and fell in, forming there quite a perceptible mound; and the pickets enclosing it also rotted away, leaving around it the embankment that had supported them in an earthen circle similar to that surrounding the great "Ceremonial" mound at Marietta, O., which to the early settlers of that region seemed so mysterious and incomprehensible.

But, long before the days of Black Hawk; long before the coalition of the Sauks and Foxes, Illinois was visited, at a remote period in the past, by a colony of Indians who had learned the art of grave-digging and buried their dead in graves from two to four feet deep, lined all around and covered over with thin, broad, flagstones. Distinguished from all other Indians of the United States by that peculiar method of burial they are known to ethnologists and antiquarians as the Stone Grave Indians. The habitat of their parent tribe was in central Tennessee, more especially in the Cumberland valley, from whence colonies migrated in various directions. The one that came to Illinois—traced by their stone-lined graves containing, with human remains, high-grade pottery and finely chipped flint implements—crossed the Ohio river at the mouth of the Cumberland, and for a period occupied the district of Salt Springs in Gallatin county. Moving thence westward they stopped for a time near the junction of the Ohio and Mississippi rivers; then followed the range of bluffs as far up as Monroe county. There they again halted for another period, when, finally crossing the Mississippi, they settled along its western bluffs from the present site of Florissant down to St. Genevieve, in Missouri, where their further trail is lost.

In southeastern Missouri and eastern Arkansas extensive cemeteries of the aborigines have been discovered similar in many respects to our own burying grounds of today. The graves they comprise, enclosing remains of deceased Indians with their domestic utensils, stone implements, and bone and shell ornaments, deposited there long ago, are not rock-lined, or disposed with any regard to uniform orientation; are but two or three feet deep and superficially unmarked. In, or near, those ancient graveyards are mounds of the ordinary conical form from four to eight feet in height, containing human remains, probably of the more distinguished defunct personages of the same tribe; or it may be they were erected by later Indians who observed the mound mode of burial and knew nothing of grave-digging. No prehistoric cemeteries of that kind have thus far been found in this State, but their presence here may yet be brought to light by future investigation. Grave digging, however, was not altogether unknown to the earlier Indians of Illinois, although they very seldom had recourse to that mode of interment. And for the occasional rare exceptions to their usual custom of mound burial there cannot now be discerned any apparent reason.

The invariable manner for disposing of their dead by almost all prehistoric Indians of the Mississippi valley was, first, to place the body, securely enveloped and bound in deer and buffalo skins, on a scaffold or in the branches of trees, beyond the reach of wolves and other carnivorous animals, to remain there until decomposition and desiccation rendered it no longer alluring to birds and beasts liable to prey upon it. Then, either singly or with the dried skeletons of other deceased members of the family or gens, it was taken down and removed to the spot selected for its last resting place. That was usually an elevation of the ground, a prominent peak or ridge of the bluffs if conveniently accessible, though the flat, sandy bottoms bordering rivers and lakes were often chosen, but the high, open prairies always avoided. The surface at that place was then prepared—sometimes with a layer of sand spread over it, but more often with a bed of dry grass and bark—to receive the mummified remains, which, if of more than one individual, were placed compactly together, either at full length or doubled up, in the embryonic position, and covered with broad pieces of bark. Then clay from the bluffs or the subsoil, scraped up with mussel shells and flint implements, was brought in deer skins and willow baskets, in many instances from a considerable distance, and heaped upon the grewsome pile until a mound was formed, as represented by Fig. 1, Pl. 33, of sufficient magnitude to protect its contents from molestation. This process, as a rule, permanently concluded the burial. Occasionally, however, but rarely, the same Indians dug the mound down again from the top almost to the enclosed remains, and there placed the bodies of other kinsmen since deceased, over which they rebuilt the mound as before.

The small conical, or oblong, mounds of this type are seen on hilltops near water-courses in all parts of the country formerly inhabited by the red race. They were constructed in the same way from a remote period to sometime after the white race had secured a foothold upon this continent, as is attested by the numerous instances in which articles of European manufacture occur in them as part of their original contents. Excepting in sandy districts, or other localities where clay was entirely absent, no Indian mound of any description was ever made altogether of the surrounding surface soil. The reason for this is obvious: the mound-builders having learned by observation and experience that clay, impervious to water, would resist the erosive action of rains and frosts and afford permanent protection to the relics it covers, when mounds of sand or loam, readily permeated by water, could offer no such protection or well withstand the wearing down effects of winds and storms.

The "Memorial" or "Monumental" mounds—a classification somewhat arbitrary—primarily sepulchral in purpose, differ from the ordinary burial mounds in size and in relative arrangement of the objects they were built to enclose and preserve. They also differ from them in technique of construction, having grown so much larger by successive additions of material in course of years, while the common burial mounds were usually completed at once. This is plainly indicated in vertical sections of many of the large memorial mounds by well-marked lines of curvilinear stratification, as shown in Fig. 2, Pl. 33. The dark lines in the cut represent accumulations of surface soil formed by growth and decay of vegetation in long intervals of suspended labor.[15] The first step in the erection of a stately tumulus of this kind was careful preparation of the chosen ground, in some instances by maintaining on it for some days a brisk fire; in other instances by spreading over it a layer

---

15. Memorial mounds are found in Ohio with "mysterious stratas" an inch or two in thickness, generally of sand, sometimes of river shells or water-worn pebbles, laid in close contact, thought to have had some occult sacred or religious significance. But they, perhaps, only denoted intervals of cessation for a period in the building process, marked in that manner to protect them from molestation during the absence of the builders.

of sand, clay or bark. Upon that base were deposited, either with or without the agency of fire, but doubtless with weird savage ceremonies, the bones of the dead with accompanying offerings. Their preliminary protection was generally an enclosure of heavy logs or rough stones—often both combined—over which sufficient clay was thrown to cover them. The Indians then left for their annual hunt, or upon some predatory expedition, and were gone for a season, and sometimes for several years. Returning to that locality, as they eventually did in course of time, they immediately resumed the piling of more clay upon the sepulchre, each individual contribution brought in deer skin or basketful being yet well defined as dumped down in parts of the structure.

This work was prosecuted, with more or less diligence, until the close of the season, when the Nomads sought other districts for special food supplies, or to engage in aggressive warfare, then continued it again upon their return. By periodical accretions gained in that way the monument finally attained the proportions deemed to be a worthy tribute to the fame of the warrior, or merits of the many Indians and value of the propitiatory offerings, therein interred, and was forever after regarded by all Indians who saw it as sacred and inviolable. In the progress of upbuilding the great mound it served as the camping ground for some of the builders, as is evidenced by beds of ashes and charcoal interspersed with burnt stones, mussel shells and bones of various animals, met with at different levels all through it above the log crib work at its base. And not infrequently there is encountered near by one of those camp sites a lone human skeleton, perhaps of a clay carrier who died there and was buried where he fell.

Very few prehistoric Indian earthworks were projected and built with mathematical precision. The few describing accurate geometrical figures in their structural proportions are exceptional and accidental. The greater number of memorial mounds are oblong in form, more or less regular in outline; but the most symmetrical and conspicuous are conical with bases approximating true circles. When exploring memorial mounds the human remains and associated objects they inclose are often found near one end, or the edge, instead of under the center, the builders having lost their exact location as the process of heaping on more earth advanced. A large mound of that class, two miles west of La Grange, in Brown county, examined by the writer a few years ago, well illustrated this erratic architecture, and also disclosed a remarkable departure from the hereditary Indian custom habitually observed in monumental mound burials. Situated at the verge of a prominent point of the bluff, irregularly oblong in shape, as seen in diagram, Fig. 1, Pl. 34, it was 125 feet in length, 80 feet in breadth at the widest part, with an average height of 20 feet, and made altogether of bluff clay.

Excavations carried down, at different points, to the bluff surface failed to discover the objects so sacred to the Indians, or so revered by them, as to demand for their commemoration a monument comprising 13,000 cubic yards of earth. A trench was then cut through it longitudinally which revealed little more than two or three intrusive superficial burials. However, at a short distance from the eastern end a space 8 feet long by 7 feet wide in the solid bluff surface was observed to be soft and yielding, indicating that the ground there, at some former time, had been disturbed. That fact was soon apparent when on digging at that spot the loose earth was found to be intermixed with potsherds, flint chips, bones, mussel shells, etc., and on the firm sides of the pit were plainly visible marks of the ancient flint or copper implements employed in its excavation. At the depth of five feet the broken horn of a deer was thrown out. Ten and a half feet down, a layer of large rough rocks was encountered a foot in thickness. When that mass of rocks, and all the loose earth, were carefully removed there appeared eight human skeletons, much decayed and crushed by the weight of the superincumbent stones and earth. The bottom of the pit—which was fully twelve feet in depth—was covered with two inches of dark loam, the decomposed residium of the bed prepared for the dead, presumably of bark, skins and prairie grass.

With only one of those entombed bodies had been interred worldly possessions that resisted the gnawing tooth of time; and he, in life a large, burly man, occupied the central position on the floor, lying full length on his back. Crouched around him the other seven may have been his wives, or slaves, buried with him to attend him in the mythical future. From his extraordinary obsequies and the magnitude of his monument, it may be inferred that he was the head grand chief of the tribe and a copper magnate of distinction. Near his head was a nodular nugget of pure native copper, weighing 24 pounds; ranged along his sides were ten finely wrought copper axes; around his neck were three necklaces, one of large oblong beads made of the columella of marine shells perforated longitudinally and polished; another of over 200 incisor teeth of squirrels bored at the base; and the third composed of 283 globular copper beads, solid, perfectly spherical, as though cast in

247

moulds and highly polished. They ranged in size from two-thirds of an inch in diameter in the middle of the necklace to three eighths of an inch at either end; and on his breast was a splendid ornament or insignia of authority, consisting of five plates of fluor spar, each six inches in length, two and a half inches wide, a quarter of an inch in thickness, as smooth as glass and resplendent as mirrors. In each was drilled a hole two inches from either end for cords to suspend them an inch apart, and for attachment to the clothing.[16]

In the diagram, Fig. 1, P. 34, the letter B designates the bluff, M the mound and P the burial pit. Some idea may be formed of the fervor of esteem or superstitious veneration entertained for the principal individual buried there, by his tribe, when considering the prodigious amount of manual labor expended in sinking that pit with only the mechanical aid of mussel shells and implements of stone and copper, and of piling up that immense quantity of earth by the primitive methods they employed. But it is difficult to detect the motive impelling them to exercise such extraordinary precaution for the safety of their chief's body and his wealth of copper by that mode of burial; for they must have known that, although Indians frequently buried their dead superficially in mounds erected by other Indians, Indian custom and superstition universally safeguarded all original mound burials from desecration or despoiling, even by the most inveterate enemies. No buried Indian was ever known to be disturbed by Indians. That this monument was not built in conventional form and immediately over the remains it was intended to commemorate, was perhaps not because the builders forgot the precise location of the burial pit, but that the point of bluff there was too narrow to afford a sufficient width of base for a regular cone-shaped mound of the magnitude required.

There is occasionally found upon examination a large memorial mound that was raised over the remains of but one individual; and in some no human remains, or other object whatever, can be discerned as the incentive for erection of the monument. In this latter class of works the motive is sometimes discovered by exhaustive exploration of the ground beneath the base of the tumulus, as in that shown by Fig. 1, Pl. 34. It is well known, however, that mounds of great magnitude were built for other purposes than commemoration of the dead—as signal stations, elevated bases for wooden buildings, etc.—

16. American Archaeologist. Columbus, Ohio, 1898. Vol. II, pp. 22–23. [See p. 207 above.]

but, as a rule, the Indians were never prodigal of labor excepting when incited by fear, necessity, or superstition. The thought that they toiled at scraping up clay with mussel shells, and carrying it long distances, in deer skins, to pile it up into mounds, merely for diversion or pleasant recreation, is totally at variance with Indian nature. Every earthwork had its definite purpose, though in some instances that purpose is now not readily apparent, as numerous products of their handicraft, of daily use in their domestic economy, are to us unsolvable puzzles, because of our ignorance of many of their habits and methods of life.

Notwithstanding the identity of purpose of all memorial mounds they present much diversity, not only in size and form, but also in their internal design and structure. While they all are sepulchers no two are exactly alike, and often are, internally, so dissimilar as to warrant the conclusion that their builders were of different tribes, each having its peculiar mortuary customs, and evidently not contemporaneous. Many years ago a large mound of this class at East St. Louis was demolished, as it stood directly on the line of a new railroad then in course of construction. Over thirty-five feet in height and cone shaped, it was built throughout of bluff clay, on the sandy alluvial soil of the American Bottom, within half a mile of the Mississippi river. The hidden secrets it had so well guarded in the by-gone ages, were revealed by its sacrifice to the spirit of modern civilization, and shed a broad light upon the savage faith that prompted its building.

As the work of destruction progressed it was found that about the mound's surface several Indians of later date had been buried in shallow graves, some of whom still wore ornaments of shell and bone, together with glass beads brought to Canada by early French traders. Nothing unusual, beneath those remains, was observed in the huge mass of compact earth, as it was shoveled down, until approaching its base, when several upright cedar posts, in fair state of preservation, were encountered. More careful and complete removal of the remaining clay then laid bare the design and motives of the ancient authors of the work, plainly showing the inception and details of the impressive barbaric obsequies preceding and occasioning the erection of that majestic earthen tomb. The final disposition there of a great number of dead bodies—more probably their dried skeletons—was a modification of the community funeral practiced in 1775 by the Choctaws, as described by Bartram. He says the bones of the deceased were brought in from the field scaffolds and placed "in a curiously wrought chest or coffin, fabricated of bones and splints," and then "deposited in the bone-house, a building erected for that purpose in every town. When this house is full, a general, solemn funeral takes place." The coffins are then carried out "to the place of general interment, where they are placed in order, forming a pyramid, and lastly covered all over with earth, which raises a conical hill or mount." [17]

Centrally on the site of the East St. Louis mound a "bone-house" was built, twelve feet square and seven feet high. The corner posts, of cedar, were still in place; the other uprights and roof timbers, of softer wood, were reduced to dust. The side walls of the house, constructed of poles planted perpendicularly and interlaced with long slender willow sprouts, or reeds, had disappeared, leaving only here and there their impression in the adjacent dry clay. In that charnel-house had been gathered from the scaffolds and stored the remains of all members of the tribe who died within a certain period; but if each one was encased in "a curiously-wrought chest or coffin," the corroding touch of time left not a distinguishable vestige of it. At that stage of the burial rites, when the bone-house was filled, instead of carrying the corpses out "to the place of general interment," as the Choctaws did, the Illinois Indians brought clay from the bluffs and heaped up this mound over the house and its contents where they were, and thereby "raising a conical hill or mount." When all had been cleared away, the bottom of the space bounded by the four cedar corner posts defining the area of the buried bone-house was found to be covered, to the depth of eighteen or twenty inches, with a mass of mingled human bones so far decayed—with exception of the teeth—that their separation and removal for careful inspection and preservations was utterly impracticable. From among them, however, were recovered many valuable relics of aboriginal art to enrich the private collections of Dr. John J. R. Patrick, of Belleville, and that of the writer of this paper.

During that progressive period three other mounds there of the same general character, varying in cubic dimensions and inclosed relics, were torn down and incorporated in the grading of new railroad lines, without record of their structural peculiarities having been preserved—if at all closely observed—by any one.

17. Travels through North and South Carolina, Georgia, etc. By William Bartram. London. 1792. pp. 514–515. [The quotation differs slightly from the wording of the 1793 edition; probably the changes were made by Snyder and are not due to variations in the text of the editions.]

By far the finest and most perfect example of the prehistoric earthen monument in the Illinois river valley—a district abounding in aboriginal earth works—was situated immediately on the left bank of the Illinois river, half a mile below its ancient junction with the Sangamon; that junction having since been changed by natural causes to a point six miles farther up. As is often noticed in river bottoms, the land next to the stream is higher than that farther away from it. Such is the topography of that mound location, which is now occupied by the city of Beardstown, in Cass county. Formerly a channel, now filled up, carried part of the waters of the united streams from the mouth of the Sangamon to the south, then westward, to where it rejoined the Illinois several miles below, converting an extensive area there— especially during the rainy seasons—into an island, elevated considerably above the line of highest overflow. From the river there a sandy alluvial plain stretches four miles in width to the eastern range of bluffs, and across the river westward a similar flat bottom, a mile wide, separates the stream from the bluffs on that side. The many advantages for savage life presented by that island; the natural beauty of its wild surroundings, and the limitless resources there of fish, game and indigenous fruits, rendered it an attractive abiding place for the Indian. From time immemorial, reaching far back into the dim ages of the past, that place was occupied by successive tribes of aborigines.

This is evidenced by the fact that for quite a distance back from the river front the sandy surface soil has been artificially raised twenty or more inches by the accumulation and admixture of ashes, charcoal, fire-stained rocks, bones of various birds, beasts and fishes, mussel shells and other refuse common about all old Indian camp sites. The vast length of time required for an addition of that depth to the original surface, to be made by that process of gradual accretion, can only be conjectured. The great mound there (Fig. 2, Pl. 34) was another silent witness—of undoubted high antiquity—of the centuries passed since the first Indian village was pitched upon that island. The smaller adjacent mounds may have enclosed the dead of the tribe that built the large one; or, perhaps, were of more recent construction.

When the vanguard of the horde of immigrants that began pressing into the "Sangamon country" in the first years of the nineteenth century, came to that place they found a village of Kickapoo Indians, who had been there but comparatively a short time, and who possessed not the slightest tradition of their predecessors on the island or of the mounds. The early white settlers designated the collection of buffalo and elk skin lodges there, "The Mound Village," until, in 1826, Thomas Beard established a flatboat ferry across the Illinois river at that point, when the name of the embryo white settlement he started there was changed to Beard's Ferry; and again changed in 1829, when the town was platted and recorded as Beardstown.

There is no one now living who saw those mounds in the completeness of symmetrical proportions they had when seen by the earliest settlers of this region. They have long since totally disappeared, and are now only ideally restored, as seen in Fig. 2, Pl. 34, from descriptions and accounts of a few of the oldest residents of the county.[18] They were all conical in form; the large one fully sixty feet high, with base four hundred feet in diameter. The burial mound almost contiguous to it was fifteen feet in height, with corresponding width of base. About forty yards to the west stood an ordinary burial mound ten feet in elevation; and farther down the river was another, the smallest of the group, about eight feet high. The three smaller mounds were destroyed early in the history of Beardstown, their removal being deemed necessary for opening and properly grading the road leading down the river, and the clay of which they were made was needed for filling up sundry holes and depressions in the principal streets of the village. By 1837 Beardstown had become quite an important trading point. It was situated on a drift deposit of sand, which in summer time, when dry, was blown by the winds in stifling clouds in all directions; and at all times rendered traveling and teaming through the town slow and laborious. To remedy that condition some bright genius, who had discovered that the great mound was composed of clay, suggested to the town trustees the idea of "macadamizing" the sandy streets with that material.

That expedient was at once adopted, and the criminal folly of digging down the mound—one of the grandest and most perfect specimens of its kind and the second in magnitude in the State—was commenced that year and continued for years, until the last vestige of it was hauled away to "clay" the deep sand of the streets and about two miles of the main road to the eastern bluffs. At that time Beardstown had several citizens of culture and education;

18. The drawing of them, copied in Fig. 2, Pl. 34, and their measurements, as above stated, were furnished by Mr. H. F. Kors, for years circuit clerk of Cass county, who was born and raised at the southern margin of the mound adjoining the large one; whose account of them is, in the main, corroborated by the few remaining citizens of Beardstown older than himself.

but American archaeology had not yet been elevated to the dignity of a distinct science, and Indian antiquities were then so commonplace that the extraordinary opportunity afforded by the mound's removal for investigation and study of the spiritual ideation and sepulchral arts of the aboriginal red race was practically unnoticed. However, from reliable sources—particularly from Mr. John Davis, a native of the county, town marshal of Beardstown for many years, and superintendent of the mound's destruction—it was learned that all over it were many superficial intrusive burials of later Indians, accompanied, as usual, with their implements and ornaments of stone, shell and bone. Among them was found the remains, evidently of a missionary priest who had long ago penetrated the wilderness thus far, and there laid down his life in exercise of his faith, and was entombed by his converts in that majestic sepulcher of their unknown predecessors. Around his skull was a thin silver band an inch in width; on his skeleton breast reposed a silver cross, and near by were the jet and silver beads of his rosary.

Fragments of broken pottery, flint chips and mussel shells occurred all through the homogeneous mass of clay, with here and there the ash beds, charred wood, animal bones and other debris usual about old Indian camp fires. At the base of the mound, about its center, resting on the ground surface, the workmen uncovered a pile of large, rough flagstones, which proved to be a rude vault, six feet square and four feet high, enclosing five human skeletons, far decayed, and "a quantity of relics" buried with them; the reliquiae, doubtless, of renowned chieftains, to whose memory their tribe had reared this imposing monument.

Fig. 1, Pl. 35, is the copy of a sketch by Mr. Kors of what was left of the mound in 1850; a section of it on the north side, next to the river, having been specially excavated for the building there of the four-story grain warehouse shown in the cut. When I first visited it, in the spring of 1865, the buildings seen in this cut had been destroyed by fire, and the mound's obliteration was complete, with the exception of remnants, from three to five feet in depth, about its margins, sufficient to define its original line of circumference. Those remnants of the mound, and much of the same material that still covered the sandy streets, were seen at a glance to be earth of a very different kind from that of the ground upon which the mounds had stood. In a vertical section of the geological formation at Beardstown, as shown by Fig. 2, Pl. 35, the letter C denotes a limestone ledge of the lower coal measures; B, a deposit of true till, or boulder clay; DD, a stratum of fine brick clay; SS, drift, or diluvial sand, from six to fifteen feet in depth; M, the large mound; and R, bed of the Illinois river, at that point over a quarter of a mile wide. The clay composing the mounds was upland (tertiary) loess, identical in color and ingredients with the "bluff formation" constituting all the (earthen) river bluffs of Illinois as far south as glacial action extended. The brick clay (DD) at the bottom of the river, exposed at either bank in low stages of water, differs from that of the mounds in color, texture and analysis.[19]

No depression of the land in the near proximity of the mounds could be discovered from whence material of their bulk could have been taken for their construction. The inference must, therefore, be held conclusive—until more exhaustive investigation refutes it—that those Beardstown mounds, located at the verge of the river bank on a base of loose sand, were built of clay, almost impervious to water, brought there for that purpose from the bluffs four miles east, or from those across the river one mile west. If this deduction is correct, a conception may be formed of the fervor and tenacity of Indian veneration for illustrious leaders—that impelled them to perform the stu-

19. Quantitative Analyses. By Dr. John J. R. Patrick.

	Bluff Loess.	Brick Clay.
Coarse sand	0.10	0.05
Fine sand	13.02	15.15
Silt	41.01	28.46
Clay	40.51	51.84
Water and loss	5.36	4.50
	100.00	100.00

Chemical analysis of bluff loess. From the U.S. Geological Survey. M. 38.

SiO_2	64.61
Fe_2O_3	2.61
TiO_2	.40
MnO	.05
MgO	3.69
K_2O	2.06
CO_2	6.31
C	.13
Al_2O_3	10.64
FeO	.51
P_2O_5	.06
CaO	5.41
Na_2O	1.35
H_2O	2.05
SO_3	.11
Total	99.99

Chemical analysis of brick clay. Illinois University.

SiO_2	56.74
Fe_2O_3	2.82
CaO	7.64
SO_3	.07
Na_2O	.93
Water 100°	.21
Al_2O_3	10.36
MnO	.04
MgO	4.70
FeS_2	1.21
K_2O	1.86
Ign. loss	13.35
Total	99.93

pendous labor of carrying over 50,000 cubic yards of earth that distance to construct a monument for the safe keeping of their remains and the perpetuation of their memory. Possibly superstition, or other consideration besides the preservative or lasting properties of drift clay, influenced them to adopt it for that purpose at the cost of such arduous toil.

The large sepulchral Indian mounds, dotting our Illinois landscape in homely grandeur, are geographically distributed also throughout the eastern and middle portions of the Mississippi valley and the Gulf States. In this State they are seen in proximity to all the principal streams, particularly in the valleys of the Wabash, Kaskaskia and Illinois rivers and on the bottoms and bluffs of the Ohio and Mississippi, from Shawneetown and Cairo to Galena. The intrinsic evidence of great age they present on investigation suggests the probability that the custom of building this class of anamnestic monuments was in decadence, or had entirely ceased, before the invasion of America by Spanish adventurers. All artifacts associated with the human remains they contain are of distinctively native Indian type. In none of them so far examined has any article of European manufacture been discovered; but in a few have been found devices wrought of sheet copper of unquestioned Mexican or Central American origin. And in many occur [a] profusion of sea shells, implements, ornaments and weapons made of copper, hematite, catlinite, mica and obsidian, transported from far distant regions.

They are all of essential mnemonic intent, and were the material expression of the same sentiments that have actuated civilized peoples in all countries to rear splendid granite monuments and shafts of sculptured marble over the graves of their dead. Properly interpreted, they legibly reveal many of the Indian's mythological and religious conceptions. The basin-shaped "altar" of burnt, or otherwise indurated clay, at the mound's base, filled with ashes of the funeral pyre; the charred remains of astonishing sacrifices of the finest and most beautiful articles of personal adornment, and their wealth of implements and utensils, cast in the seething fire; the thousands of artistically chipped flints [20] and other rare objects fashioned by months—perhaps years—of patient labor and brought from great distances, there deposited as votive offerings or to appease supernal wrath—all testify to the Indian's faith in immortality and belief that his destiny was controlled by contending, all-powerful good and evil spirits.

20. *Primitive Man in Ohio.* Warren K. Moorehead. Cincinnati, O. 1892. pp. 186–190.

The builders of those mounds in Illinois—doubtless of various tribes and probably of different primitive stocks—were in the neolithic stage of culture when they arrived. Their arts were not developed here from crude beginnings, as they had already attained elsewhere superior skill in chipping flint, as well as in shaping and polishing the hardest and most refractory stones into forms of grace and beauty. But notwithstanding their surprising proficiency in the technical, and even esthetic, manipulation of such materials as nature furnished them, the structure of their skeletons found in the oldest mounds—the ape-like prognathism, the flattened tibiae, perforated humerus, retreating forehead and prominent supraorbital ridges—places them low in the scale of humanity, physically and mentally. The problem of their origin remains unsolved. It may be that it never will be satisfactorily explained. But some light may yet be shed upon the dark page of their ethnography and migrations by persistent, systematic and intelligent study of the broad and inviting archaeological field our State presents. With some highly creditable exceptions, antiquarian research in Illinois has heretofore been conducted principally by curiosity mongers and mercenary vandals for selfish gain only. It demands and should receive, before it is too late, the earnest attention of active, scholarly workers in the interest of science.

PART THIRD: TEMPLE OR DOMICILIARY MOUNDS [*]

The large level-top mounds built by Indians, known to antiquarians as Temple or House mounds, are in this latitude an exceptional class. There are less than fifty of them in the State of Illinois; but in that limited number is included the largest earthwork of the aborigines in the United States. They are not regarded as memorial monuments; nor are they believed to be sepulchers; but whether or not they were primarily projected to entomb the dead is not known, as not one of them has yet been fully explored. In form they are either truncated pyramids, square or oblong—the "teocalli" of the Mexicans—or describe the frustrum of a cone, with circular base. They vary in outline, as well as in dimensions, from low platforms elevated but a few feet above the surrounding surface, to huge structures elaborately terraced and provided with broad ascending roadways.

In the Wabash valley, it is said, are two mounds of this kind, but the

[*] Reprinted from *Journal of the Illinois State Historical Society*, Vol. II, No. 2 (July, 1909), pp. 71–92.

report of them is too vague and unreliable to be available in this paper. There is one near Mill creek in the northeastern corner of Alexander county "nearly square and some 6 or 8 feet high" on which is now a dwelling house.[21] It may, however, not be of the class under consideration, but a buried aggregation of stone graves, as were two others in its immediate vicinity. On the Illinois river bottom two miles below La Grange, in Brown county, is a circular plat-form mound ninety-eight feet in diameter, originally eight feet in height, having yet the vestige of a graded way leading to its top from the surround-ing level plain. It is made of compact clay taken from the bluffs near by, and when first observed, thirty years ago, there was scarcely a perceptible abra-sion in its vertical periphery.[22] Apart from the few truncated mounds above mentioned, it is only in the American bottom, and in one of the upland prairies a short distance farther east, that the true type of temple mounds are found in Illinois. If there are others in the State they are only locally known, and have not been brought into general notice.

For form and magnitude, and for surprising numbers in such a limited area, the well-known group of Indian mounds in the northern end of the American Bottom is the most remarkable of all aboriginal works in the United States. In their explanatory note of the very accurate and reliable map of that wonderful antiquarian district, published in 1906 for private distribution by Dr. Cyrus A. Peterson and Clark McAdams, of St. Louis, they say of the great Cahokia mound, that it is "treble the size of any other similar structure" in this country, and "was originally the central feature of several hundred mounds within a radius of six miles." As sixty-nine mounds are figured on their map within a radius of two miles, their estimate of the probable number once occupying a circle of twelve miles does not seem extravagant.[23] Bracken-ridge, who visited that district in 1811, says: "I crossed the Mississippi at St. Louis, and, after passing through the wood which borders the river, about half a mile in width, entered an extensive open plain. In fifteen minutes I found myself in the midst of a group of mounds, mostly of a circular shape,

21. Twelfth Annual Report of the U.S. Bureau of Ethnology, p. 149. [Quotation cor-rected.]

22. The Archaeologist, Columbus, O., 1895. Vol. III, p. 77. [See p. 193 ff. above.]

23. Timothy Flint, writing in 1830, stated the number of mounds on the American Bottom adjacent to Cahokia creek to be two hundred. Quoting this statement of Flint's, Dr. John Mason Peck says, in his New Guide for Emigrants, p. 164, that he "has counted all the elevations of surface [there] for the extent of nine miles, and they amount to seventy-two." [The quotation is from the 1837 edition. Snyder had the bracketed word in parentheses.]

and at a distance, resembling enormous hayricks scattered through a meadow. One of the largest, which I ascended, was about 200 paces in circumference at the bottom, the form nearly square, though it had evidently undergone considerable alteration from the washing of the rains. The top was level, with an area sufficient to contain several hundred men. . . .

"Around me I counted forty-five mounds, or pyramids, besides a great number of small artificial elevations; these mounds form something more than a semi-circle, about a mile in extent, the open space on the river. Pursuing my walk along the bank of the Cahokia I passed eight others in the distance of three miles before I arrived at the largest assemblage. When I reached the foot of the principal mound, I was struck with a degree of astonishment, not unlike that which is experienced in contemplating the Egyptian pyramids. What a stupendous pile of earth! To heap up such a mass must have required years, and the labors of thousands. . . . Nearly west there is another of a smaller size, and forty others scattered through the plain. Two are also seen on the bluff, at the distance of three miles. . . . I everywhere observed a great number of small elevations of earth, to the height of a few feet, at regular distances from each other, and which appeared to observe some order; near them I also observed pieces of flint, and fragments of earthen vessels. I concluded that a very populous town had once existed here, similar to those of Mexico, described by the first conquerors."[24]

Many of the mounds seen there by Brackenridge in 1811 have long since vanished before the inexorable agencies of civilization; and many of those still there are rapidly yielding to the disintegration of natural causes accelerated by the plow and harrow. In that Cahokia creek district may yet be counted a dozen mounds of the domiciliary type—square or circular with flat tops—the most noted of which is, of course, the great Cahokia mound, deriving its name from that of the creek near its base that formerly joined the Mississippi at the old village of the same name, six miles below their present junction. On the crest of the bluffs three miles directly east of the great mound there were formerly situated two "sugar loaf" mounds overlooking, on opposite sides, a wide ravine formed by a small rivulet that cut its way at that place through the bluffs in its course from the higher lands beyond. They were signal stations, as is shown by the following report of the thorough ex-

24. Views of Louisiana, etc. By H. M. Brackenridge, Esq., Pittsburgh, 181[1?], pp. 187–188.

amination of one of them, in 1887, by employes of the Bureau of Ethnology: "This was conical in shape and formed a landmark for some distance around. At the depth of about three feet the earth, which was a yellowish clay, became dry and very hard and quite different in character from the loess of the bluff on which the mound stands. At the depth of about twelve feet [farther down] a layer of ashes, nearly an inch thick, was disclosed, and a foot below this another layer of ashes a foot or more in thickness. Excepting some thin, flat pieces of sandstone there were no relics nor other remains, not even a portion of bone." [25]

In the early settling of that part of the State there was still plainly seen a well-worn trail, or road, leading from the mound village on the banks of Cahokia creek to the eastern bluffs, and up that ravine between the two lofty signal stations, and on through the timbered hills and across Silver creek, to another square mound in the western edge of Looking Glass prairie, a distance of fifteen miles. Known in early pioneer days as the Emerald mound because of its dark green color in the spring and summer seasons, it was a conspicuous and attractive object in plain view for many miles to the northeast and southward. It is situated at the eastern end of a high wavelike swelling of that beautiful prairie, a mile from the (then) timber line, and two and a half miles northeast of Lebanon—the seat of McKendree college—in St. Clair county. It is the most perfect and best preserved mound of its class in the State; a truncated pyramid in form, approximately true mathematical proportions, each line of its quadrilateral base measuring almost exactly 300 feet, and its level top 150 feet square. Its height is within a few inches of 50 feet, rising from the ground surface on each side with the even grade of a modern railroad embankment. As shown by Fig. 1, Pl. 36,[26] it has survived the passing of centuries with but little abrasion, still retaining to a marked degree the integrity and symmetry of all its outlines and angles, due to the tough clay of which it is made. And of that, it is computed to comprise 56,787 cubic yards; much of it doubtless brought from a distance or scraped up from the subsoil of an extensive area of surrounding country, as no corresponding excavations can be seen in its vicinity. Its corners directed to the four cardinal

25. Twelfth Annual Report of U.S. Bureau of Ethnology 1890–91, p. 133. [Quotation corrected.]

26. The drawing of Fig. 1, Pl. 36, was copied from a photograph of the mound, but denuded of the building, fences, trees and other "improvements," accumulated on and around it during the seventy-five years it has adjoined the homestead of a large farm.

points of the compass indicate that it was projected with regard to correct orientation, vaguely suggesting worship of the sun by its builders.

Extending a hundred feet from the base of the mound, on its northwestern side, there was originally an artificial terrace 280 feet wide and two or three feet high, marked T on the diagram, Fig. 2, Pl. 36, upon which an inclined way 20 feet wide ascended to the top. In all directions from the mound, excepting the west, the ground slopes down as gradually and evenly as a shelving beach of the ocean; on the west it continues with but slight depression to the timber. A hundred yards to the north is a small brook that drains a portion of the prairie, and wends its course westward to Silver creek. Near the bank of that rivulet, beneath the spreading branches of stately old elms and oaks, there gushed from the earth—at S on the diagram—a bold spring of clear, cold water in the days before the era of well-digging and corn-raising. It furnished the water supply of the colony of mound builders whose lodges were pitched all around it on both sides of the branch, as was attested by the numerous hut rings and fire-places, obliterated only after many years of annual plowing.

Directly in front of the northeastern side of the square mound, and 350 feet from its base, there stood a circular mound, 75 feet in diameter at the ground, 12 feet in height, with a level top 30 feet across. East of the east corner of the large square mound, and 300 feet from it, was conical mound No. 2, the exact counterpart of No. 1. Both were carefully constructed of hard, tenacious clay, and described true circles, both at their bases and flat summits. On the broad undulation to the west of these works, and 600 feet distant from the western corner of the truncated pyramid, is mound No. 3, presumably artificial and perhaps sepulchral. It is of the ordinary rounded form, ten feet in height, 150 feet in length and 100 feet wide at the base. West of it a hundred feet is another similar but smaller mound, No. 4, in length 75 feet, by 50 feet in width, and 6 feet high. No exploration of that very interesting assemblage of Indian earthworks has ever been made. In 1840 Mr. Baldwin, then proprietor of the premises, built a dwelling house that encroached several feet upon the large square mound near its eastern corner. In excavating for the cellar and foundations of that building he unearthed, from about a foot beneath the mound's edge, sixteen large flint spades, from ten to eighteen inches in length, smoothly polished at their broad ends by long continued use—evidently tools of the mound builders, secreted there after their work was done. Forty years later a narrow trench, two or more feet deep, was cut into the northeastern side of that mound in which to embed an iron pipe for supplying water to a distributing reservoir placed on its top. Only dense, solid clay was penetrated in digging that trench, and not an object of human fabrication was discovered in it; but about the center of the square top was found a bed of ashes and charcoal, a few inches below the surface, denoting that, long ago, fire had been maintained there for an indefinite period of time.

There is not another instance in the State of Illinois of an Indian mound approximating this one in dimensions, and certainly not one of its technical form, situated, as this one, on the broad, open prairie. The numbers of ancient lodge rings, with their central fire beds, and the camp refuse and the many fragments of pottery and flint, scattered far and wide around these mounds, as seen there at an early day, prove that locality to have been occupied for a long time by a numerous population identical in characteristics and culture and contemporaneous with the Indians of the American Bottom, who built the great mounds of the Cahokia creek district. Assuming they were the same people, the conclusion is justified that they erected the Emerald mound pyramid, on the most elevated point of their vicinity, with its view of the eastern horizon and the rising sun unobstructed, for a specific purpose connected with their forms of worship and religious rites.

Passing southward from Cahokia creek, where it joins the Mississippi at East St. Louis, on down to the lower extremity of the American Bottom at Chester, Indian mounds are occasionally seen on the alluvial plain, but limited in numbers and far apart. The first American settlers in that region— subject to overflow by the Mississippi—selected, when they conveniently could, those artificial elevations to build their dwellings upon. Reynolds says, in his *Pioneer History*, page 115, that Robert Kidd, one of Colonel George Rogers Clark's soldiers, located on the American Bottom in 1781, and "lived many years on a mound near Fort Chartres." That mound was probably "the eminence near Fort Chartres" from which Captain Bossu in 1752 witnessed the massacre of a band of Cahokia and Michigami Indians by a foray of Foxes, Kickapoos and Sioux, that came down the Mississippi in 180 bark canoes to wreak vengeance upon that unfortunate remnant of the once powerful Illinois confederacy. In his charming book on *The Far West*, Edmund Flagg, in 1836, says (Vol. II, p. 225): "As I journeyed leisurely," from Columbia to Cahokia ". . . . here and there upon the extended plain stood out in loneliness like a landmark of centuries, one of those mysterious tombs of a departed race. Some of them were to be seen rearing up their summits from the hearts of extensive maize fields; and upon one of larger magnitude stood a white farm house, visible in the distance for miles down the prairie. The number of these ancient mounds upon the American Bottom is estimated at three hundred."

That farm house mentioned by Mr. Flagg, shown in Fig. 1, Pl. 37, was made of brick, with only its woodwork painted white. The mound *in* which it was built is the only one of the distinctively temple class now known in the Bottom south of those in the Cahokia creek district. It is in St. Clair county, within less than a mile of the Monroe county line, five miles south of Old Cahokia and three and a half miles southeast of Jefferson Barracks, in Missouri. A truncated pyramid in form, it is 30 feet high, 180 feet square at the base, and each side of its square top measures 80 feet. The ground all around it is level as a floor, with general altitude considerably above the flood line of the Mississippi. Less than a mile to its south was formerly a long, crooked, dismal sheet of water known as Back Lake, now well-nigh drained; and for a distance around that was a very dense forest of large trees, mainly oaks, hickories and pecans. For quite a distance to the north the view up the Bottom was unobstructed except by scattered patches of crab apples, persimmons and hazels. On sandy loamy soil, the well-preserved mound, composed altogether of clay, is correctly oriented, each side facing one of the cardinal points of the compass. The house upon and partly in it, built in 1825, is still in fairly sound condition.[27] When excavating on the south side for the building and cellar, human remains, with primitive artifacts of archaic types, are said to have been discovered, doubtless from intrusive burials of more recent Indians than the builders of the mound.

About six miles east of the ancient village of Cahokia the rounded bald bluffs defining the limits of the American Bottom on that side are suddenly replaced by a perpendicular wall-like escarpment of rock, rising to the average height of 200 feet. A mile and a half farther down is the famous "Falling Spring," where a moderate stream of water, from an opening in the massive strata of carboniferous limestone, leaps eighty feet to the ground below. That

27. The house was built, and part of the land around it put in cultivation by Adam W. Snyder, who named the farm "Square Mound," and there the writer of this paper passed the first three years of his life.

lofty mural barrier extends down to a point a mile and a quarter east of the Square mound (Fig. 1, Pl. 37), there terminating in a projecting vertical cliff over 200 feet high, to reappear in the same rugged grandeur at Prairie du Rocher. Perched upon the verge of that towering terminal precipice is a noted signal station of the prehistoric Indian, known far and near for more than a century as "The Sugar Loaf." It is a conical mound, thirty feet high, made of clay, tramped so solidly as to have—in its exposed position—successfully defied for ages the destructive forces of the elements. The view presented to the eye from its summit on a clear day is truly magnificent. Below, the American Bottom, for miles around, dotted here and there with groves and farms, lakes and villages, and in the distance the spires and domes of the city of St. Louis and its thriving neighbor, East St. Louis, and of Jefferson Barracks, almost opposite, with glimpses of the Mississippi and its bold, rocky cliffs beyond, make a picture of unsurpassed splendor.

From beneath the great ledge of rock surmounted by this signal mound there issues a large spring of pure cold water, which has (or had) the strange peculiarity of regular ebb and flow, as the ocean tides. At a short distance from the spring commences a foot-worn path leading, by a steep, tortuous way, up to the mound above. So conspicuous and familiarly known is that noted landmark that the district in which it is situated was long ago officially named "Sugar Loaf township."

The American Bottom—particularly that part of it north of a line drawn from the mouth of Cahokia creek east to the bluffs—was, and still is, the richest field for archaeological research in the State of Illinois, if not in the entire United States. It was for a protracted period the abode of Indians much higher in the scale of barbarism—as judged by their progress in mechanical arts—than the tribes surrounding them; and far in advance of those found there upon discovery of the country. When the white race came into possession of that region, there were in the area specified three groups of ancient earthworks, extraordinary in dimension and numbers, and many of them of forms seldom seen elsewhere north of the Ohio river. The first group, of forty-five, described in 1811 by Brackenridge as placed in a semi-circle of a mile or more in extent, with the open side to the (Mississippi) river, have all totally disappeared and are replaced by the buildings and paved streets of East St. Louis.

"Some twelve miles north of East St. Louis a sluggish creek or slough with high banks, called Long Lake, joins Cahokia creek; and on its banks, near the point of juncture, stands a group of some thirteen or fourteen mounds, circled around a square temple mound of moderate height." [28] That collection of mounds, the second and smallest of the three groups mentioned, has also, since the above was written, completely vanished; the material of which they were made and valuable relics they contained having long ago been utilized for grading the road-beds of several railroads passing that point. Only the third and largest group farther east remains intact. Of all those splendid earthworks at East St. Louis and Long Lake, recklessly destroyed and gone, the technical structure and enclosed objects of but three or four were critically observed and reported by persons versed in the lore of American antiquities. Mr. Howland, from whose paper the above quotation is taken, commenting upon the grandeur of this system of aboriginal remains as it appeared thirty years ago, says: "Lines of mounds at irregular intervals serve to connect these groups; and scattered over the entire extent of these rich lowlands are mounds standing alone or in groups of two or three, while occasionally one may be seen surmounting the bluffs, and upon their very verge, two hundred feet above the bottom land. It has been stated that there are two hundred in the series, but from personal observation I am inclined to think that this falls far short of a correct estimate, and that a survey would show that a much larger number may still be plainly traced, for it must be remembered that many of the lesser tumuli have been so altered by the plow that they are not now discernible." Of the central square temple mound at Long Lake, mentioned by Mr. Howland, nothing further is known than his brief statement; not so much as its external measurements have been preserved.

Only one other mound in that cluster was partially examined by competent observers while it was in process of being demolished.

In his paper, before quoted, Mr. Howland says: "At the western border of this group, and close to Mitchell Station, stood originally three conical mounds of considerable size, which were first cut into some years since in laying the tracks of the Chicago & Alton Railroad. On the 20th of January, 1876, I visited this group, and found that the largest of these three mounds was being removed to furnish material for building a road dike across Long

28. Paper read by Henry R. Howland before the Buffalo, N.Y., Academy of Science March 2, 1877.

Lake, replacing an old bridge. The mound was originally about 27 feet high and measured 127 feet in diameter at the base. . . . During the present excavation the workmen found, at a height of four or five feet above the base of the mound, a deposit of human bones from six to eight feet in width and averaging some eight inches in thickness, which stretched across the mound from east to west, as though the remains had been gathered together and buried in a trench. On this level, scattered about within an area of six or eight feet square, were discovered a number of valuable relics, together with a large quantity of matting, in which many of them had been enveloped."

The relics there discovered were chiefly of copper, including a number of small imitation tortoise shells "made of beaten copper, scarcely more than one sixty-fourth of an inch in thickness," remarkably true to nature in form, proportions and external markings. Among them was the front end of a deer's lower jaw, with its incisor teeth intact, finely plated all over with sheet copper as thin as tissue paper. There were also pointed implements of wood and bone, polished discs of bone and other articles, copper plated in the same manner—"the entire workmanship evincing a delicate skill of which we have never before found traces in any discovered remains of the arts of the Mound Builders." [29] These singularly exquisite products of ancient Indian art were separately enclosed in three envelopes; the first, a fine textile fabric made of bark fibre; the second, woven of rabbit hair; and the third, outer wrapping, a coarse grass and split cane matting. The small number of them Mr. Howland was so fortunate as to secure were perhaps but a fraction of what the entire mound contained, which, with the great mass of human bones they were associated with, were ignominiously shoveled into the slough. What treasures of similar or analogous kind the other conical mounds of that group may have contained must forever remain a matter of conjecture.

Until a comparatively recent period there was much diversity of opinions regarding the origin of the mounds. Those who believed they were artificial attributed their construction to a semi-civilized race here, antedating—and in every element of culture superior to—the Indians by whom they were displaced, and in some mysterious manner totally exterminated. Others, among whom were the most intelligent and best educated of our early settlers, maintained—and proved to their own satisfaction—that the mounds were products

---

29. This was written before Prof. Moorehead unearthed the wonderful artistic productions in copper from the Hopewell Mound in Ohio.

of natural geological forces. Prof. John Russell, the brilliant writer and scholar of Bluffdale, contributed to the March, 1831, number of the *Illinois Magazine* a paper embodying an array of facts and arguments he considered unanswerable, in support of his view that the mounds were merely natural 'elevations. All around his home, at the foot of the Illinois river bluffs, were mounds of various dimensions, several of which he carefully examined, and was convinced that "they were not the productions of human art." Dr. John Mason Peck expressed, in his *Gazetteer of Illinois* and his later *New Guide for Emigrants,* the decided opinion "that the mounds of the west are natural formations." They both pronounced the human bones found in the mounds the remains of recent Indians, whose custom was to bury their dead in elevated places wherever convenient. Prof. A. H. Worthen, State Geologist of Illinois, a man of broad learning and eminent in science, declared that ninety per cent of the mounds were natural formations, and the great Cahokia mound simply an outlier of the glacial drift.

But at present it is positively known that the mounds—with some exceptions—are genuine antiquities, made long ago for special purposes by American Indians. Ninety per cent were primarily built for depositories of the dead and human remains were interred, either originally or intrusively, in almost all of them. That the earthworks now under consideration—the temple and domiciliary mounds—are correctly classified is well established, not only by ocular proof, but by abundant historical evidence. All mounds having flat, level tops were erected, or adapted by change of other forms, for platforms, or bases, for buildings of some description. Those of that class in Illinois examined before they were defaced or mutilated by the inroads of civilization, exhibited the fire-beds and other unmistakable remains of human habitations, seen in and about similar structures in the southern States through which DeSoto passed in 1540–41. The chroniclers of that marvelous expedition give highly interesting, though sometimes conflicting, accounts of Indian villages and village life they saw there; but all agree in their descriptions of the temple or domiciliary mounds then occupied by their builders.

The Inca, La Vega, says: "The natives always endeavored to build upon high ground, or at least to erect the houses of the cacique (chief) upon an eminence. As the country was very level and high places seldom to be found, they constructed artificial mounds of earth, the top of each being capable of containing from ten to twenty houses. Here resided the cacique, his family and attendants. At the foot of this hill was a square, according to the size of the village, around which were the houses of the leaders and most distinguished inhabitants. The rest of the people erected their wigwams as near to the dwelling of their chief as possible. An ascent in a straight line, from fifteen to twenty feet wide, led to the top of the hillock and was flanked on each side by trunks of trees, joined one to another, and thrust deep into the earth; other trunks of trees formed a kind of stairway. All the other sides of the mound were steep and inaccessible." [30]

Du Pratz wrote in 1758: "Thus, when the French first arrived in the colony, several nations [still] kept up the eternal fire and observed other religious ceremonies, and many of them still continue to have temples. The sovereign of the Natchez showed me their temple, which is about thirty feet square and stands upon artificial mount about eight feet high, by the side of a river." [31]

In the account of his journeys through several of the southern States, in 1773–1777, William Bartram makes frequent mention of Indian temple mounds, upon some of which the buildings surmounting them were still standing. In his travels about the source of the Tennessee river he remarks: "On these towering hills appeared the ruins of the famous ancient town of Sticoe. Here was a vast Indian mount or tumulus and great terrace on which stood the council house." Again, at Cowee, he says: "The council or town-house is a large rotunda, capable of accommodating several hundred people. It stands on top of an ancient artificial mount of earth, of about twenty feet perpendicular, and the rotunda on the top of it being about thirty feet more, gives the whole fabric an elevation of about sixty feet from the common surface of the ground." At the ancient town of Apalachucla, he says: "We viewed the mounds or terraces on which formerly stood their town-house or rotunda, and a little back of this on a level height or natural step above the low grounds is a vast artificial terrace or four-square mound now seven or eight feet high." Of Whatoga he further says: "Riding through this large town, the road carried me winding about through their little plantations of corn, beans, etc., up to the council house, which was a very large dome or

30. Book 2, chap. XXVII. Also Conquest of Florida. Theodore Irving, M.A., New York, 1851. Pp. 129, 241, 310, 317, 347.
31. History of Louisiana. Le Page Du Pratz. London, 1774. P. 351. [From p. 333 of the 1947 reprint of the 1774 English edition. Snyder did not indicate the omission of several phrases; otherwise, the quotation is substantially correct.]

rotunda, situated on top of an ancient artificial mount, and here my road terminated." [32]

As the flat-top mounds of the American Bottom and vicinity are in every respect similar to those in the southern States seen with houses upon them, as described by the followers of DeSoto, by Du Pratz, Herrera, Bartram and others, there is little room to doubt that the purpose of *their* construction was also to serve as elevated platforms or foundations for buildings. The object of this paper, however, is not to enter the tempting field of speculation and discuss the questions, *why* or when or by whom the mounds of the American Bottom were built, but to consider technically *how* they were built. The few in the East St. Louis and Long Lake groups critically examined when demolished, of which we have any record, were undoubtedly wholly artificial and—with one or two exceptions—made of loess or the "bluff formation"; at any rate, not of sand, silt or loam. Inferentially, therefore, those still undisturbed are also wholly artificial and identical in composition. But this is not a demonstrated fact, as there has yet been no systematic investigation of any of them. Much has been written of the central figure of the remaining group, the great Cahokia mound, and yet nothing is positively known of its actual structure.

"When we stand at the base of the great Cahokia mound," says Prof. Cyrus Thomas, "and study its vast proportions, we can scarcely bring ourselves to believe it was built without some other means of collecting and conveying material than that possessed by the Indians. But what other means could a lost race have had? The Indians had wooden spades, baskets, skins of animals, wooden and clay vessels, and textile fabrics; they also had stone implements. Moreover, the fact should be borne in mind that this great mound is unique in respect to size, being more than treble in contents that of any other true mound in the United States. Nor has it yet been ascertained with satisfactory certainty that it is entirely artificial." [33]

Its size has been variously estimated. Brackenridge and Dr. Peck thought it was about ninety feet high. Featherstonhaugh, the English geologist, who saw it in 1834, says, "Its summit is 115 feet from the ground." William McAdams of Alton, having surveyed it, says: "It covers 16 acres, 2 roods and 3

32. Travels through North and South Carolina, Georgia, etc. By William Bartram. London, 1792. Pp. 345 [343], 365, 367 [388], 384 [348]. Snyder's transcriptions have a few minor variations from the text of the 1793 edition.
33. Twelfth Annual Report of U.S. Bureau of Ethnology; p. 631. [Quotation corrected.]

perches of ground, with base 998 long by 721 feet wide, and is 100 feet high."
The dimensions given it by Dr. Peterson and Clark McAdams, on their map,
are as follows: Length of base, 1080 feet; width, 710 feet; area covered by
base, 17 acres; altitude, 104 feet; and cubic contents, 1,500,000 yards. In 1882
a careful survey of the mounds in the Cahokia creek district was made and
platted by Dr. John J. R. Patrick, an enthusiastic archaeologist residing at
Belleville, six miles east of the American Bottom. In connection with that
work he employed C. H. Shannon, then chief engineer of the Wabash Railroad, to specially examine and measure the great mound. By the method of
triangulations familiar to civil engineers Mr. Shannon found the greatest
height of the mound to be a fraction over 97 feet. Measured with an engineer's chain, and making due allowance for the indistinct line of junction of
the mound's lower edge with the common surface of the plain, he ascertained
the extreme length of its base to be 1010 feet and its width 710 feet. The
area it covers—by his calculation—is 13.85 acres; the rectangular plateau of its
summit comprises 1.45 acres and the earthen material of the mound "ap-
proximates very closely 1,076,000 cubic yards."

To form an adequate conception of the immensity of this earthwork, by
comparison, it may be stated that the most gigantic achievement of aboriginal
labor in the United States (next to the Cahokia mound) is Old Fort Ancient,
in Warren county, Ohio, whose four miles of huge embankment and included mounds contain—as estimated by Prof. Moorehead—738,000 cubic
yards of displaced earth. The basal area, 760 feet square, of the pyramid of
Cheops, in Egypt, one of the "seven wonders of the world," is just 13 acres.

The Cahokia mound, at its base and for the first 37 feet of its height, is a
rectangular parallelogram. Fig. 2, Pl. 37, is Dr. Patrick's ideal restoration of its
appearance when its builders left it. "From the top to the base," says Mr.
Shannon's report, "toward the west the slope is quite flat, being about one
perpendicular to 3.8 horizontal; while to north, northeast and east the slope
is more abrupt, being 1.75 horizontal to one perpendicular. At the south end
of the mound is a terrace, 60 feet below the top, having an area of one and
three-quarter acres. The slope from this second plateau to the east, west and
south is the same as above, viz., 1.75 horizontal to one perpendicular. Sup-
posing the material for its construction to have been procured from the immediate vicinity, and estimating the barren pit was excavated to an average
depth of three feet, it would have exhausted the soil to that depth from the

surface of a little over 222 acres; while if the barren pit had averaged but two feet deep, it would have extended over 333 acres. . . . The weight of a cubic foot of common soil is about 137 pounds. A man can carry 70 pounds, or half a cubic foot, in addition to the weight of the receptacle he carries it in. This is a fair estimate, when the weight now carried by hod-carriers is considered. Assuming the material was carried from a distance of not more than the quarter of a mile, and that the Indian worked 10 hours each day in the year, carrying each day 13½ cubic feet, or half a cubic yard, of earth, he could have completed the job in 5898 years; or 2448 [sic] of them, working at that rate, could have done it in two years."

There is little probability, however, that any Indians of the mound-building era worked on the ten-hours-a-day system. Attaching no value to time, their labor was desultory and fitful; persistent for periods, then suspended for long intervals. The moving of all the earth comprised in the Cahokia mound, by their methods, could only have been accomplished by the united efforts of a numerous tribe during a great many years. And was then never completed. The inequalities of level, or offsets, in the upper part of the truncated pyramid evidently mark unfinished stages of construction. For it must undoubtedly have been the architect's design to carry the four lateral slopes up to a plane uniform with that of the present highest plateau. Hence, the inference follows that before that design could be executed the tribe became demoralized and abandoned the work. The arrest of their labors may have resulted from one of two causes. They were, perhaps, overwhelmed and dispersed by an incursion of wild savages; or, owing to the incoming herds of the buffalo, they relapsed from their higher development of semi-sedentary life and agricultural pursuits back into nomadic savagery and subsistence by the chase.[34]

Until the Cahokia mound is thoroughly and scientifically investigated the problem of its construction will never be determined with certainty. That it is entirely a product of human agency has seldom been doubted; and that belief seems to be confirmed by its regular geometric form; the exact coincidence of its long axis with the north and south points of the compass, and the fact that the mounds around it that have been examined proved to be unquestionably artificial. On the other hand, its extraordinary bulk and the character of the material largely employed in its composition justify the assumption

34. Nature and Man in America. N. S. Shaler. New York, 1891. P. 182 et seq.

that it may be, in part, a natural elevation modified in shape by the Indians—a parallel instance to that of the celebrated Selsertown mound of Adams county, Mississippi. Certain elements of probability apparently sustain Professor Worthen's contention that it was originally an "outlier of the bluff formation," left there by the surging torrents that plowed out the American Bottom in pleistocene times.

In 1905 the few of us still devoted to the study of American antiquities were startled by a well written description, in an eastern magazine, of an Indian mound of enormous magnitude in Illinois, that we had never before heard of. The author, modestly styling himself an "amateur," named it "The Kaskaskia Mound," and says of it: "One mile to the west of the little town of Damiansville, in Clinton county, is situated the monarch of all mounds—the masterpiece of monumental structures at the hands of the prehistoric race of mound builders. It is, in fact, the largest mound in the world. It excels the great Cahokia mound both in altitude and area, having a height of 105 feet and covering a total of 14 acres of ground. It is conical in shape, its extreme surface resembling a perfect table-land, and is resting serenely in the midst of an ideal fertile prairie. It is undoubtedly the largest structure of ancient times, and quite possibly of our modern era." [35] It is represented by Fig. 1, Pl. 38. Having passed all the years of my boyhood within twenty-five miles of that marvelous mound, in profound ignorance of its existence, its discovery at that late date was astounding. I sent the publication to Dr. Cyrus A. Peterson of St. Louis, who, as soon as practicable after receiving it, with Dr. W. J. McGee, Clark McAdams and one or two other scientists, hurried over to Clinton county to inspect the new-found wonder. A brief investigation satisfied them that it is a "natural hill," an outlier of the loess or bluff formation, unchanged by prehistoric aborigines, excepting by building a signal mound upon its summit. Possibly a similar outlier may have formed the nucleus of the Cahokia mound. That suggestion is not entirely visionary. From the foundation of that great tumulus up for two-thirds of its height the earth of which it is made is identical with that of the bluffs, so far as has been ascertained. Several years ago its proprietor, Hon. Thomas T. Ramey, dug a tunnel 90 feet in length in direction of its center, on the north side, about 30 feet above the base. In that exploration a small cube of lead ore was discovered, but no charcoal or ashes; nor a flint, pot sherd or bone was found to

35. The Dental Brief. Philadelphia, Sept., 1905. P. 529 *et seq.*

indicate that the solid bluff clay excavated had ever been previously disturbed. But in that clay taken out of the tunnel I afterwards detected and secured several specimens of the small semi-fossil fluviatile shells, often occurring in the drift deposits of the bluffs, namely, *psysa heterostropha, limnea humilis, helix concava, succinea obliqua, helix striatella* and others. In the same drift deposits fragments of galena are not uncommon. Close observers of the great mound have noticed that the south terrace and the lower part of the pyramid (made of clay) have retained comparatively well the integrity of their original design; but the upper parts—particularly about the northeastern angle of the summit—are deeply seamed and gashed by action of rain and frost. They have further noticed that the yawning channels of erosion seen there were cut through sandy soil and black silt. From this it is conjectured that the builders, becoming weary of carrying clay from a distance, concluded to complete the mound more speedily with such surface soil, sand or loam they could more conveniently scoop up near by. Fig. 2, Pl. 38, is a bird's-eye view of the mound as it appears at present, well displaying the effect of centuries of rains and storms in wearing away and washing down the lighter and less coherent materials of its upper section.

The meager facts I have cited regarding the composition of the Cahokia mound are all that are positively known. It may be but a bluff outlier *in situ;* or every pound of it may have been placed there by human labor and much of it brought by the Indians from the bluffs three miles distant. The definite solution of this problem will be a distinct gain for science. The technical construction of Indian mounds probably appears to many a matter of trivial consideration, but is really an important preliminary step in the systematic investigation of their history, by which there may be learned something of the motives and characteristics of their builders.

Our desultory study of the American Bottom antiquities leads to the conclusion that in the remote past that interesting region was for long periods of time occupied by two different colonies of aborigines, not contemporaneous, but both having migrated there from localities south of the Ohio river. The earlier of the two were the builders of the large mounds—people of semi-sedentary habits, depending in great measure for subsistence upon the products of the soil, particularly the cultivation of corn. For many years, perhaps centuries, they were numerically strong enough to defend themselves from incursions of aggressive enemies and enjoy the peace and quietude necessary for the very considerable advancement they made in the rudiments of civilization. The other—more recent as well as more limited—occupants, who buried their dead in stone lined graves, built only such mounds as served to inclose certain aggregations of their cist burials.

And at this unsystemized beginning of individual inquiry into the aboriginal savage life all knowledge of the builders of temple or domiciliary mounds in Illinois ends. Active research in this embryonic stage of Illinois history should not thus be abandoned. It is the obvious duty of the State to revive and vigorously prosecute it, which can best and most appropriately be done by delegating the work, with ample appropriations, to the Illinois State Historical Society.

Illustrations

FAMILY
PORTRAITS

Adam Wilson Snyder,
from an ivory miniature
painted in 1837

Dr. John Francis Snyder,
an 1877 photograph

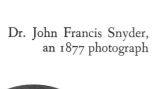

Mrs. John Francis Snyder

PLATE I

PLAN OF FORT CHARTRES

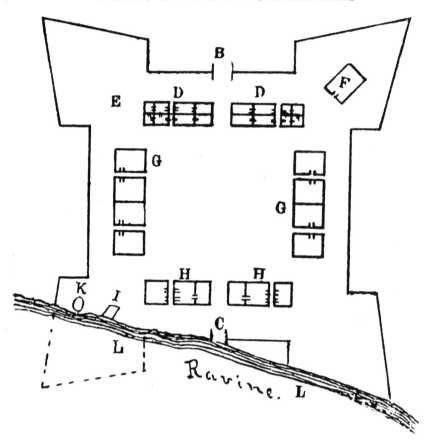

    B. Main gate; facing the east.

    C. The river gate.

  D. D. Officers' quarters, hospital and store rooms. Each 96 feet in length and 36 feet in breadth.

  G. G. Soldiers' barracks. Two stories high, 135 feet in length and 36 feet in breadth.

  H. H. Storerooms and guardhouse. Each building 90 feet long and 24 wide.

    E. One of the several wells.

    F. The magazine.

    I. The wine and kitchen cellar.

    K. The bake oven.

  L. L. A ravine marking the limit of erosion by the river in 1772, and the portion of the walls then washed away.

The large council hall back of the officers' quarters, is not shown in the cut.

The bastions were more nearly square than the artist has represented them [in] the above diagram. [This caption was written by Dr. Snyder.]

PLATE 2

View of Kaskaskia, drawn and lithographed by J. C. Wild and published
in *The Valley of the Mississippi* in 1841

Ruins of the powder magazine at Fort Chartres
from J. C. Wild's *Valley of the Mississippi*

PLATE 3

The Mansion House, in Belleville, where Charles Dickens
was entertained in 1842

The Mermaid Tavern, in Lebanon
from a 1935 photograph in the Historic American Buildings Survey

PLATE 4

James Harvey Ralston

Richard Montgomery Young

PLATE 5

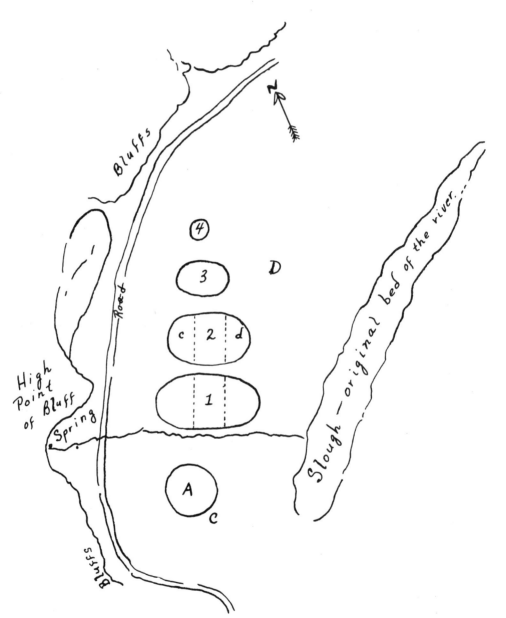

THE BAEHR AND HEMPLULL SITES

Sketch map of five mounds (A, 1, 2, 3, and 4) at the Baehr site
on the Illinois River thirteen miles below Beardstown—
A was a temple mound; 1, 2, 3, and 4 were sacred burial mounds.

PLATE 6

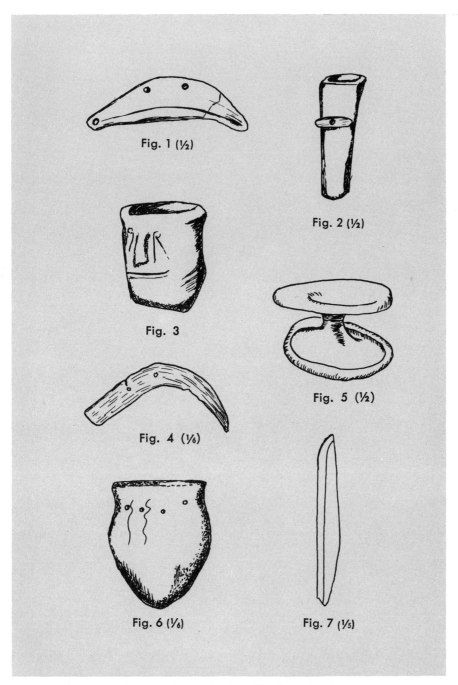

Fig. 1 (½)

Fig. 2 (½)

Fig. 3

Fig. 4 (⅙)

Fig. 5 (½)

Fig. 6 (⅙)

Fig. 7 (⅕)

Artifacts from mounds at the Baehr site (see Pl. 6): 1, bear's tooth, drilled and perforated; 2, stone pipe; 3, clay pipe; 4, copper plume or headpiece; 5, copper ear ornament; 6, pottery vessel; 7, copper ax or gouge

PLATE 7

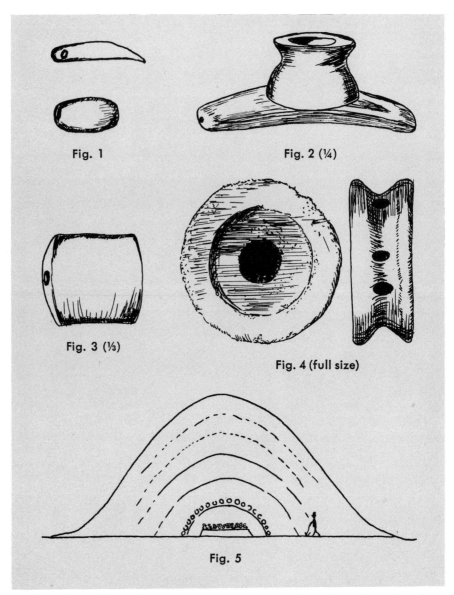

Fig. 1

Fig. 2 (¼)

Fig. 3 (⅓)

Fig. 4 (full size)

Fig. 5

Artifacts from Illinois River mounds: 1, top—animal tooth, perforated at base for use in a necklace, bottom—large oblong shell bead from the Hemplull Mound, a mile north of the Baehr site. Dr. Snyder, here as elsewhere, made his illustrations do double duty. In his article in the April, 1895, *Archaeologist* (p. 109) he identified the tooth in Fig. 1 above as a raccoon tooth found in Mound 2 at the Baehr site, and in the January, 1898, *American Archaeologist* (p. 23) he calls it a squirrel tooth from the mound a mile north. Fig. 2, "mound" or platform pipe of white marble; 3, pink jasper bannerstone; 4, bone ear rings. Fig. 5 is a center cross-section drawing of Mound 1 at the Baehr site. The vault of logs and stone was covered with twenty-five feet of clay on the sides and top.

PLATE 8

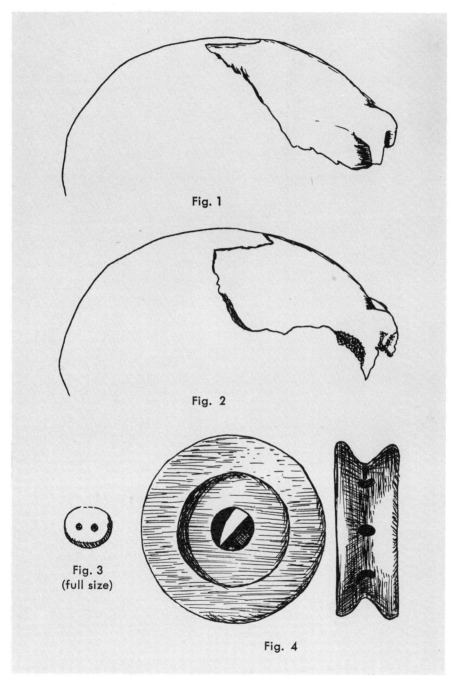

Fig. 1

Fig. 2

Fig. 3
(full size)

Fig. 4

Figs. 1 and 2, skulls reconstructed from fragments found in the mounds
at the Baehr site (the sloping forehead is a result of faulty alignment
of the fragments); Fig. 3, flat shell bead, drilled for jewel setting;
Fig. 4, ear ring of polished black wood (?)

PLATE 9

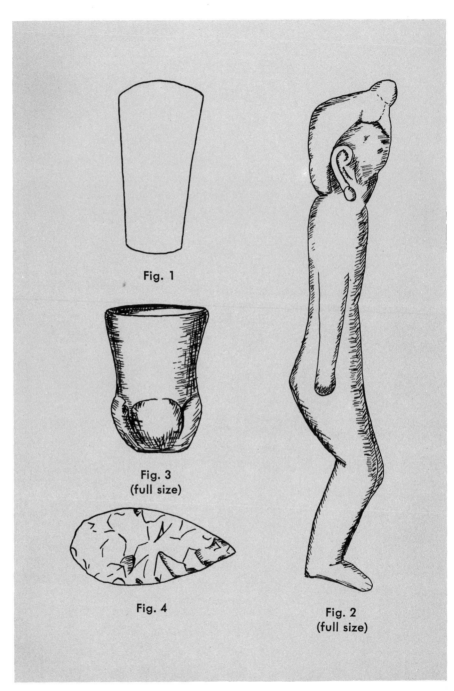

Fig. 1

Fig. 3
(full size)

Fig. 4

Fig. 2
(full size)

Fig. 1, hammer-marked copper ax; Fig. 2, terra cotta image; Fig. 3, hard-burned, polished terra cotta vase; Fig. 4, flint blade (which Dr. Snyder called a black hornstone implement) of the type found in Mound 2 at the Baehr site

PLATE 10

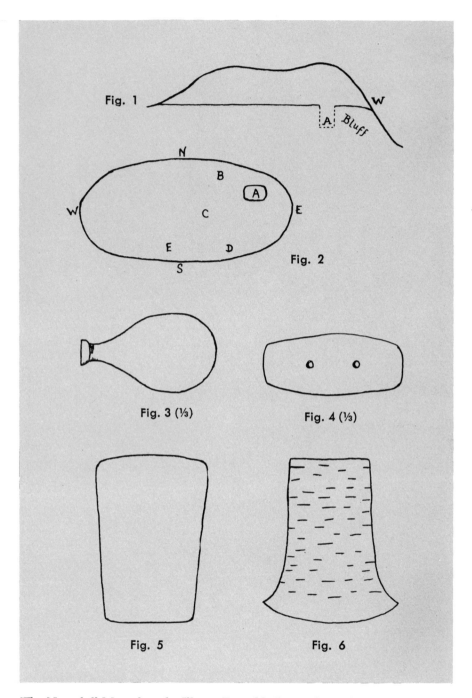

Fig. 1

N

B

A

W

C

E

E

D

S

Fig. 2

Fig. 3 (⅓)

Fig. 4 (⅓)

Fig. 5

Fig. 6

The Hemplull Mound on the Illinois River bluffs, a mile north of the Baehr site: 1, longitudinal profile; 2, horizontal plan; 3, one of three stone plummet-shaped pendants found at C. Also taken from the mound were a bar gorget (4, bottom view); 5, a celt-shaped copper ax; and 6, a flaring-edged copper ax.

PLATE 11

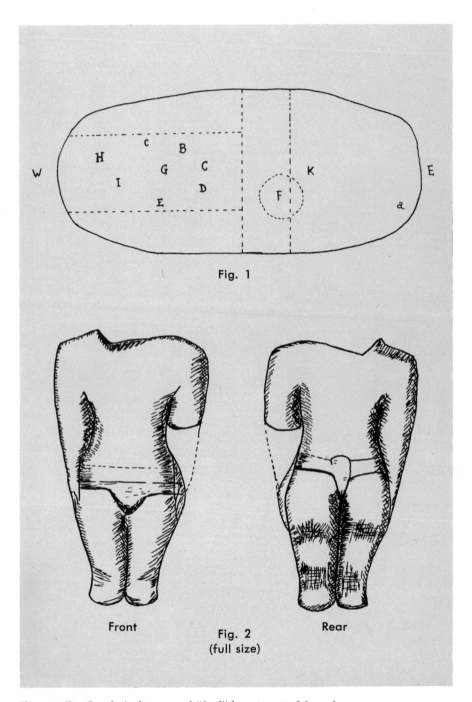

Fig. 1 is Dr. Snyder's diagram of "find" locations in Mound 1 at
the Baehr site. Fig. 2 is the headless pottery figurine found at the place
marked with a capital C on the diagram.

PLATE 12

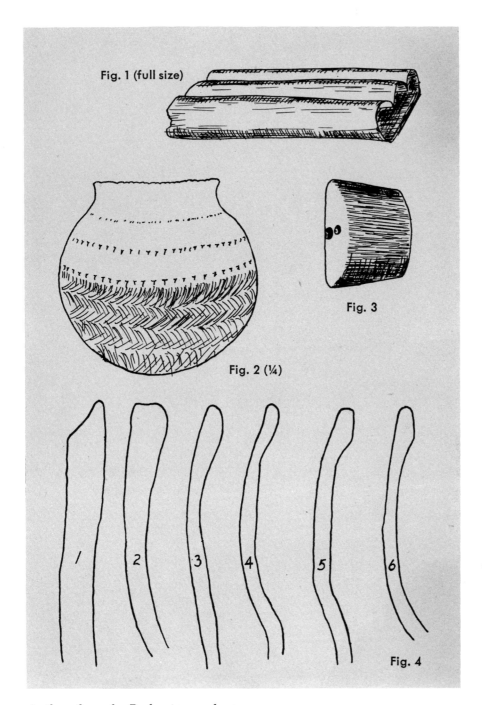

Fig. 1 (full size)

Fig. 3

Fig. 2 (¼)

Fig. 4

Artifacts from the Baehr site: 1, sheet copper ornament;
2, decorated clay vase; 3, polished and partially drilled stone;
4, outline drawings of cross sections of rim sherds

PLATE 13

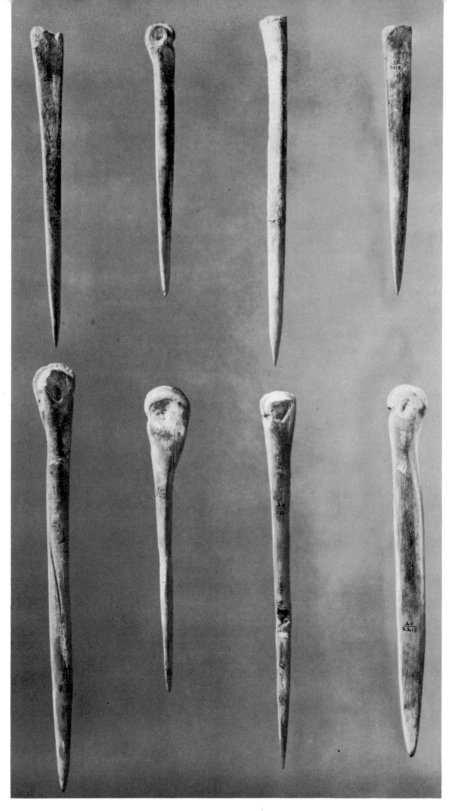

Large metatarsal skewers or awls from the Baehr site
(Courtesy of the American Museum of Natural History)

PLATE 14

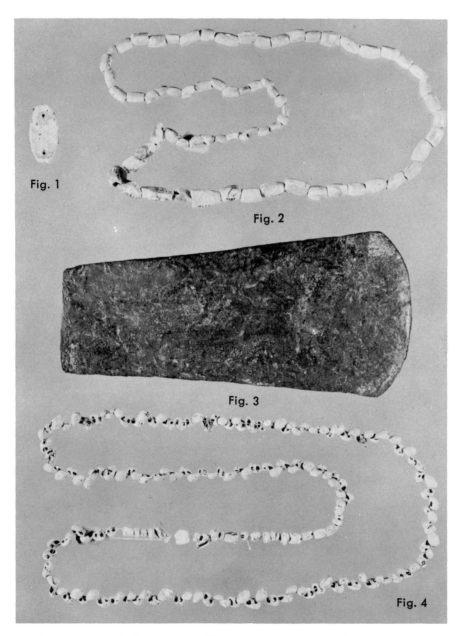

Artifacts from the Baehr site: 1, shell ornaments; 2, shell beads;
3, copper ax, 23.1 cm. long; 4, shell beads
(Courtesy of the American Museum of Natural History)

PLATE 15

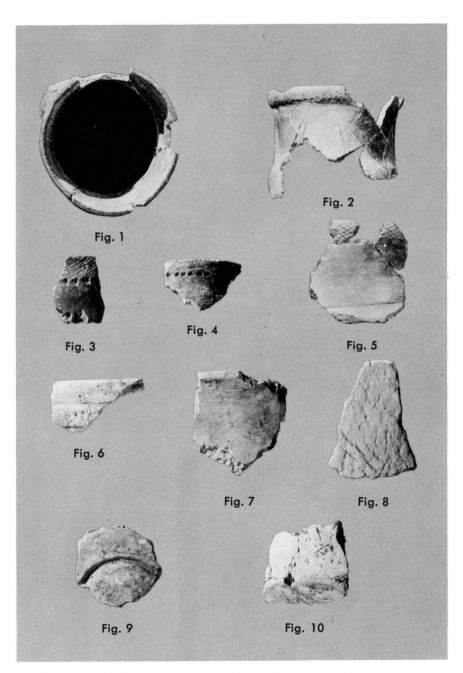

Fig. 1

Fig. 2

Fig. 3

Fig. 4

Fig. 5

Fig. 6

Fig. 7

Fig. 8

Fig. 9

Fig. 10

Sherds from the Baehr site: 1–6, Hopewell zoned incised rim sherds; 7, 8, 10, Woodland rim and body sherds; 9, Hopewell zoned incised body sherd (Courtesy of the American Museum of Natural History)

PLATE 16

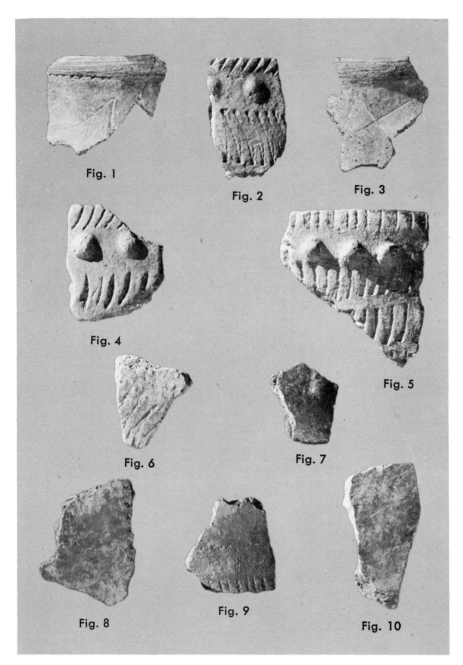

Sherds from the Baehr site: 1, 3, Hopewell zoned incised rim sherds;
2, 4, 5, 7, Naples stamped rim sherds; 6, 8–10, Woodland body sherds
(Courtesy of the American Museum of Natural History)

PLATE 17

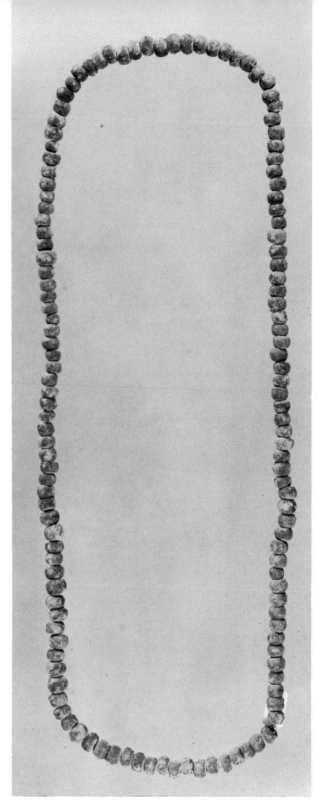

Copper beads
from the Hemplull Mound
(Courtesy of the
American Museum of
Natural History)

PLATE 18

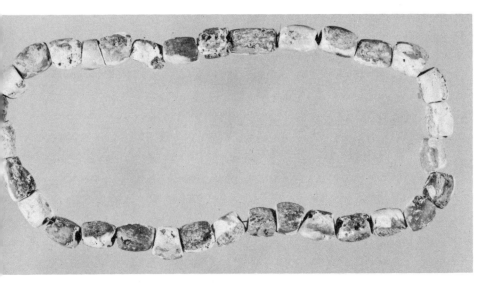

Fig. 1. Shell beads from the Hemplull Mound
(Courtesy of the American Museum of Natural History)

Fig. 2. Double-conical copper beads from the Hemplull Mound
(Courtesy of the American Museum of Natural History)

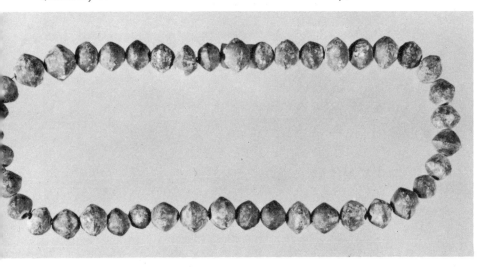

PLATE 19

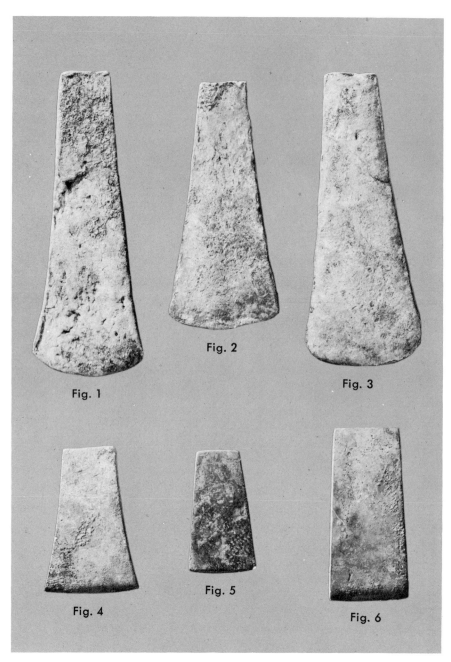

Fig. 1

Fig. 2

Fig. 3

Fig. 4

Fig. 5

Fig. 6

Copper axes from the Hemplull Mound
(Courtesy of the American Museum of Natural History)

PLATE 20

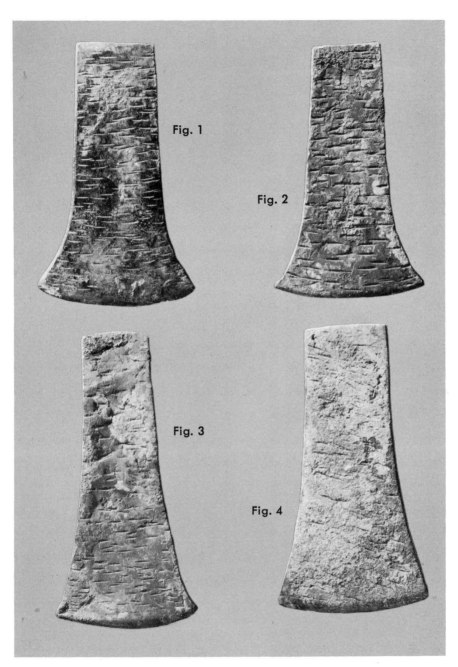

Incised copper axes from the Hemplull Mound
(Courtesy of the American Museum of Natural History)

PLATE 21

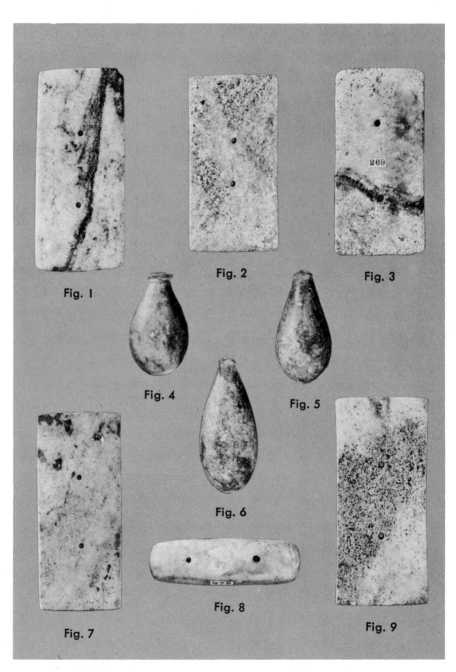

Stone artifacts from the Hemplull Mound: 1–3, 7, 9, fluorspar gorgets;
4, 5, 6, stone plummets; 8, plano-convex bar gorget
(Courtesy of the American Museum of Natural History)

PLATE 22

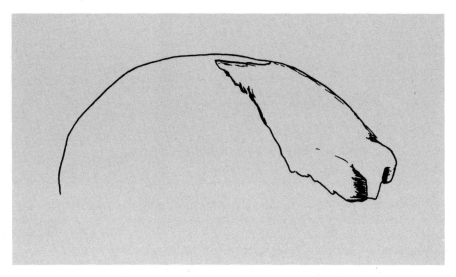

Fig. 1. Skulls, above and below, reconstructed from fragments found in mounds at the Baehr site in 1893. Complete skulls found later in the ossuary on the Crabtree farm are shown in Fig. 2, Pl. 24.

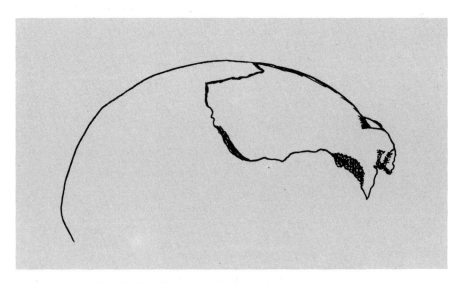

Fig. 2. Dr. Snyder's faulty alignment of the skull fragments led him to the conclusion that the people buried in the mounds must have been as "hideous as the gorilla." Actually, the skeletal remains are of modern man.

PLATE 23

Fig. 1. Residence of Mrs. Margaret Crabtree, eight miles north of Mt. Sterling, with a long burial mound, the Brown County ossuary, in the background. The mound was ninety-five feet long and five feet wide, and its highest point was about five feet above the surface of the natural bluff on which it stood.

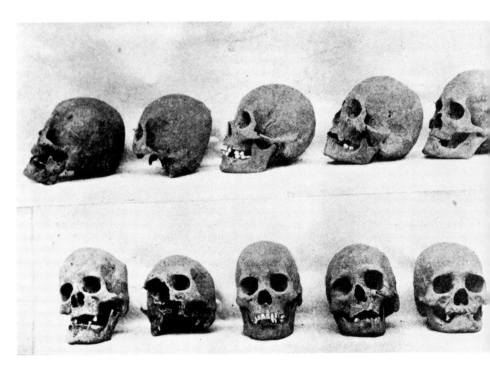

Fig. 2. Skulls from the Brown County ossuary—
more than 350 skeletons were found in the mound.

PLATE 24

Fig. 1. Pottery from the Brown County ossuary—
note the spoons made from mussel shells, at bottom.

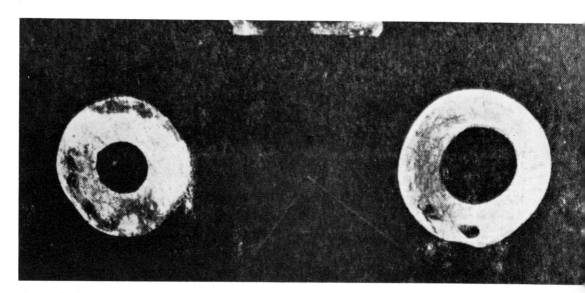

Fig. 2. Shell ornaments

PLATE 25

PLATE 26

Fig. 1, right, full size, and
Fig. 2, below, enlarged ½,
are shell gorgets from
the Brown County ossuary.
These pictures are
larger than those
used by Dr. Snyder.

Fig. 2. This gorget and the one above were found on the breasts
of adult skeletons. They were worn by chiefs as totems
or tribal symbols of the spider gens to which they belonged.

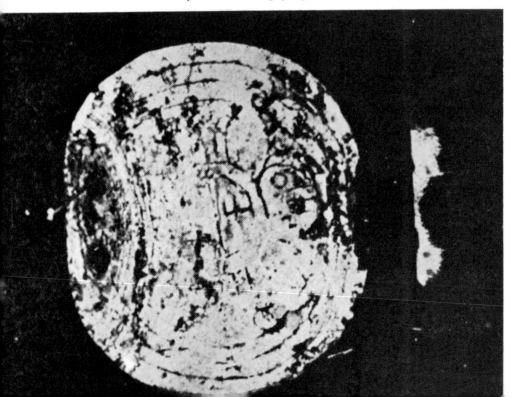

Pottery, in Dr. Snyder's collection, from mounds
in northeastern Arkansas—
compare with that from the Brown County ossuary,
Pls. 25 and 28. The numbers were added
by Dr. Snyder, but are of no significance here.

PLATE 27

Pottery from the Brown County ossuary

PLATE 28

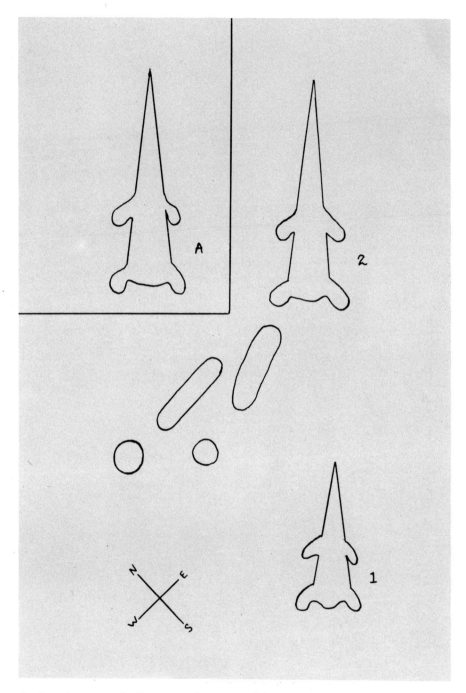

Outline drawings of effigy mounds near Rockford. Mounds 1 and 2 were
five miles south of Rockford; nearby were four ordinary mounds — two circular
and two oblong. Mounds 1 and 2 were identical in contour with the lizard
or turtle mound (marked A) that once stood in the city of Rockford.

PLATE 29

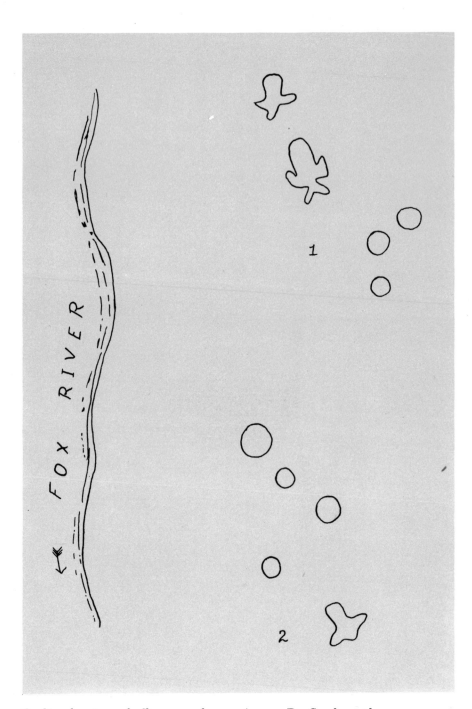

Outline drawings of effigy mounds near Aurora. Dr. Snyder said that these mounds were "presumed to portray birds flying south."

PLATE 30

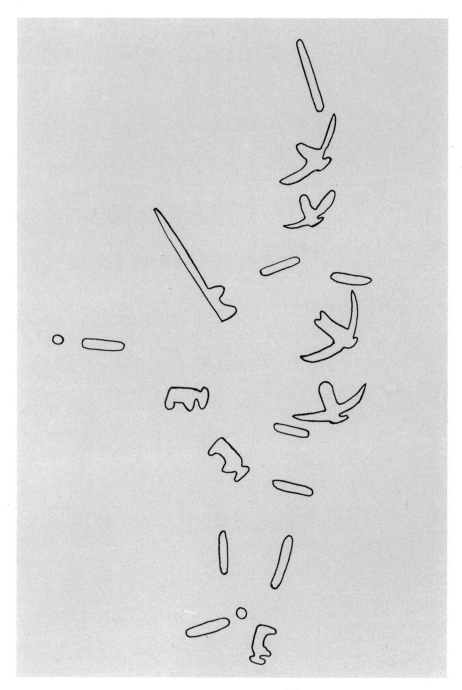

Outline drawings of effigy mounds in southwestern Wisconsin

PLATE 31

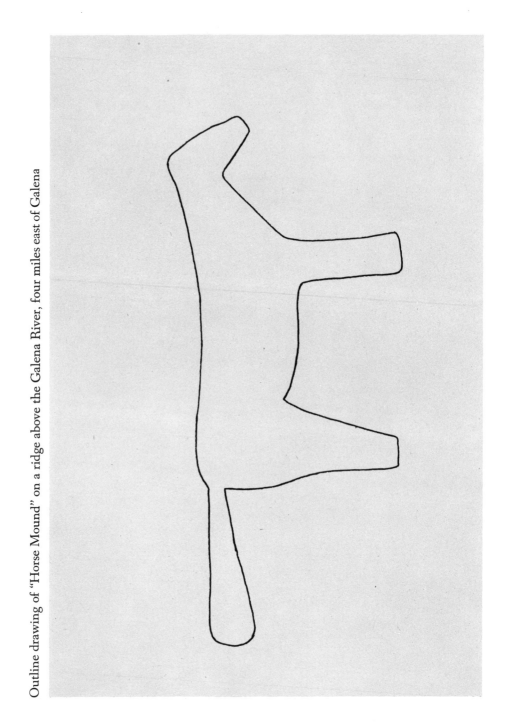

Outline drawing of "Horse Mound" on a ridge above the Galena River, four miles east of Galena

PLATE 32

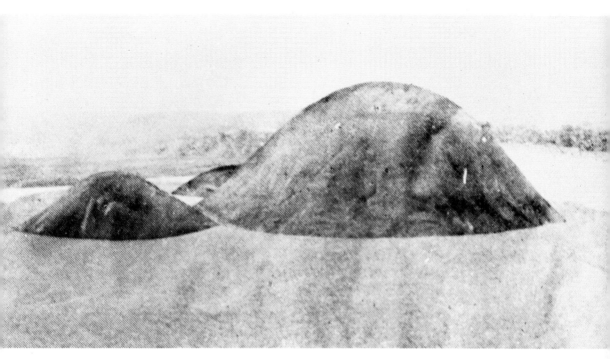

Fig. 1. Common burial mounds

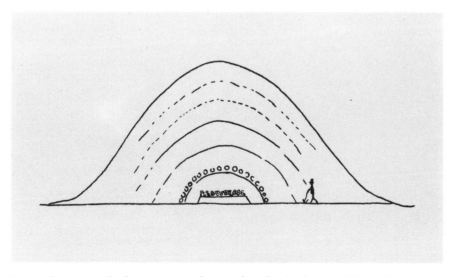

Fig. 2. Structure of a large memorial mound at the Baehr site. The dark lines represent "accumulations of surface soil formed by growth and decay of vegetation in long intervals of suspended labor."

PLATE 33

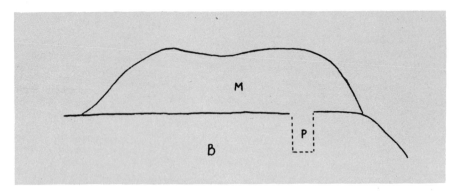

Fig. 1. The Copper Mound—so named by Dr. Snyder because it was the grave of a "head grand chief" who was a "copper magnate of distinction." The mound, more commonly known as the Hemplull Mound, is located two miles west of La Grange in Brown County. The letter B in the drawing designates the bluff, M the mound, and P the burial pit.

Fig. 2. The Beardstown mounds in 1817, as "ideally restored" from accounts of old settlers. This drawing and Fig. 1, Pl. 35, were made by H. F. Kors, who lived near the mounds.

PLATE 34

Fig. 1. The Great Beardstown Mound in 1850. A section had been excavated
for the grain warehouse shown in the drawing. By 1865,
when Dr. Snyder visited the site, the mound was completely destroyed.

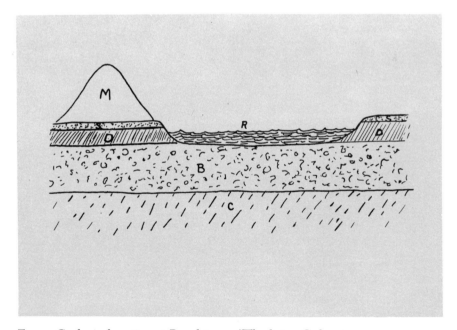

Fig. 2. Geological section at Beardstown. "The letter C denotes
a limestone ledge of the lower coal measures; B, a deposit of true till, or
boulder clay; DD, a stratum of fine brick clay; SS, drift, or diluvial sand . . .;
M, the large mound; and R, bed of the Illinois river."

PLATE 35

Fig. 1. Emerald Mound, two and one-half miles northeast of Lebanon, was, according to Dr. Snyder, "the most perfect and best preserved" temple mound in Illinois. The drawing was copied from a photograph but "denuded of the buildings, fences, trees and other 'improvements.'"

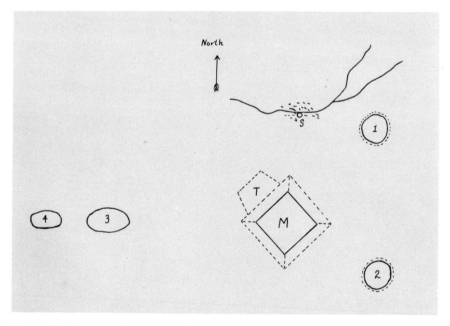

Fig. 2. Sketch map of area around Emerald Mound (M). The letter T marks the location of a terrace, two or three feet high, upon which a twenty-foot-wide road ascended to the top; at S, near the bank of Silver Creek, was a spring. Nos. 1, 2, 3, and 4 are sepulchral mounds.

PLATE 36

Fig. 1. Square Mound, a temple mound in St. Clair County, five miles south of Cahokia and three and one-half miles southeast of Jefferson Barracks, Missouri. The house was built by Adam W. Snyder, and there Dr. J. F. Snyder was born and spent the first three years of his life.

Fig. 2. The Great Cahokia Mound, now known as Monks' Mound. This drawing was made by Dr. John J. R. Patrick, an archaeologist of Belleville, Illinois.

PLATE 37

Fig. 1. Kaskaskia Mound, in Clinton County

Fig. 2. Drawing of Monks' Mound, as it appeared in 1909

PLATE 38

Appendix

BIBLIOGRAPHY OF THE GENERAL
AND ARCHAEOLOGICAL WRITINGS OF
JOHN FRANCIS SNYDER

General Works

"The Aborigines of Minnesota" (book review); *Journal of the Illinois State Historical Society,* IV (Jan., 1912): 513–18.

Adam W. Snyder, and His Period in Illinois History, 1817–1842. Springfield, Ill.: H. W. Rokker Co., Printers and Binders, 1903. Pp. 394. Second and revised edition, Virginia, Ill.: E. Needham, Bookseller and Stationer, 1906. Pp. 437.

"Alfred Cowles," *Transactions of the Illinois State Historical Society,* XIV (1909): 167–78.

"The Armament of Fort Chartres," *ibid.,* XI (1906): 219–31.

"The Army Led by Col. George Rogers Clark in His Conquest of the Illinois, 1778–9," *ibid.,* VIII (1903): 166–78.

" 'Battle of Osawatomie,' " *Missouri Historical Review,* VI (Jan., 1912): 82–85.

"A Belated Book Review: The School Advocate, an Essay on the Human Mind and Its Education, by John Reynolds," *Journal of the Illinois State Historical Society,* VIII (April, 1915): 69–78.

"Bernard Stuve, M.D., 1829–1903," *Transactions of the Illinois State Historical Society,* IX (1904): 374–77.

Captain John Baptiste Saucier: At Fort Chartres in the Illinois, 1751–1763. Peoria, Ill.: Smith & Schaefer, Printers, 1901. Pp. 93. Revised edition in *Transactions of the Illinois State Historical Society,* XXVI (1919): 215–63.

"The Capture of Lexington," *Missouri Historical Review,* VII (Oct., 1912): 1–9.

"Charles Dickens in Illinois," *Journal of the Illinois State Historical Society,* Vol. III, No. 3 (Oct., 1910), pp. 7–22.

"Col. Risdon M. Moore" (obituary), *ibid.,* Vol. II, No. 1 (April, 1909), pp. 38–39.

"The Democratic State Convention of Missouri in 1860," *Missouri Historical Review,* II (Jan., 1908): 112–30.

"Doctor James D. Robinson," *Journal of the Illinois State Historical Society,* IV (Jan., 1912): 446–58.

"Dr. Robert Boal, 1806–1903," *Transactions of the Illinois State Historical Society,* IX (1904): 378–83.

"Forgotten Statesmen of Illinois: Hon. Conrad Will," *ibid.*, X (1905): 349–77.

"Forgotten Statesmen of Illinois: Hon. Jesse Burgess Thomas, Jesse Burgess Thomas, Jr., Richard Symmes Thomas, Jr.," *ibid.*, IX (1904): 514–25.

"Forgotten Statesmen of Illinois: Hon. John McLean; — Hon. Thomas Sloo; — Hon. Charles Slade," *ibid.*, VIII (1903): 190–210.

"Forgotten Statesmen of Illinois: James Harvey Ralston," *ibid.*, XIII (1908): 215–32.

"Forgotten Statesmen of Illinois: Richard M. Young," *ibid.*, XI (1906): 302–27.

"Fort Kaskaskia," *Journal of the Illinois State Historical Society*, VI (April, 1913): 58–71.

"Governor Ford and His Family," *ibid.*, Vol. III, No. 2 (July, 1910), pp. 45–51.

"An Illinois Burnt Offering," *ibid.*, Vol. II, No. 4 (Jan., 1910), pp. 23–35.

"In Memoriam: Mary Nash Stuart," *Transactions of the Illinois State Historical Society*, VII (1902): 154–55.

"An Incident in the Early History of Morgan County, Illinois" (written by J. F. Snyder from the account given to him orally by Mr. John Yaple), *ibid.*, VI (1901): 108–10.

"An Inquiry" (concerning the *School Advocate: An Essay on the Human Mind and Its Education* by John Reynolds), *ibid.*, IX (1904): 59–61.

"The Old French Towns of Illinois in 1839: A Reminiscence," *Journal of the Illinois State Historical Society*, XXXVI (Dec., 1943): 345–67.

"The Organization of the Illinois State Historical Society," *Transactions of the Illinois State Historical Society*, VI (1901): 16–18.

The Relation of the Public Press to the Illinois State Historical Society (an address delivered May 16, 1903, at Cairo, Illinois, to the members of the Illinois Press Association), n.p., n.d. Pp. [8].

"Response of Dr. J. F. Snyder" (to the address of welcome by Lieutenant Governor W. A. Northcott to the Illinois State Historical Society, at Springfield, January 27, 1903), *Transactions of the Illinois State Historical Society*, VIII (1903): 12–15.

"Response of Dr. J. F. Snyder" (to the address of welcome by Mr. George P. Davis to the Illinois State Historical Society, at Bloomington, January 27, 1904), *ibid.*, IX (1904): 21–24.

"Shickshack in Romance and in Real Life," *Journal of the Illinois State Historical Society*, Vol. II, No. 3 (Oct., 1909), pp. 14–28.

Archaeological Works

"Anchor Stones," *Annual Report of the . . . Smithsonian Institution, 1887* (Washington: Government Printing Office, 1889), 683–88.

"The Burial and Resurrection of Black Hawk," *Journal of the Illinois State Historical Society,* IV (April, 1911): 47–56.

"The Burial of Black Hawk," *Magazine of American History,* XV (May, 1886): 494–99.

"Buried Deposits of Hornstone Disks," *The Archaeologist,* I (1893): 181–86.

"Buried Deposits of Hornstone Disks," *Proceedings of the American Association for the Advancement of Science,* XLII (1893): 318–24.

"Buried Flints in Cass County, Illinois," *Annual Report of the . . . Smithsonian Institution, 1881* (Washington: Government Printing Office, 1883), 563–68.

"Deposits of Flint Implements," *Annual Report of the . . . Smithsonian Institution, 1876* (Washington: Government Printing Office, 1877), 433–41.

"Field for Archaeological Research in Illinois," *Archaeological Bulletin,* Vol. I, No. 2 (1900), pp. 52–53.

"The Field for Archaeological Research in Illinois," *Transactions of the Illinois State Historical Society,* IV (1900): 21–29.

"The Great Cahokia Mound," *Journal of the Illinois State Historical Society,* X (July, 1917): 256–59.

"A Group of Illinois Mounds," *The Archaeologist,* III (March, 1895): 77–81.

"A Group of Illinois Mounds," *ibid.,* III (April, 1895): 109–13.

"A Group of Illinois Mounds," *The American Archaeologist,* II (Jan., 1898): 16–23.

"An Illinois 'Teocalli,'" *The Archaeologist,* II (Sept., 1894): 259–64.

"Indian Remains in Cass County, Illinois," *Annual Report of the . . . Smithsonian Institution, 1881* (Washington: Government Printing Office, 1883), 568–79.

"The Kaskaskia Indians: A Tentative Hypothesis," *Journal of the Illinois State Historical Society,* V (July, 1912): 231–45.

"The Ohio Llama," *The Archaeologist,* I (1893): 235–41.

"Prehistoric Illinois: Certain Indian Mounds Technically Considered; Part First: The Effigy Mounds," *Journal of the Illinois State Historical Society,* Vol. I, No. 4 (Jan., 1909), pp. 31–40.

"Prehistoric Illinois: Certain Indian Mounds Technically Considered; Part Second: Sepulchral and Memorial Mounds," *ibid.,* Vol. II, No. 1 (April, 1909), pp. 47–65.

APPENDIX

"Prehistoric Illinois: Certain Indian Mounds Technically Considered; Part Third: Temple or Domiciliary Mounds," *ibid.*, Vol. II, No. 2 (July, 1909), pp. 71–92.

"Prehistoric Illinois: Its Psychozoic Problems," *ibid.*, IV (Oct., 1911): 288–302.

"Prehistoric Illinois: The Brown County Ossuary," *ibid.*, Vol. I, Nos. 2–3 (July–Oct., 1908), pp. 33–43.

"Prehistoric Illinois: The Great Cahokia Mound," *ibid.*, VI (Jan., 1914): 506–8.

"Prehistoric Illinois: The Primitive Flint Industry," *ibid.*, Vol. III, No. 2 (July, 1910), pp. 11–25.

"The Prehistoric Mounds of Illinois." Published by "The Monks of Cahokia," 1913. Pp. 8.

"A Primitive Urn Burial," *Annual Report of the . . . Smithsonian Institution, 1890* (Washington: Government Printing Office, 1891), 609–13.

"Were the Osages Mound-Builders?" *Annual Report of the . . . Smithsonian Institution, 1888* (Washington: Government Printing Office, 1890), 587–96.

"Who Were the Mound Builders?" *Kansas City Review of Science and Industry,* V (1882): 661–67.

Index

INDEX

This book was designed, printed and bound for The Illinois State Historical Society at The Lakeside Press, R. R. Donnelley & Sons Company, Chicago, Illinois, and Crawfordsville, Indiana